WEHRMACHT PRIESTS

Wehrmacht Priests

CATHOLICISM AND THE NAZI WAR OF ANNIHILATION

Lauren Faulkner Rossi

 Harvard University Press

Cambridge, Massachusetts · London, England
2015

Copyright © 2015 by the President and Fellows of Harvard College
All rights reserved

Second printing

Library of Congress Cataloging-in-Publication Data
Faulkner Rossi, Lauren.
  Wehrmacht priests : Catholicism and the Nazi war of annihilation / Lauren Faulkner Rossi.
      pages cm
  Includes bibliographical references and index.
  ISBN 978-0-674-59848-5 (alk. paper)
  1. Catholic Church—Germany—History—1933–1945. 2. Priests—Germany. 3. Catholic Church—Germany—Clergy. 4. Germany—Armed Forces—History—World War, 1939–1945. I. Title.
  BX1536.F38 2015
  282'.4309044—dc23
                                                            2014031312

For my parents

CONTENTS

ABBREVIATIONS USED IN TEXT ix

Introduction 1

1. Catholic Bishops and Catholic Youth in Germany after the Great War 13

2. Pastoral Care in the Wehrmacht 64

3. Priests and Seminarians in the Wehrmacht 112

4. Religion, Nationalism, and Why Priests Went to War 154

5. The German Catholic Church and the Reality of Defeated Germany 192

Conclusion 239

APPENDIXES
 1. German Church Provinces, Dioceses, and Bishops in the Third Reich 257
 2. April 1944 Overview of Catholic Priests, Members of Religious Orders, Seminarians, and Theologians in Military Service for Greater Germany (Including Austria and the Sudetenland) 259
 3. Chaplain Rankings and Equivalents 263

NOTES 265

ACKNOWLEDGMENTS 325

INDEX 329

ABBREVIATIONS USED IN TEXT

BVP	Bavarian People's Party *(Bayerische Volkspartei)*
DNVP	German National People's Party *(Deutschnationale Volkspartei)*
HJ	Hitler Youth *(Hitlerjugend)*
NSFO	National Socialist Leadership Officer *(Nationalsozialistische Führungsoffizier)*
NSV	National Socialist Social Services *(Nationalsozialistische Volkswohlfahrt)*
OKH	Army High Command *(Oberkommandes des Heeres)*
OKW	Armed Forces High Command *(Oberkommando der Wehrmacht)*
OKW/AWA	General Office of the Armed Forces
RSHA	Reich Security Main Office *(Reichssicherheitshauptamt)*
SA	Stormtroopers *(Sturmabteilung)*
SD	Security Service *(Sicherheitsdienst)*
SiPo	Security Police *(Sicherheitspolizei)*
SPD	Social Democratic Party of Germany *(Sozialistisches Partei Deutschland)*
SS	Protection Squad *(Schutzstaffel)*

WEHRMACHT PRIESTS

INTRODUCTION

MORE THAN 17,000 Catholic priests and seminarians were conscripted into the German Wehrmacht during the Second World War.[1] The vast majority never served officially as chaplains. Instead, they were assistants in field hospitals, stretcher-bearers, radio dispatchers, or even general infantry, depending on their level of ordination.

Only one refused to serve; he was executed.[2]

They served in all theaters, from Norway to North Africa and from France to the easternmost stretches of the embattled Soviet Union. Hundreds were killed, wounded, or went missing. Others, fewer in number, abandoned their vocation and occasionally their faith, but most believed that they stayed true to both. Not surprisingly, almost all who spoke of their experience after the war identified their time in the Wehrmacht as life altering; the majority even insisted that it was integral to their commitment to the priesthood. In other words, participation in the war in a German uniform, laden with Nazi insignia, somehow underscored their devotion to a religious life of service to others. Put simply, they did not view what the uniform represented as incongruous with the vocation they treasured.

This book studies Catholic German men who aspired to be priests in the 1930s and early 1940s, and who, with but one exception, did not have serious qualms about serving in the Wehrmacht while purporting to stay true to their vocation. It also analyzes the milieu that produced them. It underscores the unstable and contentious interplay between Catholics (as represented by a selection of priests and seminarians from the above-noted group) and the Nazi regime. It explores the motives that impelled these religious men not only to participate in a war led by Hitler, but even to somehow endorse it. It examines the culture of the men who provided pastoral care to soldiers during the course of the war and genocide between 1939 and 1945. Finally, it attempts to understand the experience of the war from the point of view of a small subset of its German soldiers, whose spiritual vocation undoubtedly influenced those around them. For all of their mutual antagonism, the Nazi regime and the Catholic Church also had points of shared interest. This, above all else, enabled Catholic German priests to embrace the war.[3] This book is not a social history; there is no rigorous exploration of the backgrounds of the various men in question, nor of how regional differences accounted for distinct, even contradictory impressions they had of Nazism or the war experience. The statistics regarding seminarians included in the appendixes are taken from a single seminary in Bavaria. They are meant to serve as the basis for a case study rather than as a comparative or comprehensive investigation.

Why they served; what their experiences were; how they made sense of the war; how they justified their role in the military, both at the time and in the following years and decades: these are the central questions that animate this book. After all, this was the second great global war with Germany at its center in less than three decades. It saw the mobilization of millions of men and women, challenged existential arguments on all sides about the life-and-death nature of the confrontation, and resulted in atrocious suffering and misery that, in the postwar period, would defy easy belief. What place did clergy have in this setting, especially clergy who were not formally part of a chaplaincy? Attempting to trace their actions and decisions, and to comprehend why they acted as they did and how they reconciled their wartime actions with their vocation and principles, is important to understanding the possibilities and limits of conformity and autonomy for men who were both deeply spiritual (in the Catholic sense) and proudly German.

Such questions drive us toward an understanding of how these men were thinking about and making sense of the reality in which they found themselves, as well as their psychological and emotional coping strategies—in other words, their worldview. Ultimately we cannot know what went through the mind of even one of these priests save for what they chose to write down or share in recorded conversation (words that themselves may be vulnerable to revision and self-deception). Still, this book endeavors to "re-create the mental horizons of the years before" the Second World War.[4] In other words, its central task is to reconstruct the frameworks that these men adapted, sometimes repeatedly, to process what they were witnessing and surviving.

These experiences were by no means universal. Just as any individual relies on multiple reference points and influences (culture, family, friends, religion, politics, social mores, formal education) to engage with and function within the contours of her world, so too were the identities of these men determined by their own prewar life experiences. As such, they were a heterogeneous group, difficult to study as a whole and about which it is perhaps impossible to arrive at any general conclusions. Within these diverse experiences, however, two recurring themes emerge: faith and national identity.

These two terms require careful definition. By faith, I refer to a system of religious beliefs that included several overlapping elements that contributed to how these individuals understood the word: professed religion (Roman Catholicism) and its formal theology, or ecclesiology; its institutional structure (the Roman Catholic Church); and the institution's leaders (the bishops in Germany and the pope in Rome). One's faith was and is an intensely personal matter bound up with, but not exclusively dependent on, external conditions and regulations as well as social and communal interactions. Their faith was embedded in language and ritual, in tradition and culture, and in the local community. While even clergymen differed among themselves in how they practiced their faith, all professed to belong to the same Catholic community.

The concept of national identity poses a similar definitional challenge. Like faith, it is at once a private matter and a public, political affair. It is no easier to delineate what constituted being "German" in the 1930s than it is to explain any other national identity—French, American, Brazilian, Chinese—at a specific point in time. German nationalism, however, had faced particular challenges even before 1933, by which time it had already shown itself to be a force at once unifying, divisive, and destructive. National unification in 1871 may have been a top-down process that the Prussian minister-president (and subsequent imperial chancellor) Otto von Bismarck and his supporters orchestrated in the aftermath of three successful wars. But by then German nationalist sentiment had become widely enough felt that most individuals in the new empire (regardless of religious or political affiliation, social status, or economic class) could abide by it.[5] How agonizing it was, then, for Germany's Catholics to experience a deeply personal persecution based on nationalist principles: Bismarck's definition of a German was, significantly, a Protestant German whose absolute loyalty was to the German *Volk* and the German nation—and, by implication, not to a foreigner in Rome. During the years of the Kulturkampf, or "culture war," Germany's Catholics were told repeatedly that they were not true, patriotic Germans. Although the Catholic population resisted the discriminatory laws that Bismarck and his circle passed aimed at eradicating the Catholic clergy in Germany, they did not abandon the national identity in which they felt at home. They would spend the next several decades trying to prove that they were as loyal to the Fatherland as any Protestant.

Roman Catholic faith and German national identity in the first decades of the twentieth century intersected with the Catholic youth movement. It formed one of the largest and most well-maintained organizations of young people in the world at the time. Most priests and seminarians were involved directly with some branch of the movement at some point before 1939, when the Nazi regime dissolved the last of the independent Catholic youth groups in the German Reich. Outside of their families, schools, and churches, vast numbers of Catholic boys and girls (including many youths who went on to become priests) found a sense of community and belonging in these youth movements. The Catholic youth movement decisively shaped both religious and national identity for many young Germans who ended up in the Wehrmacht after the war broke out.

A final point of unity for this otherwise diverse group of men, divided by different socioeconomic and regional backgrounds, personal interests, and life experiences, was their commitment to their vocation. When confronted with the conscription order, all of them were either fully ordained priests or in the process of becoming priests. Most would make use of this calling at least in part to explain to themselves and others why their service in the Wehrmacht was integral to their spiritual and priestly development. How exactly did they formulate these explanations? How did they understand the nature of their vocation? How did their understanding change during the war, and in what ways did their military service inform their conception of their priestly life after the war was over?

The small size of the group in question—slightly more than 17,000, out of about 17 million men who served in the Wehrmacht[6]—means that their experiences cannot be taken as representative of German soldiers writ large, especially considering that I primarily focus on only two dozen of them in the pages that follow. But their value for historical inquiry has nothing to do with whether and to what extent their experiences were emblematic. These experiences engage three distinct but overlapping themes of inquiry in relation into the Third Reich. The first is the ever-shifting, fluid negotiation of national and religious identity under the Nazi regime. The second is the capacity for individual action, or what historians like to call agency, for German soldiers during the Second World War. My subjects' experiences definitively demonstrate the limits of Nazi ideology in the military sphere and the endurance of traditional expressions of religious belief among soldiers. The final theme is context. These men did not act in a vacuum; understanding why they did what they did depends on how accurately we can apprehend the world in which they acted and the pressures to which they were responding. As twenty-first-century readers, we must consciously distance ourselves from our own expectations about Catholic priests living under an ultranationalist, xenophobic, and murderous dictatorship. Instead we must frankly acknowledge that the Church's moral theology, the training of its clergy, the expectations placed on them, and even the way that Catholics lived their faith were very different in Germany in the 1930s.

The kind of military service that these men provided and the ways in which they made sense of it raise questions about the nature of the relationship between Catholicism and Nazism, about pastoral care within and beyond the chaplaincy in a time of war, and about the justifications for such service. Perhaps the most pressing of these questions concerns how Germany's Catholic priests, from bishops at the top of the Church hierarchy down to novices in the seminaries, made sense of Nazism before and after 1933. German nationalism and Roman Catholicism did not stand in static relation to each other even after the 1933 concordat between the Vatican and Germany sought to stabilize the relationship. Rather, the men who embraced both identities constantly negotiated, reworked, and redefined them. They rarely abandoned one wholly in favor of the other. How did this occur in practice, though? How did priests and seminarians resolve conflicts? Their orders ultimately came from diverse political, military, and religious authorities. These included the Nazi Party, the high commands of the military (Oberkommando der Wehrmacht, or OKW) and the army (Oberkommando des Heeres, or OKH), and the Catholic episcopate in Germany. These groups in turn both competed with each other for influence over priests and accommodated each other to avoid direct conflict.

The experience of these priests and seminarians also raises questions about the authorities they may have turned to for guidance and advice. Their counselors were not military; in fact, few of the men featured prominently in this book conceded, implicitly or explicitly, that military figures had any great bearing on their comport and decision making. But they did have spiritual leaders (the heads of the chaplaincy) and, before they were in uniform and when they were on leave, they had the leaders of the Church at home. These leaders informed the behavior of clergy in the Wehrmacht. How did the Catholic Church's leaders in Germany react to and interact with Nazism? To what extent can we categorize their behavior as resistance, as collaboration, or as something less easily delineated, such as conformity or complicity? What example did they set for Germany's Catholics to follow? A vast and rich historiography on these questions has produced fierce divisions. One of the deepest separates those, on the one hand, who are critical of the Church's failure to speak against Nazism with one voice from those, on the other hand, who have tried to understand the motives behind compromises without falling into apology or becoming overly defensive.[7] (The Church is defined variously, most often either as the pope himself or as the pope and German bishops in tandem.) Seminal studies have focused on the impact of Nazism on Catholic Germans' everyday lives. More and more historians are also now attending to the actions of priests and other lower clergymen, both those who stood by the Nazi Party and those who rejected it.[8] Yet we still have much work to do in understanding the situations, motives, and behavior of such clergy—and what they tell us about the larger meanings of tyranny, war, and mass desolation. The decisions of individual priests and seminarians either to promote Nazism or to condemn it do not appear to have been determined by their vocation. For every clergyman who openly resisted—the Jesuits Rupert Mayer and Alfred Delp; Bernhard Lichtenberg, provost of Berlin's Catholic cathedral; Cardinal August von Galen, bishop of Münster; Konrad von Preysing, bishop of Berlin—there was a "brown priest," such as Albanus Schachleiter or Philipp Haeuser, who touted Nazi ideology and promoted antisemitism. Most fell between these two poles, choosing to work within the political circumstances without displaying either open fervor or contempt for Nazism.

The presence of priests and seminarians in uniform also underscores questions about the cultural history of the German military. How these priests and seminarians understood their role in the armed forces during the war and how they articulated their importance vis-à-vis other soldiers and officers adds to our understanding of the roles that religion and religious men played during Nazi Germany's wars of conquest and annihilation.[9] The degree to which the conditions of their wartime service affected their chosen vocation and their religious beliefs address the ways in which faith and traditional spirituality endured, mutated, or dissipated beneath the overwhelming pressure of total war.

The focus of this work is the relationship between Catholic faith and Nazi ideology, as exemplified by the behavior of selected priests and seminarians, from the ascent of Nazism to the downfall of the Third Reich. The postwar world and the multiplicity of roles these men played in it is a story beyond the scope of the book. Our story ends in the summer of 1945 amid what another scholar calls the end-of-war period (in contrast to the postwar period).[10] Thus it finishes in some ways where it begins: the immediate aftermath of war and catastrophe.

Conventional periodizations tend to produce uncritical categorizations and underemphasize contingency. From our contemporary vantage point, the years 1933–1945 in Germany are self-explanatory, constructing an obvious and self-contained story, as do the years 1919–1933 and 1914–1918. Historians have employed these periodizations for decades. This book examines the uncertainty and immediacy that characterized the lives of its subjects. In 1919, could they have predicted the rise of Nazism in fourteen years? In 1933, could they have foreseen the existence of death camps in eastern Europe by 1942? In the spring of 1941, no one in Germany was speaking of military defeat; in fact, for many, victory was imminent. The actions of German priests and seminarians depended on what they knew and understood of the world in which they lived. It is this "sense of the present . . . that could not anticipate the future" that this book aims to convey.[11]

For this reason, 1919 marks the departure point for an examination of the ways that some priests and seminarians negotiated religious and national identity during the Third Reich, even though Hitler's rise to power was still fourteen years in the future. One cannot understand the reaction of clergymen to National Socialism without considering what predisposed them to work with the regime: the preceding years of social and economic instability, political radicalism, the perceived evils of cultural modernism, and the rise of communism. On one level, 1919 is misleading as a starting point. All the Church leaders under scrutiny in the first chapter were born before 1900, several prior to the unification of Germany. Many had personal memories of the experience of living under a non-Nazi German government that persecuted Catholic priests. Most went through the First World War in leadership positions either in their dioceses or in seminaries. One did double duty as bishop of Speyer and head chaplain of the Bavarian army and finished the war as archbishop of Munich and Freising.[12]

The focus of the first two chapters is the relationship between Catholic religious faith and German national identity. Groups and associations integral to the construction of Catholic German identity, including the Catholic German youth movement, are analyzed. Chapter 1 examines the issue of generations in Catholic Germany, scrutinizing in particular the older generation of spiritual leaders—the Catholic German bishops—and their young charges, the Catholic youth, among whom could be found the future priests of Germany. The bishops, in communication with the pope in Rome, supplied the spiritual compass and moral authority of Germany's Catholics. Not only all priests, but even all Catholic Germans relied on them for spiritual guidance. The pattern of behavior they adopted vis-à-vis the state was a model that other priests and seminarians later looked to (though did not always follow). This paradigm reinforced the majority's decision, in most cases, to acquiesce to the Nazi regime and to conform to its policies and goals. These men, from older bishops to impulsive adolescents, were not only Catholic clerics, making choices on the basis of an active faith, but also Germans and not above the emotional, even intoxicating pull of nationalist sentiment. One did not need to admire the Nazis to feel proud of being German.

The development and maintenance of a functioning Catholic military chaplaincy is the focus of Chapter 2. This is a vital context, since the priests and seminarians serving in the Wehrmacht fell under the jurisdiction of the Reich Catholic field bishop and his field vicar-general, whether chaplains or not. The men responsible for the chaplaincy's construction looked to previous chaplaincies for guidelines; the German military of the First World War had a well-staffed chaplaincy that continued, much diminished, into the Weimar era. Although the vast majority of priests and seminarians who served in the Wehrmacht during the Second World War were not chaplains, they were affected by the rules and regulations that governed the chaplaincy; and the chaplaincy's leaders, Field Bishop Franz Justus Rarkowski and Field Vicar-General Georg Werthmann, felt responsible for those clergy and seminarians officially outside of their jurisdiction.

In Chapters 3 and 4, I address some of the most difficult questions raised by the involvement of Catholic priests and seminarians in Hitler's army: Why did they participate willingly in a criminal and genocidal military undertaking? In what ways did they contribute to the war effort? And how were they able to justify this service well into the postwar period, when the fullest extent of the Wehrmacht's crimes had become widely recognized? Recently, historians have argued that priests and chaplains furthered Nazi wartime goals by providing a "(self-) deception, an opium" to soldiers with the belief that the courage and self-sacrifice demanded of them during the war came from God.[13] Although the experience of each individual was unique and any attempt at generalization presents its own problems, at times the men under scrutiny come close to acting as a cohesive whole: the difficulties they faced, the methods they used to cope, and even the language they adopted during and after the war to describe their experiences were common characteristics. Underlying these characteristics was the formal training for the priesthood that they had received up to that point, some as fully ordained priests, others as seminarians before the interruption of war. They entered war with a worldview shaped substantially by their seminary training and immersion since childhood in Catholic moral theology, with its distinctive conceptions of good and evil, right and wrong, the role of the sacraments, and the duty of a priest.

Chapter 5 delves into the immediate end-of-war period during which the fighting ceased and the German military capitulated. It considers the reality of Germany at the end of the war in 1945 and the situation of the Catholic Church in Germany, especially its leaders: their experiences in the final months of the conflagration; their public pronouncements; their understanding of Nazism, so recently defeated; and their ideas about the future of Germany and the role of the Church therein. It focuses deliberately on the initial weeks and months after the cessation of fighting, before a true "postwar" period had set in, with more stability for occupiers and occupied alike. This chapter pays close attention to Georg Werthmann during his internment, which lasted from the end of April to the end of July 1945. Werthmann, second-in-command of the Catholic chaplaincy for most of the war, is a slippery, enigmatic personality. Deeply devoted to his vocation and the priests and seminarians with whom he worked, not above the fervent aggrandizement of his *Heimat* and Fatherland, at times given to pompous sermonizing, he is difficult to empathize with and at times exceptionally frustrating to study. But his centrality to pastoral care in the Wehrmacht is undeniable.[14]

I have chosen to focus exclusively on Catholic seminarians and clergy, both within and outside of the chaplaincy, for two reasons. The first is the unique nature of this large group of men, which derives from their military status. Theology students and seminarians who had not been ordained to the subdeacon level were eligible for military service upon conscription, but authorities accorded men who had been ordained beyond this point (as well as conscripted Catholic priests) special status: they did not have to bear arms. This was the direct result of a secret appendix to the 1933 concordat between the Vatican and Hitler's new government, signed by Secretary of State Eugenio Pacelli, later Pope Pius XII.[15] Those priests who did not serve in the chaplaincy were usually assigned to the medical service, where they worked as doctors' assistants in field hospitals or as stretcher-bearers. Their Protestant counterparts, in contrast, were eligible to carry arms as regular military.

The second reason is availability of source material and, more specifically, the personal records of one man who left a wealth of written observations about his service in the army and his understanding of the Third Reich. Georg Werthmann spent his internment and many years afterward making copious notes about his experiences during the Third Reich, in preparation for a projected mammoth history of the Catholic pastoral care system in the armed forces of Nazi Germany. He never wrote the book, but his voluminous notes for it have survived, mostly intact and newly reorganized, in the Catholic Military Bishop's Office in Berlin.[16] Historians have underutilized these notes, which embrace sources as diverse as military reports, personal observations on individuals' personalities, official letters and memoranda, and reflections about Nazism and its impact on Germans. Historical literature on the chaplaincy rarely mentions Werthmann himself, and it does so almost always in passing. His personality, unmistakable in these documents, and his importance as a leader of Catholic pastoral care in the military under the Third Reich entitle him to a more prominent role in the historiography, which my work seeks to accord him.[17]

This book uses the examples of priests and seminarians to investigate the negotiation of religious and national identity in a wartime setting. The decisions these men made—to collaborate with Nazism, or, to phrase it differently, their decision not to dissent or resist—aided and abetted Nazi wartime goals by providing a "moral numbing"[18] at the front in the form of a "salve for Catholic consciences."[19] The analysis of these men's experiences, yet to be included in the historical record, expands our understanding of the unstable, contentious interplay between the Nazi regime and the Catholic Church as well as the motivations for religious men not only to participate in a war led by Hitler, but even to sanction it. Looking more closely at these experiences may also help us to comprehend *why they insisted, perhaps inexplicably, forty years later that they would behave the same way if they had to do it again.* That this affirmation makes them complicit with all that the regime stood for registered for some, but not all, of these veterans. Some scholars might insist that this evidences a persistent, long-term myopia, willful ignorance, or a determination to evade the lessons of the past. Detractors have applied such criticism, harsh but no doubt deserved in some cases, to the Church as an institution in the aftermath of the Third Reich and the Holocaust. I am concerned here neither with combating these scholars nor with adding my voice to their chorus. Whence comes this myopia, this ignorance, this unwillingness or perhaps inability to earnestly confront and engage a dark past? This book attempts to provide the answers.

1

CATHOLIC BISHOPS AND CATHOLIC YOUTH IN GERMANY AFTER THE GREAT WAR

The story of what motivated young Catholic German priests and seminarians to serve in the armed forces of the Third Reich begins in 1919, the year after the Great War ended. For most Germans, the end of the war must have seemed like the end of the world as they knew it. The military dictatorship that had run the country for much of the war abruptly ceded to a civilian government. The German armies, built on the famously triumphant Prussian model, surrendered before their enemies breached German borders. After four years of hardship, destruction, and death, revolution erupted in multiple cities across the country. Soldiers mutinied at Kiel in October 1918. In Berlin one month later, two different socialist republics declared their sovereignty on the same day. Before November ended, the five-centuries-old Hohenzollern dynasty crumbled. Emperor William II fled to the Netherlands. The monarchy vanished.

As 1919 dawned, chaos continued. A global influenza epidemic peaked, eventually claiming more victims than the war. Civil war threatened, with street fighting from Berlin to Bavaria. Hundreds of thousands of demobilized soldiers needed food and jobs. When such security proved lacking, many turned to violent paramilitary groups such as the Freikorps or the Stahlhelm, where they found at least a sense of belonging and worth. In Paris in June, the Allies forced the German delegation to swallow a peace treaty that Germans across the political spectrum denounced as harsh and humiliating. Whispers of a stab in the back grew louder. Had weak-kneed politicians sued for peace, betraying the army? Such sentiments weakened the credibility of the new republic before it found its feet.

The leadership of the Catholic Church in Germany felt keenly its obligation to shepherd its flock through this turbulence. The episcopate's first postwar pastoral letters, between December 1918 and August 1919, expressed gratitude for the end of the war while acknowledging the heartbreak of the "ignominious peace," the tremendous sacrifices of the soldiers and their families, and the ongoing demoralization of society.[1] Though careful not to criticize the fledgling government openly, the bishops nonetheless voiced concern about the new state of affairs. They repeatedly wrote of their discomfort with socialism in Germany, symbolized by the parliamentary Social Democrats, and its imagined connections to the Bolshevik revolution in Russia. This theme expressed itself as anxiety over the separation of church and state in the new constitution and the controversy about the possible elimination of religious education in schools. By August 1919, the bishops made so bold as to refer to "a new Kulturkampf against Christianity and Church."[2]

Ever conservative, the Catholic bishops after 1918 remained primarily, even obsessively focused on protecting the rights and rhythms of the Church in Germany. This goal united men who could be fractious and given to independent decision making, but who were emotionally bound to each other by their dedication to preserving dogmatic education and the traditional practice of Catholicism. Their emotional intimacy also grew from the survival of numerous crises, both internal and external, and the resolution of conflicts posed to Church leaders by the Weimar-era government and its Nazi successor.[3] It allied them more often than not with Eugenio Pacelli, who after 1918 advanced from nuncio (Vatican ambassador) in Bavaria to nuncio in all of Germany to secretary of state at the Vatican in 1930 and finally to pope in 1939.[4] Like the bishops, Pacelli concerned himself first and foremost with legally guaranteeing the rights of Catholics in republican Germany. His conviction that Bolshevism had to be fought to the death, and that

Christian Germany was a prerequisite in this fight, was a mainstay of his tenure as papal secretary of state and his papacy as Pius XII. It is for this reason that Germany's Catholic leadership, like Church leadership in the Vatican, did not seriously resist Nazism when it came to power. The bishops' decision to accept most of the regime's policies echoed after 1939 as a model of obedience to state authority for the thousands of priests and seminarians drafted into the army.

"Church leadership" in interwar Germany (as always and everywhere) is a fuzzy and complex term, including secular and spiritual, official and informal leaders. Here the term refers exclusively to the episcopal head of each of Germany's Catholic dioceses as those governing units existed from 1919. (The territorial redistributions of the Treaty of Versailles removed a significant percentage of Germany's Catholic population to Poland.)[5] In 1933, Germany's annual episcopal conference, the Fulda Conference of Bishops, was composed of six archbishops (three of them cardinals), eighteen bishops, one prelate, and two vicars general. The bishop of the diocese of Meissen was also invited to attend, though he was not technically a member of the conference. Following Germany's *Anschluss* with Austria in 1938, a further six dioceses and two apostolic administrative districts became part of Greater Germany and their leaders were invited to join the conference, though their bishops and dioceses remained relatively nonintegrated.[6] For this reason, they are not part of the Church leadership under discussion.[7]

Although the German bishops officially acted as a cohesive whole, they were never a monolithic group. Whether responding to the Treaty of Versailles in 1919, the emergence of Nazism as a political force in the early 1930s, or the concordat in 1933, the individual bishops were influenced by regional pressures, class, age differences (the oldest bishop in 1933, Sigismund Freiherr von Ow-Felldorf of Passau, was born in 1855; the youngest, Joseph Vogt of Aachen, was forty years his junior), political affiliation, and—in some cases—doctrinal divergence.[8] To speak generically of Catholic German clergy, its political aspects, or the episcopate at any given moment inevitably generalizes. In issuing official proclamations regarding National Socialism or its policies, however, the bishops maintained a united front in spite of internal tensions. Moreover, the emotional intimacy mentioned above ensured that no individual bishop ever broke rank to gainsay his peers, at least publicly.

The episcopate is only part of the picture. An investigation of the episcopate alone cannot explain the behavior of all Catholic Germans. While the bishops no doubt influenced their flocks—like any person in a position of authority and guidance—this influence could in turn be minimized, twisted, or even obviated by innumerable other factors: region, age, social status, political leanings, even personalities. Just as the bishops did not always agree wholeheartedly with the Holy See, or with each other for that matter, so individual Catholics, motivated by diverse pressures and circumstances, sometimes made decisions and adopted attitudes at odds with pronouncements of bishops and the pope. No single inducing entity—whether ecclesial authority or something else—can account comprehensively for what individuals believed or how they behaved. We must look beyond the Catholic leadership for a more complete grasp of the Catholic German weltanschauung.

If not the model set by their spiritual fathers and guardians, what else might have swayed Catholic Germans, especially the younger cohort? The term "younger" is key here. The majority of the men who serve as the subject of this study—those priests and seminarians conscripted between 1939 and 1945—were born during the First World War or in the first few years immediately following the war. Their formative years as children and teenagers occurred during the nadir of the culturally effervescent, politically and economically turbulent Weimar Republic, the ascent of Nazism, and, especially for the younger seminarians, the Third Reich's half-decade of peace. In this latter period, between 1933 and 1939, German society, as Mary Fulbrook states, "was fundamentally transformed from within: there was a rapid, progressive, 'racialization' and brutalization of German society from which no one could stand aside."[9] While traditional distinctions such as class, gender, and social status endured, a rigid hierarchy of race geared toward the production of a superior "Aryan" nation trumped these others. All sections of German society were oriented toward this, resulting in new stratifications and regulations that challenged the cohesion of traditional social units such as the family. Young Germans were no exception: the regime courted children and teenagers aggressively and expected them to embrace enthusiastically the new future that Nazism was offering, via affiliated organizations such as the Hitler Youth (Hitlerjugend, or HJ). As Gerhard Rempel has argued, in the eyes of the regime, "there was to be no significant life for young people [in Nazi Germany] outside of the Hitler Youth."[10]

The study of generations is not new, but recent scholarship in German history has utilized this lens to sketch the development of a common collective identity. This identity was based on "'key formative experiences' (Schlüsselerlebnisse) which allegedly stamped their mark on members of a cohort, cutting across social or religious differences, at a crucial stage in youth." Mary Fulbrook calls this common collective identity a social generation.[11] While its members shared common experiences at particularly important stages of their lives (in terms of development and maturation), this generation was neither cohesive, united, nor monolithic; on the contrary, there was no single generation in Germany that was not deeply divided internally.[12] This is why the term "generation" is so difficult to define. Rather, the idea of "generation" provides another shared element, in addition to religion, by which the behavior of individuals in this group during the war can be analyzed. If we accept that religion was important to them, ergo the leaders of their religion carried some influence, then the ways that they were socialized during their childhood and adolescence also reveal spiritual, mental, and emotional influences that molded them into the adults that they became. Alongside the study of the bishops, the youth movement, one of the most significant social influences for young Germans in the 1920s and 1930s, must also be studied.

Young Catholic Germans had been raised in a country with a highly developed and well-organized youth movement that incorporated several different, even competing, groups representing sundry interests. Local clergy often played prominent leadership roles. The movement's relative insularity and the involvement of priests (usually older than their charges) aided in the resilience of these groups, even after the Nazi regime attempted to subvert them via the HJ leadership. When priests and seminarians received the conscription order in 1939, their only model of consistent (if passive) opposition to regime policies was the youth leaders. By then, that model had succumbed to the regime's dissolution of all non-Nazi youth groups. If they looked to their spiritual leaders to mold their response, they found men who reliably accommodated the regime. If his superiors were willing to accept the aims of the Nazi government, how could a young seminarian say otherwise?

Overview: Church-State Relations to 1919

In 1919, Catholic Germans could reflect that the Church's current relations with the state in Germany were unstable at best, and that this accurately reflected much of the previous fifty years. On 11 August 1919, the new constitution effectively separated church and state in the fledgling German republic, stipulating in Article 137 that there was no state church. Although the constitution also guaranteed freedom of conscience and worship, and that civil rights and duties would neither condition nor limit religious freedom, the announcement perturbed many German bishops deeply. The first post-constitution pastoral letter of the Fulda Conference alluded to a new Kulturkampf, asserting that "the more we bemoan how the separation of church and state shall be executed even now, when the greatest conciliation and centralization of our vital energies is demanded, the more assiduously intent we will become . . . on preserving the sanctifying and salubrious influence of Church and religion on the life of the family and the people, in particular on its schools and youth education."[13] The bishops' words turned out to be prophetic. From the early months of the republic to the end of the Third Reich, the episcopate was consumed with the struggle to safeguard the life of the Catholic Church in Germany, especially to preserve religious education in schools.

Their use of the term *Kulturkampf* was deliberate. Translated literally as "culture war," Kulturkampf recalled for many older Catholic Germans dark memories of the first dozen years of the Second Reich. Beginning in 1871 and enduring into the following decade, the years were marked by lay Catholics protesting the actions of the state, political resistance and agitation, arrest and exile, and the continuous negotiation of religious identity and political boundaries for Catholic Germans. Nowhere else in Europe at that time did the clergy of a religious minority fight to retain their spiritual particularity while simultaneously attempting to prove their national loyalty as citizens to their Protestant counterparts.

The nineteenth-century culture war between the Catholic Church and the imperial state manifested itself primarily in legislation passed between November 1871 and May 1875. The architect of these laws, Otto von Bismarck, the first chancellor of a united Germany, was above all anxious to preserve the fragile young empire he had helped create. In his concurrent post as minister-president of heavily Protestant Prussia, geographically the largest and the most populous of the empire's states, he saw a chance to do something about this. Many of his Protestant compatriots shared his conception of Roman Catholics: backward, antimodern, loyal ultimately to Rome, and therefore dangerously subversive. In Bismarck's mind, the primary menace to the young German empire was its sizable Catholic minority. He regarded its clergy in particular as a roadblock to the assimilation of Germans into a fully integrated empire. He designed the "internal preventive war," which he launched in Prussia, against what he saw as Catholics' revolutionary potential, to amalgamate the remaining disparate elements of the empire—and eradicate whatever resisted union.[14]

The most significant problem was the political involvement of the clergy, and it was this thorn that the Kulturkampf laws were designed to pluck out. Some of these laws were effective on a national level, including the prohibition on speaking from the pulpit about political matters (the so-called Pulpit Law of 1871), the 1872 expulsion of the Jesuits, and the abrogation of diplomatic relations with the pope that same year. Other laws were implemented only in Prussia, such as the 1873 May Laws, which put the training and appointment of clergy in the hands of the government and resulted in the closure of about half of Prussia's seminaries within five years. By 1875, marriage had become a mandatory civil ceremony across the German Reich and laws had abolished religious orders and curtailed state subsidies to churches in Prussia. Other German states such as Baden and Hess followed Prussia's lead and were preparing similar legislation.

The results of the laws were staggering. By 1875, the high point of the struggle, 241 priests had been arrested for violating the laws and 103 expelled or interned, including several bishops. Nearly 1,000 parishes lacked priests. Politicians and the media also felt the sting of the legalized discrimination: 136 newspaper editors and 210 delegates in the Prussian legislature from the Center Party, which represented Catholic interests across Germany, landed in jail.[15]

Nonetheless, the Kulturkampf failed. The legislators meant to direct the laws specifically against the political activities of clergy, not against Catholics in general. But Catholics in Germany perceived the laws as an assault on the life of the Church, especially as their effects were not limited to Prussia's borders. Where it had legal effect, the Kulturkampf threatened an integral part of Catholics' lives. A parish with no priest was a sacramentally lifeless, effectively dead parish, and a diocese with no bishop was leaderless. The state was attempting to extinguish the nerve center of Catholic public, not merely political, life. Throughout Germany, the diverse Catholic population, irrespective of locality, cultural and ethnic background, economic status, or political affiliation, identified wholeheartedly with the targeted priests. The Kulturkampf therefore bred the opposite of what Bismarck had intended: instead of pushing Catholics to assimilate to a generic German identity, a new, closer, and more exclusive sense of Catholic community emerged, defined against a putatively hostile non-Catholic majority.[16]

This sense of community, with its closeness and exclusivity, enabled Catholics to resist the state. Instead of being intimidated, the Catholic laity, even in states untouched by Kulturkampf laws, found many ways to fight back: individuals aided fugitive priests and harassed clerics who cooperated with government policy; they circulated petitions of protest; they participated in clandestine religious ceremonies and rituals; they fired signal guns and displayed flags and lights in honor of their church leaders; they used vandalism and boycotted patriotic celebrations and national holidays.[17] It was an extraordinary period of resistance to the state, both concerted and spontaneous. As one historian has noted, "So dramatic in fact was the agitation of the Catholic population that it was not until the outright revolution of 1918 that imperial Germany would again see such levels of collective action against state authority."[18]

By the end of the 1870s, the Kulturkampf was winding down. When a conciliatory Leo XIII became pope in 1878, his accession heralded a new era of papal diplomacy. Moreover, Bismarck, the architect of the Kulturkampf, was becoming preoccupied with other perceived domestic enemies of the Reich, namely the Socialists, whose recent electoral successes concerned the chancellor. In 1879, the government adopted a series of modification laws to the May Laws, and by 1887 the pope himself declared the Kulturkampf finished.[19] For all the ferocity of anti-Catholic legislation and the equally vehement Catholic reaction to it, the Kulturkampf did not last very long. But its implications, and the memory of its immediate repercussions, endured for generations.

One of the most obvious consequences of the Kulturkampf was to reinforce the confessional divide across Germany. Though German nationalism at this time was deeply rooted in both Protestant and Catholic communities, fostering a sense of Germanness that could supersede religious differences, deep divisions between the two religious groups remained.[20] For many Protestants, their faith was central to German national identity as well as to emerging national narratives that traced German nationhood back to the Reformation. Catholic foils, however, were more difficult to find.[21] Additionally, a basic apprehension lingered about the Catholic connection to the papacy. The Evangelical League, one of the most vociferous Wilhelminian-era Protestant institutions, was founded in 1886 with the explicit goal of defending "German Protestant interests" against "false parity and tolerance concepts" and to bring "more light into the Roman darkness that still lies over fully a third of our people."[22] It is not surprising that even long after the Kulturkampf, Catholic Germans still felt pressed to prove that they were as loyally German as any Protestant, particularly in obedience to the state and in service in time of war.

The waning of the Kulturkampf had another important ramification. The existence of an external enemy brought Germany's Catholics together, providing enough commonality among radically different social, economic, and ethnic groups in the 1870s that religious identity was generally underscored at the expense of other community-forming factors. When the external threat disintegrated, these alternative self-identifications resurged, revealing deep fault lines within German Catholicism. The post-Kulturkampf discord within the mostly Catholic Center Party is one example that demonstrates the deepening rifts among politically active Catholics before 1914.[23] But it also serves to illustrate the point that religion was never the sole identity of Catholic Germans, including priests; distinctions of class, geography, gender, and social position, in addition to regional nationalisms and the pull of the progressively more powerful Social Democratic Party, played increasingly determinant roles. Most Germans who voted for the Center, particularly during the 1870s and first half of the 1880s, did so for religious reasons. This was "the single factor uniting the leadership and the voters, who were otherwise extremely diverse."[24] It explains why, after less than half of eligible Catholic voters chose the Center in 1871, three years later over 80 percent cast their votes in favor of the denominational party. By 1912, the number of eligible Catholic voters supporting the Center had dropped close to the 50 percent mark again.[25] So long as the religious issue dominated the political scene, internal differences were downplayed or overlooked by voters. Without unifying religious concerns, however, class and social interests began to take over, with the result that the Center vote slowly declined even as the total number of voting Catholics increased.[26]

The lessons of this period of prolonged strife with the state returned to Church leaders after the Great War. As they discussed in their pastoral letters the potential horrors of the new constitution and its separation of church and state, they were reminded that standing up to the state and protecting Church rights could bring victory, but that such opposition incurred a cost. Questions of accommodation and dissent, conformation and opposition, required thinking of the price to be paid. This was possibly the most important lesson of the Kulturkampf for Church leaders. The bishops recalled parishes without priests and bishoprics with no bishops; they remembered broad swathes of the Catholic population with no access to the sacraments and other pastoral care. Consequently, they would choose carefully the points over which they were willing to defy the state. They would push just far enough to preserve the religious rights and freedoms of Germany's Catholics, but no further. This strategy continued to define their course after the rise of Nazism.

The Episcopate at the Beginning of the Weimar Era: The Evils of Communism

So it was that the bishops viewed with alarm the postwar upheaval and the turbulence responsible for separating church and state. A mere five weeks after the end of hostilities, the Prussian bishops, leaders of the dioceses of Breslau, Ermland, and Berlin, proclaimed that those who agitated for such a separation sought to divide "what in the eyes of God and in legal recourse belongs together, want to cut asunder [*auseinanderschneiden*] what has grown together and into each other."[27] This was tantamount to a direct assault on the life of the Church, which was in danger of becoming "nothing more than a private association, as something of an enterprise [*Gesellschaft*], cultivated for the sake of amusement."[28] A year later, they acknowledged the provisions in the constitution that guaranteed freedom of worship and conscience, but they asserted in a letter to the Prussian state assembly that it was imperative to reinstate articles from the 1850 Prussian constitution that pledged to the churches in Germany complete freedom in their own administrative affairs.[29]

While the bishops' earnest efforts to bolster the status of the Church in Germany never wavered, by the end of the 1920s their attention had shifted from the dangers of a secular republic to a rising menace in the east, whose tendrils they saw spreading inexorably into German society. Church leaders had long opposed socialism and its more violent sibling, communism. Pope Leo XIII wasted little time in sounding the alarm upon his ascent to the papal throne in 1878—the first explicit papal condemnation of socialism. In the first encyclical of his reign, Leo decried it as "the deadly plague that is creeping into the very fibers of human society and leading it on to the verge of destruction . . . a new species of impiety, unheard of even among the heathen nations."[30] Nor was this his last word. Thirteen years later, in less inflammatory language, the pope clarified the Holy See's stance on capital, labor, and unionization. In it, Leo denounced unrestricted capitalism and declared that workers had the right to safe working conditions, a living wage, unionization, and reasonable hours. He also condemned socialism for its attacks on private property, enshrined as just and necessary in both sacred and natural law. He exhorted his audience to remember that inequality and suffering were intrinsic to the human condition, and that it was the Church's responsibility, in its use of the Gospel, to end conflict and bring enlightenment.[31]

Leo XIII's fin-de-siècle charge against socialism moderated in the first two decades of the twentieth century. His successor, Pius X, chose to focus on the evils of modernism, among which he included socialism, and Benedict XV, whose papacy lasted through the unprecedented carnage of the Great War, made a passing reference to socialism before promoting brotherly love and peace.[32] In the wake of the Russian Revolution and through the chaos of the civil war that followed, Benedict XV and his successor, Pius XI, attempted to reach a private agreement with the Soviet state. From the end of the war through the 1920s, no explicit judgment of the socialist or communist movements, or the latter's Russian variant, Bolshevism, came from the Holy See. In 1929, however, the

Vatican recognized its failure to secure an agreement and severed relations with the Soviet Union.[33]

This breakdown freed Church leaders once more to denounce socialism in all of its forms, led by Pius XI's call for a "crusade of prayers" against the Stalinist regime's violent religious persecution.[34] In Germany, bishops and Catholic lay leaders formed a chorus decrying in unflinching terms the assault on the Orthodox Church in Russia. Their rhetoric framed the atrocities as part of a larger struggle between good and evil, represented by Catholicism and Bolshevism. (The doctrinal differences between Roman Catholicism and Russian Orthodoxy conveniently vanished.) The episcopate released a lengthy report following its annual conference in August 1930 about the danger that Bolshevism posed beyond Russia's borders, in particular for Germany. The report was both descriptive, outlining the bishops' understandings of Bolshevism's spiritual and moral aberrations, and prescriptive, reiterating the Church's role in "initiating the spiritual reorientation of the masses" and supporting the traditional family unit through the promotion of "rootedness to the ground and the settling on rural ground [*die Sesshaftigkeit auf dem Lande und die Siedlung auf ländlichem Boden*]."[35]

Nor was it merely the highest echelons of the Church that denounced Soviet communism. Religious and lay groups disseminated countless pamphlets, magazines, and newspaper articles, often with grainy photos of desolate Russian villages and burning churches. One of the first long brochures on the subject, compiled by Cologne-based priests Joseph Froberger and Stephan Berghoff, circulated in more than 300,000 copies and two editions, its blood-red title, "Night over Russia: The Battle of the Bolshevists against Christianity," stark on a black background.[36] Bolsheviks "in the best case scenario would destroy religion with one fell swoop." The sixty-page tract, detailing the persecution and murder of Russian bishops, priests, and other clergy, the obliteration of churches and icons, and the annihilation of the family and marriage, finished with the sobering announcement that "two worlds fight each other: belief and unbelief. Light and dark. Life and death. Both powers compete for existence, not only in Soviet Russia, *but also among us*. We too must make up our minds."[37] In this totalizing worldview, there was no room for passivity or indifference.

Catholic newspapers continued to feed Catholic anxieties about Bolshevism in 1930, and not just in Germany proper. One of Vienna's oldest

Catholic journals labeled Soviet communism an "un-culture" that propelled the most brutal unbelief.[38] Shortly after, the German circular *Umschau* (Survey) declared, "Bolshevist culture is ultimately a culture markedly directed against God, not merely a culture without God. Atheism is the essential element in the composition of Bolshevism."[39] In March 1930, Munich's largest Catholic weekly, the *Münchener katholische Kirchenzeitung* (Munich Catholic News), devoted an entire issue to the persecution of religion in Russia. Twenty-eight bishops and 1,200 priests, the paper reported, had been murdered up to 1928, and thirty more bishops "disappeared in mysterious ways [*auf geheimnisvollen Wege verschwunden*]" between 1928 and 1929, in addition to 1,348 more priests. By the end of 1929, 1,386 Orthodox churches and 762 houses of prayer had been forcibly closed.[40]

Newspaper articles during the first half of 1930 emblazoned headlines designed to cultivate trepidation: "The Antichrist on the Move," "Russian Misery without God," "Moscow against God and Humanity," "Letters from Soviet Hell," "The Bolsheviks Are Sons of the Devil."[41] While stoking fears, the Catholic press also sought to assuage them by highlighting the Church's battle against the Bolshevik threat. Headlines such as "German Women against the Persecution of Christians in Russia," "The Holy Father against Bolshevik Atrocity," "Church and Stahlhelm in the Battle against the Bolsheviks," "The Papal Crusade," "The Cross over Hammer and Sickle" reinforced the notion that the Church was acting in unison to defeat its enemy. The multilingual Cardinal Michael von Faulhaber, archbishop of Munich and Freising, kept track of American views; his files contained an article from the *New York Herald Tribune* reporting on the "indignant protest among Protestants, Catholics, and Jews" in the United States.[42] The major German Socialist paper *Die Rote Fahne* (The Red Flag) noticed the commotion and snorted about "the international priest conference against the Soviet Union" and "the black counterrevolution assembling for a global battle [*Weltkampf*] against Bolshevism."[43]

Catholic Youth during the Weimar Period

While the bishops battled the evils of communism in the press, German youth, including Catholics, were swept up in the vast youth movement. An early historian of the youth groups ascribed the proliferation of such groups before and after the First World War to two causes. First was generational conflict—fathers versus sons. Second was a general meaninglessness in German society that began with rapid industrialization and modernization before the war and that became more pronounced after the war had ended. Young men and women flocked to clubs, leagues, and unions that operated outside of school and the family because they found "little emotional satisfaction and no moral inspiration" in the political vacuum and social upheaval of the twentieth century.[44] The turn-of-the-century Wandervogel (Wandering Birds) of Hermann Hoffmann had an influence on youth organization disproportionate to its membership (estimated at 25,000 by 1914). Rooted in the Wandervogel, youth groups expanded and flourished despite the Great War, during which as much as a quarter of Wandervogel members fell in battle.[45]

The postwar youth movement was hardly the homogeneous, coherent organization that the term suggests. It is more accurate to speak of youth *movements*, with diverse bases, interests, leaders, and goals. Most Weimar-era youth groups did share a love of the outdoors (hiking and camping), weekly meetings, and camaraderie as well as an investment in promoting different kinds of reform. Groups that complemented and competed with the Wandervogel flourished after 1918. They included confessional and political youth groups affiliated with the churches and political parties as well as the *Bündische* Youth, comprised of numerous smaller organizations reflecting a variety of orientations: political, confessional, paramilitary, nationalist, racist, liberal, democratic, socialist, sports, even Pfadfinder (the German equivalent of the Boy Scouts).[46] Indeed, one scholar who was part of the German youth movement as a boy suggested that the movement, while always a minority, was nonetheless "a microcosm of modern Germany."[47] The explicit programs and activities of prewar youth groups tended to be humanitarian rather than political, revealing themselves to be part of a "social movement of profound idealism"[48] growing out of disillusionment and boredom with the status quo. After 1918, however, politics became more pronounced, or rather, various youth groups became less concerned with remaining apolitical. Various branches of the youth movement acquired prestige and consequently the ability to influence important changes, such as the *Bündische* Youth's contributions to educational reform. Thus it is difficult to underestimate the movement's impact on its individual members, many of whom went into politics as adults.

Catholic youth tended to organize (though not exclusively) in groups formally sponsored by, or informally affiliated with, the Catholic Church. There were myriad options during the Weimar years for them to choose from. They included the Quickborn movement, the Catholic equivalent of the Wandervogel, with an emphasis on abstinence and pacifism; the Neudeutschland Bund (New Germany League), a "less buoyant and exuberant," more monastic version of Quickborn; and the largest, the Katholische Jungmännerverband (Catholic Young Man's League), which in 1933 had some 365,000 members.[49] Like their secular and Protestant counterparts, these groups created an atmosphere in which youth could express themselves independently from parents and schoolteachers, though Catholic youth tended not to disavow authority explicitly. In fact, members of Quickborn after the war pledged themselves to familial, state, church, and school authorities.[50] Like other youth groups, their activities included walks, hikes, excursions, camping, games (including war games), and singing. Their Catholic nature also encouraged their members to deepen their faith through frank spiritual and moral discussions with others their own age as well as with clerical leaders. They also took part in pilgrimages, both within Germany and to other destinations such as France. The Catholicity of many of these groups meant that they operated in relative segregation from non-Catholic youths; just as there was virtually no ecumenical dialogue between Catholic and Protestant clergy in Germany at this time, so too did youth groups of a clearly confessional nature tend to stick to themselves. One estimate states that somewhere between 1 and 1.5 million Catholic boys and girls belonged at some point to one or several Catholic youth organization in the 1930s.[51]

The Catholic youth groups' most formidable opponents, even before Nazism came to power, were the Nazi youth organizations, led by the indomitable Hitler Youth. The HJ was founded in 1922, then formally refounded in 1926, after Adolf Hitler's release from prison following the failed 1923 Beer Hall Putsch and the reorganization of the Nazi Party. Its membership grew steadily after 1925. Between 1929 and 1932, it ballooned from 13,000 to 99,586, reflecting the climb in popularity of the Nazi Party in general. Baldur von Schirach replaced the first leader, Adolf Lenk, in 1932; he retained the post until Artur Axmann supplanted him in 1940. About the time Schirach took charge, the HJ counted a little fewer than 100,000 members, spread across five different groups.[52] By mid-1934, more than 3.5 million German youths claimed membership in the HJ or one of its affiliates, and its ranks had grown so quickly that it temporarily banned new members to allow its organization to catch up.[53]

The Rise of National Socialism

The exploding membership of the Hitler Youth makes it clear that the Nazi Party pulled a considerable segment of the German population into its orbit, even if it failed to persuade a majority to vote for it in 1932. Perhaps this is part of the reason why the bishops never employed the kind of alarmist language to describe Nazism that they used for Bolshevism and communism. Though they never indicated enthusiasm for the extreme right movement, either among themselves or to their parishioners, there is little evidence that, at the end of the 1920s and into the early 1930s, they understood it to be as lethal a threat to the Church as Bolshevism. Not surprisingly, the clergy in Munich and the surrounding area were the first to concern themselves with the new player on the political scene. Munich, after all, was the birthplace of Nazism and the site of Hitler's infamous failed putsch in 1923. It was also where, prior to 1925, individual lay Catholics had been active proponents of the young Nazi movement, depicting it as a Catholic-oriented segment of the radical racialized *völkisch* movement.[54] The Nazi Party attracted the negative attention of Church leaders only after 1928, when Nazi politicians, infused with a new anti-Catholic rhetoric that estranged most of its previous supporters among Bavarian Catholics, began to make strides in the political arena.[55] Church leaders viewed Nazism as one option among several, and not necessarily a viable one due to its extremism and its anti-Catholicism. Nonetheless, Nazism did not present the same kind of menace that they saw in Bolshevism.

Such views of Nazism may seem naïve, but only in hindsight. The evidence suggests that individual priests and bishops were well informed about the goals of Nazism, its inherently racist and antisemitic ideology, and its violent methods. Many clergymen found these elements problematic enough to keep their distance before 1933. In one of the early detailed discussions of the Nazi Party program among clergy, Father Philipp Jakob Mayer pointed out two problematic elements in the program: its attitude toward Jews and its promotion of so-called positive Christianity. After delineating the relevant points of the program concerning Jews, including their depiction as a foreign race living in Germany, Mayer declared that the "surge of nationalism leads to the disdain and hate of foreign peoples, in particular the Jewish people, and *ultimately also to the contempt and persecution of Catholics*, whose religion contains Jewish elements, as Nazi writers allege." The party's understanding of "positive Christianity," as trumpeted by Gottfried Feder, an early member of the party and one of the drafters of its 25 Point Program, reinforced this. Feder did not hesitate to borrow Catholic terminology for his own purposes, as Mayer paraphrased, "One day the German *Volk* will also certainly find an expression of gnosis and spiritual life suitable to its northern blood [*nordisches Blutsteil*], and only then will the trinity of blood, belief, and state be consummated." Mayer, a vicar-general in Mainz, insisted, "Such assumptions cannot be reconciled with Catholic teaching."[56] Mayer's discomfort with the party's notion of "positive Christianity" and its exaltation of race is the core of his condemnation of Nazism, an attitude that many Catholic clergy shared. This does not mean, however, that Germany's Catholics took a stand against the Nazi Party because of their aversion to its racism or antisemitism.[57]

No less a figure than Faulhaber followed up, sending a letter to the Congregation of the Council, the Holy See's administrative body charged with supervising discipline of the secular (diocesan) clergy and their parishioners. The immediate occasion for the letter was the presence of SA men at a funeral for a Catholic Nazi, and the local priest's subsequent prohibition of their attendance. But Faulhaber took the opportunity to assert episcopal authority vis-à-vis the Holy See. Evincing an interest in the pope's opinion whether a Catholic might licitly support the Nazis, the archbishop of Munich also pointed out that the bishop was leader of his diocese and that the faithful were duty-bound to obey his religious decisions—implicitly, not the Congregation's.[58] As Catholic leaders in Germany became increasingly concerned over the political and social clout of the Nazi Party, they seemed equally anxious to preserve their spiritual autonomy, even from the pope, to deal with such issues.

Qualifying the Bishops' Independence

As the preceding pages demonstrate, this spiritual independence was not unprecedented in 1930. While they tended to act as a unified body that usually followed papal guidance, the Catholic bishops of Germany had in the past occasionally issued decisions independently of (or in angry reaction to) the pope or even each other.[59] After 1930, the bishops showed a pressing awareness that an external threat required a united front, no matter how superficial—and this threat, initially conceived almost exclusively as Bolshevism, gradually became in the latter 1930s a double menace, with Nazism nearly as ominous. Their autonomy also ensured that the bishops were not aimless or disaggregated after 1939, when wartime exigencies diminished but did not entirely silence the pope's voice. For Church leaders, a unified front's past success returned vividly after Hitler became chancellor and the Nazi Party proved to be a political force that they had to face.

This independence, however, was not limitless. Three significant factors restricted the behavior of the bishops and, by extension, the lower clergy in Germany. The first was that, as a result of the nineteenth-century Kulturkampf and the state's vicious persecution of Church leaders, the bishops understood that taking a stand against the state bore serious consequence. They were slow to resist the state, even when a regime was peppered with openly anti-Catholic leaders, and they would not risk retaliation on behalf of groups not among their flock, notably Protestants and Jews.

Second was internal disagreement among members of the hierarchy about Nazism and Hitler, a constant throughout the Third Reich. The twenty-seven men who met regularly before 1939 remained united in emphasizing the preservation of dogmatic teaching and education and the traditional practice of the faith, but often disagreed on how best to pursue these goals.[60] Moreover, a kaleidoscope of opinion existed about cooperation with Hitler's government, ranging from early open support of Nazism by Archbishop Conrad Gröber in Freiburg—who by 1935 had reversed course—through the more persistent cooperation of Adolf Cardinal Bertram, bishop of Breslau and chairman of the Fulda Conference of Bishops, and the studied official neutrality of Faulhaber in Munich, to the consistent anti-Nazi attitude of Bishop Konrad von Preysing, whose seat moved from Eichstätt to the more turbulent Berlin in 1935.

The final factor limiting episcopal independence was the concordat signed in 1933 between Hitler's six-month-old government and the Vatican. Understanding the attitudes of the Catholic leadership, and by extension its priests, to the ascent of the Nazi Party and Hitler's installation as chancellor is bound up inextricably with the story of this concordat.

A History of Concordats

When in 1933 the opportunity arose to sign a concordat, the leaders of the Church preferred the measure of certainty it brought to lingering in political limbo, uncertain about the future care of Catholic German souls. Of course, Catholic leaders in Germany were not blind to the Nazis' anti-Christian activity; the party and its leaders surfaced repeatedly in correspondence between bishops in the late 1920s and early 1930s. Bishops also fretted over the party's exuberant racist rhetoric. They supported the Roman curia's condemnation of Alfred Rosenberg's deeply anti-Christian *The Myth of the Twentieth Century*.[61] Yet from other angles, Catholics found much about Nazism reassuring. In particular, bishops and priests were susceptible to the Nazi Party's unflinchingly anti-communist and anti-Bolshevik ideology. Clergy and laity alike also warmed to the idea of a strongly centralized, even authoritarian government, which in the twilight of the Weimar era seemed immensely preferable to the atheistic liberalism and chaotic parliamentarianism that had reigned in Germany since the end of the First World War. Nor did the party's antisemitic rhetoric estrange Church leaders.[62] The Church was no stranger to such sentiments. The only time that clerics felt pressed to defend Jews from the regime was when those Jews happened to have converted to Catholicism and were, in the eyes of the Church, no longer Jews. For these various reasons, Church authorities turned a blind eye when the Nazi Party breached the concordat. They did so even when the breaches became increasingly blatant.

The *Reichskonkordat*, as known at the time, had enormous consequences for Catholics in Germany and for clergy in particular. One of the first international treaties signed with the young Nazi regime, it was a Vatican act recognizing Hitler's government that Church leaders and priests in Germany accepted.[63] But the concordat was also the endpoint of a process that unfolded over more than a decade. It involved several German states and the efforts of key individuals determined to bring about an official agreement between the government and the Church. Also critical was the determination of Pope Pius XI and his secretary of state, Eugenio Pacelli, to reach an accommodation with the German government that would safeguard the rights of Germany's Catholics.

The Church's attempts to reach such an accommodation predate Nazism. The 1933 concordat can be fully grasped only within the context of church-state compromises that had evolved over centuries. Concordats were diplomatic tools used by various popes to obtain guarantees of the rights of Catholic subjects from a secular ruler or state. Pope Pius VII and Napoleon Bonaparte signed the first concordat of the modern era, three years before Napoleon crowned himself emperor in 1804. This agreement ended the revolutionary chaos and religious persecution that had plagued the Church in France since the revolution.[64] The 1801 concordat legitimated the Catholic Church in France and recognized the authority of the pope. While the pope had to make some concessions to achieve these gains, he secured the future of the French Catholic Church. Napoleon would later misinterpret and misapply some of the concordat's revisions, but a Catholic revival in France nevertheless began that strengthened the Church's position throughout the nineteenth century. The concordat, furthermore, became a model for several subsequent agreements, which helped to regulate Church-state relations in Europe and beyond.[65]

The immediate precursor to the *Reichskonkordat* was the Lateran Accord of 1929, signed by Pope Pius XI and Italian fascist leader Benito Mussolini. The treaty had its roots in the struggle for Italian unification, when the Papal States were seized and incorporated into what emerged as modern Italy in 1870–1871. In reaction, the pope at the time, Pius IX, retreated into the Vatican and declared himself a prisoner. His successors sought redress from different Italian governments, without success, until Mussolini took power and expressed a desire for reconciliation. He took this action largely out of the same motivations that would steer Hitler towards accommodation with the Vatican in 1933: both dictators recognized the potential support to be gained from tradition-minded, conservative segments of the population. The *Conciliazone,* as the treaty was called, settled the old "Roman question" by guaranteeing papal sovereignty in Vatican City in return for the pope's recognition of an independent Italy. It also paved the way for broad popular support for fascism in Italy and—drawing comparison, again, to Hitler in 1933—legitimacy for Mussolini as its head of state.[66]

The man chosen to act as the first nuncio to Germany after the First World War had held that station in Bavaria since 1917; Eugenio Pacelli was appointed to his new post on 30 June 1920. From this early date, his priority was a concordat to safeguard the rights of Catholic Germans to their religion. Nor did Pacelli act alone. With the establishment of a republic, several Catholic politicians and clergymen who recognized the need for a formal revision of church-state relations saw an opening to accomplish that goal. The Weimar Constitution of August 1919 guaranteed freedom of belief and conscience and the unimpeded practice of religion.[67] These provisions seemed to open the way for a concordat, which in the Church's eyes would effectively bind the state to upholding such constitutional guarantees. It would, moreover, bring to an end the history of futile attempts to achieve a nationwide agreement between the Vatican and the German state.

On a federal level, this goal proved impossible during the Weimar Republic. Given the inability of the plethora of political parties in the Reichstag to form durable coalitions, concordats became possible only at state level. In fact, it had proved easier for the Vatican to pursue such contracts with authoritarian regimes than with democratic governments. In the latter anticlericalism and political diversity often made negotiating with the pope, let alone arriving at a consensus, nearly impossible, as was the case in the Reichstag.[68] Pacelli therefore directed the Vatican's attention to Bavaria in 1920. Bavaria was a predominantly Catholic state where the strongest party in its parliament was the conservative Catholic Bavarian People's Party (BVP). Furthermore, Bavarians had a precedent: a concordat signed in 1824. Pacelli was familiar with Bavarian parliamentary politics from his years as nuncio, and he believed it would be wise to "first guide the concordat with Bavaria to its end . . . since a majority for it will be found more easily in the state legislature. This Bavarian concordat could then serve as a model for the other German states and as a precedent."[69] Five years later, the Bavarian parliament voted seventy-three to fifty-two in favor of a concordat. The treaty was signed without official Reichstag approval but with informal assurances that it did not violate the federal constitution.[70]

A second concordat, "a tenaciously negotiated agreement"[71] at the end of a more vigorous battle, was Pacelli's second triumph. It was also a near polar opposite experience, negotiated between the Prussian state government and the Vatican. Unlike Bavaria's legislature, dominated by a Catholic party, in the Prussian parliament the powerful forces of the Social Democrats (SPD) and the German National People's Party (DNVP), a predominantly Protestant conservative party, distrusted Catholics and opposed a concordat. Moreover, throughout the 1920s delegates of the Catholic Center Party feared that agitating for one might provoke reactions reminiscent of the 1870s.[72] But the achievement of the Bavarian concordat, and a 1925 concordat with Poland affecting formerly Prussian areas of Germany, persuaded pro-concordat delegates to try. The Center made the concordat a condition of coalition: "If the SPD did not want to lose their most important and reliable partner, and thereby the precondition of their long-standing ruling power, they had to consider the problem fully [*näher treten*]."[73] After a bitter battle in parliament and, decisively, the sacrifice of any mention of the education system in the text, the Prussian parliament ratified the concordat in July 1929.

The third and final provincial concordat was signed with Baden. Its supporters had to make the same concession as in Prussia, namely the exclusion of education. The Center in particular found this hard to swallow, because regulating denominational schools and sustaining religion in the education system had long been one of its top priorities. However, conditions were otherwise optimal for an agreement in August 1932, when the SPD, the Center's traditional coalition partner in the state, agreed to a draft. Ultimately the concordat passed in October that year by a mere two votes.[74] The parliament ratified it in March 1933 and the state president signed it hours before the Nazis removed him from office as part of their sweeping seizure of power.

Attainment of these three state-level concordats had little to do directly with the bishops and even less with the Catholic German population, lay or clerical. These concordats illustrate the power brokering needed to produce them: a handful of men with political clout in German governments and the Vatican cooperating to make the deals. The process underscores the marginalization of the German episcopate and priests, which set an alarming precedent for the 1933 concordat and subsequent events during the Third Reich. The episcopate as a group had no pull, though bishops in two states—Faulhaber in Munich and Archbishops Fritz and Gröber in Freiburg—had enough clout to exert limited influence. Faulhaber and Pacelli were friends from Pacelli's days as nuncio in Munich. Their warm relationship, evident in the frequent letters the two exchanged from the 1920s to 1945, ensured no diocesan roadblocks for the Bavarian concordat.[75] Archbishop Carl Fritz of Freiburg im Breisgau, on the other hand, was "always openly cool" toward Pacelli's aims. Fritz kept Pacelli from making real headway until the bishop died at the end of 1931. A more amenable Conrad Gröber replaced him, opening the way for the concordat with Baden several years later.[76]

The *Reichskonkordat* emerged, as had the three state concordats, through a diplomatic power play engineered by a handful of men who nominally acted on behalf of Catholic Germans while excluding them from the deal making. Even the episcopate, not to mention the lower clergy and laity, were held at arm's length during negotiations. The treaty's very existence was the subject of agitated, though mostly unconfirmed, rumors until the bishops saw a draft at their annual conference in May 1933, mere weeks before the final version was signed.[77]

Although Hitler's explicit enemy before 1933 was primarily communism and its sympathizers, not the Church, the Nazi Party's success in the 1932 Reichstag elections pushed Pacelli to resume efforts to secure a national concordat. He feared for the rights of the Catholic Church in Germany and a continued loss of Catholics to an openly anti-Christian ideology. He found an ally in the Catholic politician Franz von Papen, who became chancellor in July. After stepping down in January 1933 to make room for Hitler as chancellor, Papen served as the middleman between the Nazi government and the Vatican, represented by Pacelli.[78]

The Bishops and the *Reichskonkordat*

The concordat came into existence almost entirely without the bishops' input. Hitler had partially pacified the episcopate in his speech to the Reichstag in March 1933, leading to the Enabling Act. Then he had called the Christian churches in Germany "the weightiest factor for the maintenance of our nationality."[79] The bishops still worried, however, and in mid-April 1933 Bertram wrote to Hitler expressing his apprehension about the future of Catholic lay organizations in Nazi Germany. Neither his letter nor Hitler's response mentioned a concordat.[80] At some point toward the end of that month, though, Catholic leaders learned of concordat negotiations; the minutes of a meeting of representatives of the Church provinces on 25 and 26 April 1933 recorded that a *Reichskonkordat* was being reconsidered at a meeting that included leading Nazis.[81]

Some of the bishops felt increasing urgency to secure an official modus vivendi with the regime in order to safeguard the Church's activities in Germany. Though Hitler spoke positively about the role of the churches under the Third Reich, the behavior of some of his minions told another story. Not-infrequent anti-Catholic actions, including the arrest of nearly 100 priests in one week, led Faulhaber to beseech the Bavarian minister of state "not to allow the fight against so-called political Catholicism to become a fight against Catholicism, tantamount to a camouflaged Kulturkampf."[82]

Thus one would expect the dominant emotion of Church leaders responding to the concordat signing in July 1933 to be relief. This is certainly evident in their correspondence. But alongside relief ran strong currents of nervousness and skepticism mixed with gratitude. While Bertram thanked Pacelli for his work, he simultaneously urged his fellow bishops to convene to deal with outstanding questions and the implementation of the concordat. Faulhaber was even bolder in his congratulatory letter to Hitler, hoping that "the articles of the concordat will prove to be worth more than the paper they are written on [*auf dem Papier nicht stehen bleiben*]."[83] Publicly the episcopate stood with Bertram when he exclaimed in a thank-you letter to the chancellor, "What the old parliaments and parties could not achieve in sixty years, your statesmanlike foresight has realized on a world-historical level in six months."[84] Hitler himself had had very little to do with the drafting of the concordat. But his assumption of the chancellery—and the dismantling of democracy—opened doors that had remained shut throughout the Weimar era.

The bishops did appreciate the concordat's guarantees, several of which Catholic German lay and spiritual leaders had sought for decades. These included religious freedom and the right of the church to manage its own affairs (Article 1); the right to free communication between the Holy See and the Catholic bishops, clergy, and populace of Germany (Article 4); clarification of the legal status of the clergy (Articles 5 through 10); guarantees of property, juridical rights, and finances tied to the state (Articles 15 through 18); pastoral care for the army, prisons, and hospitals (Articles 27 and 28). In the eyes of the bishops and many Catholics who had feared the Nazis, the two most important guarantees concerned religious education (Articles 19 through 25) and the right to organize and maintain Catholic lay organizations, including the Catholic youth movement (Article 31).[85] These articles clarified the ambiguities in the Weimar constitution and expanded on the Bavarian, Prussian, and Badenese concordats. Some concluded that a "dishonorable 'horse trade'" had been made, in view of the fact that the dissolution of the Center and, indeed, democratic practices in the Reichstag in general took place almost simultaneously with the signing of the concordat. But most saw the agreement as a victory for Catholic Germans.[86]

Initially the concessions the Church made to secure the concordat appeared to ease Nazi strictures on Catholic involvement in public life. The Catholic German population, or at least its leaders, could, it seemed, live without fear of state-directed persecution. Now legally bound to respect the rights of Germany's Catholics, Hitler's government would leave organizations and religious education alone, and the Church would exercise unquestioned authority in its own affairs. Events immediately in the wake of the concordat's signing suggested that the Nazis would indeed play by the rules. Hitler declared dissolved Catholic organizations free to reorganize; he suspended coercive measures against priests; and he promised to stop persecuting Catholic leaders.[87] Bishops and priests offered masses of thanksgiving, and Catholic theologians stepped forward to proclaim their cooperation. New pro-Nazi Catholic periodicals and organizations sprang up, reflecting a remarkable, if limited, ideological *Gleichschaltung* pursued by some Catholics.[88]

The more astute bishops, however, were convinced that the concordat did not really change Nazi Church policy. Nor was Pacelli naïve. A concordat would keep the party from attacking Catholicism and the institutional Church too openly or aggressively, not because the party felt duty-bound to honor the terms but because Hitler was sensitive to international opinion. In a report to the Foreign Office, Ivone Kirkpatrick, the British chargé-d'affaires in the Vatican, related a conversation with Pacelli, in which the future pope insisted that the Church had no political angle in pursuing the concordat. Rather, "the spiritual welfare of 20 million Catholic souls in Germany was at stake," and when the Nazis violated the agreement—"they were certain to do so"—the Church had a legal foundation for protest.[89] Pacelli continued to speak in these terms after the war, long after he became pope. Addressing the College of Cardinals in 1945, he chose to ignore the Church's enthusiasm for a concordat with the Nazi government and emphasized that

> the stimulus came from the side of National Socialism itself, so that in the case of a rejection, the entire responsibility for its consequences would fall on the Holy See. At the time, to be sure, the Church itself was not deluded or misled about the true lessons and goals of National Socialism. However, through the existing concordat, all kinds of mischief could, at least in the first years after 1933, be prevented.[90]

This line of argument downplays Pacelli's role as a highly adept political player in securing the agreement, but it also highlights the difficulties that the Church faced—and chose to engage. This would not be the only time Catholic leaders combined willful myopia and strategic decision making when it came to the welfare of Catholic German souls. Nor would it be the only example of claims to neutrality or apolitical thinking contradicted by subsequent behavior. But what the Catholic signatories sought was a defensive maneuver, "a juridical instrument [rather than] a moral endorsement," against a regime that they knew was hostile to religion in general and the Church in particular.[91] In this way, Pacelli hoped to attain the best possible legal standing for the Church with the new regime, including an independent sphere for the activities of its spiritual and lay leaders—even while expecting the Nazis to flout their obligations.[92]

The concordat was an important milestone in another way, one that the episcopate and Pacelli could not ignore, particularly when two Nazi circulars audaciously proclaimed the concordat as a triumph for the regime. The *Nationalsozialistische Parteikorrespondenz* (National Socialist Party Correspondence) asserted: "The fact that the Vatican has closed a deal with the new Germany signifies the recognition of the National Socialist state by the Catholic Church. This agreement makes it clear and beyond doubt to the whole world, that the assumption that Nazism is an enemy of religion is a lie which was devised for the purpose of political agitation." The Nazi Party's chief organ, the *Völkischer Beobachter* (People's Observer), was more succinct but no less powerful: "National Socialism in Germany has been acknowledged by the Catholic Church in the most solemn way possible."[93] Very few in 1933 understood the lengths to which the Nazi Party would go to realize its weltanschauung. Those who compromised with dictatorship and racism in the early years of the Third Reich did so for a variety of reasons. Some, but not all, were devoted Nazis; others cooperated for more opportunistic reasons. These early collaborators came from all sections of society—journalists and lawyers, teachers and bureaucrats, merchants and factory workers. They did not perceive Nazism as intrinsically evil; instead, they thought that through compromise they could get what they needed with little to no inconvenience to themselves. Only over the next dozen years were they to learn the magnitude of their mistake. The Church's leadership was no exception.

Breaking the *Reichskonkordat:* The Disintegration of the Catholic Youth Movement and Other Anti-Catholic Measures

It did not take long for Faulhaber's apprehensions about Nazi contempt for the concordat to be proven correct. Other bishops and many lay Catholics assumed that the Nazi regime would hold the agreement as inviolable, or infringe upon only a few articles. But the regime had quite the opposite idea. The state began to break its own commitments in August 1933, requiring church groups to meet only within church buildings, in contravention of Article 31. There followed a decree against double membership (*Doppelmitgliedschaft*), barring Catholics from belonging to both a Catholic association and the Nazi Party. Nazi agents, including the police and the Gestapo, forcibly entered diocesan offices across Germany and turned them upside down. The regime attacked denominational schools at all levels and on multiple fronts: state governments suddenly dismissed their professors and teachers, denied them their promised subsidies, and rigged school board elections.

In June 1933, Hitler elevated Schirach to the ranks of Nazi leaders with dual party-state roles by naming him the Youth Leader of the German Reich. Schirach had worked against the Catholic youth movement for a year by this point, and he quickly ramped up the HJ's hostile tactics. In a move targeting Catholic youths explicitly, in July 1933 the Hitler Youth organization, like the party, prohibited simultaneous membership in a Catholic youth organization and the Hitlerjugend. This greatly affected both Catholic youth and Nazi-affiliated youth, as the leaders of each locked their opponents out of certain activities; HJ members, for example, could no longer serve as altar boys, and many boys and young men, when forced to choose, went with the Catholic groups. Eventually HJ leader Baldur von Schirach decreed, "All activity which is not of a purely ecclesiastical or religious nature, in particular political and various sport activities, is forbidden to denominational youth associations even if formed for the occasion."[94] This was in July 1935.

In fact, from 1933 to 1936, in direct contradiction to the concordat, a fierce battle was waged between the HJ and Catholic clergy for "control" of German youth. German boys and girls caught up in this battle, no matter on which side, would have been indelibly marked. Either a youngster joined the state-sponsored youth, giving up activities run by the Church, or he or she stuck to the circles run by the priests and lay leaders of the community, risking state retaliation. Nonmembership in the HJ became increasingly disadvantageous in the 1930s. Most damaging, jobs, especially in the civil service, were open only to Germans who had been members of the HJ. More lucrative career paths through the Nazi Party required several years' membership in the HJ.[95] The goal of the *Gleichschaltung* of German society was to bring all disparate elements into the party's orbit and eradicate not just opposition but also potential dissent and marked difference; the youth were no exception. Schirach and other Nazi leaders intended to starve Catholic youth into submission.

But the Catholic youth groups of Germany did not subside quietly. Until 1936, evidence indicates that the HJ barely weakened them. In spite of harassment by the HJ, SS, and Gestapo; confiscation of goods and property; searching of houses and arresting of leaders; even pitched scuffles in the streets, Catholic youth membership numbers did not decline. In many west German dioceses in 1934 demonstrations in the form of pilgrimages and processions supported the youth movement, often with the bishop present.[96] Priests and other youth leaders even contravened the concordat in defense of the youth groups' autonomy, actively discouraging their charges from joining the HJ. In this they were aided considerably by the leaders of the HJ, who tended to be provocative, undisciplined, and disorganized. Religious instructors used their positions to recruit new members for their Catholic organizations. To some degree, inviting comparison with the effects of the Kulturkampf, the *Gleichschaltung* had the opposite effect: distinctions between the different Catholic youth groups, which competed with each other before 1933, melted away under external hostility. So, too, did the insularity of the Catholic youth movement. As non-Catholic youth groups were obliterated or "coordinated," including the Protestant Free Youth and the youth wings of the socialists and communists, Catholic youths no longer shied away from working with them as they went underground.[97]

After the *Anschluss* the Nazi regime also closed theological faculties in Austria, and it left posts both there and in Germany vacant when it refused to approve the proposed candidates. The state curtailed subsidies for churches as early as 1935; it severely limited the circulation of pastoral letters by the bishops and papal encyclicals; it reduced the Catholic press steadily, forcing a decline from 435 periodicals in 1934 to just seven in 1943. All these moves directly violated the concordat.[98] Finally, priests and bishops faced constant ridicule in the pro-Nazi press and harassment from the Gestapo. Newspapers such as the *Völkische Beobachter* and *Das Schwarze Korps* (The Black Guards), the SS organ, waged a determined fight against the Catholic Church and its practices, taking aim in particular at the German hierarchy and the pope. It soon became obvious that the party would use every opportunity to circumvent the concordat. Pacelli himself spoke of a new Kulturkampf in 1934, ruing that the Nazis wanted capitulation, not compliance.[99]

The push for submission continued. By the end of 1936, service in the Hitler Youth became compulsory for boys. Steadily from 1936, the state forced Catholic lay organizations to disband; this once vast network had disintegrated by the onset of the war. In May 1936, the regime's attacks on religious orders mounted with the start of the so-called immorality trials, avidly followed by the Nazi press, which alleged that "Catholic monasteries were . . . breeding places of filth and vice."[100] Though these trials continued sporadically up to the outbreak of war, most took place in 1936 and 1937. While it is difficult to assess overall public reaction to the Nazi offensive against monks and nuns, Catholic Germans seemed to have imitated their spiritual leaders: the bishops privately protested, but publicly said little.[101]

Another pastoral letter shortly before Christmas 1936 complained about Nazi concordat violations, including the attacks on denominational schools and youth groups. It nevertheless urged Catholic Germans "to support unstintingly the head of the German Reich in the defensive struggle against Bolshevism." The infringements on the 1933 agreement were unacceptable, but the letter stated, "We Catholics will be ready, *in spite of the distrust with which we are confronted*, to give to the state what belongs to the state, and to support the Führer in repelling Bolshevism and [his] other tasks."[102] The bishops set the example for their flocks that would persist through the war years: equivocation was justified, even if the regime undermined the Church, because the larger threat was the complete abrogation of religious freedom and, even worse, godless communism. In this, the episcopate, led by its conference chairman Adolf Cardinal Bertram of Breslau, consistently modeled the practice of German Catholicism from 1933 on. The bishops stressed the maintenance of order, obedience to legitimate authority, and submission to God's will. Whatever problems priests and bishops faced with the regime were to be dealt with through the proper channels, which usually involved a great deal of letter writing.[103]

The Spanish Civil War

In 1936, however, the bishops had an opportunity to publicly nuance the Church's submission to the regime. When the Spanish Civil War broke out in July of that year and Germany allied with the nationalists, the bishops stressed their loyalty to the state and their antipathy for communism. They first addressed the Republican atrocities in

Spain at their annual conference in Fulda in August. Shortly thereafter, they issued a pastoral letter highlighting the plight of Spanish Catholics in their fight against "the Bolshevik anti-Christ." But they then emphasized the conscientious fulfillment by so many Catholic Germans of "their duties as citizens and soldiers" despite the unjust, anti-Catholic accusations made by "our rivals" (the Nazi government was never explicitly named). The letter cautiously disowned the regime's racial ideology, commenting on the nonsensical idea of replacing the Christian God with a racial "German god." Though conceding that the fourth commandment required Catholics to obey the state, the bishops recalled St. Paul's gloss, "Man must obey God more than men."[104]

They must have been stung, though not entirely surprised, when in September a Hitler Youth leader attacked both the pope and the German bishops for supposed silence and willful distraction in the face of Spanish communist atrocities. The ardent Nazi Gustav Staebe published his lengthy critique, "Great Anxiety in Fulda," in Würzburg's Nazi daily *Mainfränkische Zeitung*. After laying out in gruesome detail atrocities against the Spanish Catholic Church, including desecrating tombs and burning and hanging priests and nuns, he asked plaintively, "Where is the pope, where is the battle cry of the Fulda Conference of Bishops, where is the conspicuous, audible activity of the Church and all her organs? But the pope does not weep, the German bishops don't weep either. At present they have no time for it. They hold multiple meetings on the confessional schools question, which at the moment is without doubt the most important thing in September 1936." Staebe was no stranger to priests or bishops in Nazi Germany. He had kept an eye on relations between Catholic clergy and the Nazi movement since at least 1933, when he had encouraged priests who supported Hitler to submit their names to his newspaper, the southern edition of the *Völkischer Beobachter*. He was "pleasantly surprised" by the number of submissions he received.[105]

The German bishops defended themselves in October 1936 through their spokesman, Bishop Matthias Ehrenfried, pointing out their strong condemnation of Russian Bolshevism and the Spanish massacres months earlier as well as the pope's call to the world to defend the victims of Bolshevism in Spain.[106] Concerning the civil war, they followed the pope's example and condemned explicitly the atrocities perpetrated by Spanish "Bolsheviks." Pope Pius XI devoted an entire encyclical in March 1937 to "the scourge of communism" in Spain.[107] In the eyes of some Nazis, however, the Church was nowhere near strident enough in its condemnation. The Vatican did not officially break with the Republican government, although Rome posted no nuncio to Spain due to the war. The Holy See was (and remains) slow to formally withdraw an ambassador unless forced to do so, as it was by the Soviet Union.[108] Rumors prompted Faulhaber to meet with Hitler in November 1936 to reaffirm the Church's anti-communism and to protest the calumnies spread by the Nazi press, particularly concerning the pope. Faulhaber wrote a memorandum the next day detailing his exchange with the Führer. He recalled arguing,

> In his speeches of February 1930 and of this year, given before Spanish refugees, Pope Pius XI labeled Bolshevism the deadly enemy of every Christian culture, and at Fulda, the German bishops expressed themselves identically in this year's pastoral letter and in earlier proclamations.... You can imagine, Herr Reich Chancellor, how painful it had to be for us Catholics to hear and read the untruth that is still spread in today's German newspapers and educational addresses: the pope stands silently in league with Moscow, he thinks ever on closing a concordat with Moscow, and for this reason he was silent at the beginning about the atrocities in Spain, and hopes increasingly that Bolshevism will destroy the Third Reich.[109]

Faulhaber's intervention was futile. Nazi journalists continued their attacks on the pope and the Catholic Church in Germany throughout the Spanish Civil War, undeterred by the bishops' protests of their consistent, deep-seated antipathy for all things communist.

Some dared to speak out against these lies. Faulhaber's record vis-à-vis Nazism is inconsistent, but he disagreed vocally with the regime often enough to have the Gestapo raid his office several times. He was to become a favorite target of the ire of *Das Schwarze Korps*.[110] Galen, in Münster, is well known for his sermons in August 1941 explicitly attacking Nazi "euthanasia" of the physically and mentally handicapped. Konrad von Preysing, bishop of Berlin after 1935, most dedicated of the anti-Nazi bishops, at one point threatened to resign his seat in protest.[111] But most bishops seemed willing to cease engaging with the regime in order to safeguard their spiritual influence and preserve their flocks' access to the sacraments. Thus, the concordat was a decisive turning point in the regime's quest to neutralize potential adversaries. The Church leadership played no part in any sustained resistance to Nazism after it pledged itself to the treaty.

The "Silence" of the Bishops

The bishops' quietism was evident in their reaction—loud public silence—to various blatantly illegal, discriminatory, even murderous events before the outbreak of the war in 1939, including the Röhm putsch in June 1934, the pronouncement of the Nuremberg Laws in September 1935, and the nationwide pogrom known as *Kristallnacht* in November 1938. Unofficially, the bishops grumbled. There was furious letter writing and sermonizing, complaints from individual clergy and laity, and no doubt feelings of resentment and betrayal. But at no time did anyone who might have had some influence attempt serious, sustained, and stubborn resistance that might have accomplished what letter writing could not. Despite the increasing hostility of the Nazi Party and its organizations to institutional religion, the Church, from the bishops down, did not break ranks to confront it. In what has been called a "lopsided, unrequited love affair," the majority of Catholics in leadership positions (both secular and ecclesiastical) found ways to acclimatize to the new regime.[112]

For many, this was not difficult. Hitler's movement had paraded as the guardian of conservative, antimodern values, opposed to liberalism and communism, advocating a return to order and a reassertion of traditional ideals, emphasizing family, discipline, and strong authority: all virtues that Catholics could appreciate.[113] Even when the highly racial 1935 Berlin exhibit *"Das Wunder des Lebens"* ("The Miracle of Life") promoted nonmarital sex ("immaculate and holy is the conception out of worthy love—immaculate and holy is the birth of life of a healthy type"), the only objection that Church authorities seem to have raised was that the exhibit omitted references to God as the originator of life.[114]

Why did not bishops, and the priests who looked to them for guidance, more aggressively dissent from the regime's offenses? The answer must be an amalgam of German nationalism, religious antisemitism, and fear of Russian Bolshevism. The importance of the Bolshevik threat cannot be overstressed. The degree of danger that most Catholics saw in communism is difficult to imagine today. This fear of Bolshevism persuaded many devout Catholics and their leaders to accept Nazism. It may help us understand why bishops and priests felt it necessary to remain silent when concentration camps opened in 1933. Even those wary of Nazism treated it as the lesser evil—at least it was not official Nazi policy to torture priests, burn churches, and eradicate the religious beliefs of the people. Faulhaber reminded his clergy in 1933 of their debt to the earlier Bavarian parliament, "which in the last decade barred the threats of communism and Bolshevism from our homeland and which stood up for the religious, moral and socio-economic recovery of our people. However, we must also accept the basic laws of Christian political science with regard to the new government and give civil obedience to the lawful authorities."[115]

Faulhaber was not alone in this advice. The first pastoral letter of the German episcopate after the triumph of Nazism, in June 1933, sounded downright optimistic:

> To our great happiness, the leading figures of the new state have expressly declared that they and their movement stand on the foundation of Christianity alone.... No more, therefore, shall the unbeliever and the immorality unleashed by him poison the marrow of the German people, no more shall the murderous Bolshevism with its satanic hatred of God threaten and devastate the soul of the German people.[116]

Pope Pius XI chimed in, too, labeling communism "the first, greatest and universal danger" because it threatened "personal dignity, the sanctity of the family, the order and security of civil life, and above all ... and in particular the Catholic religion and the Catholic Church."[117] Even when the regime began to violate the concordat more frequently, Catholic leaders in Germany firmly believed that Hitler's movement was necessary to combat the greater evil of communism. The *Münchener Beobachter* (Munich Observer) was adamant that "we were and even now are always prepared to work together with state authorities in the struggle against Bolshevism and still repudiate decisively all Muscovite ingratiation [*Anbiederungsversuche*]."[118]

Mit brennender Sorge and the End of the Catholic Youth Movement

Only once did Church leadership either in Germany or Rome abandon its policy of "no comment" regarding Nazism. In March 1937, the Vatican released the German-language papal encyclical *Mit brennender Sorge* (With Burning Anxiety). Released a mere five days before Pius XI's encyclical condemning communism, *With Burning Anxiety* denounced the Nazi regime's habitual breaches of the 1933 concordat, its unrelenting attacks on the Church in Germany, and its neo-pagan ideology, without ever including the word "Nazi." The target was clear enough. Pius's letter began by explaining why the Vatican had signed the concordat, then moved on to point out the violations. It denounced in no uncertain terms the exaltation of race and the German state, the center of Nazi ideology. These doctrines, the letter said, directly contradicted the Christian belief in equality and, more importantly, the possibility of redemption for any baptized person. Though the encyclical did not discuss German legislation and discrimination against Jews, it did underscore the equality of all human beings before God and rejected the misappropriation of religious language and imagery to create a national religion. It also condemned the Nazi drive to purge the "Jewish" Old Testament from the Bible.

The encyclical outlined in detail infringements of the concordat, including closing confessional schools, harassing clergy, dissolving lay religious organizations, and trying to gain control of Catholic youth. In a section directed to Catholic parents, the pope declared that the bitter campaign to curtail their rights as religious educators "could hardly be considered more fateful"; he assailed so-called religious lessons in schools that systematically disparaged religion. In the letter's concluding sections, he encouraged Catholic Germans to remain faithful to God and the message of Christ despite their suffering. Their anguish even offered an opportunity for spiritual purification to those who patiently endured it.[119]

Historian Emma Fattorini uses newly available documents from the Vatican Secret Archives to elucidate the encyclical and its context.[120] In January 1937, the pope granted an audience to five German bishops (three of them cardinals)—Bertram, Faulhaber, Galen, Preysing, and Schulte, archbishop of Cologne—to hear their grievances about the concordat violations. The encyclical emerged from their lengthy conversation. Officially attributed to Pius XI, gravely ill with diabetes and heart disease, the encyclical reflected his desire to issue a spiritual (as opposed to a political) condemnation of totalitarianism. Faulhaber penned the words initially; he and Bertram especially wanted to avoid conflict with the Nazi government. Pacelli added sharper, even accusatory elements to Faulhaber's conciliatory draft before submitting it for the pope's signature.[121] The group arranged for it to be smuggled into Germany, printed by twelve different presses, and delivered by courier, on foot, often by boys or young men—the cooperation of Catholic youth was essential, which provoked the lethal ire of the Nazi Party—so that it could be read from every pulpit on Palm Sunday, 21 March.[122] And priests and bishops did read it, everywhere in Germany, in stark defiance of Gestapo agents surveilling their parishes. According to Fattorini, not a single priest failed to incorporate it into his sermon that Sunday.[123]

Much like the 1933 concordat, *Mit brennender Sorge* attracted attention worldwide. It clearly rebuked Nazi policy in respect to the Church in Germany. The encyclical pinned blame for the injustices and indignities afflicting the German Church directly on the Nazi regime. The sixth section pointed out that "the reinterpretation, circumvention, erosion, and finally the more or less open violation of the concordat by the treaty's other signer has become the unwritten rule of thumb."[124] The letter did not condemn explicitly the persecution of German Jews, which the Nuremberg Laws legalized in September 1935. It did not mention the plight of the *"Reichsfeinde,"* or enemies of the empire, including Jews, socialists, communists, and other political and "racial undesirables" languishing in concentration camps. But it did address the racial basis of Nazi ideology and uphold the Christian dogma that God's laws "are effective independent of time and space, land and race.... His law knows neither privilege nor exception. Rulers and ruled, crowned and uncrowned, rich and poor, high and low are subject in equal measure to His word."[125]

Many in Europe hailed the encyclical as a welcome protest, the strongest official reproach that the Holy See could deliver to the Nazi regime. Hindsight has not been so enthusiastic. Some historians continue to praise it as the only way in which the Holy See could rebuke

Nazi policy. They argue that the German bishops, through the pope, pushed as far as they dared without endangering their increasingly constrained sphere of action within Germany. To go further—to name Hitler or to discuss Nazi ideology explicitly—would invite irrevocable damage, such as cancellation of the concordat or open assault on the Church and its members, like the persecution during the Kulturkampf years. For other historians, the encyclical did not go nearly far enough. These historians have dismissed *Mit brennender Sorge*, called apologetic, conciliatory, or circumlocutory, as a half-measure that underplayed the serious dangers of the Nazi weltanschauung, that ignored the plight of Germany's Jews, and that achieved little more than snarls of consternation from uncompromising anti-Catholic Nazis.[126]

If Nazi reaction is any measure of how damaging the party deemed the tract, however, then those historians who argue that it had little effect underestimate its impact in the eyes of Hitler and his cronies. What the encyclical did do incontrovertibly was ignite the fury of the Nazi Party, which regarded *Mit brennender Sorge* as deeply subversive, offensive, even treacherous. The Nazi response also showed what the party would do when the Vatican growled once, leaving one to wonder what it might do if the pope more consistently snapped at Nazi policies. The regime quickly closed the firms that had printed the document, and it vigorously renewed the immorality trials that had been briefly suspended during the 1936 Olympic Games.[127] The Gestapo harassed the clergy full-time; its agents interfered with the publication of pastoral letters in weeklies and censored those Catholic presses still open.

The backlash killed the youth movement. Already in 1936, the Nazis had arrested fifty-seven Catholic youth leaders on charges of cooperation with the outlawed communist youth groups.[128] By 1939 the remaining Catholic youth newspapers had been liquidated. In December 1936, the Hitler Youth Law made membership in the HJ compulsory, requiring all German youth in the Reich to be "educated physically, intellectually, and morally in the spirit of National Socialism to serve the community and the people."[129] Although career advancement had earlier depended on HJ membership, this was the first time the regime made the obligation legally binding. The regime limited parades, processions, retreats, pilgrimages, camps, confirmation classes, and day hikes, moving steadily to eliminate the remaining autonomous youth groups. They managed to endure just over another two years before the regime dissolved the last one, the Katholische Jungmännerverband (Catholic Young Men's Association), in February 1939.

Nazi agents including the Gestapo oversaw the amalgamation of Catholic organizations—not just youth groups—with their Nazi counterparts. This process occurred with alarming rapidity: Catholic professors and teachers were fired; Church-sponsored educational courses on themes such as marriage and childcare were prohibited. When the bishops protested, they found no support from the minister for ecclesiastical affairs, official liaison between the government and the churches. Hitler even entertained the idea of doing away completely with the concordat. Although in the end he did not, persuaded by others not to risk exacerbating domestic tensions in light of his foreign policy plans, he did pointedly avoid meeting with Pope Pius XI when he visited Rome in May 1938.[130]

After the encyclical Hitler gave free rein to the anti-Catholic activities of Heinrich Himmler's SS. The SS used all methods at its disposal to further its agenda to pound Catholics, continuing to cooperate closely with the HJ, a "generational alliance between key [Nazi] affiliates" that shared an aversion to all things Catholic.[131] It was obvious to the bishops who was responsible. In October 1937, Preysing prepared a private memorandum for the episcopate, specifying the SS's supervision:

> The SS leads the sharpest and most ruthless battle against the Church. The Reichsführer-SS [Himmler] views 99% of ministers as swine, as he expressed it to one of his adjutants. . . . It is not beyond the realm of possibility that the most radical wing of the party, under the leadership of the SS, will take every opportunity to drive the battle of annihilation [*Vernichtungskampf*] against the Church to its finish.[132]

Nor did Preysing exaggerate the open battle against the Church in Germany. Arrests, dismissals, and harassment, specifically of parish priests crucial for holding together spiritual communities at the local level, showed the struggle to be life-and-death. Nazi reports at the end of 1937 reveal the regime's depth of concern about Catholic reaction to the resumption of the immorality trials. A local Security Service (Sicherheitsdienst, or SD) office in Koblenz reported that in "some areas of the Reich, in strongly believing Catholic circles, signatures were being collected for a statement which asserted that the immorality trials against priests and other clergy were led by the German government in order to destroy religion."[133] The statements would eventually be presented to the pope, an action that stimulated the SS-*Hauptsturmführer* (equivalent of a captain) to urge his men to find these lists, or at least obtain a photocopy. Six months later, the same SD office reported that the Catholic Church was building a priest-fighter organization [*Priesterfrontkämpferorganisation*] to challenge the Nazi-run War Victims Provisions (NSKOV) as well as to ingratiate themselves with the officer corps of the armed forces. The organization would be kept under close surveillance.[134] Even criticism that seemed safely hidden in sermons in small towns was liable to be reported to the local Gestapo office, as Father Franz Bungarten in Bad Neuenahr, near Koblenz, discovered in November 1938. Several SS and Hitler Youth reports quoted his Sunday sermon that "many today are being persecuted for the sake of their beliefs, in Spain, Russia, and *even in our Fatherland*."[135]

Between the release of Nazi wrath following *Mit brennender Sorge* and the outbreak of the war, relations between the regime and the Catholic Church changed little. The state worked steadily to limit the autonomy of those nominally independent Catholic groups left (for example, the youth groups) and continued to attack individual clergy. Church leaders protested these measures but offered little resistance. No doubt they privately discussed Hitler's foreign political intrigues— the *Anschluss* with Austria and annexation of the Sudetenland in 1938 and the taking over of the rest of Czechoslovakia in early 1939— but publicly they offered no comment. Not even the nationwide pogrom on 9 November 1938 prompted an official pronouncement from the episcopate. *Kristallnacht* made international headlines and shocked even some Germans with the wanton violence.[136] Church leaders were likewise silent about the regime's other blatant antisemitic behavior, including the 1935 Nuremberg Laws, the 1936 banning of Jews from professional jobs, and the gradual segregation of Jews in German public life between 1935 and 1939. Their disregard would persist to the end of the war, when, lamenting the regime's victims, they failed to include Jews.

War

In 1939, war arrived. The regime had dissolved the last of the Catholic youth groups half a year earlier, shortly before promulgating the first of a series of decrees restating its 1936 rule requiring compulsory service in the HJ for all Germans between ten and eighteen years old regardless of parental approval. The regime thus assumed responsibility for all German youth outside the walls of school and home.[137] Boys and young men in the Catholic groups were shuffled into the HJ or its affiliates and, sooner or later, found themselves in the Wehrmacht. For the Catholic episcopate in Germany, the outbreak of hostilities altered little initially. Conscription orders were sent out, but they would really bite only in 1940. The regime briefly toned down its anti-Catholic rhetoric and behavior, but it eventually resumed its vitriol and antipathy. The year 1941, more than 1939, was the real turning point for the bishops; it saw the invasion of the Soviet Union and the dramatic surge in implementing the goals of Nazi racial policy, including the murder of mentally and physically handicapped Germans and commencement of deportations of German Jews. Not themselves combatants, the bishops were directly affected by the war only insofar as their parishioners and priests took part or, after 1942, when Allied bombing began in earnest. Their primary concerns, therefore, remained administering spiritual care to their flocks and ensuring that they gave no reason to the Nazis to further diminish their sphere of spiritual authority.

The episcopate openly supported the war's outbreak in 1939, though, like most other Germans, not with particular enthusiasm.[138] They issued a pastoral letter shortly after the invasion of Poland, encouraging Catholics to perform their duty to Führer and state and appealing to their flocks "to join in ardent prayers that God's providence may lead this war to blessed success and peace for Fatherland and *Volk*."[139] Neither the bishops nor Pope Pius XII, who had ascended the papal throne in March 1939 and whose first encyclical, in October, dealt with the eruption of war, mentioned German aggression or provocation. Nor did they allude to the plight of the Polish Catholic Church during and after the invasion, in striking contrast to their vehement condemnation of the Bolshevik treatment of the Orthodox Church in the late 1920s.

In the first days of the war, the Wehrmacht and Himmler's SS arrested and murdered without mercy Polish priests, victims—like Jews, communists, and the intelligentsia—of the Führer's order to eliminate perceived enemies of Germany in Poland. Here Polish clergy were caught in a triple bind, targeted not only because of both their vocation and their religion—German soldiers, who used "Catholic" as a slur, viewed them as guilty of "nationalist rabble-rousing" and fomenting resistance—but also because of their ethnicity, as Poles.[140] By the end of 1939, the German military and SS in Poland had executed more than 200 priests, and they had imprisoned approximately 1,000 more.[141] In fact, the anti-Church policies in Poland were so relentless that two years later, a report out of the diocese of Posen-Gnesen declared that only thirty churches out of an original 431 remained open.[142]

Announced mere days before the invasion of Poland, the Molotov-Ribbentrop Pact (formally known as the Treaty of Non-aggression between Germany and the Union of Soviet Socialist Republics) would have come as a shock, even an insult, to the episcopate, who had unwaveringly opposed Bolshevism since the end of the previous war. But no comment on the unexpected truce between Germany and the Church's most loathed temporal enemy surfaced, even in passing, in the correspondence between the Holy See and the bishops or among the bishops themselves. In fact, the historian searching for some indication of the reaction of the Catholic Church's leadership, either in Germany or in the Vatican, is hard-pressed to find anything conclusive. The pact is simply not acknowledged. Perhaps the regime's about-face was too upsetting for the bishops to trust any words put to paper, let alone spoken from the pulpit. Perhaps some of them recognized the pact for what it was: a way for the Nazi regime to buy itself time and avoid a two-front war after Germany's invasion of Poland.[143] It is unlikely, given the seemingly genuine abhorrence and fear in the writings of individual bishops since the 1920s, that they accepted the Stalinist regime as a true ally.

In spite of the brazen anti-Catholic activity in Poland, Catholic Germans continued to serve their country. All bishops and most priests, regardless of their views of the Nazi regime, did the same. Some advocated improving conditions in Poland, and a few, such as Cardinal Adolf Bertram, vigorously protested restrictions on Polish forced laborers in their diocese, who were prohibited from receiving pastoral care from German priests. But as a group, the bishops declared the war in 1939 justifiably defensive, and they encouraged loyalty to the regime over solidarity with Poland's suffering Catholics.[144] In their national identity as Germans, they were no different from their lay counterparts. This distinction between the state, directed by Hitler and the Nazi Party, on the one hand, and the Fatherland, Germany, *Heimat*, on the other—notions all larger than Nazism—was so effectively ingrained in Church leaders that they supported the war with no apparent qualms. Otherwise some at least would have questioned a war led by a regime that had spent six years systematically violating the concordat and that murdered, imprisoned, or drove into exile their co-religionists in Poland. Attacks on German Catholic clergy, organizations, and property temporarily ceased. Hitler was not stupid enough to continue harassing the churches when he needed their work for the war effort.[145] But he did not need to buy the bishops' support. No evidence exists that any bishop ever considered opposing the war.

German nationalism was not the whole story. Pius XII did not exactly model opposition to Nazi aggression, though he by no means remained silent. His October 1939 encyclical lamented the "tragic whirlpool of war" and the killing of "noncombatants" in Poland, but he identified the war's cause as the unlimited exercise of the "autonomous will of [the State]"—perhaps a veiled reference to Nazi Germany, which he otherwise did not explicitly mention.[146] Neither the encyclical nor his letters of condolence in May 1940 to Luxembourg, the Netherlands, and Belgium, after their fall, gave much inducement to the German bishops to change their policy of cooperation.

Indeed their policy—if the episcopate can be described as having deliberately decided to accommodate the wartime regime—easily survived some internal discord. Most bishops individually, in their dioceses, prayed regularly for victory, for the fighting men, and for their Führer. But there was no unanimity about acceptable behavior vis-à-vis the Nazi Party. Bertram took it upon himself to send birthday greetings on behalf of his colleagues to Hitler in April 1940. Preysing, a diehard foe of Nazism, reacted with such indignation that only the pope's refusal to accept his resignation kept him in office.[147] Though other bishops sympathized, including Faulhaber and Preysing's cousin Galen,

Preysing's act of outrage did no more than estrange him from Bertram, who remained head of the Fulda Conference. The bishops did not formally discuss the incident.[148]

The Invasion of the Soviet Union

It is understandable—in terms of patriotic duty, national sentiment, and the example set by their spiritual leaders—why priests and seminarians supported the war, even if they opposed Nazism. Indeed, they willfully misunderstood or ignored some of the war's goals, perhaps a necessary precondition of their support. That they did, in fact, support it vigorously and deliberately became obvious in June 1941, when Germany invaded Soviet Russia and dramatically escalated the war. Even as the regime resumed its attempts to limit the wartime ministry of the Church—in 1941, a decree from the OKW summarily discharged all Jesuits serving in the army[149]—the bishops depicted the expanded military actions in the best possible light. Bolshevism, absent from sermons and pastoral letters since September 1939, became once again a familiar theme. In a formal letter to the pope, the bishops pronounced the war to be "in a new phase, maybe in its end-stage."[150] They quickly issued a pastoral letter urging Catholic Germans, both soldiers on the Eastern Front and civilians back home, to stand firmly against Bolshevism, "of which we German bishops have warned German Catholics, and called them to vigilance in countless pastoral letters, between 1921 and 1936."[151]

Some bishops also saw the invasion of the Soviet Union as an opportunity to protest state-directed harassment of the Church in Germany. Somewhat slackened, persecution had persisted into the war years. The Bavarian bishops, agitated by continued removal of crucifixes from schools at a time when the German military was engaged in its all-or-nothing battle against Bolshevism, condemned the policy in August 1941. The OKH, the letter pointed out, had ordered the graves of fallen soldiers to be marked with crosses. Yet simultaneously, "fathers and brothers of our schoolchildren depend on the prayers of the *Heimat* . . . that are being offered in the schools [where crucifixes are being removed]."[152] Galen's famous sermons that summer against the Nazi T-4, or "euthanasia," program did not mention the fight against

Bolshevism, but he contrasted with euthanasia the legitimacy of "killing an armed enemy soldier in a righteous war." Catholic Germans would not have missed the outrage in Galen's supposition that a program targeting "unproductive life," taken to its logical conclusions, would eventually zero in on "our brave soldiers who return home, severely wounded, crippled, sick."[153] The protests of the Bavarian bishops and Galen achieved their purposes: the purloined crucifixes were rehung, and the regime temporarily abrogated the T-4 program in the wake of the controversy Galen's sermons created (before relocating it outside Germany).

Of atrocities on the Eastern Front and rumors of industrialized mass death, the bishops had a good idea what was going on as early as the first months of 1942. A few of them conjectured that German war plans called for the extermination of Jews in the East, but they failed to imagine the immense scale of the operation. As for the more verifiable stories of the murder of noncombatants, the execution of hostages, and the slaughter of POWs, the bishops categorized these as the "unfortunate side-effects" of a brutal war.[154] From 1942, their pastoral letters emphasized the immorality of killing innocent people, echoing the pope. These ambiguous references to the slaughter of civilians and the existence of extermination camps remained, in the words of one historian, "cautious and abstract," designed to avoid provoking the regime.[155]

The bishops were less cautious during the war about Jews who had converted to Catholicism. They labeled these Catholics "Catholic (or Christian) non-Aryans," adopting the Nazi terminology for them. Because of their concern, the bishops received as early as 1942 all but definitive proof about the atrocities inflicted on Jews in the East. Before 1939, Church leaders had maintained consistent public silence about the increasingly harsh persecution of Germany's Jews. Faulhaber typified the bishops' outlook. In 1933, he wrote to a priest who had tried unsuccessfully to publish a newspaper article opposing the boycott of Jewish businesses:

> These proceedings against the Jews are un-Christian in that every Christian, not merely every priest, must act against them [*dagegen auftreten*]. [But] there are far more important problems presently for

the ecclesiastical authorities. The schools, the continued existence of Catholic associations, and sterilization are more important for Christianity in our *Heimat*. Above all *we can assume—[as we've] already seen, to some extent—that the Jews are able to take care of themselves*. Therefore we have no reason to give the regime a reason to turn the anti-Jewish agitation into an anti-Jesuit agitation.[156]

As Church leaders had done for centuries during periods of tension with secular authority, Faulhaber and his fellow bishops strove to protect the autonomy of the Church. They combated direct threats to Church doctrine, such as sterilization and, later, mercy killing. Abuse of Jews, however un-Christian, did not figure into this priority. The common, casual antisemitism of bishops like Faulhaber reinforced the Church's self-absorption.

What did become increasingly urgent was protecting Jewish converts to Catholicism. In the eyes of the Church, baptism drained these former Jews of their Jewishness and made them full-fledged Christians. To the Nazis, a baptized Jew remained racially a Jew—and subject to legal discrimination and, after the war's outbreak, deportation. The bishops' concern predated the war. The Relief Committee for Catholic non-Aryans was formally organized in 1935. But an informal group had begun work two years before that, aiding ex-Jewish Catholics who had converted from Judaism who had been expelled from their jobs in the wake of the first race laws of the Third Reich. By 1937, the committee helped Catholic Germans victimized by compulsory sterilization laws or exiled due to political affiliation.[157] The bishops, in conjunction with the *Caritasverband* (German Charity), undertook the initiative of forming the Relief Committee.[158]

The bishops' annual conference met in August 1939, days before the war broke out. Toward the end of the meeting, the bishops noted that the Gestapo had confiscated relief money for the support of non-Aryans. Catholic non-Aryans were being expelled from their homes, and emigration aid and other kinds of support were becoming harder to give. The bishops, however, were more concerned with the regime's directive requiring all Jews to adopt the names "Israel" and "Sarah." The bishops wondered, "Also for the baptized?"[159]

An indefatigable opponent of Nazism, Konrad von Preysing, bishop of Berlin, quietly set up his own relief association. His assistant, the equally tireless Catholic social worker Margarete Sommer, helped to run it. They founded the Relief Organization of the Episcopal Chair of Berlin in 1938, officially to help "Catholic non-Aryans." After September 1939, when Jews could neither emigrate nor work, Sommer's organization unofficially gave money, food, and clothing to Jews as well.[160] With Preysing's approval, Sommer set up a network stretching across the German capital that helped to hide Jews (who thereby escaped deportation and certain death). Because her network included informants connected to the Gestapo, Sommer compiled four very accurate reports in 1942 and 1943 about conditions during the deportations. The reports in February and August 1942 detailed the fate of deported Jews. It is not clear if Sommer knew about the extermination camps, but she described in great detail the lethal conditions in the ghettos and the mass shooting of Jews in Lithuania: "Not only the Jews of the great Kovno ghetto have been shot in the tens of thousands, but also Jews who had been deported there from Germany." The executioners, she reported, were SS-men, members of the SD, and local Lithuanians, all dressed in Lithuanian uniforms because the slaughter was filmed "to prove that Lithuanians, not Germans, shot the Jews."[161]

Sommer and her superior, Preysing, did not stay idle. After Sommer's final report in March 1943, they drafted a petition on behalf of the bishops. It began: "With deepest pain, even with holy indignation, we German bishops have learned of the evacuations of non-Aryans, evacuations that mock all human rights. . . . The world would not understand if we did not raise our voices loudly against such treatment of innocent people." It went on to list five demands centered on the material and spiritual care for inmates of the camps and ended with the firmest admonition yet offered to Hitler by the bishops: "We shall not fail to point out that the fulfillment of our stipulations would be the surest way to invalidate the incessant crescendo of rumors about the mass death of evacuated non-Aryans."[162] Preysing and Sommer continued to use the regime's euphemism for deportations—"evacuations"—despite Sommer having earlier documented the inappropriateness of the term. In any case, the letter, short as it was, represented a remarkable moment for Preysing and the bishops who sided with him. It proves that they knew enough about the wartime genocide in the East to have spoken out against it.

They were a minority. Bertram's notes about the draft reveal his worries. He feared that, by making demands about matters beyond the Church's jurisdiction (i.e., the more humane treatment of mostly non-Catholic "evacuees"), the petition left the Fulda Conference open to attack. Moreover, he insisted that an earlier petition from the bishops had already addressed the Reich ministries on the topic and "was sufficient."[163] This March petition had confined itself almost entirely to "Catholic non-Aryans" and deportees in mixed marriages and was far less strident in tone. After Bertram quashed the August 1943 petition, Sommer and Preysing, working largely on their own, gave up attempting to persuade the bishops to speak out in unison against the atrocities in the East.

Preysing was the second bishop to be disappointed on this matter. Faulhaber had also worked on behalf of Jews in his diocese, as shown in voluminous correspondence during the early years of the war. In November 1941, he drafted a letter to Bertram, urging him to take a harder stance against anti-Jewish discrimination and deportations occurring in Germany. He described the initial transports from Munich as scenes of utmost brutality and inhumanity "that will be placed in the chronicle of history in parallel with the transports of African slave traders." He underscored the obligation of the bishops to protect Jews who had become Catholic. He paraphrased Scripture: just as the Church did not distinguish between Greek and Jew after baptism, so must the German bishops welcome all baptized Jews into the Church. The bishops were their spiritual fathers, whether conversion had taken place before or after the Nuremberg Laws. The letter ended with an appeal to solidarity, urging Bertram to sign an unambiguous declaration in the name of the Fulda Conference of Bishops, so that Bertram would not have to carry full responsibility for suggestions in the declaration.[164] No reply from Bertram survives in the file, and the German bishops took no concerted stand against the deportation of "Aryan non-Christians," as they might have done had the regime threatened "Aryan Christians" with deportation.

Discouraged but undeterred, Faulhaber drafted more letters. One he sent to a bishop in his archdiocese during the Easter season of 1943. In it he pointed out that every " 'non-Aryan' in Germany today has fallen among murderers [unter die Mörder Gefallene], and we are asked whether we face him as a priest and Levite, or as the Samaritan. No 'Jewish question' can relieve us of this decision."[165] Faulhaber quietly continued to exhort his colleagues to consider their spiritual duty to stand up for those being persecuted by the Nazis. Whatever they managed to do as individuals, from 1943 to 1945, did not alter the ultimate outcome. The final year and a half of war proved hell, with communications unstable and infrequent, with the Vatican nearly unreachable, and with their own churches and homes being bombed to ruins around them. The bishops' world-weariness in the spring of 1945, at the very end, is evident in their writings and sermons.

* * *

Few Catholics identified Nazism as evil in the 1930s. Nazism was not yet commonly understood, within Germany's borders or without, as a universal threat engaging in mass murder to achieve its goals. Nazism and Catholicism, as two distinct worldviews, had much in common: neither had any love for the chaos of democratic republicanism, which had paralyzed German political life and fanned social divisions to the point of civil war. Both categorized liberalism and socialism as fundamental threats to German *Kultur*. Both desired a strong, centralized leadership that would seek to amend the indignities Germany had suffered in 1918 and 1919. Moreover, Hitler's ascent to power had resulted in a concordat, something that the Church had pursued for years but that was frustrated by the inadequacies of the Weimar system. Church leaders regarded Hitler's movement warily, but he was preferable if it came to a choice between Nazism and Bolshevism. Taken together, these rationalizations may have justified for bishops and priests the Church's failure to protest the moral crimes of the regime more vigorously between 1933 and 1939, specifically the discrimination against Jews and the eugenic policies. And of course, it did nothing to discourage some clerics from engaging in anti-Jewish and antisemitic rhetoric of their own.[166]

The regime violated the concordat repeatedly during the six years between its signing and the outbreak of the war. The bishops reacted with protests and letter writing and little else. The palpable tension between secular and religious authorities, reminiscent of more than fifty years earlier, when Bismarckian Germany had ascribed ulterior and treasonous activities to Catholics, left Catholic Germans in an uncomfortable situation that colored the years preceding the Second World War: on the one hand, the regime guaranteed them more rights in the realm of religious practice than any other group in Germany received under the Nazis; on the other hand, their traditional political affiliations, their ultimate subservience to the pope as head of the Catholic Church, and their "inferiority complex," an inheritance from the Kulturkampf, pressured many Catholic Germans to prove that they were loyal Germans, even as the Nazi movement repeatedly violated the guarantees in the concordat. This constant and occasionally bloody struggle between Nazism and Catholicism was interrupted, very briefly, by the outbreak of war. Even then the antagonism did not end; it merely took fresh form in the new situation, as Catholic priests and seminarians serving in the military became targets of Nazi anti-Catholic wrath.

During the war, the Church was still too important an ally for the party to confront directly. Hitler himself decreed that the final reckoning would have to come only after the war was decided, stating in 1942 that until then, "all provocative steps had to be avoided."[167] Hitler was forced to rein in some of his more fanatical underlings during the war, who wanted to keep persecuting the Church. But many Catholic Germans feared that they would suffer the same fate as the Jews once Germany won the war.[168] Even if the ultimate battle had to be delayed and, consequently, anti-Church measures during the war decreased, evidence was overwhelming that the regime had become fixedly anti-institutional: attempted expulsions from the Nazi Party of clergy who were members, as well as a mass exodus of people from both Catholic and Protestant churches, point to a fundamental rupture in church-party relations instigated by the Nazi Party.[169] Yet none of these attacks persuaded the bishops—or their flocks—to abandon wartime support for their Fatherland. The timelessness of the institutional Church, its higher goal of protecting and caring for the souls of Catholic Germans above and beyond temporal politics, and their allegiance, as Germans, to their country and its *Volk* led the bishops to believe that the Nazi regime had to be endured but not necessarily protested. They never encouraged active opposition.

Controversy still rages about the extent to which the Church's silence, spotty protests, and lack of resistance in the face of overt racism, human rights violations, and genocide contributed to these evils. It is similar to questions of how or whether more active Church opposition might have altered the course of Nazi war crimes and the genocide. Pope Pius XII presents the most distinct target for critics of the Church during the Third Reich, both because of his position at the time and perhaps because, in hindsight, a single individual can be more easily blamed than a large group. His actions between 1939 and 1945 have not been my focus because they present a distinct story, embedded in a voluminous and growing historiography that cannot be encompassed within the story of Germany's bishops.[170]

The episcopate proves problematic enough. Those seeking to defend the bishops' behavior in Germany usually resort to highlighting the actions of one or two bishops, Galen's 1941 sermons against the T-4 program foremost among them. Preysing and Faulhaber were also notable exceptions to the norm. As a group, however, the bishops are difficult to defend. They were unable to decide unanimously how to respond to the regime and its policies; they consistently defended the terms of the concordat, even as it became increasingly apparent that the Nazis had no intention of honoring it; they praised Hitler's anti-Bolshevik rhetoric and action; and they failed to defend—or even protest on behalf of—non-Catholics whose lives were imperiled by the regime's racial policies. With at least older clerics hamstrung by memories of the price for defying the state, and with all persuaded that Bolshevism, an atheistic, anti-Catholic movement, had to be defeated at all costs, Church leaders moved between passive acquiescence to and outright cooperation with Hitler's government. Dissent came very infrequently in the form of ineffectual letter writing and, occasionally, the more dangerous sermonizing. The two times a bishop or a group of determined Catholics stood against a particular Nazi policy (Galen and the T-4 program and the removal of crucifixes in different dioceses, both protests taking place during the war), the regime backed down. A third instance in which the regime was broadly criticized (though not by name), in the 1937 encyclical *Mit brennender Sorge* (notably before the war), increased state-directed discrimination and persecution until the regime had all but obliterated the guarantees of the concordat.

This, then, was the example set by the Church's spiritual leaders. The bishops were the role models and the arbiters to whom priests and seminarians looked for guidance. Yet one more authority must also be considered as a crucial influence on those clergymen conscripted into the Wehrmacht: the leadership of Reich Catholic Field Bishop Franz Justus Rarkowski and Georg Werthmann, his field vicar-general of the Catholic military chaplaincy.

2

PASTORAL CARE IN THE WEHRMACHT

From 1939 to 1945, between 17 and 18 million German men served in the armed forces of the Third Reich.¹ According to one of only two Nazi censuses, in May 1939 the German population hovered around 80 million. This included the populations of the annexed territories of Austria and the Sudetenland. About 38 million of these were male. Therefore, just under half of the men living in the Greater German Reich served at some point in the Wehrmacht.² It was on their shoulders that the future rested. Only by righting the perceived wrongs that the Treaty of Versailles inflicted, racially purifying the *Volk* and acquiring living space for its expansion, and eradicating the eternal enemy of German civilization, namely Judeo-Bolshevism, could Germany have a future. The mission entrusted to Wehrmacht soldiers was a most sacred one. They could not be left without the necessary moral support and spiritual care needed to carry out their task.

Many German words were used to describe the support systems for German soldiers, suggesting that both the Nazi Party and Wehrmacht leadership took the issue of troop morale very seriously. Many of these terms are difficult to translate into English while retaining their distinctive meanings. Wehrmacht officers, Nazi Party leaders, and priests tended to use *Seelsorge* most often in discussions of pastoral care, though *Truppenbetreuung* and *wehrgeistige Führung* also surfaced. Less specific than *Militärseelsorge* (pastoral care in the military), and *Feldseelsorge* (pastoral care in the field), *Seelsorge* refers to pastoral care in a general religious sense. Depending on context, *Betreuung* suggests assistance, support, supervision, mentoring, and care. When applied to troops, as in *Truppenbetreuung*, its immediate meaning is entertainment or distraction, but in the larger sense it includes all methods for supporting and sustaining morale, from film and literature to formal lectures and informal conversation. *Geistig* in German can denote the spiritual, intellectual, or mental aspect of something. In the context of the Wehrmacht, *wehrgeistige Führung* indicates either ideological or spiritual leadership (after 1943 this became a highly politicized term wedded to indoctrination).

This chapter examines the antecedents of the Catholic chaplaincy in the German military, its reconstruction during the 1930s, and its struggle to maintain its existence during the war. The number of Catholic chaplains was disproportionate—significantly smaller—to both the number of priests and the number of priests-in-training (seminarians and theology students[3]) who wore the Wehrmacht uniform between 1939 and 1945. It was also disproportionate to the number of Catholic soldiers to whom chaplains administered. The chaplaincy, therefore, was not the sole source of spiritual sustenance for Germany's fighting Catholics. In addition to Catholic priests serving outside the chaplaincy, there were also Protestant chaplains and pastors as well as civilian priests across occupied Europe. However, the Catholic chaplaincy was the only sanctioned system of such support.

The Catholic chaplaincy in the Wehrmacht was erected on the edifice of earlier systems of Christian pastoral care in Germany. The most immediate precedents were the Catholic and Protestant chaplaincies of the kaiser's armies during the First World War.[4] However, after 1933 the chaplaincy was subject to new political and sociocultural pressures. Now part of a Nazi war machine, the chaplaincy was governed strictly by Nazi rules and regulations. More importantly, the chaplaincy had to cope with the fact that the German army during the Second World War was fully complicit in war crimes. Accordingly, the priests and seminarians in the Third Reich's military found themselves furthering the war aims of a criminal, expressly anti-Christian regime. Eventually those aims evolved to include genocide.

The chaplains and their leaders, Reich Catholic Field Bishop Franz Justus Rarkowski and his second-in-command, Catholic Field Vicar-General Georg Werthmann, offer examples of how to negotiate a world whose borders were determined by the army and, ultimately, the Nazi weltanschauung. They did so to care for the religious needs of soldiers, and they believed that this higher religious mission removed them from temporal—political—concerns. For this reason, few viewed their willingness to adapt to this new environment as a form of collaboration with a loathed enemy.

No historian can successfully get inside the head of her subjects, particularly a group as large and diverse as Catholic priests (both chaplains and non-chaplains) in the Wehrmacht. So their motivations may prove too elusive to grasp definitively. But a genuine devotion to the soldiers, ardent faith, and cunning opportunism are perceptible. In the case of Werthmann, there was also a certain satisfaction with his influence over Catholic soldiers. Above all, he was dedicated to his chaplains, as they were to the troops. The fruits of these labors resulted in a functioning, albeit embattled, military chaplaincy.

Given the Nazi regime's anti-Catholic proclivities before 1939, it is not immediately apparent why Werthmann—or any Catholic priest—served in such a regime's army. However, in 1939, the German military was not a criminal organization, overtly racist, or a mere stooge of the Nazi Party. To the contrary, the army, in addition to the Catholic Church, was the only social institution that could claim any autonomy from the tremendous reach of the Nazi Party. (Admittedly its independence was diminished in the wake of the 1938 scandals that resulted in the forced resignation of Wehrmacht commander-in-chief Werner von Blomberg, the dismissal of army commander-in-chief Werner von Fritsch, and the voluntary resignation of army chief of staff Ludwig Beck.[5]) Its highest echelons remained relatively independent of party control, and Hitler still had to tread carefully with the army generals in foreign policy decisions, for they were the only group in the latter 1930s capable of deposing the Führer had they been so inclined.

Though it was notably hostile to institutional religion throughout its tenure, the regime permitted the existence of a chaplaincy for three vital reasons. First, as Hitler asserted more than once, religion was an essential element for cultivating loyalty and motivation in soldiers. Although he showed little religious inclination, Hitler made such utterances to pacify the leadership of the churches and, by extension, the religious sensibilities of much of the German population, including the many army officers who were still devout Christians. Second, through the outlet of faith, nurtured by the presence of priests, a chaplaincy was a means of control over soldiers and their morale for the party and military officers. The clergy who staffed the chaplaincy cooperated in this venture. Either they saw no conflict in collaborating with the state and the military or they understood that they had more to gain through acquiescence than any alternative. Simply put, Catholic souls were at stake. To not have a chaplaincy meant that Catholics serving in the military—many of them conscripted—would have no recourse to spiritual care. The final impetus was nationalism, which fueled the conviction of many Germans that the war that broke out in 1939 was necessary and justifiable. German civilization (viewed as inseparable from the Christian tradition) itself was at stake, and every defense, including religious ardor, was to be utilized.

A closer inspection of the chaplaincy both affirms what previous scholarship has highlighted and provides new perspectives on the effects of Nazi ideology and why Germans, priests included, participated in the war. The presence of priests at the battlefront reveals that the Nazi dictatorship was no top-down organization, impervious to on-the-ground developments. Nor was it oblivious to the religious inclinations of the fighting men. While several Nazi leaders developed a clear antipathy to chaplains and priests in uniform and tried to restrict their religious activities after 1941, it is a mistake to understand either the party leadership or the military leadership as monolithic and totalitarian. Both were composed of individuals with divergent interests, running the gamut from aiding and abetting the spiritual work of priests to attempting to undermine the entire system of pastoral care.

There were also limits to the reception of Nazi ideology among soldiers. Historian Thomas Kühne has recently argued that the concepts of togetherness, belonging, and the unity of brotherhood are central to produce "a mass murder–generated sense of community." While not pervasive, this "grand brotherhood of crime" created enough cohesion among its members that "its crucial social dynamic made complicit even those who did not want to become complicit."[6] Taking this valuable argument further, religion also fueled a kind of community among the soldiers. It is evident that, with priests among them, troops found consolation in religion during the final months of the war, particularly when belief in the war's necessity and the regime's ideology had waned. This was why the chaplaincy persisted, and why chaplains displayed such tremendous devotion to their mission. This was also why traditional elements of pastoral care were important to German soldiers in the Second World War, at least in the eyes of the men who provided it—they never felt unwanted or useless within "Hitler's army."

Focusing on the priests and seminarians in close physical proximity to the war amplifies our understanding of the Catholic Church's relationship with Nazism. The bishops offered no resistance to the regime. Chaplains and their leaders as well as priests and seminarians conscripted into the military behaved no differently. Given the impetuses of putting soldiers' spiritual needs ahead of their own political concerns and of a vocational training that emphasized obedience and submission, Werthmann, Rarkowski, and the priests in Wehrmacht uniform likely did not consider any other option.

The Basis for Pastoral Care in the Wehrmacht

An entire article of the 1933 concordat dealt with spiritual guidance for Catholics in the armed forces. Article 27 guaranteed pastoral care to all Catholic officers, personnel, and other officials serving in the German military, as well as their families. The leadership of this care was incumbent upon the Reich field bishop, whose appointment fell under the jurisdiction of the Holy See, "after the latter has contacted the Reich government, in order to appoint, in agreement with the government, a suitable candidate."[7] Thus, the position required a double approval, from the pope and from Hitler. Such a stipulation underscores the equal importance given to two potentially contradictory authorities. Franz Justus Rarkowski, the man who eventually won the nomination and was the Third Reich's first and only Catholic field bishop, was never in the position of having to choose between them.

The article further specified that the military chaplaincy be accorded exempt status, meaning that the bishop in charge was independent of the German Catholic hierarchy, and directly responsible to the government and the pope.[8] Thus he had nothing to do with the German episcopate—he did not even attend the annual Fulda conference. He was called a field bishop, a more distinguished title than his predecessor's, the field provost of the Reichswehr.⁹ If there were misgivings about the autonomy of the field bishop, given that the position was so decisively separated from the rest of the Church in Germany, the concordat's signatories conceded the point. They did so for assurances in other matters, namely the provision of religious education and the maintenance of Catholic youth groups.¹⁰

The Catholic field bishop was the highest spiritual leader for Catholic soldiers in the Wehrmacht. Once they were in uniform, soldiers were no longer part of their home dioceses, and censors made communication with their home bishops and parish priests difficult.¹¹ Perhaps the bishops were persuaded to acquiesce to the government's request for an exempt military chaplaincy because they assumed that they would have a say in choosing the field bishop. Perhaps they had confidence in the pope's influence. As we have seen, several bishops had close ties with Eugenio Pacelli, who was Vatican secretary of state in 1933. Moreover, in July 1933, when the concordat was signed, the bishops were preoccupied with the dissolution of the Center Party and the imperiled autonomy of Catholic education and youth groups. The organization of pastoral care in the armed forces was important, but it was hardly pressing.

The Concordat's Secret Appendix

When the concordat was signed, few people beyond those party and Church leaders involved in the negotiations knew of an appendix, which was meant to be kept secret until the situation it addressed—total war—came about. Those with direct knowledge of the appendix included the drafters of the concordat, Pacelli and Pope Pius XI; Ludwig Kaas of the Center Party; Franz von Papen, the German vice chancellor and a Catholic; and Rudolf Buttmann, a minister working in the Interior Ministry in 1933. The appendix detailed how clergy, seminarians, and students of theology would be affected by universal conscription. The only clergy excepted from the draft were ordinaries, the heads of monasteries and seminaries, and others in leadership positions as well as those employed in diocesan administrations or otherwise engaged with diocesan work. Seminarians and theology students were eligible for weapons-bearing duty (philosophy students were also included). Priests not employed in diocesan positions were "to dedicate themselves to the pastoral care of the troops under the ecclesial jurisdiction of the field bishop, if they are not drafted into the medical service." Any remaining clerics who were not fully ordained were to serve in the medical service.[12]

That the secret appendix existed already in July 1933 indicates that Hitler was preparing for the eventuality of war at this early period. He was anxious to utilize every available source of manpower, including that found behind seminary walls and in Roman collars. Its strict secrecy is also revealing, as the bishops did not know of it until the nuncio informed them at the beginning of the war.[13] Its details about the conscription of priests, seminarians, and students in times of war were another indication that the Nazi regime had ideas different from Weimar and imperial practices about the use of clergy and clergy-in-training in the armed forces. The compliance of the concordat negotiators with these conditions is also telling. Perhaps Pacelli did not fear the threat of war in 1933. Kaas, Papen, and Buttmann must have felt justified in demanding that men with religious vocations be treated as other Germans when it came to conscription, for priests and seminarians were also German. No doubt this was the regime's stance, and the complete absence of protest to the appendix suggests considerable ecclesiastical sympathy with it.

Pastoral Care in the Military before 1933

A chaplaincy for Catholic German soldiers had operated continuously since the First World War, when a federal chaplaincy based on the Prussian example was organized for the first time. Prior to 1914, priests and volunteer laymen and women served in state armies to tend to Catholics in uniform. From 1864, the prestigious Order of Malta directed volunteer hospitals and chaplains in the German states.[14] During the first of Germany's wars of unification, a total of 157 sisters and brothers from various orders, as well as fifty-six priests, worked in fourteen hospitals performing nursing and pastoral care. By the end of the Franco-Prussian War in 1871, the Rhineland-Westphalian Order of Malta listed sixty-seven deputies, 565 nursing sisters, 206 brothers, and eight chaplains, in addition to eight doctors, thirty-two stretcher-bearers, and other volunteer personnel.[15]

This background was a solid basis upon which the Catholic military chaplaincy evolved during the First World War. The statistics alone demonstrate how much it grew, although the sheer scope of the war ultimately exceeded the supply: 788 sisters and brothers, 227 chaplains in the field, 100 front-line altars, 243 hospital chaplains attending a total of 14,000 beds.[16] Soldiers had their wounds looked after in hospitals that priests and nuns ran; priests carried their letters from the front to the army post; chaplains nursed them upon request in their sick and dying hours. Because they were Catholic, soldiers could also attend mass, receive communion, have their confessions heard, and even be granted general absolution (that is, without individual confession) in extraordinary circumstances.

The terms of the 1919 Treaty of Versailles seriously affected the chaplaincy's size, as it did all German military institutions. The manpower strength of the Reichswehr itself was whittled down to 100,000 men divided among seven infantry and three cavalry divisions, and a navy of only 15,000 men.[17] Unlike the air force, the chaplaincy escaped total elimination and operated during the Weimar Republic, though in a much-diminished capacity. At its head was an acting field provost, Paul Schwamborn, who had served during the war as field vicar-general under War Field Provost Peter Heinrich Joeppen.[18] Under Schwamborn, military chaplains—priests who catered to Catholic men and their families serving in the Reichswehr—were the main practitioners of pastoral care. Contracted part-time priests aided them. Full-time chaplains were not employed by the army because they were not considered military officials, but they were classified as "public servants [*Zivilbeamte*] in the army administration." The state paid their salaries. Although the chaplaincy continued to exist after 1919, the number of full-time chaplains was minimal, such that each of the seven infantry districts possessed only one chaplain. For example, the entire army district of Bavaria employed a single Catholic chaplain. Part-time chaplains performed the majority of pastoral activity, and they were considered church officials [*Kirchenbeamte*] with no formal relationship with the military. Clearly the chaplaincy was stretched thin. In January 1930, Rarkowski estimated that 33,469 Catholics serving in the army and navy received pastoral care and another 9,174 women and children made up their families. The number of full-time chaplains just over a year later was estimated at twelve (including the acting field provost), with an additional 154 part-time chaplains.[19]

Though substantially downsized, the German military remained intact throughout the Weimar era, and the chaplaincy persevered. With Nazism's accession to power in 1933, the role of the military in revitalizing the country was reconceptualized. Hitler did not intend to leave the troops without recourse to spiritual care. As early as April 1933 Hitler said to a bishop, "Trouble with Poland is on the horizon. We need soldiers, devout soldiers. Devout soldiers are the most valuable. They put in everything [they have]."[20] He was referring specifically to the question of confessional schools, a debate that shaped a considerable part of the concordat, and may have applied the word "soldiers" to German society as a whole and not just the military. In the early years of his dictatorship, Hitler evidently recognized the importance that faith could play in the training of steadfast, reliable soldiers. A few years later he would remark to Cardinal Michael von Faulhaber, archbishop of Munich, that "the soldier who for three or four days lies under intense bombardment needs a religious prop,"[21] a statement that affirmed Hitler's belief in the importance of religion for men at war. The chaplaincy was to provide this support. However, the man chosen to lead the chaplains was, according to most critics, eminently unsuitable for the role despite a lengthy history of working in the military chaplaincy.

The Field Bishop

The most important figure in the chaplaincy's construction was the field bishop. From the beginning of the German drive to rearm, one individual was a favorite of both the Nazi regime and the military. Franz Justus Rarkowski was born in Allenstein, East Prussia, in 1873 and, after his ordination in 1898, was employed in various positions, including hospital chaplain and curate. He joined the military chaplaincy in Berlin when war broke out in 1914 and became secretary to Field Provost Joeppen. Upon Germany's defeat and the downsizing of the Reichswehr, he remained devoted to serving in his capacity as chaplain.[22] Because of his lengthy experience in the chaplaincy, as well as his family connections (his father, a landowner and representative in the Reichstag for the Center Party, was a friend of Paul von Hindenburg, the celebrated First World War general who served as the second president of the Weimar Republic), the Nazi government put Rarkowski's name forward as early as 1933 as candidate for the leadership of an exempt military chaplaincy. He appeared to be a logical choice.[23] He had been serving as leader of the chaplaincy since 1929, when he started to reorganize pastoral care for the army.[24] However, the episcopate reacted with protests not merely because the regime supported Rarkowski's candidacy, but also because the bishops strongly objected to his personality and education. Specifically, the bishops considered Rarkowski's training inferior to their own; all of them had gained distinction as seminarians, many of them had studied advanced theology in Rome, and most of them had worked as university professors or seminary directors before becoming bishops.[25] Rarkowski's candidacy added to their reservations about the proposed system of pastoral care in the military and the field bishop's role therein.

The bishops believed that, on nearly every level, Rarkowski was unfit for the job, a conviction that both chaplains and Werthmann, Rarkowski's own vicar-general, would later echo. Concerning his religious education, "it was known that Rarkowski had managed to be admitted to the study of theology without graduation from high school. He had studied for the priesthood in Switzerland rather than in Germany, had left a religious order, and was generally considered by the bishops to be an upstart without the requisite educational background."[26] Rarkowski never attempted to conceal his lack of the German equivalent of a high school diploma, but his religious training was marked by indecision. After nine years in a *Gymnasium*, he received a dimissorial letter from his bishop in Ermland, which gave him permission to study in England, where the Marist Fathers accepted him as a novice.[27] Over the next few years, he applied to several other orders, suggesting that his commitment to the Marists was not a firm one (what follows is chronological). His alleged—and failed—attempt for admittance to the famous Trappist monastery at La Chartreuse, France, was followed by several months with the Carthusian monks in Düsseldorf before he returned once more to the Marists. He subsequently applied to the Benedictine order, which rejected him for health reasons, before finally requesting permission to be released from his order-vows in 1901. He returned to Ermland and, in quick succession, became the personal chaplain of a housekeeping school, a local hospital, and an epilepsy institute.[28]

In addition to questions about his religious training, the bishops also expressed reservations regarding his character. These reservations arose in part from discrepancies between Rarkowski's official personnel file and other evidence about his history. By 1933, even Rarkowski's predecessor as acting field provost, Paul Schwamborn, who had retired in 1929, was concerned enough about these discrepancies to write to a ministerial council pointing them out. He was worried about Rarkowski's foreign training (in England) with the Marists and his apparent failure to take the entrance exams for the priesthood. The fact that Rarkowski was allegedly unable even to remember which bishop had ordained him in 1898—he had written in his file "ordained to the priesthood by the bishop of Ermland" when in fact it had been the bishop of Brixen—aroused further apprehension. Schwamborn noted with some asperity, "I believe that it is unique that a Catholic priest doesn't know which bishop ordained him to the priesthood."[29] Even more damning, Schwamborn suggested that Rarkowski had deserted his post in August 1914 in fleeing from Lötzen to Berlin. A second letter revealed that another priest, Joseph Mühlenbein, had brought charges against Rarkowski, including the use of false titles as a chaplain in the Great War.[30]

Closer scrutiny, however, revealed that the majority of these accusations were either misunderstandings or distortions. While the bishop of Brixen had indeed ordained Rarkowski, he had done so on behalf of the bishop of Ermland. Rarkowski had provided information that was incomplete but not untrue. With respect to his leaving Lötzen in 1914, Rarkowski explained that he was attending someone on a sick visit when military authorities evacuated the city. The commander of the nearby fortress of Boyen offered him residence, but Rarkowski elected not to accept, as his own military superiors had not given him orders. Rather, he had joined some refugees heading for Königsberg, unsure of what else to do.[31] He employed false titles because he had been incorrectly instructed to do so by his superior—who was, ironically, the same Schwamborn who later turned against him.[32] Schwamborn's concerns appear to have been borne of personal animus that stemmed from a falling-out with Rarkowski between 1929 and 1933, the reasons for which remain unknown.³³ Rarkowski pointed out that Schwamborn previously had been supportive of his career, and that Rarkowski himself had wondered if his education and religious training might eventually pose problems. Schwamborn had admitted that "that could be the case, and he encouraged me to accept the appointment [as his successor to the post of field vicar-general of the Reichswehr]."³⁴ Furthermore, several of Rarkowski's wartime military superiors, including Wilhelm Groener, then defense minister, praised his abilities highly. Groener cited his "affectionate good will" and his "readiness to help," calling him a man who "is tirelessly active in his calling," who "fulfills his obligations fully" and was "not only extraordinarily beloved as a priest, but also as a man and companion." Rarkowski was "a distinguished personality whose strong character was suffused with the most ideal disposition and highest patriotic spirit.... He has earned for himself in a short period of time the deepest trust of the soldiers in his care. He has zealously and successfully tried to give them his best."³⁵

Given such high acclaim, why did the episcopate object to Rarkowski's appointment as field bishop? They might have been suspicious of his connections to the Nazi movement. They definitely viewed him as a social inferior, tainted by his East Prussian origins. They were certainly uncomfortable with the Nazi Party's vigorous promotion of his candidacy. He was unabashedly and sometimes radically nationalistic and believed that the German military was an essential national institution. In the introduction to a small book that Werthmann published in 1936 for military recruits, Rarkowski wrote, "With the expansion of Germany's Wehrmacht, the Führer has laid out the basis for German security and given back to free German men the right and the responsibility to protect and honor the Fatherland with body and soul."³⁶ Later he cited *Mein Kampf* in his effusiveness for military education: "In the school of the army, the boy will become a man; in this school he should learn not only to obey, but also thereby to acquire those prerequisites necessary to prepare him for later orders."³⁷ He went on to describe the Führer in his first wartime pastoral letter as the "luminous model of a true warrior ... of the first and bravest soldier of the greater German Reich, who from now on resides with you at the battle front."³⁸ He never offered a word, explicit or implicit, that was critical of the regime. He was not a member of the Nazi Party, although he did belong to the National Socialist People's Welfare (NSV) and the Reich Air Defense Organization [Reichsluftschutzbund].[39]

One historian has claimed that the bishops' antipathy "stemmed from [their] feeling that he was their intellectual inferior and a threat to their status rather than from the unacceptability of his political ideas."[40] In short, he was an outsider. This likely exacerbated their discomfort with the exempt status of the chaplaincy, since it kept him beyond their ecclesiastical reach. Only guarantees to respect the autonomy of Catholic schools and Catholic youth groups mollified them when the concordat confirmed that the chaplaincy would be exempt. Rarkowski was not even a bishop when he was nominated for his post. The pope appointed him titular bishop of the defunct ancient diocese of Hierocaesarea only in 1938 and only on a technicality since the field "bishop" required a diocese to merit the title.[41] To the bishops, not only was Rarkowski an outsider who had failed to earn his episcopal stripes, but also, as head of the chaplaincy and all of the military's Catholics, he was in no way responsible to them.

In the end the bishops lost the argument about Rarkowski. He had been acting as chaplaincy leader since 1929 in addition to holding duties as chaplain in Army District III, Berlin. Following the debates over his nomination, in 1936 the regime and the Holy See jointly agreed to appoint him provisional field bishop. Two years later, they recognized him as the head of the Catholic chaplaincy. He selected as his vicar-general Georg Werthmann, who had succeeded Rarkowski as district chaplain in Berlin.[42]

Rarkowski's Critics

It was not only the bishops who complained about Rarkowski. While Werthmann's postwar notes suggest that no major difficulties arose between them during their work together, other comments he made indicate that their relationship was not always easy. Rarkowski's deficiencies were hard to overcome. His pro-Nazi promulgations aside, Rarkowski suffered even in the judgment of his chaplains, some of whom felt he did not measure up to his Protestant counterpart, Field Bishop Franz Dohrmann. Bonifaz Pfister, a conscripted seminarian who served as a medical orderly and sexton from 1940 to 1945, informed

Werthmann that chaplains "sharply criticized" Rarkowski, "above all for a lack of decisiveness, as well as the nonchalance with which he represented the interests of the army chaplaincy to higher-ranking posts."[43] Several decades after the war's end, former chaplains made similar observations about Rarkowski's character. Otto F. stated, "Let's say he had no great charisma."[44] Kunibert P. remembered that he was less well-spoken of than Dohrmann, whom he saw along with Rarkowski in Paris during the war. Egon Schmitt echoed this, insisting, "From the outset he made an outstanding impression neither in what he said nor in what he presented. He was an amiable man, but he had no leadership qualities, no authority."[45] Martin Z. likewise did not mince words, describing him as "a weak man; today one doesn't really know at all how he became field bishop."[46]

Temperamentally the two were very different: Rarkowski exhibited an uncritical approval of the war and the Nazi regime, whereas Werthmann was less overtly patriotic and showed more reserve vis-à-vis National Socialism. However, they were able to construct a functional chaplaincy together and to complement each other's strengths in carrying out their respective offices. Werthmann did not commit to paper his judgment of Rarkowski until the end of the war, in the first weeks of his internment—the first opportunity that he dared to criticize his former superior, when the war was lost and the chaplaincy all but dissolved. He tried to present a balanced evaluation, beginning with the admission that Rarkowski was "friendly in intercourse with his brethren, [and] he knew how to encourage in his own kindly manner, and to lead those who erred back to the way of truth."[47] He characterized his working relationship with Rarkowski as efficient and amicable.

When reflecting on his superior's character and comportment, however, Werthmann was less generous. Rarkowski lacked the sober objectivity that bishops required. He occasionally displayed an "almost volcanic" asperity that was "insurmountable."[48] Cheap flattery won him over easily, leading to a loss of respect from chaplains. Rarkowski seemed aware of these faults, remarking to Werthmann in conversation that he "simply couldn't understand how I completely disengaged myself from subjective, personal experiences with the individual involved when it came to judgment." He also suffered considerably from a lack of self-confidence, and he lived in constant fear of disgrace and dismissal, or worse, arrest and confinement in a concentration camp. This might explain his eagerness to support National Socialism. Werthmann surmised in conclusion that this "helplessness" and "unreliability," which those around him could often perceive, were rooted in "pathological disorders." He suggested that, coupled with the bishop's frail health in 1944 and 1945, this indicated the onset of senility.[49]

According to his own testimony, Rarkowski expressed an open support for Nazism to avoid the greater evil. "I know that the others condemn my attitude," he stated to Werthmann, "but what should I do? If I oppose, then I will have absolutely no influence. In this way, I can prevent some evil."[50] While his dedication to Germany and the chaplaincy is evident, Rarkowski was never the authority figure that others expected him to be. He was more anxious to please his superiors than to challenge Nazism's anti-Catholicism or criminality. As one historian has pointed out, "any soldier so troubled who turned to the Military [sic] Bishop and his published pronouncements would find his problem swept away in a torrent of nationalistic outpourings."[51] Virtually all of the postwar scholarship in which he features depicts Rarkowski as a weak, ineffective chaplaincy leader.[52] Theologian Heinrich Missalla declared him to be a loyal follower [treuer Gefolgsmann] of the law: "church law and concordat regulation, state law and Wehrmacht law."[53] Historian Hans Jürgen Brandt renders probably the most generous judgment, remarking, "Perhaps Rarkowski esteemed precisely those qualities in Werthmann that he himself lacked: the ease and pleasure of communication, rapid comprehension, the firm ability to make judgments and decisions in the face of all hardship."[54]

Georg Werthmann

Though Werthmann lacked the family connections that Rarkowski enjoyed, his youth paralleled that of the field bishop's in one fundamental aspect: he also served his country in the First World War, though as a soldier, not a chaplain. Born in 1898 in Kulmbach, in Upper Franconia in Bavaria, he was a *Gymnasium* student in 1916 when he volunteered for duty, whereupon he served in several infantry regiments and received steady promotion.[55] In December 1917 his superiors awarded him a second-class Iron Cross for bravery in battle, and in August 1918 he became an NCO. In September 1918, after he was badly wounded, the French took him prisoner; after the war ended, he moved about between different POW camps and was an interpreter before his release in January 1920. One unpublished biography speculates that Werthmann's decision to become a priest stemmed from his experiences in the Great War, particularly his time in French captivity. Certainly it familiarized him with an institution—the German military—that he would spend the greater part of his life serving.[56]

During the Weimar era he was not involved with the Reichswehr or its chaplaincy. Instead he studied for the priesthood and was ordained in July 1924 in the Bamberg cathedral by Archbishop Jakobus von Hauck. He was then deeply involved in the Catholic youth movements, including Quickborn and Bamberg's regional branch of the Sturmschar (Storm Band).[57] He held various positions in and around Bamberg for the next several years, including chaplain for the Order of the Brethren at the Hospital of the Virgin Mary—more commonly known as the Teutonic Knights—in 1931, and religion teacher at a Catholic *Gymnasium*.[58] For a short time, he was a member of the Bayerische Volkspartei (the Bavarian People's Party, or BVP, an offshoot of the Center Party during the interwar period), and in January 1935 he joined the Nazi Civil Servants Union (NS-Beamtenbund) and, like Rarkowski, the Nazi Social Services (NSV) and the Reichsluftschutzbund.

In all likelihood, Werthmann joined these groups as a result of the nationwide *Gleichschaltung* that the Nazi Party engineered in the 1930s. As a teacher and, therefore, civil servant, this was the only way that he could retain his position. Such membership was not necessarily indicative of a genuine adherence to Nazi ideals. In fact, his diocesan superior, the archbishop of Bamberg, was so concerned that Werthmann's anti-Nazi behavior was endangering the school that in 1935 he advised Werthmann to report for service in the military chaplaincy in Berlin.[59] Here he met Rarkowski, to whom he delivered a trial sermon on Saint Francis of Assisi as part of his application process. Despite their numerous differences in character, Rarkowski was impressed enough to recommend him for the field bishop position. When authorities rejected this recommendation on the bases of inexperience and youth, Werthmann became a full-time chaplain instead, and Rarkowski worked to appoint him his second-in-command. There were concerns with this as well, as Werthmann was relatively young (at thirty-seven, he was the second-youngest priest in the chaplaincy), but Rarkowski held his ground.[60] In September 1936 Werthmann became chaplain of Army District III, Berlin, and one month later, on 21 October, he became field vicar-general.[61] He was now the second most powerful man in the Catholic leadership of the Wehrmacht's chaplaincy, based permanently in Berlin.

Werthmann did not remain tethered to his desk behind the battle lines; he saw active service and traveled extensively during the war. From June to October 1941, he was based at the Fifteenth Army headquarters near Lille, France. In December 1941, he received the prestigious War Merit Cross, second-class with swords (roughly equivalent to the American Distinguished Service Cross). Six months later the Holy See awarded him an honorary papal title.[62] In June 1943 he journeyed to Riga, Latvia; in March 1944 to Cracow, Poland; in April 1944 to Prague and Holoubkov (Hloubka, Czech Republic); in June 1944 to Orscha (Orsza, Belarus) and Biala Podlaska, Poland.[63] In January 1945, because of Rarkowski's failing health, Field Marshal Wilhelm Keitel, head of the OKW, informed Werthmann that he was temporarily in charge of the offices of the Catholic field bishop.[64] In March he fled Berlin, mirroring other Germans moving south and west away from the invading Russians, and, while so doing, the Allies intercepted him. He spent his internment from the end of April until 27 July 1945 under the supervision of the American Twenty-sixth Infantry Division at the Benedictine monastery in Niederalteich, in eastern Bavaria. He was detained along with the Protestant field bishop, Franz Dohrmann, and Dohrmann's field vicar-general, Friedrich Münchmeyer.[65]

The Nazi Party seemed to have gained the upper hand with Rarkowski's appointment, but the Church recovered some control of the situation with Werthmann's appointment as field vicar-general. Werthmann worked tirelessly during the war to protect chaplains and other priests and seminarians in German army uniforms from the anticlerical malevolence of party higher-ups and OKW personnel. For this reason he became in the eyes of many—priest, bishop, minister, even general—the true leader of Catholic military pastoral care.

Despite his behavior before entering the chaplaincy, Werthmann seemed at ease working with the regime and did not criticize Nazi policy after 1935. Such behavior invites comparisons to the placating accommodation of Cardinal Adolf Bertram of Breslau rather than the public anti-Nazi adamancy of Konrad von Preysing, bishop of Berlin. Moreover, Werthmann's personality was much stronger and more impressive than Rarkowski's. Chaplains who worked under him remembered Werthmann fondly years later. Otto F. stated that the chaplains had little contact with Rarkowski, who was an "unobtrusive man," in contrast to Werthmann, "who really had an active personality."[66] Richard S. also remembered, "One got a bigger impression, a better impression, from Vicar-General Werthmann. One noticed immediately that he had things in hand, he led the department, he did the work."[67] Egon Schmitt described Werthmann as "a rational, objective man and no doubt the actual leader of the shop [Leiter des Ladens]."[68] Josef P., who met Werthmann during his chaplain training in 1941, recalled that the vicar-general "really radiated something and impressed me very much."[69]

In the scant postwar historiography in which he surfaces, Werthmann is portrayed as a hard-working, intelligent man who maneuvered his way between the demands of the Nazi Party and the OKW to protect chaplains and other Catholic priests and seminarians in the military. He and Rarkowski made the Wehrmacht's pastoral care system into an efficient part of the war machine. During the war, however, Werthmann in particular worked to sustain the chaplaincy in the face of hostility from anti-Catholic Nazi leaders such as Martin Bormann, Heinrich Himmler, and Hermann Reinecke. His attitude toward serving in the armed forces and the necessity of pastoral care for Christian soldiers exemplifies the justifications that most priests used when donning the Wehrmacht uniform to serve in "Hitler's army."[70] He empathized with priests and seminarians in the military, and he showed an ability to negotiate with military personnel, even those with whom he disagreed. Thus, Werthmann wrote to a colleague in January 1943: "The world wants to be deceived, so let's get on with it."[71] Beyond this frank acknowledgment of the necessity of working with the Nazi Party to achieve his own aims, no evidence has surfaced that he otherwise questioned the regime's larger ideological goals or its treatment of Jews, foreign civilian populations, or Soviet POWs.

Setting Up a Chaplaincy

The field vicar-general, chief aide to the field bishop, was also liaison between the field bishop and the military office in charge of pastoral care, the Pastoral Care Group, under the Office for Replacement and Military Affairs in the General Army Office.[72] Werthmann's responsibilities, therefore, overlapped to some extent with those of Rarkowski. His office was responsible for organizing chaplain support; their assignment and transfer; their training to deal with soldiers and specific wartime situations; the supply of organizational necessities, such as mass kits, vestments and other liturgical materials for the chaplains; and the printing and distribution of field hymnals, religious writings, rosaries, and other devotional objects.[73] In addition to these duties, Werthmann undertook administrative correspondence, including with Karl Edelmann, department chief for replacement and military affairs and Werthmann's liaison in the OKH. He also responded to private letters from chaplains and priests conscripted into the medical service.

Prior to the outbreak of war, Rarkowski and Werthmann focused on getting the chaplaincy running smoothly. In September 1935, Pope Pius XI released a list of statutes applying to Nazi Germany's fledgling military chaplaincy in the official gazette of the Holy See, *Acta Apostolicae Sedis*. Included were details about the jurisdiction and duties of the field bishop, the legal status of chaplains, and instructions for the effective execution of pastoral care.[74] The field bishop appointed all chaplains, though the involvement of state and military authorities was nothing short of intrusive. Priests who applied to the chaplaincy before 1939 required permission from their diocesan bishop in the form of an ecclesiastical nomination. The army's Pastoral Care Group then subjected the applicant to an investigation that included a recommendation from the Reich Ministry for Church Affairs and reports from the applicant's regional Gestapo or *Kreisleiter* (county leader; a Nazi Party office) offices, or the SD. The latter was essentially a thorough background check, with questions about possible membership in former political parties or Freemason lodges, a signed declaration ascertaining that the individual was of Aryan descent, and an investigation to determine whether the individual had ever conducted espionage activities or demonstrated inappropriate political (anti-Nazi) behavior.[75] This briefing was even more complicated for priests who became chaplains after 1939: in addition to the above, each applicant had to provide a detailed personal history, declarations concerning their membership in any religious societies or clubs, a declaration of citizenship, a certificate of good conduct from the police, and reports from military superiors.[76] Like all army recruits, chaplains had to take the army oath, swearing allegiance to Hitler. Chaplains may not have had to demonstrate support for the Nazi movement, but they certainly had to meet its ideological requirements.

The authority of the field bishop and the duties of chaplains evolved over the years leading to the war in ways that Werthmann documented extensively. His notes, as well as surviving memoranda and other records, suggest that both the chaplains and the military authorities that oversaw them frequently required clarification on the scope of such duties. The two groups did not always work smoothly together even in the initial stages of the war. In response to questions from the OKH, Rarkowski wrote a detailed list of regulations in January 1937.[77] He reported that, according to the 1917 Code of Canon Law, civilian bishops could determine if new pastoral care positions needed to be established in certain areas, but that the field bishop had the final say. He defended the exempt chaplaincy, arguing that it worked more efficiently without the interference of the bishops, though he did not elaborate on this. He delineated a series of "specific obstructions" that the chaplaincy struggled with, including "endeavors of a negative kind in religious areas that have not stopped. . . . To give one example, brochures were distributed unimpeded throughout the armed forces in which not only Christianity as such, but also the religious tradition of the German army was attacked, and the heroic Christian deaths of German soldiers were vilified."[78]

Rarkowski then addressed his understanding of the chaplain's importance, situating the office within the turbulence of Germany. The chaplain, he explained, "is at the focal point of massive contention. . . . He stands before a young man who has experienced the emotional agitation of our time more strongly than any other generation." To be something of a role model for these youths at a time of upheaval and change, or at least a credible advisor, a chaplain needed a "lively inner connection to the . . . historical situation, to the spiritual structure of the young soldiers of our time, as well as to today's soldierly way of life, which encourages and nurtures new ideology and ambition ahead of tradition." To convey religious and ethical values to his charges properly, the chaplain required an education that included familiarity with the military lifestyle ("the young soldier wants to experience a piety in the attitude and proclamations of his priest that corresponds to his own disposition, which is oriented toward the most soldierly way of life"), ideological training[79] ("personally the chaplain has no political mission, but the young men for whom he works have gone through ideological training and live in a defined political-ideological realm, which must be recognized to make religious values effective in soldierly thinking and desire"), religious education, and familiarity with the Wehrmacht's most important regulations. To ensure that chaplains were properly trained, Rarkowski called for courses taught at regular intervals. This would engender both a uniform approach to training as well as a sense of community among the chaplains themselves before they went to their respective units.

The OKH and the Field Bishop's Office also distributed prewar regulations regarding military-ecclesiastical matters for Catholics in the Wehrmacht.[80] This was the first of several lists of rules meant to encompass all aspects of religious life in the military. The first section summarized the membership, duties, and rights of the military congregations of the armed forces. The second section outlined the authority of the field bishop, emphasizing his independence from the other German bishops and his executive power as head of the military chaplaincy. A second brochure expanded on the initial list, suggesting that some issues needed clarification. For example, irrespective of ecclesiastical jurisdiction, a secular judiciary had to delineate new rules to guarantee the effectiveness of pastoral care within the armed forces.[81] These rules provided further details about military congregations for short- and long-term tours of duty; the availability of naval chaplains for Catholic soldiers, as fewer chaplains were stationed with naval units; and the availability of army chaplains for Catholic members of the Luftwaffe, since, as per Luftwaffe leader Hermann Göring's prewar ruling, no chaplains were to serve in the air force. These regulations clearly signified the army's attempt to bring the chaplaincy and all of its activities under its firm control. This aim is further evident in the bulletin issued in August 1939, an especially important document that is set out more fully below.

The August 1939 Bulletin

The first detailed list of OKH regulations relating to pastoral care in the field came in August 1939, just days before the announcement of the Treaty of Non-aggression between Germany and the Soviet Union and less than two weeks before the invasion of Poland.[82] Hereafter referred to as the Bulletin, its title was "Character and Tasks of Pastoral Care in the Field." The OKH distributed 15,000 copies to all army group and general headquarters, cavalry, artillery, and tank officers, engineer corps and intelligence units, the OKH staff departments, and rail engineers, in addition to all army district chaplains and both field bishops—in short, any unit that could be stationed with chaplains in the event of mobilization. Its most controversial section dealt with a joint Protestant-Catholic worship service, which will be discussed in greater detail below.

While we do not know Rarkowski's reaction to the Bulletin, Werthmann did not approve of it. In spite of the OKH's recognition of the importance of pastoral care during the war, he described it as "one of many items that were part of the hapless experimentation of the military leadership" on the chaplaincy.[83] It is not difficult to understand his reaction. The Bulletin contained a detailed treatment of religious affairs in military life, and it marked the OKH's bold attempt to at least complement, if not undermine, the field bishop's authority in preparation for the coming war. The Bulletin described pastoral care in terms of military strength, as "an important means for the fortification of the army's vigor" that would serve "to maintain and nurture the inner fighting strength of German soldiers."[84] Duty and devotion to the Fatherland was a mandate from God. The Bulletin exhorted the chaplain to always make best use of his services, neglecting neither the fighting troops nor the sick and wounded in base hospitals.

The Bulletin also detailed the relationship between chaplains and military leaders. Troop commanders from large army groups to the smallest units were to view the chaplains as helpers: "A leader concerned with the spiritual comportment of his troops will notify the chaplain of every opportunity to serve, and will apprise him of observations pertaining to the mindset of the troops, of previous experiences, and of upcoming orders." The higher commanders and the chaplains were to work together to ascertain, preserve, and reaffirm the spiritual and emotional strength of their units. In certain circumstances, these commanders could assess the individual chaplain's "particular abilities and disposition" and apply for an exchange or discharge as needed.[85] So the chaplaincy was not strictly about the religious needs of soldiers; it was a military department like any other and an instrument for supervising the morale of soldiers.[86]

Werthmann's notes and the Bulletin indicate that the chaplaincy, and by extension all priests in the army, whether chaplains or not, came under attack frequently during the war, and it had relatively few vocal defenders among officers. Werthmann identified individuals at the leadership level who led the attacks and tried to defend chaplains and priests from them and singled out two men in particular who were resolutely anti-Catholic and against pastoral care from the outset. He called Wilhelm Keitel, head of the OKW, and Hermann Reinecke, the chief of the General Office of the Armed Forces (OKW/AWA), "satellites of National Socialism" because both attempted "to bring to fruition the wishes of the Party [against the chaplaincy] through obsequious compliance. They were never satisfied with measures against chaplains of both denominations." He singled out Reinecke as virulently anti-Christian, whose widely known statements about Wehrmacht chaplains documented "a blind will to destruction," presumably of anything related to the churches.[87] Werthmann was unsparing in his criticism, labeling Reinecke "an aspiring careerist and a kind of business trooper" who lunged at "anything brought to him—grievances about chaplains and the chancellery's plans for the down-sizing [of the chaplaincy]—with the fire of zealous and obnoxious impracticality."[88]

Anti-Catholicism in the Wehrmacht and Karl Edelmann

Werthmann noted an exception to the OKH's general hostility toward Catholic priests. He characterized Karl Edelmann, the department chief in the OKH, as "a true friend of the Wehrmacht chaplaincy." Edelmann was responsible for developing pastoral care in ways that "only he could," presumably due to his position within the OKH, and he "gave a shape to the chaplaincy that persisted amazingly well in the years of harder tribulation after 1942."[89] Edelmann is a minor figure in the historiography outside of texts dealing with the military chaplaincy, perhaps because his rank, though high, did not place him at the zenith of military leadership. In September 1943 he was transferred from his position within the OKH, and by October he was leading an infantry division in Norway. In one of the few surviving reflections written during the war, Werthmann was uncharacteristically emotional about Edelmann's transfer, revealing the depth of their relationship as well as the degree of trust and mutual dependency between the two: "Major-General Edelmann gave his farewell address today [1 October 1943].... The father, organizer, and custodian of our armed forces chaplaincy for the last three and a half years is leaving us. There is no one who can replace him in the sense of his campaigning on behalf of the chaplaincy. He established and strengthened it."[90]

Edelmann also played a central role in drawing up various regulations for Wehrmacht chaplains and priests: his office issued the 1939 Bulletin (of which Werthmann was so critical) and subsequent supplements up to the end of 1941. The latter included an undated draft, likely from early 1941, of pastoral duties for Protestant and Catholic chaplains with supervisory duties that were not integrated into any official military regulations. That this draft was neither precisely dated nor formally written suggests that it emerged from oral remarks that Edelmann made to the chaplains. The content of the draft reveals a commitment to respecting and enhancing the chaplain's position within the army. To this end, Edelmann noted, "Even in this war, pastoral care is an essential aid to military leadership, to educate men to be enthusiastic to the end, even to the point of surrendering one's own life . . . and so to contribute to the strengthening of spiritual deportment among German soldiers at the front."[91] As these remarks make clear, however, this essential aid was always subordinate to military control. Edelmann consistently conceptualized pastoral care within the framework of military necessity.

Edelmann's concern and enthusiasm for the office of the chaplain was thus based on its military value. Pastoral care was a necessity for men at war. Accordingly, he devised many ways to make pastoral care more meaningful, for the priests and especially for soldiers. Catering to soldiers' spiritual needs was not merely about satisfying their desire for religious meaning. It was about providing them with the mental support for the important task at hand: fighting a war on behalf of German civilization. The most effective way to accomplish this was for the chaplain to develop "a soldierly, militant personality, passionately devoted to his task and ready with his whole being for any situation with inexhaustible commitment, even to the end." Even more succinctly, the chaplain's political loyalties were to be beyond reproach: "that the chaplain possess boundless love for the Fatherland and accept the current state and National Socialism without any inner reservation is a self-evident requirement." In this sense, Edelmann was always loyal to the Nazi cause, and integrated the chaplaincy seamlessly into the exercise of maintaining morale.

It was also the chaplain's responsibility to promote attendance at religious services. Here Edelmann was full of advice on how priests were to conduct themselves, stating that their purpose would be achieved only if they abandoned orthodox preaching and stood "as comrade[s] and counselor[s] at the side of [their] comrades." In his view, divine service should be neither too long nor too informal, and ideally not scheduled during soldiers' free time. If services were poorly attended, it was the chaplain's fault, and he needed to remedy the problem. Edelmann even had advice to share about the art of preaching, with an unsurprising emphasis on a divinely sanctioned war and a Führer sent from on high:

> Every sermon must sustain close contact with the troops. It must be popularly [volkstümlich] tailored to the men and absolutely preserve a soldierly character. Troops will always reject religious lectureship, a dogmatic reading-aloud of a text, and outdated, doctrinal-style sermons. Every sermon must be adapted to the outlook of the soldiers and attuned to the practical life of a soldier at the front. It must sermonize the soldierly virtues of courage, bravery, and readiness for action as desired by the divine world order. It must situate this war over German living space and the rewarding struggle as sanctioned by God. It must depict the Führer as a man blessed by God.[92]

Edelmann's notes confirm his commitment to National Socialist ideology, and, if he is representative of the individuals in the OKH, suggest how deeply that ideology had permeated the army's highest echelons. They also demonstrate the manner in which he was a disciplined, professional soldier anxious to utilize every possible resource to advance the might of the Wehrmacht. The religious language he employed, and his description of the regime's goals as divinely sanctioned, testify to the ease with which he cloaked military aims with religious sentiment. To Edelmann, the chaplains' ultimate purpose was to promote the will of the Führer because it was approved by God. Priests and soldiers also subscribed to this confluence of Catholicism and Nazism: the "'belief' in Hitler, in an increasingly religious, metaphysical sense," became indistinguishable from belief in God.[93]

Nondenominational Services

In an innovative step, Edelmann promoted nondenominational services (*interkonfessionellen Gottesdienste*), which consisted of mixing Protestant and Catholic soldiers into one congregation.[94] This is unsurprising since he was directly involved in authorizing them in the first place, in the Bulletin.[95] He stressed in subsequent supplements that such services "have found special approval among the troops," and that the commander-in-chief (which at that time was Walther von Brauchitsch) declared that the "cornerstone of pastoral service in the field will always be the celebration of divine service, which corresponds to the inner unity of the troops, who, as a rule, are not separated according to confession. Rather, the service is held for the entire community."[96]

According to Edelmann's statements, troops gravitated naturally, even enthusiastically, to nondenominational services. Through this group activity, the cohesion of and "inner peace" among soldiers was best preserved. Whether it was before, during, or after a battle, "the troop belongs together . . . without distinction of denomination. Just as the troop steps into battle, so they will step before God. . . . The interest of the troops in these nondenominational services is unquestionably greater than those of purely denominational devotions." The nondenominational service was thus the best way to achieve a rapport with soldiers because this activity successfully achieved "the most cohesive participation of the group."

Protestant and Catholic chaplains were to work together to emphasize similarities and minimize doctrinal distinctions. Thus, while opportunity was "always to be given to soldiers to participate voluntarily in denomination-specific ceremonies such as confession, communion, etc.," the OKH ordered that "as a rule, divine service was to be held for the entire unit, and not divided by denomination, in order to reflect the inner uniformity of the troops." This not-so-subtle privileging of national over religious identity reflected the instrumental purpose of religion: soldiers could be Catholic or Protestant, but, above all, they were German.

Edelmann wrote at length about other topics, including the attitudes of soldiers toward religion, the relationship of the Luftwaffe with the chaplaincy, and nondenominational services at the front. He divided army soldiers into three types: the smallest number of individuals, those who rejected pastoral care completely; the slightly larger number of "positive believers," those who sought it out (more often Catholic than Protestant); and the greatest number, those who were "disinterested in the face of" pastoral care. While the members of this last group adopted a largely positive attitude toward participating in divine services, they "required a certain animus and incentive" to do so, which the chaplain was to provide. Edelmann also reminded priests that "the contemporary soldier has gone through the Hitler Youth, the Sturmabteilung (SA), and the labor service, and is no longer uncritical and without certain prejudices toward priests." This statement was the closest that anyone in the OKH came to recognizing the latent hostility among younger soldiers toward institutional religion. It was also a tacit acknowledgment of the effectiveness of Nazi indoctrination both at home and at the front. Concerning the Luftwaffe, Edelmann encouraged chaplains to ensure that divine services were available to air-force soldiers stationed in their army districts, declaring that this did not contradict the November 1939 decree abolishing pastoral care in the Luftwaffe.

Edelmann (and by extension the OKH) wanted to use religious services for military reasons. For those soldiers who chose to participate, such an atmosphere contributed actively to the maintenance of morale and solidarity, gave soldiers another foundation upon which to build an active and healthy *Volksgemeinschaft* free of religious division, and served to foment a hatred for Bolshevism. However, like Werthmann, most Catholic priests were keen to safeguard specifically Catholic spiritual care in the army and to guarantee sacramental access for Catholic soldiers. Hence, they viewed the nondenominational services with ambivalence and suspicion. Bolshevism was to be fought at most, but not all, costs. In their view, the price was high if distinctly Catholic pastoral care was abrogated in favor of a watered-down prayer service that Catholic Church authorities would have seen as illicit and spiritually dangerous.[97] The Protestant-Catholic divide in Germany was alive and healthy up to 1933, with memories of the Kulturkampf not that distant. Even after Nazism attempted to supplant religious distinctions through the construction of a people's community predicated on race, no rapprochement took place between Protestant and Catholic bishops or their respective clergies on the home front. In the military, it was not Christian fraternity or interest in ecumenism but pure necessity that drove the two denominations to work together. Catholic priests were well aware that Church authorities would not recognize the nondenominational service that Edelmann promoted as legitimate. Most of them did everything they could surreptitiously to offer alternatives.

Modifications to the Bulletin labeled "secret" (hereafter referred to as the Modifications) that were released in February 1940 indicate that chaplains were exceeding their jurisdiction and encroaching into areas that the OKH claimed exclusively as its own.[98] Chaplains were prohibited from disseminating religious information of any kind (whether it was personal writings or printed texts) absent prior approval from military authorities and the field bishop. That an order was required to curb such action reflects both the considerable dearth of written religious material at the front as well as the demand for it. The few materials that did exist consisted mostly of hymnals or pastoral letters from the field bishop.[99] In addition, the Modifications decreed that the armed forces chaplaincy "has a religious duty whose resolution is to be incorporated as much as possible into the patriotic exigencies of the war. The military authorities alone are entitled to the political training of soldiers."[100] If there was any lingering doubt about the relationship between politics and religion in the military, and whether one outweighed the other, the Modifications confirmed that the "patriotic exigencies"—political indoctrination and the ideology of the Nazi movement—took precedence. Furthermore, chaplains were not permitted to address questions of a general political or (even more surprisingly) an ecclesiastical nature in training seminars. The goal of these sessions was simply spiritual instruction in the context of the war effort and the exchange of military experiences through oral discussion. Chaplains were the exclusive attendees of such seminars; there was no supervisory military authority. For this reason, the OKH wanted as much as it could to control the discussion topics among priests, including those of a purely religious nature, for these men were crucial in the maintenance of troop morale.

But more than just rule-breaking led to the Modifications. As the Polish occupation unfolded and the German field of battle progressed into western Europe, it became imperative for military authorities to adjust regulations accordingly. The Modifications clarified points that were previously ambiguous—attendance of divine service was to be voluntary, not ordered by troop commanders; chaplains were to hold nondenominational services and be recognizable by small color details on their uniforms; the chaplain's first priority was always to assist in the burial of a Christian soldier. The Modifications also attempted to prevent non-chaplain priests from taking on a chaplain's duties. For instance, *only* chaplains were to give pastoral care within the army. Spiritual care performed by "priests serving as soldiers [i.e., outside the chaplaincy] should occur only in exceptional circumstances, with the approval of the unit commanders." These exceptional circumstances included death, a solemn feast day, and the specific request of soldiers before or after battle, and only if the chaplain was unavailable. This rule attempted to prevent priests serving outside the chaplaincy, who by far outnumbered actual chaplains, from acting as priests during their military service. The logistics of battle made it unlikely that a priest would obtain permission from his commander in time to administer the last sacraments to someone dying, to hear confessions, or to grant absolution to soldiers about to engage in battle.

In mid-1941, the OKW suddenly discharged all members of the Society of Jesus—Jesuits—from active service. About this incident Werthmann had surprisingly little to say, and Rarkowski mentioned nothing about it in his circulars. But it affected the Jesuits profoundly and not only because they were removed from physical battle. The release was one more volley in the battle between the Nazi regime and the religious order, and it came mere weeks before the invasion of the Soviet Union, a battle for which the Jesuits had been preparing for years. Jesuits interpreted their release as a "stigmatization" that "pushed us into line with Jews, the mentally ill, and violent criminals."[101] While at this point in the war the army may not have been lacking soldiers—the catastrophic losses had yet to be suffered on the Eastern Front, which did not exist when the Jesuits were discharged—the removal of the Jesuits was in any case relatively minimal, with only 405 men affected.[102] Like other decrees that Werthmann cited, this was followed with consternation and disappointment from fellow soldiers, who admired the Jesuits as "good comrades" and "good soldiers"; the officers reacted more ambivalently, affirming that they either "did not understand or in any case did not want to know . . . it was an order from the Führer, and therefore inscrutable [unhinterfragbar]."[103] In any case, the OKH was not directly involved in the decision. Its noninvolvement in decrees and decisions would become more commonplace at the end of 1941, after hostilities had taken a turn for the worse for Germany.

With their entrance into the chaplaincy, chaplains were responsible to two authorities that articulated rules and guidelines for pastoral care in the army: Rarkowski (their spiritual director) and the OKH (their military leader). By the end of 1941, however, two significant developments led to the interference of a third authority, the Nazi Party. The first development was the May 1941 flight of Deputy Führer Rudolf Hess, the third most powerful man in Nazi Germany after Hitler and Göring. The flight of Hess paved the way for the reorganization of the staff of the deputy führer, which was renamed the Party Chancellery. Martin Bormann came to dominate that office. A ruthless opponent of the Christian churches, he soon controlled all access to Hitler.[104] The relief of Walther von Brauchitsch from command of the OKH in December 1941 constituted the second development. In the wake of this event, Hitler appointed himself supreme commander of Germany's armed forces, and the OKH, until then still a relatively autonomous entity, lost much of its independence. The increase in influence of Bormann, on the one hand, and Hitler's assumption of control of the Wehrmacht, on the other hand, all but guaranteed an augmented Nazi

Party intrusion into the chaplaincy's affairs. A new set of guidelines heralded such an involvement in 1942.

The 1942 Guidelines

Werthmann's notes describe the 1942 "Guidelines for the Performance of Pastoral Care in the Field" (hereafter referred to as the Guidelines) as an attempt to conciliate Party Chancellery wishes with those of the army regarding the military chaplaincy.[105] The Guidelines were meant to replace the Bulletin, the Modifications, and other supplements as the official list of regulations. They reflected the Nazi Party's growing hostility to Christian traditions within the army—a reflection of Bormann's power—as well as heightened concerns from both party and military leaders about the direction of the war.[106] Their issuance was the first direct intrusion of the party into the wartime chaplaincy. The timing coincided with the first major Soviet counteroffensive and the deep crisis of the German army in the throes of a harsh Russian winter during 1941–1942. These military setbacks constituted the first substantial reverses suffered by the Wehrmacht since the opening of the war in 1939. The Guidelines' tone was more obviously militant, and the emphasis on the authority of military leaders was heightened as was the subservience of religious issues to national, political, and ideological exigencies—again, all indications of the ascent of Bormann.[107]

In one sense, the Guidelines tread little new ground. The Bulletin and the Modifications had already elaborated on most of what the Guidelines contained. Participation in spiritual activities was to be strictly voluntary; the individual soldier's choice, either to participate or to not participate, was to incur no disadvantage from a military superior or a chaplain. The chaplain was to cater to Christian soldiers who desired pastoral care (it was not to be given when not requested), and the elision of denominational differences, reflected in the active collaboration of Protestant and Catholic chaplains, was highlighted. Only OKW-approved written material could be distributed to soldiers. In one of the few changes that the Guidelines introduced, stress was placed on the responsibilities of military commanders to educate and maintain morale and positive attitudes toward the war effort. Now the chaplain was limited to handling concerns of a strictly religious nature.

The Guidelines had more distinctly propagandistic overtones than preceding lists of regulations. At the height of fighting in Europe, and just as the "final solution to the Jewish question" became fully operational, the OKW wrote that "the victorious outcome of the National Socialist struggle for freedom" was "decisive for the future of the German *Volksgemeinschaft*, and with it for every individual German."[108] Pastoral care was to serve this ultimate aim. The Guidelines further underscored the separation of religious and military matters. Chaplains could not perform religious ceremonies together with military activities and could not have processions outside of a church. Moreover, the Guidelines outlined a more stringent attitude toward the civilian population and its churches in occupied territory: religious activities or writings of any kind (including propaganda) for these occupied populations were illegal, and soldiers could not partake in civilian church services in occupied areas. In some cases in enemy territory and occupied areas, however, "appropriate churches or accommodations can be seized for the particular use of troops. These buildings as well as the religious sentiments of the populations are to be spared when possible." The prohibition on sharing churches as well as joint services with the civilian populations of occupied territories, however, was explicit.

On this point no room for flexibility was given: churches in eastern occupied areas, that is, the Soviet Union, were not to be used for pastoral activities of any kind.[109] The OKW was unsympathetic in the fall of 1941 when both field bishops wrote to plead the lack of alternatives and increasingly cold weather as reasons to permit their men to use abandoned churches in occupied Russian territory. They received a terse response: "The attitude of the armed forces on religious questions in newly occupied eastern territories has been unambiguously laid out in the regulations of the Führer. Applications for alteration at this time promise no success."[110] While the OKW provides no written explanation as to why Polish churches could be used but not Soviet ones, the unfolding of the war might have had some influence. In Poland, the war had ended quickly and German occupying forces rapidly entrenched themselves. They dealt quickly and brutally with the resistance that flared up. In October 1941, the war had not been won in Soviet territory, and, in fact, it appeared that a decisive victory was going to take longer than expected. Especially at this early stage, Wehrmacht commanders might have wanted to avoid provoking the indigenous populations by seizing their churches.[111]

While military considerations influenced the proposed changes, Werthmann was not naïve. He was aware of the anti-Catholicism of several highest-ranking Nazis; Bormann kept company with Himmler, Joseph Goebbels, and Reinhard Heydrich. The latter, chief of the Reich Security Main Office (RSHA) and the Gestapo under Himmler, had long obsessed about the Catholic Church's "subversive power" in Europe. His perception of the Vatican's intentions in Russia drove him to write to the OKH in November 1941, alleging that the field bishop's desire to use churches in Soviet territory was meant to further the "Russia-mission of the Catholic Church."[112] Heydrich listed many "institutes and commissions" to support his theory, including a "special assignment of members of the Benedictine order" and "the ecclesiastical Oriental Institute in Rome with the definitive involvement of the Jesuits." All these bodies were working to "mount the Russia-mission and create possibilities [for themselves] by deploying legions and bringing trained missionaries into conquered eastern areas." As proof of his allegations, Heydrich cited reports in Italian Catholic papers about the distribution of holy cards and the restoration of profaned churches (that is, churches that the Bolsheviks had taken control of and used for secular reasons or shut down). While he did not explicitly mention Catholic Germans in the report, Heydrich implied to the OKH that they might attempt something similar. He ended by declaring flatly that "these plans [of the field bishop, in conjunction with the Holy See] contradicted the instructions of the Führer."

Werthmann's judgment of the Guidelines, written immediately after the war, was ambivalent. He attributed the Nazi Party's motivation for their release to its hostility for the nondenominational service that the Bulletin had promoted: "the so-called nondenominational divine service was not, as was often assumed, a form of divine service pushed by the Nazis, [designed] to wear out both denominations and establish a 'religion of unity'. . . . In contrast, the Nazis acted very early on as decisive opponents of the nondenominational divine service and attempted to eliminate it." He explained that political circles—presumably party higher-ups such as Heydrich and Bormann—interpreted the nondenominational service as "an attempt to sabotage and circumvent voluntary participation in divine service." With its elimination, Bormann and his kind hoped to prove that soldiers had little interest in religion, and, therefore, the need for spiritual care in the army was superfluous (or at least the spiritual care offered by the churches).[113] It was evidence of the party's elemental distrust of institutional religion: Nazi party leaders viewed the Church as a powerful ideological rival, and they sought to eradicate what they perceived was Catholicism's potentially harmful effects on German soldiers.[114] Their hostility toward religion prevented them from seeing the irksome effect produced by nondenominational services on at least the Catholic chaplains, if not also the Protestants. In abolishing the services, these Nazis inadvertently helped Catholic chaplains to regain some autonomy and pursue spiritual goals specific to their denomination.[115]

According to the party, the Bulletin was dangerous because the principle of "absolutely voluntary participation" in religious activities was not properly adhered to, at least "not in the Nazi sense."[116] The second decree in the Modifications stated explicitly that attendance at divine services was not to be ordered; thus, army officers must have, on occasion, ordered their soldiers to attend services, though it is hard to determine how widespread this practice was.[117] Werthmann indicated elsewhere that the field bishops made absolutely clear that attendance of services was always voluntary.[118] So there was some basis for the party's concern over the voluntary aspect of religious worship. In light of this apprehension, Werthmann conceded that the Guidelines did not constitute a direct attack on Catholics in the army. Nonetheless, they were an unambiguous move toward eliminating Christian culture and tradition within its ranks because they made it more difficult for Catholic priests and Protestant pastors to perform their duties. Attempting to bring the army in line with the party's attitude about pastoral care could occur only at the expense of the army's autonomy, even as army leadership, in Werthmann's view, clung "increasingly to the Christian tradition."[119]

Werthmann's comments suggest that the problem went deeper than this. The army needed to embrace the party's hostility toward Christianity, a view that party leaders articulated more openly, notwithstanding Hitler's earlier utterances about the instrumental value of religion. In the process of the Nazi Party's wartime *Gleichschaltung* of the army, the Church had no room to maneuver and no sphere of autonomy to retain. As a result, the OKW eventually abolished nondenominational services, and chaplains and other priests and seminarians in the Wehrmacht came ever more under attack.

Front-Line Training Seminars

In spite of the Nazi Party's intensified meddling in 1942, one of Edelmann's projects for pastoral care in the military continued undisturbed. According to Werthmann, it was Edelmann who secured permission for chaplains to attend front-line training seminars, or *Frontlehrgänge*, during their war service. These *Frontlehrgänge*, most of which occurred between 1941 and 1943, were primarily training seminars for incoming chaplains, although they also offered to chaplains an opportunity to meet for two or three days and exchange stories about their experiences. An OKH decree from February 1942 described the seminars explicitly in this way.[120] Senior chaplains led each seminar, conducted according to denomination. The occurrence of these seminars slowed notably after 1942, much to the consternation of the chaplains. However, the lack of incoming chaplains coupled with mounting military losses made the scheduling of such seminars too difficult.[121] Until then, they were hugely successful. They took place on all European fronts where German soldiers were stationed: from France to the Soviet Union and from Norway to Greece.

The chaplaincy leaders structured the seminars so that they resembled a two-day religious retreat, with their division of time and suggested curriculum reflective of army efficiency. Each seminar addressed the importance of pastoral care and elaborated on its most essential elements. Chaplains shared ideas about preaching and conducting nondenominational services and discussed their experiences in field hospitals, their relationships with military officers and superiors, and their views on the "patriotic" activities of pastoral care and the distribution of religious writings. For example, the OKH suggested the allocation of forty-five minutes to consider the question, "What do the troops expect from pastoral care?" that "an appropriate officer" was to lead.[122]

Rarkowski attended a seminar in East Prussia in March 1942, and Werthmann attended several of them on the Eastern Front in the spring of 1944. Minutes were kept for each seminar, copies of which the head chaplain of the division received, as did the field bishop's office. Werthmann made notes about his experiences at seminars held over a week in Biala Podlaska and Orscha in June 1944. He remarked on a soccer game between the Fourth Army and the Third (Panzer) Army in the area, when soldiers had warmly welcomed the participation of chaplains. Werthmann declared that his meeting with the chaplains who attended these seminars in 1944 gave him renewed energy for his duties, for "when I had these brave priests before my eyes, who have come away from the battles in the East, away from encounters . . . with Bolshevism, I know that my job in Berlin, which is often difficult, has meaning and sense. For it makes me happy to have committed myself to this with life and limb. I vow to go on, even into a dark, perhaps very difficult future."[123]

The intrusion of the Nazi Party into chaplaincy affairs in 1942 indicated a dark turn for priests in the army. To this end, the Guidelines marked the beginning of the gradual removal of priests from administrative positions in the chaplaincy and a general diminution of their roles as spiritual guides. In a secret decree in October 1942, the OKW informed the field bishops that it would no longer admit priests into the chaplaincy; the offices of fallen chaplains would not be filled.[124] The field bishops reacted with letters of shock and concern, imploring that at least the positions of chaplains who had fallen at Stalingrad be filled. Their pleas were met with unsympathetic rejection.[125] This issue resonated outside the chaplaincy. In a July 1943 report that Werthmann sent to the OKH about his activities, he made a point of mentioning that "it came up repeatedly in conversations with officers and soldiers," and that an individual as prestigious as Field Marshal Georg von Küchler was convinced that neither commanders nor troops could do without pastoral care. The situation overall was "becoming much more difficult" after the October 1942 decree.[126] In March 1944, the chief of staff of Army Group South, a Major-General Haseloff (first name not given, but likely Kurt Haseloff), told Werthmann that his soldiers' need for pastoral care was beyond question. A General Staff doctor in the same area echoed this and insisted that priests were essential for hospital work.[127] Soldiers may have clung to traditional religious attitudes and resisted attempts to eliminate that outlet, given that Germany was now losing major battles and victory was slipping away. But Werthmann's notes indicate that while widespread grumbling took place, no outright protest ensued. As a result, for the final two and a half years of war, chaplains who fell in battle or went missing were not replaced.

Anticlericalism and the National Socialist Leadership Officers

In the summer of 1944, the Allied armies made significant inroads in western Europe after the successful Normandy invasion. They had already moved into Italy, Europe's "soft underbelly." The Red Army continued its westward advance, to the terror of Germans who had resettled eastern territories, in some cases as much as five years earlier. It was at this time that the dispersion of Hermann Reinecke's National Socialist Leadership Officers (also known as *Offiziere für wehrgeistige Führung*) through the armed forces peaked.[128] After Germany's devastating loss at Stalingrad in February 1943, Hitler charged Reinecke with the task of heading the new National Socialist Leadership Staff (*Nationalsozialistische Führungsstab*). The officers attached to this staff were to be disseminated throughout the ranks of the army up to the division level. One year later, they numbered approximating 50,000.[129]

In a meeting on 7 January 1944 with Hitler, Keitel, Bormann, and three other Wehrmacht officers, Reinecke discussed the contours of his office. He believed that the war could be more than halfway won (*"mit 51 Prozent Sicherheit"*[130]) through the ideological engagement of all Wehrmacht officers. The defeat at Stalingrad was not only a decisive military turning point, he declared, but also it was evidence that the military leadership was no longer capable of providing the necessary ideological training that soldiers required (this conviction would only strengthen in Reinecke's mind after the 20 July bomb plot that nearly assassinated Hitler, following which he served as a judge at the trials of the most important conspirators, including Carl Goerdeler and Ulrich von Hassel). From now on, the important task of providing intellectual and ideological guidance for the troops was to be solely entrusted to the NSFO. This was their primary—indeed, their only—task.

The development of the Nazi Leadership Office was the first major beachhead into the internal affairs of the Wehrmacht that the Nazi Party established, and it could not have been accomplished without the enthusiasm of Keitel and Bormann (incidentally, in spring 1945 Bormann would attempt—and fail—to remove Reinecke and bring the Leadership Office directly under his sole control).[131] The NSFOs remained active until the German capitulation in May 1945. They were composed of a mix of older party warriors and young, zealous officers, all of whom had "proven themselves with the same fanaticism."[132] One scholar has argued that the only thing that prevented the gradual Nazification of the Wehrmacht's officer corps through the diffusion of these officers was the end of the war. However, the NSFO's actual effectiveness as a political officer for the year and a half the office existed remains unclear.[133]

Reinecke was convinced that his officers should not be "something of a rival with priests [because] there is very little in common between the tasks of the officer and those of the priest. The objective of our education within the troop is, on the one hand, to make soldiers fanatical bearers of faith [*Glaubensträger*] and, on the other hand, to inculcate him with hatred against our enemy."[134] Despite this "official" position of conflict avoidance, however, many chaplains found Reinecke's remarks to be a direct challenge to their role. To this end, the mandate of the NSFO included the "political-ideological leadership and education" and "care for the troops (*spiritual* care and organization of free time)." The same regulations insisted that "the NSFO is not to undertake any activity that lies beyond the sphere of political-ideological leadership,"[135] and that he had a "soldierly, but not a pastoral [*seelsorgerisch*], mission to fulfill."[136] One month earlier, an artillery general in the Sixteenth Army had referred to the "mobilization of internal readiness for battle and mental strength to persevere" as the command of the hour. He further stated that the NSFO "has merely to take the reins in hand and show that he, too, bears responsibility in the area of *spiritual* and intellectual [*gedanklichen*] leadership."[137] The kind of "faith" that the NSFOs were supposed to instill was the "Nazi" faith, in direct contradiction to the Christian faith. Despite Reinecke's perfunctory exclamations to the contrary, many chaplains saw the NSFOs in this light.

Werthmann later conceded that there was no proof that the NSFOs' primary goal was to spy on chaplains, but he did note, "Chaplains disclosed many times that this surveillance was performed." No reference has been found to any official surveillance program in the January 1944 meeting of Hitler, Reinecke, Keitel, and Bormann. Given the active hostility of the latter three individuals to the Catholic Church, any such program under Reinecke's jurisdiction likely would have been mentioned in this private conversation. Werthmann and many chaplains insisted, "It was evident that the NSFO had the assignment to slowly take over the task of the priests, and—if not directly, then indirectly—to supplant and disengage the chaplain."[138] Even if chaplains found ways to circumvent and thereby limit the influence of the NSFO, they still resented their intrusion into pastoral affairs. As Werthmann stated:

> His [the NSFO's] task was really a preoccupation with Nazi propaganda and the training of soldiers. Whole mountains of printed materials were made available for this. Even various articles for sale, writing paper, shoe polish, toothpaste and toothbrushes, soap, etc., were delivered in great quantities to the NSFO for free distribution, so that they could appear "more persuasive" with it. . . . He was meant to and had to deliver his findings for promotion. He watched over virtually all the officers; even generals were not excluded. It was self-evident that he surveilled the activities of us chaplains. . . . The belief in victory was convulsively adhered to in all imaginable ways. Lies? Truth? Neither whatsoever [Keinerlei]! I will never forget, a high-ranking general who traveled from village to village in the French back area [Etappe]. He did not depict the situation as rosy, but in the end he professed belief in the coming miracle [of victory]. . . . A high-ranking general posturing as an NSFO![139]

Much of Werthmann's criticism of the NSFO came at the end of the war. In contrast, during the war, he commented that the activities of the chaplain and the NSFOs were "unambiguously demarcated," and that in practice there were "no difficulties" between the two.[140] This discrepancy lies in the distinction between what the NSFO represented—political and ideological indoctrination, party control—and their actual efficacy. Both Werthmann and the chaplains depicted the NSFOs they encountered as mostly harmless. Despite their sheer numbers, the success of the NSFOs in carrying out their mission appears quite limited. A combination of factors made their assignment challenging, if not impossible: the lethal deprivation of living at the front (particularly the Eastern Front); the camaraderie the soldiers developed in battle prior to the NSFO's arrival; the continued turbulent relationship between party leaders and Wehrmacht officers; and the growing apathy and hopelessness of soldiers in the final months of the war, which in turn provoked murderous disciplinary measures in an attempt to discourage desertion.

As Werthmann surmised, the increased use of NSFOs peaking with the new limitations on priests was not likely a coincidence. In June 1944, a decree discharged Catholic priests, deacons, and seminarians from the officer reserve corps.[141] It is unclear how many men this affected. The OKH reiterated that priests were supposed to work as either chaplains or medical orderlies, neither of which carried officer rankings. The reality, however, was that at least some priests had ended up in full military service.[142] Werthmann remembered that even the OKW did not receive the decree well; previously the OKW had passed all manner of anti-Christian regulations. This order actually hurt the army because commanders saw it as an abnegation of "valuable military material," badly needed in the summer of 1944. At this point in the war, the Soviet Union was pushing the Wehrmacht back on the Eastern Front, and invading Allied armies were engaging German troops in western and southern Europe.[143] According to Werthmann's notes, two additional decrees followed the decision to release these men from officer ranks, both designed to further remove clergy from military service. The first of these stated that clerics who held ecclesiastical offices were no longer subject to conscription. The second decree declared that any priest who had quit his studies before his theological exams could not be conscripted. With this, Werthmann noted, "the further conscription of priests was, in practice, completely suspended. Even for work service or service in the *Volkssturm* (People's Militia), priests were no longer expressly used."[144]

Werthmann speculated on the possible reason for these developments at length. The decrees exacerbated the dire problem of insufficient troops at the front—a need that had earlier driven the regime to conscript priests and seminarians. What had precipitated this about-face in policy so late in the war? Werthmann remarked sardonically that it could have simply been the desire, fanned by anti-Catholics like Bormann and Goebbels, to shut priests out of assignments having any bearing on "*Volk* and Fatherland." He admitted that the perception existed in domestic religious circles that the terror and chaos caused by the air raids called for priests to care for the civilian population. By providing for the needs of civilians, the party may have realized that it also had an opportunity to keep priests out of the army.

A sympathetic OKH officer, Alfred Weidemann, revealed to Werthmann the party's likely motivation in adopting such policies. Weidemann confided that he had connections to the resistance circles that planned the 20 July bomb plot.[145] He explained that the party (presumably represented by Bormann) designed the decrees as a "heavy blow against the hated priestlings. A letter from the Party Chancellery to the OKW stated that Catholic priests and Protestant ministers had forfeited the right, *through their behavior during the war*, to participate in the decisive existential battle for the German *Volk*." Werthmann remembered that Weidemann "was appalled by this kind of proceeding."[146] Probably two kinds of behavior merited this punishment: one, that the OKW viewed priests in uniform as untrustworthy, given the recurrent regulation breaches due to the shrinking number of chaplains, and two, that the OKW viewed priests as insufficiently patriotic.

Moreover, Werthmann contended in the same set of notes that the party attempted an even more thorough removal of clergy in the Wehrmacht when it forcibly tried to transfer priests already serving into reserve units, effectively removing them from active fronts. Like the other 1944 decrees, possible reasons for this policy change include the conviction that priests were more useful on the home front and the worry that disloyal priests were undermining troop morale. Whatever the reason, Werthmann explained that the plan ultimately failed "in the face of passive resistance from the OKW, which could not accept it [as a responsible plan] to send this cadre of valuable manpower back home, in view of the tense overall situation and the sheer mass of men involved."[147] This resistance from a group of men who had accepted Hitler's war strategies without question for years would previously have been unthinkable. It demonstrates unexpected room for independent action as well as the gravity of the war situation. Although Werthmann did not substantiate his claim with evidence, he felt that such passive resistance from the military thwarted the party's attempt to drastically reduce the number of priests and seminarians in uniform.

This, then, was the world in which chaplains and other Catholic priests found themselves operating. Despite the constant pressures and entanglements produced by the political power play between party and military high command over the six and a half years of war, their leader, Field Bishop Rarkowski, set an example of steadfast obedience to his military superiors. His pastoral letters and circulars, essentially the only approved religious literature available to soldiers apart from the New Testament, bear this out. In June 1940 he wrote: "It now lies with you, participants in this present difficult and decisive conflict, mandated by our Supreme Commander, to play a decisive role to the best of your abilities, through your selfless commitment, in bringing about a victorious peace. This peace will give our German *Volk* that rank among the nations of Europe to which we have an intrinsic right, according to God's creative will."[148] In September of the same year, on the first anniversary of the war's outbreak, he labeled the war as just, and forced on Germany by circumstance, "broken out of the necessity of *völkisch* self-defense, out of the unlikelihood of resolving peacefully a difficult, pressing issue of justice regarding our state's existence, and of making good by other means a blatant injustice that others have done to us."[149] He praised the stalwart readiness of German soldiers to make the ultimate sacrifice for their Fatherland and depicted the war as ordained by God for the advancement of Germany. After the outbreak of war with the Soviet Union, he noted that the conflict was fateful for more than just Germans: "Even you [soldiers] who are currently fighting it out for the destiny of Europe, you have become more serious, more mature, quieter. You have encountered God. Many of you have inscribed on your souls what was shared with me from the home front: 'We drift along our path into battle and need, surrounded by danger, but we also come nearer to God, we feel that His breath fans us.'"[150] In one of his last circulars, in late spring 1943, Rarkowski was adamant that the war was justifiable, even divinely ordained, and that the soldiers engaged in these battles were comparable to their fathers' generation, who had fought in the Great War and performed similar acts of valor. He told the military chaplains,

> The German soldier of 1914 and his son, who as a young soldier in 1939 is duking it out in the great, decisive engagement of our time, may differentiate themselves in many things, since they belong to different eras of our German history. But in the essentials, there is

no difference between the representatives of these two generations of German soldiery.... The fortitude of German soldiers is known across the world. It is the same for the volunteers that marched to Langemarck and fell there as it is for the warriors at Stalingrad.[151]

The Chaplaincy Numbers

It is difficult to arrive at an estimation of the number of army chaplains through the first year of the war. In March 1939, the Catholic chaplaincy consisted of ninety-three priests, and plans called for an increase in that number to more than 1,300 when the war broke out.[152] In September 1939, the OKW mobilized 103 divisions. The year 1940–1941 alone saw the addition of seventy-two infantry divisions, three tank divisions, and twenty-one militia divisions, as well as a number of new brigades.[153] These numbers do not include field hospitals; there was at least one field hospital per division. In his postwar notes, Werthmann indicated that, according to regulations, there was to be one supervisory (or head) chaplain per army group, as well as one per army within that army group, one chaplain per division, and eight chaplains per field hospital.[154] Even after 1945, Werthmann was unable to ascertain the total number of chaplains active over the course of the war. By 1952, he estimated that it was 545, including those who fell or went missing, became prisoners of war, and were dismissed. The highest number at any one time, he reported, was 390, in the summer of 1941.[155] Thus, chaplains were stretched very thin from the beginning of the war. Not uncommonly, divisions could lack chaplains for years. This chronic shortage was reason enough for priests outside the chaplaincy to administer to their soldiers in time of need, with or without official permission. The speedy prohibition of this indicates that the OKH was both aware of the shortage and unwilling to ameliorate it.

Werthmann knew of the shortage, too, and he complained bitterly and at length in private notes that it was deliberately maintained. He pointed to the presence of priests who were not chaplains and who, under army regulations, could not administer to others as such: "So ensued such nonsense as, for example, an infantry division having, with their 12,000 to 15,000 soldiers, basically only a single Catholic chaplain, whereas in the same division, twenty to thirty Catholic priests could also be found as medical orderlies, who often performed the lowliest of services and who were forbidden to exercise pastoral care for their comrades, with the exception of very particular circumstances."[156] According to the terms of the concordat's secret appendix, these priests were stationed with field hospitals or other noncombat units because they were excused from bearing weapons. Many priests acted against the prohibition and administered to others spiritually when necessary, activities of which Werthmann had full knowledge. He took note of "the true collaboration of our medical orderlies, who themselves were priests, in the pastoral care of our wounded and dying. . . . They performed their medical and pastoral duties ceaselessly day and night from the beginning of their enlistment; they often could barely stand at the operation table because of exhaustion."[157] Werthmann's frustration is palpable that such a large number of men were prevented from acting in any official capacity as priests for their units and divisions, which often lacked the presence of a chaplain.

One reality that Werthmann refrained from commenting on was the confusion, uncertainty, and overall inconsistency in the policy of the OKH and the party vis-à-vis the chaplains. Sometimes these authorities worked in tandem to monitor and limit the activities of priests in the Wehrmacht, whereas at other times they were at odds with one another. The number of agencies involved in the training of chaplains (including party, state, and Church bodies) as well as of decrees relating to chaplains' activities issued between 1936 and 1944 amplified this institutional competition and chaos. As an organizational unit, the chaplaincy was simply one more element of military bureaucracy that the Nazis sought to control using any and all means at their disposal. Their success in this regard was not insignificant.

* * *

Is it surprising that Werthmann, who readily offered opinions about the OKW, OKH, NSFOs, and leaders such as Keitel, Reinecke, and Edelmann, did not elaborate on his personal opinions of the Führer himself, nor on specific elements of Nazi ideology? By the time he was interned in 1945, he had experienced the latter as a chaplain for a full decade. He may have been saving such reflections for a later period (some scant reflections from the 1950s and 1960s support this), or he may have been protecting himself from incrimination during the war. However, he did make three observations in May and June 1945 about the connection between Nazism and Christianity and the former's remarkable and inevitable breakdown. The first came in mid-May:

> A people can certainly improvise and our own people are richer than many others in the ability to improvise. But the spiritual formation of a people cannot be improvised. In my opinion, National Socialism broke down because it attempted to annul the essential, valuable elements of its own historically established spiritual formation. With this, National Socialism obliterated the noblest element of the *Volk* and dug its own grave.[158]

The second took up the same themes a few weeks later: "Germany is—from a historical viewpoint—a Christian nation. The renunciation of God . . . was a grievous catastrophe for our people. For us Germans, whose historical development is formed significantly on Christianity, this de-Christianization signifies the dissolution of the basis of our existence and the destruction of our being."[159] And at the end of June, Werthmann reflected,

> Why did Nazism struggle over and over against the Church with every available means? It [Nazism] appeared to be anchored in the entire *Volk* and certainly didn't cower before the small gaggle that avowed itself to Christ. The answer to this question can only run as follows: it is the curse and the fate of the blasphemous spirit to resort repeatedly to violence and persecution, almost against its own intelligent will. On its own, it is too weak to battle its opponent with spiritual weapons. So it is compelled, over and over, to make ready its opponent for the Cross and to thrust that opponent into the grave—a grave that will always be glorious.[160]

Each of the three quotes constitutes a judgment. Each quote evinces Werthmann's own reconciliation of being German and being Catholic and his views on what had led ultimately to Nazism's collapse.

Werthmann perceived the essence of the conflict between Nazism and Catholicism as one of control. In his mind as well as those of many of his religious (including Protestant) peers, Nazism's attempt to supplant Christianity was what led to the former's downfall. Less clear is the extent to which the leading members of the Nazi Party who were hostile to Christianity succeeded in their mission to displace it in Germany. It was a common chorus among the spiritual leadership in Germany at the end of the war that Nazism persecuted institutional religion. A lengthy historiography on the subject confirms that the Nazi Party never trusted the churches, and at times arrested individual members and made examples of them (albeit as resisters and not as church members).[161] Clearly the party did not consider the churches an ideal ally, even when the latter indicated that they would not object to the most heinous element of the Nazi weltanschauung, namely antisemitism, and the persecution and murder of Jews.

For Werthmann, Nazism was in essence anti-Catholic. However, this feature can hardly be described as one of its main ideological tenets. Moreover, Werthmann proved all too willing to excuse Nazism's more fundamental elements, such as biological racism, the need for *Lebensraum*, and the murder of Jews, as "lesser evils" to be tolerated to defeat a more formidable adversary: Bolshevism. For this reason, upon the subjects of biological-racist ideology, imperialist conquest, murderous economic exploitation of conquered territories, and the extermination of "undesirables," Werthmann (like the majority of his colleagues, both Protestant and Catholic) was silent.

Historians have tried to explain such silence in both apologetic and pejorative tones. For some, the silence indicated acquiescence, or at least passive toleration. For others, it was cautious self-preservation while more clandestine attempts were made to aid Jews and other victims of Nazi racial policy from annihilation. Perhaps the answer lies in the deeper meaning of Werthmann's third reflection, which did not address the Church's silence but rather Nazism's seemingly inexhaustible enmity for Christianity. By approaching the subject of Church-state relations from this oblique angle, he elided a discussion of the Church's active role in appeasing the Nazi Party, which began with the signing of the concordat in 1933. Instead, he preoccupied himself with Nazi hostility toward organized religion and God, a rejection (he concluded) that inevitably led to violence.

In all likelihood, Werthmann's counterfactual speculation in early May 1945 that "if Germany had won this war, the entire Church in Germany would have been dissolved . . . and that all clergymen, both Catholic and Protestant, would have been liquidated," would have very likely come to pass.[162] The Nazi regime exhibited an inability to coexist with any institution that it could not pull entirely into its own orbit, including other political parties, the legal and education systems, the medical profession, youth groups, and the army. All of these facets of German society were subjected to either dissolution or the process of *Gleichschaltung*. The institutional churches were left alone until after the war, when the Nazi leadership reckoned they could be eliminated without provoking resistance from the German population. Thus, even the churches would have been no exception. In the military, the *Gleichschaltung* of religious personnel did not wait: priests were successfully coordinated with Nazi ideology. However much they objected or dragged their feet, they ultimately served on the party's terms, especially after 1941. Intelligent and devoted men such as Werthmann chose to compromise for an amalgam of reasons: on the basis of their German identity, for the sake of Christians in need of spiritual care, to defeat Bolshevism. It was less important to take a moral stand against discrimination, criminality, and mass murder during the war than it was to keep one's head down and serve *Volk* and Fatherland daily for what they perceived to be the greater good.

A fundamental contradiction was inherent in the military chaplaincy of the Wehrmacht, one that manifested itself in Werthmann's notes. He and his fellow priests fulfilled their military duties in what they perceived was a defensive battle on behalf of Nazism—proof that the regime's propaganda was not entirely ineffective even in devout Catholic circles. Describing the invasion of Poland as a defensive move may now appear ludicrous. In 1939, though, the Nazis had characterized the war as an inevitable step in the process of eradicating the damage of the Treaty of Versailles and of eliminating Germany's perceived enemies, Slavs and Jews, while protecting ethnic Germans who lived within Poland's borders.[163] It is unclear whether and to what extent priests discussed the sudden truce between Germany and the Soviet Union or how they understood it. In any case, Werthmann and the chaplains found other ways of motivating themselves to serve their *Heimat*. They answered the call to serve by espousing the need to take care of fellow Germans in time of need. But in seeking to act as agents of the Catholic religion, to maintain some sense of Christian ethics among soldiers, and to provide a bulwark of faith and hope on the battlefront, these men also collaborated with an anti-Catholic regime and a war effort that can only be characterized as evil. While the devotion of the majority of chaplains to their vocation may have been genuine, and while they may have been deeply committed to their country and to God, they failed to apprehend the contradictions inherent in this dual identity.

3

PRIESTS AND SEMINARIANS IN THE WEHRMACHT

Between 1939 and 1945, more than 17,000 priests and seminarians were pulled from seminaries, classrooms, or religious orders and found themselves in military training camps and then in the Wehrmacht. By virtue of their religious vocation, they were different from the average recruit, and other soldiers often viewed them as such. Nor were Catholic priests who served as chaplains, approximately 500 men over the course of the war, "average" soldiers. As chaplains, different rules governed them, prescribing their sphere of duties and iterating what they could not do. Both within and outside of the chaplaincy, however, priests and seminarians serving in the German army during the Second World War shared the experience of wearing the uniform for *Volk*, Fatherland, and Führer. These men identified as devout Catholics who had chosen the priesthood. Some were already ordained, while others were at varying stages of preparing for ordination. All were eligible for conscription in case of general mobilization under the terms of the 1933 concordat, though this came as a surprise to many when it occurred.[1] According to the terms of the concordat, priests who did not become chaplains were stationed within the medical service, as were seminarians beyond a certain level of ordination. As a result, they did not carry weapons and were not candidates for promotion through the military hierarchy. This distinguished them from their Protestant counterparts, to whom these restrictions did not apply.[2]

Other circumstances also set them apart from their fellow soldiers. First, like other devout Christian soldiers throughout history, they found themselves serving two masters, God and Caesar. Hitler was not the first secular ruler in history to alienate members of the Catholic Church. Nevertheless, Catholic Germans, including priests, obeyed him as the lawful head of state with the encouragement of their bishops. Second, there was a small visual demarcation for chaplains: their uniforms had no epaulettes, and their collar tabs had violet markings (the chaplaincy used violet as its color).[3] This subtle visible identification made them targets for openly anti-Catholic or anticlerical soldiers as well as beacons of consolation for more devout soldiers. Finally, because of their spiritual vocation, those men with whom they served may have looked to them as examples of higher moral standards; soldiers and families back home used them as pillars of support and guidance.

These priests and seminarians shared, in nearly every sense of the word, the experiences of a horrific war with the men of their units. They slept and ate, marched and trained with the soldiers, and they experienced heady victory and abject defeat with them. They aided the sick and the dying, wrote letters home to their loved ones, and corresponded with families of fallen comrades. Some even found themselves bearing weapons and engaging in battle on the Eastern Front. Others witnessed atrocities or heard of them firsthand (though none admitted to participating in them). After the war, or in diaries, a few acknowledged that they knew about deportations and concentration camps such as Dachau, which had opened on German soil in 1933. Whether and to what extent those priests who heard confessions learned more about the crimes of German soldiers during the war will never be known. Even if the seal of the confessional were not in place, these men would not admit to knowing of crimes whose perpetrators they absolved.

How did these men relate to the soldiers around them? How did they interact with civilian non-Christian and non-German populations? What role did religion play in their daily lives in the army? How did they deal with the anti-Catholic SS and the rival NSFOs? What were their experiences of war on different fronts? In answering these questions, the ability of Catholic priests and seminarians to engage with and understand the men of Hitler's army is distinct from other soldiers. Their capacity to reconcile faith with national duty equipped them with tools to deal with the war's horror in exceptional ways. I will analyze this wartime experience and how it affected the beliefs and values of these men: how they understood the war and their roles in it, and how they reconciled Nazism and Catholicism. Using letters, journals, chaplains' reports, evaluations by military and religious superiors, and postwar writings and interviews, I reconstruct the world in which these men lived as fully as possible. Their experiences show that, although soldiers and officers consistently saw chaplains, priests, and sometimes seminarians as a "group apart," they were integral to the war effort because they influenced the morale of the men around them. In some cases, they served with as much enthusiasm as nonreligious German soldiers, even citing as motivation some of the same ideological goals as the regime they later claimed to abhor. Moreover, while their religious vocation distinguished them from other soldiers, it did not help them to withstand certain elements of the Nazi weltanschauung. They reacted like other soldiers to the bitter reality around them: with indifference, reluctance, or resignation, but rarely with protest, and never with sustained or open resistance. Instead, their dedication to their fellow Christian German men gave them an excuse that on the whole blinded them to what that service really signified.

The Absence of Conscientious Objection

Whether considering the masses of conscripted Germans as a whole or looking specifically at Catholic Germans, conscientious objection to conscription was not popular during the war.[4] The low number of conscientious objectors can be attributed partly to the regime's vigorous persecution of those who refused the conscription order. Their example showed that resisting one's national duty to defend the Fatherland would be met with the harshest disciplinary measures. The number of Catholics who repudiated the regime's conscription order was extremely small.[5] These statistics make it equally evident, however, that priests and seminarians were no more likely (and maybe even less likely) than other Germans to object to military service on religious grounds. They had a personal investment in caring for the Christian souls engaged in battle, even unto death. Accordingly, Catholic priests and seminarians reported for duty along with thousands of other Germans, with very few appearing to consider the criminal nature of the regime whose orders they followed.

Most conscripts settled into their new situation as best as they could, whether they were among the few inducted into the chaplaincy or one among the masses who became part of the medical service or infantry. The distinction here is important. Throughout the war, the OKW was concerned with minimizing the number of active chaplains. Consequently, most priests and seminarians at advanced levels of study who were drafted—17,776 men, according to Werthmann's own wartime statistics[6]—served in the medical service as stretcher bearers, doctors' assistants, and orderlies. As such, the OKH forbade them to minister to others as priests. The only circumstances in which this prohibition did not apply were for the administration of Last Rites, a special request from soldiers directly before or after an engagement, or other similarly unusual cases. For these circumstances, a priest required permission to administer as such from the commander of the regiment, who generally gave his approval only if no other chaplain was available.[7] In this limited role, it was more difficult for the *Priestersoldaten*, as I will call them, to continue their daily routine of saying or attending mass.[8] More than chaplains, they toiled side by side with the fighting soldiers on all fronts; they were "like missionaries, influencing their environment. These men went with their comrades into the horror of battle, into the hopelessness of captivity, and into death."[9] Many *Priestersoldaten* did what they could when they could to maintain the deep spirituality of their civilian lives. Most remained in the soldier's uniform until war's end or until they fell in battle. Very few of them transitioned into the chaplaincy.

Priestersoldaten: Priests beyond the Chaplaincy

It is easy to assume that *Priestersoldaten* did everything possible to obtain a position that permitted them to practice their vocation. Many priests who were not at first stationed in the chaplaincy did. Chaplain Johann S. corresponded with priests and seminarians who found themselves placed in medical companies or hospitals. From them he received several requests for aid in finding a permanent chaplain position for individual units: "I have written many times to the field bishop already and received no answer... so I would like to ask you today, dear Father, if I might have some information: Could I undertake to become active in the army's pastoral care system?" The same young man renewed his request a few months later, at the beginning of Advent.[10] Another *Priestersoldat*, Bartholomäus Hebel, wrote Schmutz, "I have now been with the army since June 1940. I participated in the campaigns in France, Greece and Crete, and I believe I am equal to the task of serving as a chaplain. Is it possible to become a chaplain? Is there nothing you can do? I would be so happy to hear from you about this matter."[11] A third, Barthl, who was also writing on behalf of a friend, asked quite plainly, "Could you tell me what conditions and requirements govern employment in the chaplaincy?... We are both of us now two years in military service, and I was ordained a priest in 1935 and active in pastoral care until I was conscripted."[12]

Some military officers worked closely with chaplains and other priests to find spiritual outlets for their soldiers. In a 1942 activity report, Egon Schmitt wrote, "With the permission of the general of the division, medical soldiers [who were priests] were occasionally allowed to help with pastoral care. The masses said by these medical soldiers in this region were not included [in official reports]."[13] In 1944, navy chaplain Dietrich H. reported, "The perpetually growing number of wounded... keeps a lone priest completely occupied. Hence it is not possible at this time to conform to all the requirements. The only alleviation is the presence of two priests in the medical service, who in most cases give spiritual guidance and support to the dying."[14] This was a common problem. While there was a constant shortage of chaplains, in any given unit there may have been one or several priests who according to the rules were not supposed to minister as priests.

As early as 1941, the chaplain shortage was apparent. By the end of the war, it was dire. Chaplain Ludwig Wellmann was exasperated enough to mention in his last report before the war's end: "Because the 211th infantry division was transformed into a *Volksgrenadierdivision* in November 1944, my position as division chaplain was cancelled. This decree from Reichsführer-SS Heinrich Himmler was strongly criticized by the soldiers. The division commander and almost all of the officers strenuously deplored the breakdown of the chaplaincy." He was able to stay with his division until February 1945 when, despite the attempts of a staff officer to secure permission for him to remain, Wellmann was ordered to leave.[15]

Other chaplains who began their war experience as medical orderlies, like Hubert L., recalled that the latter position gave them no time for pastoral care, regardless of the prohibition, and cited this as the reason for their desire to transfer: "As an orderly I stood in front of the operating table the entire day and night, for one had to care for the sick. There was simply no time for pastoral care. If someone asked for it, then naturally I granted his request, but one hardly ever asked. How was I supposed to function spiritually when I was assisting with an operation? Not possible."[16] Joseph H. also admitted to having no spare time, particularly during periods of battle, although he still officiated at burials and, directly before action, said mass.[17]

Some military authorities were willing to ignore the prohibition on the use of priests who were not chaplains. But many *Priestersoldaten* acting as stretcher bearers or doctors' assistants preferred to remain where authorities assigned them for the duration of the war, even if they could not act as priests, because they felt closer there to the soldiers. In fact, some who became chaplains recalled that their former positions had allowed them closer personal relations with other soldiers. Rudolf Peifer was initially conscripted as a medical orderly along with five other priests. When his division's chaplain suggested that he attend a seminar to become a chaplain, he declined, "because I meant to stay side by side with simple soldiers, and fulfill my priestly duty in this way."[18] Later, shortly before the invasion of the Soviet Union, he attended the seminar anyway. He did not clarify whether his chaplain had suggested him against his will. Authorities informed Wilhelm Großkortenhaus shortly after his general training was complete that he would be assigned to a Luftwaffe medical unit, from which he always refused transfers into the chaplaincy: "I lay in the mud with soldiers and shared their experiences. In this way I rubbed shoulders with people I otherwise would never have met."[19] After the war, it was not uncommon for veterans to assert that they had preferred their time in active combat units.

Relations with Officers and Soldiers

Both chaplains and *Priestersoldaten* experienced a broad variety of reactions from the men with whom they served. Some of them remembered facing difficulties from soldiers who ridiculed or harassed them. Franz E., who was a naval chaplain, remembered a range of anti-Christian comments from eighteen- and nineteen-year-old soldiers in his unit. He reported them to his commander, accusing the boys, some of who came from Münster, Bavaria, and other Catholic regions of Germany, of referring to chaplains derogatorily as "the Bible beaters in the confessional [*die Pfaffen in den Beichstuhl*]."[20] Werthmann recalled that the commander of Wilhelm F., who was stationed with a mountain division, had attempted without authorization to restrict the activities of both the Protestant and the Catholic chaplains among his men. He did not elaborate on the restrictions, but Werthmann noted that F. "had weathered it well." Werthmann added cryptically that "the resistance of the chaplains" augmented the difficulties that the commander had created for them. A transfer to another division—often the remedy to a conflict between an officer and the chaplain—was not possible. Accordingly, F. "obeyed as a matter of course" and eventually "was very thankful that he was commanded to stay."[21] Wilhelm Goderski, a priest stationed as a medical orderly, complained that a master-sergeant kept him from going to church every Sunday because he had to be on duty. This duty consisted of "an hour of singing and one and a half hours of sport.... The master-sergeant is making it hard for us because we're supposed to be on duty every Sunday, though sport and singing is half as important [as getting to church]."[22] In just over a month, the problematic master-sergeant was transferred. Under his replacement, Goderski reported that "everything is in order," and he noted that he was able to get to church more easily.[23]

After the war Bartholomäus Hebel, who spent six and a half years as an NCO in the medical service, remembered the close camaraderie with other soldiers forged through endless marches and bloody operations. Such solidarity enabled him at times to attend mass surreptitiously: "We were forbidden to leave the barracks in the early morning to attend mass, but sometimes we succeeded in disappearing through the back door of an adjoining chapel in the nursing home [in which they were stationed], whereupon a buddy had to act as a lookout to make sure the coast was clear."[24] Johann S., another *Priestersoldat* who kept in contact with a chaplain, lamented the lack of fellow priests in his unit and yearned for an opportunity to go to mass. He had been able to attend on only three occasions in four months. Despite this, his morale was good: "Even if I'm at a disadvantage, I have other things in my favor. First of all, I must say that my superiors are well disposed toward me and they have never ... treated me differently from the others. With the soldiers of the company, too, I'm on good terms, and even if there are many other worldviews, we remain good comrades and never reproach each other."[25]

Priests and seminarians sometimes made easy targets, and this proved dangerous for those who rose to the bait. Anton H. was one such example. Werthmann met him in June 1943 at a front-line seminar near Riga (Latvia), and the chaplain's fixation on "sexual matters" among the inmates of the hospital in which he worked unsettled even the field vicar-general: "He spoke out exhaustively about women coming and going in the hospital ... and expressed his outrage about the situation. ... I'm almost convinced that a sexual complex presents itself in H., which determines his totally erroneous and partial judgment of such problems."[26] Werthmann's comments stemmed from a court-martial involving H. and allegations of subversion of military morale. Ultimately the court sentenced him to a term of "protective custody." He was taken to Dachau, where, according to H.'s letter to Werthmann in 1945, he was supposed to serve his sentence working in the concentration camp's medicinal herb garden. Notes in H.'s wartime journal as well as excerpts from letters he wrote to Werthmann reveal a complicated situation. Sometime in the first half of 1943, as H. was transferred from Orel (Russia) to Riga, he encountered an intelligence officer who provoked the chaplain. H. recalled in his journal,

> The lieutenant attacked the stance of the Catholic priesthood on celibacy with broad and derogatory words. Initially I answered only to his attack, which really didn't merit a response: "I am the eighth child of my mother. If every family in Germany had enough children, then Germany could leave the celibate priesthood in peace." To which the lieutenant about-faced and described the Führer as the highest example for Catholic priests. I denied this eccentricity, be-

cause it degraded the dignity of the priesthood. By this I was alluding to the notorious lifestyle of the Führer, made known to me by an[other] officer, and to the difference between religious celibacy and mere natural celibacy.²⁷

H. did not detail what he knew of Hitler's "notorious lifestyle," but it is telling that he made a point of objecting to this and not to the discriminatory and murderous policies that the Führer and the Nazi Party directed. The result was a double-charge of public defamation of the "majesty of the Führer" [*Beleidigung der Majestät des Führers*] and continuous subversion of the Wehrmacht.²⁸ H. had no less than ten officers write letters on his behalf to his military legal counsel, including a Protestant colleague and the major-general of his division at the time, Gustav Freiherr von Mauchenheim genannt Bechtolsheim. They defended his character and asserted that the incident must have been a misunderstanding. They attested that physically he suffered from wet pleurisy and was in no condition mentally to discipline himself: "Because he served his church [so] enthusiastically, he was temperamental in his devotion, and nothing could get him carried away like an expression directed against his establishment or his doctrine."²⁹ But their pleas for mercy went unheard, and the court determined that H. be discharged from the chaplaincy. He spent the rest of the war in Dachau.

Divisional Catholic chaplain Erich B. also faced disciplinary measures for similar conduct. B. was twice accused of removing an image of Hitler from the wall of a room where he met with the priests and seminarians of his division and where he sometimes said mass. Someone (he did not say who) interpreted this action, he claimed, as a suggestion that "during mass, there is no place for the Führer among the participants." Hitler may not have cared about attending Catholic services, but the military court found the removal of the image tantamount to a "public slandering," and B. was disciplined.³⁰ But the issue did not stop there. The OKH also took the opportunity to forbid chaplains to organize other priests and seminarians together in any official way. Werthmann responded craftily: "I held it as my duty to interpret this decree at the front-line seminars [that I attended] to the effect that . . . no misgivings existed about voluntary gatherings of priests or seminarians under the guidance of a chaplain." He added that he was convinced, had he enquired with the OKH about the status of such private gatherings, that they would have been prohibited.[31]

Other chaplains and *Priestersoldaten* experienced little or no difficulty from those with whom they served. Soldiers even received some priests with enthusiasm and gratitude. In 1944, Pius Fischer, a priest in the medical service who corresponded with Werthmann throughout the war, wrote to him, "Everyone is very friendly to me personally, and I can say mass daily and help out more often around our area."[32] While later he appeared to have some problems with a new commanding officer, whom he described as "no friend to priests" and who wanted "to unhook" Fischer and another priest in the same unit, the officer was unsuccessful and eventually replaced. By the end of 1944, a new commander had granted Fischer permission to give sermons. He reported, "Daily, my chapel is full, and on Sundays, people stand outside the door."[33]

In an occurrence more uncommon and dangerous because it contravened the regulations, Rudolf Unger, a priest and private in the medical service, wrote Werthmann in late 1943 asking for an extra mass kit. His commander had requested that Unger hold services for Catholic English prisoners of war in their area.[34] In his unpublished memoir, based on his wartime journal, Unger remembered a friend named Zimmerer, a gunner with whom he spoke for hours about "mutual suffering, about the fate of our land, which Adolf Hitler had plunged into such misery." Although Unger was not a chaplain, the company commander, who was "a really dignified Catholic," invited him to say mass on Christmas Eve 1941.[35] Chaplain Otto F. went even further and characterized the Wehrmacht, "with [some] exceptions . . . as politically rather free from the Nazi spirit." The generals were good Christians and exemplary soldiers, he explained, in whom chaplains such as himself placed great confidence, and who used their authority to protect religious activities. Moreover, he remembered that the 1941 Führer decree that demobilized Jesuits was very unpopular because "their superior officers greatly esteemed priests in general and these young order-priests in particular, and they were much beloved by their comrades."[36] F.'s memory may have been faulty. Perhaps he was very lucky in that the soldiers whose paths he crossed were well disposed toward priests. Perhaps the soldiers with whom he interacted presented a "good Christian" front, deliberately toning down Nazi rhetoric and avoiding any mention of criminal undertakings. Like F., they might not have been inclined to think beyond the immediate consequences of their actions.

Gustav H. R., one of nineteen Catholic chaplains who fell at Stalingrad, wrote a letter to his family two months before his death that exhibited a staunch faith and unflinching commitment to his fellow soldiers in the midst of great horror:

> I speak from the hearts of all the men here, aged youth who have grown gray in the midst of senseless murder and inhumanity. The pen is reluctant to describe it, the most unspeakable thing, that which I have experienced here.... I am proud to live through these times with these men. My people are proud that their priest endured with them here, too. An ironclad camaraderie emerges, which helps lift us away until a happy hour arrives for us once more.[37]

His last Christmas was profoundly moving for him because of the soldiers to whom he ministered. He recounted crawling from one position to another, to men in the midst of battle:

> The shells and flares were the Christmas tree candles.... The joy and gratitude of the men, who at this time were not expecting a priest, remain unforgettable for them and for me. They sobbed like children, and shook my hand in thanks.... I moved through the night from bunker to bunker, from post to post, always accompanied by enemy fire.[38]

Martin Z. also served briefly in the Soviet Union, though he escaped the cauldron of Stalingrad, and he corroborated what R.'s testimony suggests: religion, and the men who represented it, were very precious to many soldiers. Consequently priests experienced warmth, acceptance, friendship, and appreciation. In a postwar interview, he remembered that "visits from chaplains were always well-received.... [T]his attitude was never so palpable as in Russia. There the visits of chaplains to hospitals ... were naturally, in general, treasured."[39]

The Sacrament of Penance

The Catholic sacrament of Penance (today called Reconciliation) comes up regularly in chaplains' reports and private letters. In the former, many chaplains detailed statistics about participation; in the latter, startling personal experiences are relayed that raise difficult questions about the use of the sacrament during the Second World War. Before discussing these questions in greater detail, a brief overview of Penance and its significance in the spiritual life of practicing Catholics is essential. Confession as now called informally in English, is one of seven sacraments; in it the penitent receives forgiveness for sins committed against God and others. The ritual normally involves the penitent confessing her sins. The confessor, usually a priest, acts as mediator between the penitent and God; only through the confessor can the penitent receive God's mercy, grace, and forgiveness. Thus the role of the confessor is fundamental. The penitent must demonstrate repentance for her wrongdoings and resolve not to sin again. She is given a penance (normally prayers, but sometimes acts of compensation or restitution involving those she has wronged) to perform as part of the purification.

The foundation of the sacrament of Penance lies in the words of Christ as recorded in the Bible. After his resurrection Christ declared to his apostle Peter, "I will give you the keys of the kingdom of heaven; whatever you bind on earth shall be bound in heaven, and whatever you loose on earth shall be loosed in heaven."[40] To the other apostles, he said: "Receive the Holy Spirit. If you forgive anyone's sins, they are forgiven; if you do not forgive them, they are not forgiven."[41] It was not until 1215 that the Fourth Lateran Council of the Church, meeting under Pope Innocent III, declared that individual Catholics had an obligation to confess their sins at least once a year. It recommended that they do so at Eastertime so that Catholics were sacramentally prepared to receive communion. This touched off a proliferation of confessors' *summas,* or compendiums, designed to help confessors mete out proportionate penances for the sins about which they were hearing.[42]

Little in the way of systematic training was provided for clergy beyond these compendiums until the sixteenth-century Council of Trent, the Catholic Church's response to the Protestant Reformation. One of Luther's most serious charges was the abuse of the confessional via the selling of mercy and grace, which were meant to reward true penitence, in the form of indulgences. The most important reform to emerge from the Council concerned the establishment of seminary regulations for the training of men to be priests. The administration of the sacraments was an essential part of this training, and Penance was emphasized. Religious orders such as Ignatius Loyola's Jesuits, newly founded at the time, were encouraged to hear confessions as often as possible; the Dominicans and Franciscans followed suit, as did Alfonso Liguori's Redemptorists, who treated Penance as the core of their pastoral activity.[43] In the nineteenth and early twentieth centuries, moral manuals took over from the compendiums of the earlier era. Theologians, often priests, wrote these manuals as rules for human conduct, determining whether actions were good or bad.[44]

Priestly training for administering Penance evolved between the sixteenth and twentieth centuries, but the sacrament's purpose (to give Catholics the opportunity to receive forgiveness for sins in order to come closer to God) remained unchanged. So did its significance, which was for Catholics in the temporal world to receive some forgiveness for sins before death, thereby shortening time spent being purified (in purgatory) after death before entering God's presence. Catholics were (and are) exhorted to make frequent use of the sacrament to be as prepared as possible for sudden death. This explains the urgency that priests felt to accompany Catholics into the Wehrmacht and into battle: it was their duty, as priests, to act as a spiritual guardian and confessor in any Catholic's final hours, and soldiers stood much closer to death on a regular basis than most.

Penance is a powerful means of grace meant to bring Catholics closer to God. It is limitless in its presumption of God's infinite mercy: no sin committed by humans is too great for God's forgiveness. Such a supposition invites everyone to participate, no matter how egregious the wrongdoing. In accordance with canon law, the seal of the confessional ensures that what is spoken between confessor and penitent is revealed to no one. It is a stronger seal than doctor-patient or attorney-client confidentiality, both of which can be broken if someone's life is at stake. This inviolability is designed to encourage even the most recidivist penitents to visit a confessional. Regardless of the criminal nature of the sins confessed, or the penitent's indication of future crimes, the confessor is bound to silence and at most can withhold absolution (especially if the penitent signals an intention to repeat the offense). He may also encourage the penitent to surrender to authorities. If the confessor breaks the seal by discussing the details of a confession, he risks excommunication.[45]

Priests in the Wehrmacht, both within and outside of the chaplaincy, undoubtedly heard soldiers' confessions as often as they could. What they learned in their role as confessors, they never dared reveal because of confession's inviolable seal. It is worth making two observations before relating some specific experiences: the first, that the confessor is bound to give absolution for sins confessed if the penitent demonstrates genuine sorrow and a desire to avoid sinning again (which penitents normally vocalize in the act of contrition, said immediately prior to the confessor giving absolution); the second, that, just as the moral worldview of many German soldiers shifted during the war as a direct result of their experiences, particularly on the dehumanizing Eastern Front, so did the moral worldview of priests also shift. Short of finding a written explanation, such as an unofficial, ad hoc penitential manual for the front lines, of what was considered sinful and what was considered an unfortunate but necessary aspect of an all-or-nothing war effort, one cannot be certain how a confessor characterized the sins of the penitent. Such a written explanation is unlikely to have ever existed, given the constraints under which priests were operating at the time, though it was probably discussed orally, in general terms, at the front-line training seminars. It is possible that priests classified whatever soldiers confessed during the war as an effect of war and not in and of itself a crime requiring the intervention of military authorities.[46] Indeed, it is unclear what actions a soldier might have considered wrong and worthy of confession.

Somewhat surprisingly, SS men were often the subject of chaplains' reports about confession. The SS, which by 1939 had become a "quasi-governmental conglomerate"[47] functioning as both police force and elite troop, generally reflected the extreme anti-Catholic sentiments of its leader, Heinrich Himmler. He made his feelings for Catholicism clear in a quip to a subordinate in 1937: "The predominant element of the priesthood was a homosexual association serving a form of Bolshevism that was two thousand years old."[48] However, although the SS as an organization was hostile toward the churches, there were individual exceptions. These individuals, a stark minority at the beginning of the war, increased in number toward the war's end, when even Himmler's elite outfit was forced to lay aside its strict entrance requirements to conscript replacement soldiers. In a postwar interview, chaplain Georg Paulus remembered, "A lot of SS people were lying [injured] in hospitals, and many other soldiers dreaded to reveal themselves as religious. But I witnessed members of the SS appear in their hospital gowns and receive the sacraments."[49] Egon Schmitt's religious superior asked him to say Christmas masses for Luftwaffe and navy units stationed in his region in Yugoslavia, since they had no chaplains of their own, and he reported that members of an SS-*Totenkopfdivision* showed up.[50] Chaplain Erich A. B. actively pursued attempts to say mass for units of the Waffen-SS stationed around Tourcoing, in northern France. Werthmann reported that although they made no effort to help him, A. B. encountered no difficulties from the commanders of the units, from whom he required permission. They treated him with "noncommittal commitment. It was forbidden to write the time of the services on the notice board, so that attendance, aside from some ethnic German SS men, was not observed."[51] In April 1945, Wilhelm F. served in a prisoner-of-war camp for SS men in the vicinity of Bischofswiesen, not far from Berchtesgaden. He did not leave them even after their prisoners declined from 5,000 to 300.[52] In his wartime journal, chaplain Theodor L. remarked in an undated entry, likely in 1943, that he administered the sacraments to a dying SS man. The man knew that the chaplain "could not give him redemption or healing for his ruined body, but rather redemption from guilt and sin! He confessed—took communion—received Extreme Unction."[53] L. forgave the sins the SS man had repented, and he granted him absolution.

In November 1944, chaplain Josef Seitz had a similar experience during his retreat from the Balkans, when his medical company found itself sharing territory with army and SS units. The rumor that a priest was present had barely begun to spread when

> a panic took possession of both the wounded and the healthy. Without decree, instruction, or authorization from the SS leaders, the lightly wounded men cleared a small room. It happened so quickly and de-

cisively that there was no time for Father Seitz to ask permission for the exercise of his office; the soldiers had placed before him a fait accompli.... Finally he asked if anyone wanted to confess or take communion. Almost every arm was raised, even those who with SS runes (because many had been forced into the SS [that is, conscripted])…. In a small window stood an SS officer who had followed the holy event without expressing much sympathy. After the closing song had faded ... he began a conversation with an aide of Father Seitz's. He drew his attention outside of the window, where the medical orderlies were laying the dead side by side. "I am," he began, "Catholic, thirty-three years old, and since I was thirteen, I haven't been to church. I believed that the SS was a religion and I was an enthusiastic champion of it. But I've realized that I have served Satan. I beg you, man, speak with the chaplain, ask him if he wants to listen to me."

Seitz met with him, heard his confession, and gave him communion, signifying that he had been absolved of whatever crimes he had confessed. The man was killed that same day in an attack.[54] We have no statistics about how often this kind of interaction occurred, but given how many priests wrote about it at the time or after the war, it was not uncommon. If any priest withheld confession or felt taxed about giving absolution, there is no evidence to suggest this was so. Was it possible that men who returned from participation in mass slaughter found relief and spiritual solace, even moral support, waiting for them with the priests who were endlessly ready to hear them confess? Other historians have suggested as much, and the priests themselves indicate it in their written records.[55]

Joseph H. initially served as a medical orderly, then became a chaplain and was transferred to Finland. Upon arriving at his appointed station, he could not even find a bed to claim for himself and his sexton. The cellar was full of Waffen-SS officers who greeted them rudely when they saw their crosses. Later he received a cake from his family through the post, which he immediately shared with his roommates. He recalled, "In a heartbeat, the whole mood changed." Wine was produced, and he was invited to sit and drink with them, one of whom lamented, "If only all priests were like you."[56] What exactly differentiated him from other priests was not expressed. Perhaps other clerics had avoided company with SS officers, and H.'s courage and generosity had impressed them. Even more astonishing, H. later ran into one of the SS officers on a train. He sat himself in a different corner of the car, keeping as far as he could from the "decorated SS-man" who outranked him, reflecting most priests' instinctive avoidance of the organization. He struck up a conversation with the Wehrmacht paymaster next to him when the SS officer approached and spoke, revealing himself as one of the cellar men with whom H. had shared his cake: "I'm now commissioned with SS troops in southern Norway for training. It would be a great joy to me if you would visit my men."[57]

Nor was it only the SS soldiers who approached priests in search of relief and the consolation of the sacraments. Martin S. received a letter from the parents of fallen SS lance corporal Benedikt Zimmerman, who had left the church before the war. They wrote, "It would be a great solace if Benedikt had given some sign of religious disposition during his stay at the hospital, namely between the 9th and the 26th of May 1942. If you personally have no knowledge of this, perhaps you could inquire among the hospital personnel."[58] Catholic families who had lost sons or husbands in the war made liberal use of chaplains who might have known their kin, usually asking for assurance that the soldier's spiritual needs had been met before death. In this way, priests in uniform became an essential link between the homeland and the front lines.

The NSFOs

Catholic priests and seminarians found support and sympathy from other unexpected quarters as well. At the end of 1943, following the disastrous German losses at Stalingrad and Kursk, Hermann Reinecke, chief of the General Office of the Armed Forces, was given the task of selecting, training, and dispersing the National Socialist Leadership Officers (NSFOs) throughout the army. Their purpose was to bolster morale by indoctrinating German soldiers with Nazi propaganda. One year later there were 50,000 NSFOs, vastly outnumbering the diminutive chaplaincy. Reinecke's aim was to build a "revolutionary Nazi army," a "believing Wehrmacht" that would be invincible.[59] Initial reactions of Wehrmacht officers were negative, and the effectiveness of NSFOs remained limited and dependent on several factors: the NSFO's personality, the personality of his superior(s), his relationship with said superior(s), and his relationship with the soldiers. These same conditions also determined the effectiveness of Christian chaplains, whom the NSFOs were not supposed to challenge. In reality, the NSFO's task of *Truppenbetreuung*—supporting and mentoring the soldiers to keep up morale—was very similar to that of the chaplains.

According to chaplains' reports during and after the war, the NSFOs generally caused few problems for the priests with whom they worked. This view that the NSFOs were innocuous contrasts with Werthmann's opinion of the office itself, which he viewed as more threatening. Wilhelm W. recalled in an interview that he "had good relations with [the NSFOs]," and that he never felt pressured during his time in the army to accept Nazi ideals.[60] Martin Z. declared, "They played no role. There was a first lieutenant with us as an NSFO, who was a lecturer from Stettin. . . . Maybe he was in the party . . . [but] the NSFO played absolutely no role in our division."[61] In 1944, Werthmann learned during a trip to Prague and Hlbouka that an NSFO had addressed an assembly of chaplains regarding his activities and "established clear borders between Nazi Leadership priorities and those of the Wehrmacht chaplaincy."[62] Others reported that, in contrast to their leaders' unspoken intentions to eliminate chaplains by replacing them, the NSFO had actively supported the chaplains. Johann E. K. declared, "We had one [NSFO] once, he was a good Catholic, a teacher, [this] Nazi officer, who even went to church. From this side we never had difficulties."[63] In the 1970s Joseph Ohseforth remembered that in the Thirty-fifth Infantry Division in 1943, the NSFO "supported the chaplains as an active Catholic in every conceivable way. There were neither difficulties nor even any serious quarrels. The positive attitude of commanders helped this."[64] Nor were they figures of rigid authority, always toeing the Nazi Party line: "The NSFO wasn't so sure anymore, and in order to avoid bearing witness against us, he preferred to give us a bit of the cold shoulder," Richard S. recalled retrospectively. "The closer we came to the end of the war, the more he sought contact with us [chaplains]."[65] Alois K. spoke of them as "boys" who were positioned in every hospital. The chaplains were very careful around them when they listened to news, lest they react to news items with inappropriate or suspicious emotion: "When we listened to the news, when we realized he was coming, then we always immediately turned it off. But in and of himself, he was harmless, he was not malicious."[66] Josef P. went so far as to call them "piteous" figures who went around distributing combs and mirrors and were ultimately ineffectual: "The men didn't want to know anything about Nazi propaganda. The closer one got to the front, the less one heard 'Heil Hitler.' "[67] However much the Nazi Party strove to empty the army of traditional religious influence, the soldiers themselves, including those meant to aid the party, seemed more inclined to tolerate, if not actively assist, old traditions. During the bleakest years of the war, as defeat loomed, soldiers appeared to find more spiritual assistance in the faith of their parents and grandparents than the ideology hammered into them since 1933.

In addition to describing conflicts with military officers and leaders like the NSFOs, the chaplains, priests, and seminarians also wrote about the experience of war. Formally the chaplains wrote two kinds of reports detailing their routine activities. These reports reveal starkly how similar the chaplain's task was to the NSFO's, despite Reinecke's assertions otherwise. Chaplains sent their *Tätigkeitsberichte*, or activity reports, every two to three months to Rarkowski through their head chaplains and copied relevant military commanders. They did not usually send the less-frequent *Seelsorgeberichte*, or pastoral care reports, to military superiors.[68] Sometimes, for reasons of expediency, they fused the two reports into a single *Erfahrungsbericht* (literally, experience report) and copied both religious and military superiors.[69] Within these reports, chaplains discussed their routines and remarked on unusual or worrisome experiences with soldiers. Beyond these reports, priests wrote constantly about uncommon occurrences in the line of duty, such as the bearing of weapons and interactions with foreign civilians wherever they were stationed—from France to Russia and from Norway to North Africa. They gave sermons and wrote letters to the family members of soldiers who had died. Some chaplains wrote to *Priestersoldaten* in their units or to Werthmann or Rarkowski. They were all part of a war machine, and there is no evidence that they resisted, either collectively or individually, their role within it. On the contrary, most of them understood that the fulfillment of their duties was essential to the war effort and threw themselves wholeheartedly into the project. As the regulations for their service prescribed, they attended to duties not unlike those of their military commanders or the NSFOs. Their primary concern was the men in their care, particularly that they remained fit to fight.

Barometers of Morale

The reports contain a wealth of information about the experiences of these men and what occupied them most as chaplains. These reports make clear their double duty as caretakers of Christian souls as well as boosters of morale. Many military authorities placed an unmistakable emphasis on a functional military chaplaincy, often working with chaplains to maintain soldiers' confidence and gauge their fighting spirit. For this reason, they were increasingly unhappy as the number of available chaplains decreased in the later years of the war. The chaplains' own concerns with troop morale are evident: most mention it explicitly in their reports. Chaplain Egon Schmitt, who moved between France and Yugoslavia from 1940 to 1943 (mirroring the wartime experience of most chaplains who, because of the systemic shortage, were repeatedly transferred), commented frequently on the issue. In late 1940, he found troops to be generally optimistic because of their close physical proximity to Germany. For example, the mail was reliably consistent. He complained about the poor example of officers for their men in terms of "sexual difficulties." He also reported that soldiers and their superiors lamented the prohibition on saying mass with civilian populations, interpreting it as an "unhealthy exclusion and unfounded mistrust of the Catholic soldiers."[70] Toward the end of 1941, after Schmitt was transferred east, his reports became more strained, explaining, "The hardness of battle in the Russian winter and the egregious demands on the physical and spiritual energy of the men have made them especially prepared for religious values. . . . Comrades were often 90–100% in attendance [at mass], and their attitude was unquestionably good and serious, better than I had expected given the conditions."[71] The good morale continued to surprise Schmitt into 1943. He attributed its persistence to the impact of "relations with the home front," indicating that the mail was still working well. But proximity cut both ways. Bad news from the home front, such as the bombing of certain cities, could lead to a perceptible downturn in morale.

Another discernable negative influence on morale was the inevitability of German defeat in the war. At the same time, proximity to fighting and death could lead to an intense religiosity among soldiers.[72] One chaplain reported that soldiers attended mass in high numbers because devout Christians found divine service to be "a piece of *Heimat*. Due to the long-lasting war and the difficult operational relations, the need for religion is growing."[73] Chaplain Karl Rincke wrote, "The religious predisposition of the fighting men, particularly those just returning from active engagement, was very gratifying [*erfreulich*] and displayed itself in the large numbers of men who attended mass. . . . The spirit of the troops was most apparent in individual conversations with soldiers, healthy and wounded alike. Some officers and simple soldiers came to me during mass or social evening, or in otherwise quiet hours."[74] Rincke understood the need of troops in active combat for spiritual relief, though he did not explain what subjects he touched upon in conversation. Richard S. described the link between soldiers' spirituality and their closeness to battle: "Pastoral care is more fruitful and extensive in more dangerous regions, for here the soldiers feel the necessity of religious activity with more urgency."[75] His reports became more depressed through 1944 because

> the psychological state of the men stands at a critical low, especially during disengagements. Entire groups surge backwards, apathetic and despondent. . . . Soldiers unleashed looting and wanton destruction with the justification that such goods weren't allowed to fall into enemy hands; bold acts of rape were justified because the region and the people won't be seen again after our evacuation; and in the rubble of Monte Cassino and the main chapels of Italian villas, the sacrilege of using crucifixes as targets to shoot at happened because of mounting irreverence. . . . The increase in venereal disease is a great moral instability.[76]

Even in late 1944, temporary victory could reverse such hopelessness, though the length of the war, escalating enemy superiority, and the destruction of Germany proper weighed ever more heavily on the soldiers.

These last sentences of S.'s report suggest that even the solace of religion had its limits.[77]

Johannes F. was anxious about the evaporation of Christian ethics among the men with whom he served. He blamed it on the "corrupt environment."[78] In January 1942 he wrote, "Suicide and attempts at suicide have become more common. Sexual debauchery increases daily. . . . These and many other delinquencies have their roots in the recession of Christian ethics and the anesthetizing [Einschläferung] of a religious sense of responsibility."[79] The situation steadily deteriorated. In July 1942, F. drafted a list of problems among his soldiers, problems that would have bothered army and regime leaders: "Property offenses, leave without permission, dodging duties, watch delinquency, suicide, and other issues have certainly not become more rare. At any rate, the collapse of the comrades cannot be attributed systematically to instability. The demonic influences of this environment often . . . cause them to break down."[80] By 1944, F. concluded,

> one must be blind if one thinks that war has made men better. Even in terms of religion, general apathy and dourness has crept in. It is distressing to see the stark reevaluation that ethical concepts have undergone. We live in a time of ethical inflation, to put it extremely mildly. The ultimate cause of this is not the war. Rather, the roots of this ethical inflation can be found in materialism.[81]

His solution, like his conclusion, displays a remarkable (willful?) naiveté: he urged his men attend mass more frequently and that chaplains be permitted to say more masses. To counter the erosion of ethics and the impact of the Eastern Front's "demonic influences" required more than prayer. These influences may have been an allusion to the perpetration of war crimes and crimes against humanity as well as the sheer brutalization that engagement with the Red Army had become. They also included Bolshevism, perhaps the Judeo-Bolshevism that other letters reference, as well as the "godlessness" of Nazism. But at no time did it occur to chaplains, priests, or seminarians that a shift in their own reactions may have done more than the spiritual remedies (prayer and penance) that tradition dictated.

Siegfried Döring was a priest whose major-general gave him permission to take over temporarily the divisional chaplain's duties while stationed on Crete in 1944. He reported that the soldiers welcomed him everywhere he visited because they were glad that there was a priest on the island (even if he was officially a mere NCO) and that they could once more go to mass. Troop morale, though, was characterized by "tension and agitation. Apart from thoughts on the progression of the war, the soldiers think more and more of their own fate here on the island and overall in the southeast. In addition, it will soon be three months since communication with the home front was cut off."[82] When morale dipped, the chaplain's general response was to try to focus soldiers' thoughts on God's intervention, though Döring's success here was not noted.

Other chaplains reported minor irregularities. Usually breaches in regulations occurred when *Priestersoldaten* ministered in situations that may not have qualified as an "emergency" as the "Guidelines" required. Those who reported these incidents to military superiors were sometimes motivated less by a desire to inform on rule-breakers than to persuade authorities that additional chaplains were badly needed. In December 1942, Alfred Schmidt recounted that some commanders had ordered the soldiers he visited at Christmas to attend mass, in direct contradiction to the OKH "Guidelines."[83] Dietrich H. used priests who were medical orderlies to care for the dying because there were simply too many fatally wounded men to care for on his own.[84] Karl Rincke reported that some commanders appreciated the unique situation of the *Priestersoldaten* and permitted some of them to say masses after notifying the on-duty chaplain.[85] These reports underscore the pressure on chaplains to be everywhere at once. Following a trip to the Eastern Front in 1944, Werthmann wrote from Cracow, "In a 142,000 square-kilometer area, there are ten chaplains to care for 200,000 soldiers and 80,000 casualties (sick and wounded)."[86] Nor was this serious lack of chaplains confined to the later years of the war. As early as the end of 1941, the unnamed Catholic chaplain stationed with the Eleventh Army near the Sea of Azov wrote, "Inevitably, the numerically insufficient use of chaplains shows itself by the fact that individual units have only been to mass once or twice per month."[87]

Priests in Combat

Although the terms of the 1933 concordat prohibited priests and seminarians at advanced levels of study from weapons-bearing military service, it did happen. Georg Werthmann explained that seminarians and theology students were placed in active service if they had not begun the ordination process. They then returned home during leave and completed special semesters to become either deacons or priests. But "for these new priests, a transfer from armed service into the medical corps on the grounds of new circumstances was not possible. . . . So it happened that even priests found themselves bearing weapons."[88] Furthermore, during the worst fighting of the war, when men found themselves on the Eastern Front, everyone carried a weapon on the front lines, even chaplains. Some were not up to the task. Hubert L.'s commander gave him a weapon in Riga because of local partisan activity, and "I fired this service pistol only one time: it was terrible for me to have to release a poor, sick kitten from its suffering. I then traded this weapon for a wooden gun."[89] Wilhelm Ritthaler procured a pistol under similar circumstances, as did Egon Schmitt, who remembered that it was the only protection they had as they moved through dangerous forests in Soviet territory.[90] The need to carry a weapon bothered Franz M.E. when it became a "regulation in this terrible period." After the war, he quickly asserted that he had never used it, and he was "never trained to use it, but I had to carry this damn thing around. I found it horrible to be a priest with a murderous weapon."[91]

Others reacted differently. Rudolf Peifer, a veteran who turned his wartime journals into a postwar memoir, was a stretcher-bearer in a medical company with five other priests. Although they did not carry weapons, they did practice shooting with pistols.

> In our unit there was a so-called "shooting club." . . . This "shooting club" was particularly intimidating. In the first four weeks, I had made many good friends among the NCOs, and one of them asked me to one of these shooting try-outs: "Shoot once, for fun, to see whether you can make the score." I protested that I didn't deal with guns, I had never picked up a gun, but to no avail. I had to try, at least! I couldn't be ordered to do it, but the soldiers asked me so amiably and with frank curiosity that I finally buckled. I asked for advice about

the necessary grip for the weapon, the alignment of rear and front sights, and then I lay down 100 meters from the target and shot a gun for the first time in my life—thank God the "adversary" was a mush target and not a man. I achieved the necessary score with three shots. The jubilation of my comrades was enormous. Unfortunately I hadn't reckoned on what came next: the raucous laughter that burst from the "shooting club," directed at those who had not made the required score despite longer periods of practice than I.[92]

While he may have caved in to the jovial peer pressure of his comrades, Peifer's narrative suggests that he would have been more reluctant to participate in battle. Other priests were less hesitant. This concerned Werthmann. During his internment in Niederalteich, he reflected that the Field Bishop's Office had repeatedly stressed to chaplains that "in no way was the intervention in military actions by chaplains justified as part of the exercise of their service."[93] Three chaplains had ignored this prohibition. The first was Alphons Satzger, who took a wrong turn in the thick of battle. While evacuating wounded Germans, he ended up storming an enemy bunker. Armed with only his pistol, he took no fewer than sixteen Russian soldiers captive.[94] The second was a priest Werthmann referred to as Wolff, who partook in a tank battle. The third was Karl Ernst Kuhn, who participated in nightly patrols with his unit. Satzger and Wolff did not merit further attention from Werthmann, but he made extensive remarks about Kuhn, indicating that the latter's actions or his personality—or both—had made an impression. Another priest who had served with Kuhn in North Africa laconically designated him an "aristocrat" and noted that his "enthusiastically martial comportment, which very much resembled that of an officer," put him on good terms with the English soldiers who captured them at the end of the war.[95] Kuhn "came off as vain and overbearing to other priests," and Werthmann observed sardonically that "the true greatness of man lays not in an exaggerated self-confidence, but rather in modest reserve."[96] Kuhn's divisional commander felt differently than Werthmann about the chaplain who cared for his men. He recommended him for an Iron Cross:

> In the performance of his pastoral duties, Chaplain Kuhn stood repeatedly in strong enemy fire. He had the opportunity to take part in

the necessary grip for the weapon, the alignment of rear and front sights, and then I lay down 100 meters from the target and shot a gun for the first time in my life—thank God the "adversary" was a mush target and not a man. I achieved the necessary score with three shots. The jubilation of my comrades was enormous. Unfortunately I hadn't reckoned on what came next: the raucous laughter that burst from the "shooting club," directed at those who had not made the required score despite longer periods of practice than I.[92]

While he may have caved in to the jovial peer pressure of his comrades, Peifer's narrative suggests that he would have been more reluctant to participate in battle. Other priests were less hesitant. This concerned Werthmann. During his internment in Niederalteich, he reflected that the Field Bishop's Office had repeatedly stressed to chaplains that "in no way was the intervention in military actions by chaplains justified as part of the exercise of their service."[93] Three chaplains had ignored this prohibition. The first was Alphons Satzger, who took a wrong turn in the thick of battle. While evacuating wounded Germans, he ended up storming an enemy bunker. Armed with only his pistol, he took no fewer than sixteen Russian soldiers captive.[94] The second was a priest Werthmann referred to as Wolff, who partook in a tank battle. The third was Karl Ernst Kuhn, who participated in nightly patrols with his unit. Satzger and Wolff did not merit further attention from Werthmann, but he made extensive remarks about Kuhn, indicating that the latter's actions or his personality—or both—had made an impression. Another priest who had served with Kuhn in North Africa laconically designated him an "aristocrat" and noted that his "enthusiastically martial comportment, which very much resembled that of an officer," put him on good terms with the English soldiers who captured them at the end of the war.[95] Kuhn "came off as vain and overbearing to other priests," and Werthmann observed sardonically that "the true greatness of man lays not in an exaggerated self-confidence, but rather in modest reserve."[96] Kuhn's divisional commander felt differently than Werthmann about the chaplain who cared for his men. He recommended him for an Iron Cross:

In the performance of his pastoral duties, Chaplain Kuhn stood repeatedly in strong enemy fire. He had the opportunity to take part in

Priests in Combat

Although the terms of the 1933 concordat prohibited priests and seminarians at advanced levels of study from weapons-bearing military service, it did happen. Georg Werthmann explained that seminarians and theology students were placed in active service if they had not begun the ordination process. They then returned home during leave and completed special semesters to become either deacons or priests. But "for these new priests, a transfer from armed service into the medical corps on the grounds of new circumstances was not possible. . . . So it happened that even priests found themselves bearing weapons."[88] Furthermore, during the worst fighting of the war, when men found themselves on the Eastern Front, everyone carried a weapon on the front lines, even chaplains. Some were not up to the task. Hubert L.'s commander gave him a weapon in Riga because of local partisan activity, and "I fired this service pistol only one time: it was terrible for me to have to release a poor, sick kitten from its suffering. I then traded this weapon for a wooden gun."[89] Wilhelm Ritthaler procured a pistol under similar circumstances, as did Egon Schmitt, who remembered that it was the only protection they had as they moved through dangerous forests in Soviet territory.[90] The need to carry a weapon bothered Franz M.E. when it became a "regulation in this terrible period." After the war, he quickly asserted that he had never used it, and he was "never trained to use it, but I had to carry this damn thing around. I found it horrible to be a priest with a murderous weapon."[91]

Others reacted differently. Rudolf Peifer, a veteran who turned his wartime journals into a postwar memoir, was a stretcher-bearer in a medical company with five other priests. Although they did not carry weapons, they did practice shooting with pistols.

> In our unit there was a so-called "shooting club." . . . This "shooting club" was particularly intimidating. In the first four weeks, I had made many good friends among the NCOs, and one of them asked me to one of these shooting try-outs: "Shoot once, for fun, to see whether you can make the score." I protested that I didn't deal with guns, I had never picked up a gun, but to no avail. I had to try, at least! I couldn't be ordered to do it, but the soldiers asked me so amiably and with frank curiosity that I finally buckled. I asked for advice about

the ambush [*Vorbrechen*] of enemy reconnaissance patrols and stood under strong artillery fire.... Always ready to see to the wounded, he demonstrated that he was not only a chaplain, but a soldier through and through. His attitude even in the most difficult situations was always exemplary.[97]

Almost three years later, Kuhn still impressed his military superiors, who evaluated him as a "straight, open character, modest, made of the hard stuff, physically and mentally fresh, who has dedicated himself zealously to the pastoral care of the troops and has earned their complete trust."[98] Unlike Werthmann, who found Kuhn's fervent militaristic behavior a betrayal of his vocation, Kuhn's superiors praised his ability to fit in seamlessly with his comrades, even to the point of joining them in battle.

Priests as Letter Writers

Priests and seminarians also made spiritual inroads with their comrades. Most, if not all, chaplains, and a great number of priests and seminarians, corresponded with the families of fallen soldiers in spite of numerous prohibitions. The OKW made it clear that *Priestersoldaten* were not to communicate with families back home *as priests*. The decree forbidding it, which came in 1944, relatively late in the war, was concerned that "such letters, which have been increasingly reported to various local party offices by the families involved, have an overwhelmingly religious content and thereby serve consistently to have a spiritual influence on the civilian population [back home]."[99] The decree raises several questions: were families really forwarding letters from priests at war to local Gestapo or police offices? Was the religious content of the letter somehow subversive, and if so, why were the letter writers not punished? Why would the OKW be concerned with priestly spiritual influence on the home front and give little attention to the chaplains' permissible communications? Their letters would likely have also employed religious language to convey their condolences to grieving families. Whatever the reasons for its issuance, the decree suggests that such behavior had occurred often enough to bother the OKW.[100]

Chaplains corresponded liberally both with their fellow soldiers and with the families of the wounded and fallen. The letters that survive in archives reveal how these priests became bridges between the world at war and the world at home, where anxious families awaited word about husbands, sons, and brothers. In the worst cases, when a soldier had been killed, the chaplains often corresponded with family members after the initial condolence letter, sometimes for several years. Judging from the sheer number of letters in the dossiers of some chaplains, some of them would have had time for little else. Often, the family indicated that the priest's letter had given them spiritual solace despite the bad news it had relayed. In September 1943, Stefanie Oesterle wrote to Chaplain Heinrich Müller, "I thank you on behalf of our extended family for offering a mass for my dear husband and his comrades. It is a great consolation to me to be able at least to see the memorial for my husband and his comrades, since a final resting-place was not granted to him in this terrible war."[101] A young mother wrote to Martin S., "Your dear lines were a great solace to me in my grievous suffering. I can't thank you enough for the great love that you had for my husband. I am now far more content for I know that my husband did indeed receive the holy sacrament [most likely Last Rites, which would have included both Penance and Holy Communion]."[102]

Others were grateful for the news and asked for more detail about the manner of death, revealing that communications from military authorities, containing the most dreaded of all news, were devastatingly unsatisfying. One widow, well acquainted with the suffering of war, wrote to Rudolf P.,

> First, I thank you for your consoling letter. It was a hard blow for me, for I have lost two sons in fourteen days.... At least with Karl [who P. had buried], I have the certainty that he's been buried.... Now I must withstand a difficult lesson. My husband served in the Great War from beginning to end, in August 1918 he fell into captivity, where he wasn't freed until 14 November. In November 1931 he died as a consequence of his war wounds.... Our God will strengthen my faith so that I can take on this suit of suffering, for my younger children [she had nine total] still need me. Dear Father, can you find a soldier who could photograph the grave of my son Karl, and you need only tell me what it costs, I'll gladly send it to you.[103]

Another widow expressed her gratitude that P. had tended to her husband in his final hours, but she pressed for more information: "If it's possible, please write me a bit more about our dearly departed. . . . Were you there when he died? Why didn't anyone give him his rosary, which arrived home in a case today? Please give me some answers, but only if it's no great difficulty for you."[104] Still others, in their grief, became aggressive in their search for knowledge that might soothe them. Frau Krunz sent Josef P. several letters asking for the whereabouts of her son, badly wounded somewhere in western Russia. P. had briefly looked after him. After the opening salutations, she bluntly declared:

> You wrote to us, dear Father, that you know nothing more of our dear son, Alfred. This I cannot believe, dear Father. Indeed, you were with him, and know precisely whether he was lightly or badly wounded. Only you don't want to write it to us. We know well enough that our dear Alfred's badly wounded, otherwise he would have written. Tomorrow will mark ten weeks with no letters from him.

She ended her letter by imploring him to "write us the truth" about the gravity of her son's injury. Whatever answer he sent (not contained in the file) was unsatisfactory, for her questions continued. In her final letter, she intimated that she believed her son to be in captivity somewhere, and that P. "alone was my only hope."[105] In some cases, only a chaplain could assuage the anguish of families looking for information about a lost loved one. Only a chaplain might provide any closure if that information was lacking.

Companions unto Execution

Chaplains tended not merely to the sick and those killed in battle. They also administered to soldiers whom the military authorities condemned to death for breaches in discipline. In comparison to other armies in this war and all armies participating in the First World War, the number of German soldiers killed by their own military was unprecedented: as the war became increasingly brutal and the men more prone to unchecked violence, between 13,000 and 15,000 German soldiers were executed.[106] The authorities permitted these soldiers to receive spiritual consolation, and they assigned the nearest chaplain—and occasionally another priest, if there was no chaplain—to the task. As with all activities that the chaplain undertook, the OKH carefully regulated this task, too.[107] Georg F. had just transitioned into the chaplaincy when he was sent to France in 1941. His commander charged him with caring for approximately 200 German soldiers imprisoned in Fresnes, a large prison in the outskirts of Paris, who were accused of desertion and awaiting execution. He corresponded with the families on their loved one's behalf. The poignant and at times angry letters demonstrate the gratitude of the families for F. as well as their difficulties dealing with their loved one's delinquency. In many cases they exchanged more than one letter as the courts processed the case and handed down the conviction. Some asked for advice about requesting a pardon; others expressed grief and rage; more than one was a tearstained letter from a widow concerning her only son.[108]

Fresnes was the location for another noteworthy German priest who took risks and communicated with the families of those condemned to die—and not just with German families. Authorities in Paris nominated Abbé Franz Stock to head pastoral care in Fresnes during the German occupation of France. Stock and those under him cared for approximately 2,000 French members of the Resistance and other "political prisoners." In 1945, he fell into Allied captivity and was responsible for the foundation of a "barbed-wire" theological school (*Stacheldrahtseminare*) for German seminarians interned in the POW camp where he was stationed.[109] His two aides, Theodor Loevenich and Paul Steinert, were not as well known after the war, but in some ways they took more chances than Stock. Loevenich and Steinert ignored the prohibition on communication with the families of the inmates under German rule. Both brought Bibles, cigarettes, food, and clothes to the inmates. Steinert accompanied two Jewish youths to their deaths when they asked him to. By early 1942, authorities retaliated by transferring both of them to the front lines. Loevenich was sent explicitly as a punishment for writing to the relatives of inmates. No one replaced them. From 1942, Stock alone administered to the civilian prisoners of Fresnes.[110]

Interacting with Foreign Populations

Certain behavior also distanced priests and seminarians from their fellow soldiers. Where other soldiers might have hesitated, priests in uniform were comfortable interacting with foreign civilians, whether in Belgium, Greece, or the Soviet Union, even if regulations forbade such contact. Chaplain Anton Ullrich, one of the few veterans of the Great War who was part of the chaplaincy before the war broke out, wrote about what he had witnessed during the invasion of the Soviet Union:

> In occupied Poland, the Bolsheviks left the churches alone and permitted masses to be said. But the houses of God in Russia proper appear bleak. They still stand, but have been transformed into warehouses, cinemas, sawmills, and similar buildings. The glorious beauty of the churches has been completely destroyed. In the city where we're stationed, the house of God was converted into a profane museum. We threw out all the showroom's objects and burned them in a public courtyard. The populace participated eagerly in this. Old people trampled on images of Lenin and Stalin. The following Sunday we met up with our army chaplain Walter to say the first mass for the army in this church. After long years of Bolshevik rule, the holy mass [sic] in this city. In tears, the populace brought flowers and decorated church and altar. The older people wept with joy. Many brought crucifixes and prayer books that they had kept hidden from the red menace for years, that they had taken care of surreptitiously like invaluable treasure. A great number of them gathered in front of the church. After the service for the army, another one was said for the populace. The crush of people was so great that they squeezed themselves nearly to death at the doors. In an instant, the entire church was full up to the last seat. Even young people entered awestruck.[111]

Ullrich was not the only one to witness the extraordinary desire for religion among Russians and other East Europeans previously under Soviet rule. Such expressions of religiosity so impressed priests and seminarians that they consistently overlooked the difference between the Roman Catholic rite and the Orthodox rite—a difference that would have been carefully observed in other circumstances. None of them even commented on it. An unsigned letter sent from Russia in June 1942 to the seminary director in Freising reads, "In spite of terror and death, Bolshevism has not been able to extirpate religion in the people here. On the contrary! The hunger of the Russian people for what has so long been withheld is great."[112] Chaplain Rincke echoed this finding in his reports, revealing that soldiers were also impressed by such displays: "I can ascertain repeatedly that, for officers as well as for individual soldiers, the religious demeanor of the Russian civilian population is deeply awe-inspiring, especially in connection with the opening of Russian churches."[113] Russians reportedly attended mass even when they could not participate or receive communion. In one instance, an entire company of German soldiers, including non-Catholics, voluntarily attended a mass that the local Russian community also attended. This likely happened very early during the invasion of the Soviet Union because the mood was friendly enough between soldiers and civilians that "after the mass, the people erected a dance platform. On this platform Russian girls and women danced with German soldiers. They celebrated the service like a country fair."[114] J. L., a seminarian from Freising, wrote: "Here in Russia, where Bolshevism wanted to exterminate all religion, one can observe distinctly how little this godless movement has actually achieved: in the houses of this wretched, believing people, many religious images testify to their strong religious convictions."[115] These displays of religiosity fueled the beliefs of chaplains and seminarians alike that their mission—their crusade—into Soviet Russia was not only justifiable, but also God-given. Such a conviction echoed the Church's official line about battling Bolshevism to the death to save Russia. Other Nazi propaganda claims about Russian *Untermenschen* (subhumans), as well as the immense dying of Soviet POWs, did not factor into their remarks.[116]

Encounters with civilian populations fueled some of the most vivid memories of these chaplains and priests in the postwar years. In journals, memoirs, and interviews, they recounted interactions that most soldiers evaded, particularly in the East. Franz M.E. stated simply, "It was official [that we had no contact with other Christians]. All the same, I say I was in the navy and the navy always had contact with civilians."[117] Otto F. was stationed with a Ukrainian family in Melitopol, and though he obeyed the dictates of the OKH and minimized interactions, he described relations between the Ukrainian populace and the army as peaceful until SS units moved into the area.[118] Apparently this was not particular to the Ukraine, either. A priest in Greece recalled, "So long as the German troops behaved well, the Greeks were full of praise for Germany and her soldiers. . . . Unfortunately, the day arrived when the SS spirit was felt more and more across the island, whose people until then had been well disposed to us. Raids were held. . . . The agitation of the people grew and slowly became hatred."[119] Poles in the East also originally feted the Germans as liberators, and they enthusiastically welcomed priests after two years of anti-religious persecution by the Soviet regime. Rudolf Peifer wrote of the event several decades later and could still recall how

> different the religious comportment of the Poles was, how ebullient they were in their gratitude, how almost idolatrous in their veneration of priests! They wanted to kiss my hands, to kneel before me, to send me eggs, butter, even chickens. [What became of them], those whom I baptized, those whom I married? . . . It was inconceivable to us, how many remained believers under the Soviet regime![120]

Russian civilians did not repulse all German priests and seminarians. Many such as Peifer saw an opportunity to save souls. They tested the limits of military restrictions on their activities for that purpose. Others remembered throwing caution to the wind to administer to foreign populations because there was no priest. Bernhard Häring, who after the war published a book about his experiences as a priest in the Wehrmacht's medical service, recalled how in 1943 Russian villagers asked him to assist in childbirth when they could not find a midwife. The woman delivered a baby boy, whose baptism Häring helped to celebrate.[121] In November 1944, when he was in Widrinnen (Widryny, Poland), Rudolf Ritzer wrote in his diary: "At midday mass. Some civilians. Beautiful little church. The populace very religious. The teacher and the young missus [perhaps his wife] very religious too," intimating that they may have attended the masses he said.[122] If so, he risked a great deal because he was not a chaplain; he served six and a half years as a medical orderly. Josef Vennemann also found himself in a situation in which civilians pleaded for his help. Stationed in Shitomir (Zhytomyr, Ukraine) during 1942, he witnessed the Wehrmacht help the city's Polish Catholics rebuild "their beautiful cathedral, in which solemn Latin masses could be celebrated."[123] Shortly thereafter, the Polish priests disappeared, "arrested by the Nazis or fled," he surmised. More likely they were executed along with several thousand other members of the Polish intelligentsia. He did not connect this disappearance with the German army's deliberate killing of Polish elites, including priests, or the persecution of the Jews in the German Reich and in Poland.[124] When the feast of the Assumption, a major solemnity in the Catholic Church and a particularly important day for Poles, approached in August, German-speaking Poles asked him to say a mass. They told him, "It's a high feast-day for us, for we honor the Madonna here as 'Regina Polorum,' queen of Poland." Vennemann was reluctant to breach regulations, but he was equally disinclined to refuse Catholics who beseeched him. He successfully devised a furtive solution using an ambulance and a disguise to smuggle himself into and out of the cathedral. No one caught him, and he found the experience moving: "Then I entered the church. A sea of jubilation, flowers, candles, songs—everything surrounded me."[125] Alois K. and Friedrich D. both baptized children during the invasion of the Soviet Union. As D. explained, "What became of it [the child], I don't know, but the people knew at least that the child was baptized. It was already forbidden to us [to do this], so [what we did] was already too much."[126] But they did it anyway.

Not all interactions left German soldiers with a favorable impression of Russians. Seminarians in particular could be very critical, as when G.W. observed that he had not "been able to make out much about what these people think about religion and Christ. The older generation cannot be dechristianized—everywhere icons are appearing again. But the younger generation! The prisoners of war! For the first time I encountered here people truly without God. And how terrible it was."[127] W. H. opined, "Bolshevik propaganda has made the people completely brittle and dull.... The Russian appears to have a very deep and difficult character." He then admitted, "I very much like the eastern stuff [*der östl. Bausch gefällt mir sehr gut*], especially its religiosity."[128] A third seminarian retreated into familiar cultural stereotypes, emphasizing the naiveté and primitive nature of the Russians: "The faith of this land is as enigmatic as its geography and its people.... New, childlike beliefs coexist with fanatical, passionate faith, and honest will and severe ethical principles coexist with bestial sadism."[129]

Unexpected interactions on religious grounds worked both ways. As often as civilians made requests of priests moving with German armies, priests also approached civilians with pleas for aid. Desperate to say a mass, Rudolf Unger found himself in Belgrade and visited the nearest

Catholic church. He did not speak Serbian and anticipated that whoever answered the door would not understand German, so he resorted to Latin: "A Serbian acolyte who didn't understand me and whom I didn't understand knelt at the foot of the altar and ministered and prayed the Latin responses with a voice as clear as our [own] altar boys. . . . I must also say that at that time in Serbia, particularly in Belgrade, every German soldier was hated, not well accepted at all. No German soldier could walk around in the streets without being obviously armed." He was able to do the same thing at a Franciscan monastery in Vucova, Romania, as was Wilhelm L. in Riga.[130]

Seminarians could not administer sacraments like chaplains and priests, but some of them were as eager to practice their faith, and they did what they could to evangelize. A. A. attended (presumably Orthodox) mass with Russian civilians (which was forbidden) because, he declared, "we contribute in a small way to bringing back the faith to this godless country. In a certain sense we are trailblazers for the Lord, so He can return."[131] One of his classmates prayed that he would be "a warrior in the first line in this war against Bolshevism. May our deeds be capped off with the proclamation of the Christian Gospel to these poor people."[132]

Glimpses and Omissions of Jews

Many details of the priests' wartime experiences could be revealed only after the war. Letters and journals were largely limited to a dry list of daily activities. Sometimes, if a chaplain was writing, statistics might be compiled about how many soldiers attended mass and how many received communion. There was no mention of proper names and often no indication of place (this was standard military practice due to censorship, but this was also sometimes because the author did not know exactly where he was). Unsurprisingly, there was very little discussion of atrocities committed by Germans. Even the presence of Jews was overlooked. Given that many men were on the Eastern Front between 1941 and 1944, precisely when the mass murder of Jews, Soviet prisoners of war, and other racial undesirables was taking place, this absence is notable. Part of this omission can be attributed to fear. Chaplain Friedrich D. kept journals of his activities, but he notes, "It says so little, so little and only briefly what I did: sick visits, hospital visits, etc., but nothing at all in detail. One couldn't write down the important things, only a skeleton of activity."[133] The reason for this absence may have been due, in part, to the power of the seal of the confessional: whatever soldiers confessed to priests could not be revealed.

There were few exceptions. Joseph Wassong, an older chaplain and veteran of the Great War, remarked on 20 April 1941, "I heard that a Jew in Kielce (Poland) passed by a soldier without greeting him and received a slap in the face. The Jew greeted the next soldier with particular care, but was slapped by him as well because he believed the Jew was ridiculing him. Is this true?"[134] After this entry, there is no more mention of Jews. His disbelief that a soldier would mistreat a Jew in Poland indicates a profound ignorance, willing or otherwise, about the nature of the German occupation of Poland.

Josef Menke also recalled an experience in Italy. In November 1944, he learned that German authorities were transporting an Italian nun, Sister Cressin, to an "extermination camp [run] by our SS" because she was of Jewish descent. He wrote that she "came as a two-year-old child with her Jewish parents from the Ukraine, was naturalized in Italy, and became, as far as I can recall, a music teacher. [She] converted and entered an order . . . but her Jewish descent was enough to place her on the death list."[135] Working with a local German consul and Monsignor Giovanni Urbani, who after the war became the patriarch of Venice and a cardinal of the Church, he tried to save her. On the morning of her deportation, the SS who came to pick her up discovered that she was gone. Menke reported that "only the patriarch [of Venice] knows where she is, and he certainly will keep her hiding place to himself." He learned soon after that the SS had abandoned their search for her.[136] He made no mention of the 7,000 Italian Jews who had not converted to Catholicism and were rounded up and killed in the extermination camps.[137]

Chaplain Johannes Stelzenberger, a veteran of the First World War, made the most extensive diary entries during the war about Jews and their murder. His entries, though few, constitute the richest detail and emotional reaction to the events of the Holocaust as they took place. In Smolensk in October 1941, he witnessed the terrible treatment of prisoners, some of whom were so exhausted that they collapsed in the street. Those still standing "tussled with each other for the shoes and clothes! Men have become animals here. On the highway, 30,000 prisoners went past, a train of wretchedness . . . they estimate that they haven't eaten for six days. They bawled. Whoever left the line was shot. The tramping, wailing, and shooting ululated through the night. It was a night of horror."[138] On the way to Vilna (Vilnius, Lithuania), he wrote,

> Everywhere Jewish women and children work in the streets. They are concentrated in work details. An abominable disgrace to culture! Our caretaker in Molodetschno [Molotschna, Ukraine] reported that he was supposed to provide asylum for German soldiers. In addition he had 300 workers, mostly Jews. This morning, they didn't come. From his wife he received the information that ninety of them, mostly craftsmen, were shot. Reason: a supplies warehouse had allegedly been set on fire in Minsk.[139]

Not much later, he wrote,

> Molodetschno . . . 8.30 am departure, arrival in Vilna at noon. A very beautiful, generally very interesting and rich city. Mostly Catholic populace . . . every day here, thousands of Jews were shot. Of 40,000 Jews in Vilna, now only 6,000 are still alive. How terrible is that! One is mortified that any such deed was perpetrated by German people. Food no longer tastes of anything. At any time, Jews will be picked up: men, women, and children. They are led out by the Lithuanian militia, supervised by German police, must dig their own graves, are rabidly beaten and then shot. The next row must first lay the dead in the holes, fill them up, then will themselves be shot! Blood! Blood![140]

The nightmare landscape continued as he moved south from Vilna to Tarnopol (Ternopil, Ukraine), close to the town of Zloczow (Zolochiv, Ukraine). He may have lost his appetite, an indication of physical, mental, or spiritual stress (or all three). But he still noticed the weather, "much snow," and the people shoveling it, "prisoners, Jews, inhabitants of the village." He arrived at Proskurow (Proskurov, Ukraine) in the evening and wrote, "Earlier 48,000, now 16,000 inhabitants, 3,000 of them Jews. Stationed in a soldier's shelter. The sister there complained a lot about German soldiers. The Hungarians were nicer. They didn't put their guns on the table in order to get beer."[141] Stelzenberger was another chaplain lost at Stalingrad, taken prisoner by the Russians. He was involved with pastoral care for German POWs in Soviet captivity. He returned to Germany in 1949.[142]

Some years ago, two historians unearthed separately the only evidence of clergy who tried to intervene on behalf of Jews about to be murdered. In August 1941, a pair of chaplains, one Protestant and one Catholic, found a group of Jewish children near Belaya Tserkov (Bila Tserkva, not far from Kiev), Ukraine.[143] SS and German soldiers had already slaughtered their parents, but there was some question about the children. Interestingly, it was German soldiers who heard the children crying who alerted the chaplains. Catholic chaplain Ernst Tewes and his colleague went to investigate: "We found about ninety young Jewish children, among them some tiny babies, in a pitiless situation: penned up, moaning, crying, hungry, and thirsty in the great midday heat. Some of their parents had been shot; the mothers of others were imprisoned in a neighboring room, from which they had to see the misery of their children without being able to do anything about it."[144] They persuaded an army officer to find out what was going to happen and, if possible, to save the children. But in the end, policy prevailed, and an SS unit took the children from the school and shot them.[145] It is not clear if the chaplains knew of this outcome at the time. Tewes's role in the tragic event became known only in 1968 (the same year that he was consecrated auxiliary bishop of Munich and Freising), when he testified in Darmstadt at the trial of former members of an SS-*Einsatzgruppe* unit.[146] Werthmann's postwar notes praised Tewes for caring tirelessly for the sick and the wounded, but he made no mention of the incident regarding the Jewish children. It is possible that Werthmann did not even know, especially if Tewes did not report it to him.

After the war many priests insisted that nothing about Auschwitz, extermination camps, or massacres of Jews could have been known with certainty, but some contradicted that assertion. Alfons Mende's postwar testimony reveals that, for many Germans on the Eastern Front, the "rumors" about atrocities were not rumors at all. At the same time, he stressed to his interviewer that certainty was not a part of life in battle. "Our train stopped somewhere for a long spell, this was already 1942 or 1943," he remembered.

> There were freight cars standing there, and we heard over and over, "Bread, bread!" and such things. So then we stepped outside. The

whole length of the train was full of prisoners. What that was, we knew ... [but] we couldn't see, and they begged for bread. They were going to Auschwitz, we heard. When we returned, we immediately told others. "Man, they're killing them. ...." But it was always a rumor. One never knew for sure. ... But we witnessed it. The whole freight train full of people. ... And the [unnamed] general, too: "Yes," he said, "that's right [that they will be killed and not simply taken to work camps]." "But they are rumors, one can hardly imagine it!" "No, no, it's no rumor ... you've seen it now yourself."[147]

But whether they witnessed the massacres or heard only "rumors" of shootings and Auschwitz, neither chaplain nor priest nor seminarian pushed himself to condemn the treatment of Jews. It was irrelevant whether his fellow soldiers and officers in the Wehrmacht, the *SS-Einsatzgruppen* and other paramilitary organizations, or auxiliary units in the Baltic states or in eastern Europe were involved in the extermination operations. None went out of his way to attempt to learn more about these "rumors." With the exception of Tewes and his Protestant colleague, there is no record of any cleric either questioning orders or interfering with the murder of Jews.

* * *

In September 1944, an unarmed German medical company was winding its way slowly toward Germany through the woods of eastern France. Allied air bombers and French partisans simultaneously attacked them, in spite of their prominently displayed Red Cross flag. Among them were sixteen priests, including NCO Heinrich Niewind. The attacks wounded four soldiers who fell into partisan hands; a fifth, an orderly, was killed in the air attack. Niewind oversaw the burial of this man in the nearest village, Velesmes, with help from the local French priest. After the burial, he and one lance corporal elected to remain to warn German soldiers passing through of surrounding danger. The Allies renewed the air raids overnight, and more Germans died. In the morning, German military police arrived with orders to destroy Velesmes. Trucks full of troops, weapons, and explosives began to roll into the village, whose anxious inhabitants watched nervously as Niewind and his lance corporal, Stamm, conversed with the German commander. Long hours passed. Niewind managed to persuade the officer to abandon the reprisal action, shortly before the military police confirmed that Velesmes was not connected to partisan activity. Had the measures been carried out, Velesmes would surely have been compared to similar acts of revenge in Oradour-sur-Glane, France, in 1944 and in Lidice, Czechoslovakia, in 1942. After the SS and police left, the French villagers went to mass, offered in thanksgiving for the fallen German orderly who had brought Niewind to Velesmes. Four days later, the Allies captured Niewind. His role as "the savior of Velesmes" would not come to light for another twenty years.[148]

What determined a priest's decision to object to wartime actions either unfolding or about to unfold? What moved Niewind to endanger his life for the French villagers by arguing with an officer bent on revenge, while other priests merely noted that trainloads of Jews had passed them on their way to Auschwitz, where, they were told, they would be killed? Why did priests risk their lives to break Wehrmacht regulations to baptize Russian children or to communicate with the families of executed French prisoners, but not find a way to protest the misery of Jews in the Warsaw ghetto or the shootings of unarmed civilians on the Eastern Front? Why were there not more conscientious objectors who refused the conscription order?

No straightforward or monocausal explanation can address these questions satisfactorily. In fact, the reasons that motivated these men to act as they did demonstrate the heterogeneity of the Wehrmacht. No doubt antisemitism and racism played roles in inducing some Germans, even some Catholic Germans, to serve enthusiastically. As an institution, the Church was no stranger to antisemitic discrimination. Catholic German spiritual leaders did not protest the persecution and deportation of German Jews. Priests and seminarians serving in the armed forces might have relied on this antisemitism and especially the example of their authorities, consciously or otherwise, to justify the actions taken in the name of the German people, particularly on the Eastern Front. Nor were Catholics immune to racism at this time. The Catholic Church proved more impervious than other political, social, and cultural institutions to racist language and thinking. But this immunity did not preclude Catholics in Germany from adopting certain racial conceptions or terminology prior to 1939. The use of the word *Volk* is one of the best examples.[149]

Any number of factors could explain why these men failed to stand against the crimes of the Wehrmacht and the political party that directed it: cowardice, the desire to conform, an inclination to trust in, or at least accept, orders from higher authorities. To some extent, the qualified explanations that historian Christopher R. Browning has offered are useful: wartime brutalization, racism, routinization of the task, careerism, indoctrination.[150] Browning's seminal text, however, dealt with what induced ordinary men to become killers. The question of what drove priests and seminarians—well-educated religious men and, therefore, not "ordinary" in Browning's sense of the word—to tolerate criminal, immoral activities is of a different order. It requires an answer about what displaced these priests' devotion to Christian principles.

What drove these men in their fervent dedication to the army was their desire to help the men—Christian and German—with whom they served. This aspiration engaged their religious vocation as Catholic priests and their national identity as Germans. Long into the postwar period, veterans remembered their service with pride. They declared without hesitation that they would serve in the same way again if necessary. In their own words, this solidarity with their fellow soldiers is why they chose to stay. Such camaraderie convinced them that soldiers needed their particular spiritual care. By providing this care, they fulfilled their yearning to do their national duty to the Fatherland as well as to their fellow Germans.[151] While remaining in the army and failing to protest the army's crimes are two distinct choices, in the case of chaplains and other priests, generally they were connected. By and large, these men separated their comrades and military superiors from Nazism's darker aspects without trouble. As priests, they were providing spiritual solace to the good Christian men who found themselves in a horrific war in defense of German civilization and culture. Moreover, the enemy was Bolshevism, an evil universally acknowledged by Catholic Germans, taking their lead from the pope and their bishops. Most chaplains, priests, and seminarians in the Wehrmacht consigned whatever atrocities they heard about, perpetrated by German soldiers, to the realm of unfounded rumor. When pressed with more irrefutable evidence, they found ways to set the atrocities to the side and continue their service.

Like their lay counterparts, most Catholic priests and seminarians gave little or no consideration to the potential confrontation they might have had with the Nazi movement over their military service. As one veteran chaplain later put it, "Because the men and young boys of our parishes were forced to go to the front, so we went with them as spiritual aids, according to the postulate, 'Soldiers have a right to religion.'"[152] The tradition of separating spiritual care and religion during times of war from national politics and intrigue dates back in Christian history to at least the Crusades.[153] Following this tradition, priests willingly donned the Wehrmacht uniform to provide for the spiritual needs of their fellow Christian men and to give solace and comfort when they were far from home, risking their lives. There is evidence, and other scholars have argued, that priests and seminarians who went to war between 1939 and 1945 were politically very naïve and were encouraged to be so by their superiors.[154] They did *not* put on the uniform to proclaim their support for Nazism. In 1945, Werthmann defended his decision to compromise by stating, "We felt that we could be of greater service if we remained outside [the] concentration camp,"[155] that is, if he kept his head down and remained as unobtrusive as possible.

One can debate the morality of such a decision, but for these men such rumination rarely emerged during the war. The preservation of peacetime moral codes proved difficult under wartime conditions, particularly when decrees commanding soldiers to shoot civilians on sight had inverted such codes.[156] Those soldiers looking for guidance or leadership from the religious men among them would have found it in the solace of confession. The corruption of morals went unchallenged in a war that was "perceived as a struggle of all-or-nothing [that] called for complete spiritual commitment, absolute obedience, unremitting destruction of the enemy."[157]

Seminarians, priests, and chaplains recorded extraordinary experiences as soldiers in the Wehrmacht. They developed relationships and led activities—saying mass, hearing confessions, caring for the sick and dying, ministering to prisoners and soldiers condemned to death for breaches of discipline—that distinguished them from other soldiers and their officers. Recognized as priests or priests in training, greeted with hostility or admiration, many other soldiers recognized them as integral to the machinery of war. They felt themselves to be needed and irreplaceable, and so they persisted in their dedication to the men who relied on them. For many of them, it took all of their energy, their will, and their faith in their vocation to stay this course. Like their leaders, they did not prioritize concerns about interactions with foreign soldiers, civilians, and Jews or questions about the larger ideological goals of the regime. Rather, they elided these in favor of the all-consuming needs of the Catholic men with whom they served.

4

RELIGION, NATIONALISM, AND WHY PRIESTS WENT TO WAR

Most conscripted priests and seminarians who went to war did not do so because they supported the Nazi Party. They went for a variety of reasons. Many of them saw it as a duty both to care for the Catholic German souls who were fighting and to defend their country. Religion and nationalism worked in tandem as motivation. As they performed their military service, they rationalized and justified their role in a war that was ultimately not only antithetical to their religious beliefs, but also criminal. Most lacked genuine enthusiasm for military service. But they went determined to do some good or to make a difference for the soldiers. In written testimony, particularly after the war, they consistently divorced the war, the army leadership, and the average soldier from the ideology of Nazism. Just like laymen, priests and seminarians were susceptible to diverse incentives when it came to military service. Nationalism, fear and hatred of Bolshevism, and peer pressure are a few of many factors that they shared with lay Germans. This commonality makes the commitment of these men to the army "ordinary" in every sense. However, a kind of spiritual opportunism was at work, manifesting itself in the conviction that theirs was a spiritual burden that only they could bear. To decline this duty—to neglect to look after the Catholic soldiers in time of need—was tantamount to shirking one's vocation, in both their own estimation as well as that of other members of the Church.

If these men had the same motivations for military service as laymen, this suggests that vocation and religious devotion did not differentiate them sharply from their fellow soldiers. In fact, I argue that they were a distinct group precisely because of their vocation, grounded in a thorough education and training and often deep faith, all of which are evident in their written reflections. Some men with whom they served ridiculed or harassed them, but others sought them out for spiritual support and counsel, even when they were not part of the chaplaincy. This combination of training, faith, and feeling useful helped them rationalize their complicity with a racist, murderous regime. In their view, the moral support they provided was vital. Such thinking reveals a dangerous myopia: the souls of Catholic Germans counted above all else. Their service also reveals the flawed rationalization that their actions were apolitical because they were working strictly for the spiritual benefit of Christian Germans.

This experience provides an unusual lens through which to explore how Catholic Germans resolved the contradictions between their national and religious identities. In particular, their examples show how they squared their own morality with Nazi ideology. On some points, most obviously regarding Bolshevism, Catholicism and Nazism shared an affinity that priests and seminarians in the army used to justify the inhuman conditions they encountered, particularly on the Eastern Front. On other issues, it is not so obvious how this reconciliation occurred.

This chapter investigates how the experience of a brutal war generally affirmed the religious beliefs and nationalist leanings of Catholic priests and seminarians in the Wehrmacht. Wartime correspondence and reports as well as postwar testimonies from interviews and memoirs reveal the worldview of these men, both in the way they described their war service and Nazism and in the subjects they reflected upon. Their silences are also telling. How they understood themselves, their faith and ideology, and what they did under extreme conditions help to explain why these men committed themselves to the war. For most of them, their service ultimately strengthened their religious vocation and convictions.

Priests and seminarians serving in the Wehrmacht were loyal to many war aims that the Nazi regime touted, such as the defense of German civilization and the eradication of Bolshevism. They grounded this devotion in religious fervor. Simultaneously, such a deep spiritual commitment failed to incite them to defend those human lives most in need of defense, namely Europe's Jews. In their examples, Nazism and Catholicism coexisted and even mutually reinforced each other during the war. Paradoxically, this made religion less likely to foment resistance to Nazi military policies and, in fact, more likely to facilitate cooperation.

The Impact of a Seminary Education

In addition to their Catholic faith and their vocational aspirations, conscripted priests and seminarians had all spent time in a seminary classroom before donning the Wehrmacht uniform. Generalizations about that experience are difficult, given the range of ages, differences in education and training at the time of conscription, and the diocesan variations in seminary regulations. But any discussion of the worldview of the Catholic priests and seminarians must account for the influences that helped to shape that worldview. The youth movement of the 1920s and 1930s was one defining influence. Seminary training was a second one.

Very few priests or seminarians left explicit commentary detailing their educational experiences or the ways that the seminary prepared them for war. Thus, the majority of available evidence limits this overview to a top-down investigation using secondary texts. Additionally, I have consulted contemporary analyses of teachers in German seminaries who were not conscripted during the war. Despite the lack of eyewitness testimony, it is informative to bear in mind what the seminary experience was like. How this experience molded a young Catholic's conception of the wartime world and his role in it is integral to the story of priests in uniform.

Although it was not the Catholic Church's first attempt to enforce standards for its priests, the Council of Trent's 1563 Decree on Seminaries was unprecedented. The council was the Church's response to the sixteenth-century Protestant Reformation. For the first time in

Church history, the council's members called for the maintenance of local institutions to standardize the education and training of its priests. This standardization would help combat ignorance and encourage the professionalization of clergy.[1] The decree's guidelines, gradually implemented over the following centuries, endured into the twentieth century. Stricter examinations of those entering the priesthood were created as were age minimums for the various levels of ordination. Boys had to be at least twelve years old to enter the seminary, and instructors had to hold degrees (a doctoral, master, or licentiate degree) in sacred scripture or canon law. The Church would now train seminarians in many subjects, including grammar, chanting, contemporary Church issues, Church practice, the homilies of holy men, the performance of Church rituals, and the administration of the sacraments with an emphasis on Penance. The local bishops had control of the seminaries and were also responsible for disciplinary measures and financing.[2]

In the early twentieth century, therefore, each German diocese made its own decisions about how to operate its seminaries.[3] In theory, according to the Tridentine decree, the bishop wielded a great deal of influence in the educational curriculum of future priests. In practice, it was more complicated. Germany lacked a Catholic university for the training of priests, so German clergy utilized seminaries to teach what state universities otherwise would not or could not: Catholic theology (moral, pastoral, dogmatic), ascetics, and matters pertaining to the training of priests, including pedagogy and catechetics. While each diocesan bishop made final decisions about the seminary curriculum and its directors, he worked with the seminary directors on the specifics of ordination. State universities and seminaries often shared students (many seminaries in Germany had semi-official relations with the nearest large university for financial reasons). Tensions over curriculum and training were not unusual among theological faculties in seminaries and universities, the diocese's vicariate, and the bishop himself.[4]

In 1931, Pope Pius XI issued *Deus scientiarum Dominus*, an apostolic constitution (the highest form of papal decree). Its purpose was to further synchronize priestly education globally with the 1917 Code of Canon Law.[5] Its practical effects for German seminaries were obvious. For example, in Münster, attendance at lectures and completion of academic work was now mandatory (this was only implicit in the 1563 decree). Training for the priesthood now took six years. The training included theological and philosophical education at a theological seminary (*Theologenkonvikt*) as well as more practical pastoral training and spiritual formation at a clerical seminary (*Priesterseminare*). There were additional required courses at state universities. There were more exams, and all students, with few exceptions, were required to take them.[6]

While the makeup of a seminary classroom in preceding centuries is discernable—church historian Georg Schwaiger has said, "The nineteenth century clergy [of Bavaria] was a true elite of the people: only the most capable youth were chosen and sent to the few grammar schools and seminaries"[7]—the question of who was likely to enter a German seminary in the 1920s has no satisfactory answer. Industrialization, socialism and the rising strength of the German Socialist Party (SPD), complications facing political Catholicism, continued secularization, and war were all contributing factors to a crisis in vocations by 1918–1919. Beyond the obvious religious requirement that one be Catholic with a sense of priestly vocation, generalizations about candidates are difficult. So are any assumptions about specific social, cultural, economic, or regional pressures that might have induced a young man to enter the priesthood. A recent study of the diocese of Münster suggests that a concerted effort to augment seminary applications in the wake of the Great War produced an increase in candidates that lasted about a decade. The younger clergy emerging from this upswing came primarily from urban centers and social strata that actively promoted social change.[8] To what extent Münster was representative of a trend in vocations in Germany is not clear without further social and religious studies.

Who and what future priests were reading, the reforms that these books endorsed, and the kind of Catholic worldview, framed by moral and theological concepts, are more perceptible. Two of the most significant influences were the Italian-born German theologian Romano Guardini and the theological development of *Corpus Christi mysticum*. These two influences focused on the role of the layperson in the life of the Church. They also addressed how reforms to lay participation would affect the clerical-lay relationship and the definition of the priestly vocation. Such reforms would have major ramifications in the postwar period, particularly for Vatican II. But it also affected seminarians and young priests in the late 1920s, 1930s, and during the Second World War. The clergy of this generation clung to older ideas about lay Catholics who needed the guidance of a priest-confessor. At the same time they embraced the new idea of a vast Catholic community in which lay Catholics demanded the full engagement of the clergy in all aspects of the temporal world.

Of the many theologians and moral manual authors that German seminarians read in the interwar years, Romano Guardini is mentioned frequently.[9] He was deeply involved in the German youth movement, in which he was a chaplain during and after the First World War. He was seminal to the German branch of the modern liturgical movement, in which scholars advocated over several decades for the reform of Roman Catholic worship. He was among the first to stress that the Church was not composed of the clergy alone; rather, it constituted "a living space [Lebensraum] in which all Catholics stand." He described a worldview that emphasized global homogeneity rooted in renewed religious meaning.[10] The idea that the laity had an important role in the life of the Church, equal to that of priests themselves, marked a major revision to previous conceptions of the priesthood. Before, a priest's pastoral skills were evaluated on the basis of the religious and social health of lay Catholics in his care. Moreover, a priest had to distinguish himself from those he guided; he was to be their model for emulation. Early-twentieth-century moral manuals (textbooks, focused on sin, conscience, authority, and virtue, used in seminary classrooms to teach the fundamentals of moral theology) echoed this view. They stressed the priest's duty to keep the penitent safe from falsehood and evil.[11]

While Guardini did not compose moral manuals, his writings were read with them. Thus his ideas contributed to their eventual reform. Catholic moral theology, defined as a systematic treatment of ethics or how to live as a morally upright Roman Catholic Christian, is not a static construct. Moral theology developed over several centuries and had many diverse contributors. The prototypes of modern moral manuals emerged in the medieval era, with collections of summary statements (summas, or compendiums) about morals and ethics (there were also more academic compendiums about theology, such as Thomas

Aquinas's thirteenth-century *Summa Theologicae*). Up to the twentieth century the authors of these compendiums presented their writings as ahistorical, timeless principles.[12] Priests and monks used the manuals to teach and to assist a Catholic priest in his duties, particularly as a confessor. Contemporary Catholicism's emphasis on charity as rooted in the words of Jesus Christ, on the sanctity of human life, and on the personal conscience as the epicenter of moral judgment are relatively recent, post–Second World War axioms of Catholic moral theology. They were not at the center of moral teaching in the first half of the twentieth century, when moral theology more frequently stressed sin, authority, and penitence as well as the priest's responsibility as caretaker. Conformity with Church regulations was to be preserved at all times rather than ad hoc or spontaneous responses to temporal, and thereby fleeting, challenges. In this sense, Guardini served as a harbinger.

Contemporary Catholic ethics is a product of both current pressures and key historical events in preceding decades, especially the Vatican II reforms. Accordingly, priests and seminarians who were educated in the 1920s and 1930s and who went to war in the 1940s did so formed by a Catholic worldview and identity that were decidedly distinct from that found today. The Catholic Church had yet to embrace the ecumenical movement, so official Protestant-Catholic dialogue was nonexistent. Obedience to spiritual and political authorities was the hallmark of a good Catholic; one simply did not question the duties and demands that a legitimate authority made. Thus, so many priests and seminarians unquestioningly put on a Wehrmacht uniform and did not question the meaning of the war or Germany's right to wage it.

Finally, bishops and priests in Germany in the late 1930s and 1940s had a specific interpretation of the war and the suffering it caused that was closely connected to the popular theology of *Corpus Christi mysticum*, or the mystical body of Christ. This theology's origins are rooted in Paul's epistle to the Corinthians about the relationship between Christ and the Church on earth, called the Church militant. Paul delineated this relationship as a body, with Christ as the head and all of Christ's followers (Christians) as the (mystical) body.[13] The significance of this theology lay in its stress on the unity of all Christians who profess faith in Christ. Eventually the theology evolved to include specifically those Christians who recognized the authority of the pope—in other words, Catholics. In the 1920s, the theology of the mystical body of Christ reemerged with renewed emphasis in France, Germany, and Italy as a widespread popular devotion.

Pope Pius XII's 1943 encyclical with the near-identical name, *Mystici Corporis Christi (On the Mystical Body of Christ)*, elevated this theology to Church doctrine. It was one of his most important encyclicals, one that addressed the magnitude of Christian unity in the midst of war, the responsibility of all faithful Catholics (not just clergy) to work toward the perfection of the Church on earth, and the importance of receiving the sacraments regularly. He made no direct reference to Nazism or communism. In those few sections that dealt with contemporary political concerns, he underscored the grave errors of forced conversion, discrimination based on race and nationality (Jews were not specifically mentioned), and the murder of mentally and physically handicapped people. But the encyclical was primarily an explication of a theological doctrine, and, as such, it was profoundly spiritual. Particular emphasis was placed on charity as the hallmark of a life that imitated Christ and on the importance of suffering like Christ. This delineation of suffering was important, reinforcing what devout Catholics across Europe already believed about the meaning of the war in which they were caught up. It likely bolstered what seminarians and young priests had learned about suffering and its meaning.

The encyclical contains numerous references to suffering and how Catholics were to handle it: "The greatest joy and exaltation are born only of suffering . . . we should rejoice if we partake of the sufferings of Christ"; "if the sorrows and calamities of these stormy times, by which countless multitudes are being sorely tried, are accepted from God's hands with calm submission"; "these heavenly gifts will surely flow more abundantly if . . . we humbly accept as from God's hands the burdens and sorrows of this present life"; "there was never a time . . . when the salvation of souls did not impose on all the duty of associating their sufferings with the torments of our Divine Redeemer; but today that duty is more clear than ever."[14] The war had caused much of the suffering and pain that the encyclical mentioned. Pius XII did not have to instruct Catholics on how to absorb this, as the German bishops stepped in readily. In many reports, the SiPo (Security Police) noted what they heard from the pulpit: the war stemmed from the wrath of God as a punishment for the godlessness and immorality of Nazi leadership; it was necessary for the betterment of Germany. With words like guilt, punishment, plague, penitence, and atonement spread liberally through their sermons and pastoral letters, Catholic bishops and priests asked their flocks to unite in suffering and offer that suffering to God.[15] The opportunity to suffer was not to be avoided. On the contrary, it was to be embraced, pursued, even glorified, for the sake of perfecting both the Church, as the mystical body of Christ, and the individual's own soul. For priests and seminarians in the Wehrmacht, this was the most commonsensical explanation of both their temporal and their spiritual predicament.

Failed Priests and "Brown Priests"

A minority of conscripted priests and seminarians lacked the courage to stay true to their faith and vocation. One response to the dehumanizing effects of war was suicide, and some priests were no more immune to this than the common soldier. Other priests found solace in alcohol. Battle and alcohol have naturally paired since long before the Second World War. Nor was this something that soldiers concealed from military authorities. In some instances, their commanders even encouraged moderate alcohol consumption as a way for soldiers to deal with participation in brutal battle or mass slaughter.[16] That a small number of priests resorted to intoxication is probably unsurprising, but it did pose special problems for religious authorities such as Werthmann, who wrote apologetically: "Unfortunately it must be said that some colleagues, whose grievous crimes consist of perverse fornication [likely a reference to sodomy or bestiality] and defeatist expressions, were under the influence of alcohol when they exercised their misdeeds . . . this put them in the situation in which they were no longer masters of their own senses."[17] He did not offer details about who he was describing and what they did, and he was careful to qualify the statement. Not all priests who succumbed to sexual deviance or defeatism could plead the excuse of intoxication.

Elsewhere, Werthmann related the adventures of Chaplain Franz Schmitz, who spent time with the interned former vicar-general at the

Benedictine monastery in Niederalteich in May 1945. A religious superior's assessment of Schmitz described him as a chaplain who "loved his duty, and also alcohol," but who was still functional as "an enthusiastic Catholic priest . . . [whose] men treasure him."[18] Because of his struggle with alcohol, Schmitz told Werthmann, he experienced problems at the end of the war. Authorities had imprisoned Schmitz in Vienna for defeatist remarks. In the confusion of converging Russian and American armies in the Austrian capital, Schmitz became displaced. Werthmann wrote, "It's regrettable that this reliable and efficient chaplain made his defeatist remarks against the state in a condition of considerable drunkenness. Schmitz is by nature sober, but the difficult battles he's been in since the evacuation of Bessarabia [modern-day Moldova and Ukraine] were probably crucial in determining his addiction to alcohol at the time."[19] What Werthmann knew about alcohol addiction and the nature of the Eastern Front is ambiguous, but he seemed to connect these two in the figure of Schmitz. Whether Schmitz continued drinking after his escape and as he made his way back to Germany is unknown. During his flight from the Russians, who had taken away his clothes, he stumbled, literally, into an SS *Totenkopf* division (SS-Division Theodor Eicke), who almost shot him under suspicion that he was an enemy.[20]

Others responded to the situation by either converting to Protestantism or leaving the priesthood altogether. Werthmann remembered chaplain Johannes F. as a "little conman [*Hochstapler*]," who confided to a Protestant chaplain that he wanted to become Protestant. In early 1944 he had become romantically involved with a young German woman. By late summer 1944, military authorities in conjunction with the Field Bishop's Office discharged him from the chaplaincy and returned him in his earlier position in the medical service. He was killed in March 1945.[21] Chaplain Franz K. became so ill in October 1942 that he lost forty pounds and requested sick leave. In a brief postwar note, Werthmann remarked that K. was attempting to leave the priesthood.[22] That these men, and others like them, became disillusioned with their vocation as a direct result of their war experiences is not definitively proven. But it is equally difficult to believe that the war played no role at all.

Other priests also proved incapable of handling the stress of their new situation close to or at the war's front lines. Their inability to perform their duties reflected this. Superiors, most often another chaplain or the hospital staff doctor, subsequently reported this in their evaluations. Young chaplain Franz E. was unable to please his authorities. Another chaplain wrote, "I have known E. since 1942 and was never satisfied with his work. In the summer of 1943, the chief doctor who was working with him complained that he could not even fulfill his modest obligations at the hospital. Exhortations, expositions, even brotherly attempts on my part have had no luck in inspiring him to do his work."[23] The doctor with whom E. was working also wrote, "He had no initiative in concerning himself with the housing, provisioning, and care of the numerous wounded. He was completely unmoved by the miserable looks of the starving, suffering, wounded soldiers, who only wanted some support. He didn't lift a finger, as each of us did day and night."[24] In 1944 he was transferred no less than six times. He finished the war in Soviet captivity, which he survived.[25] Ludwig E.'s chaplain superior also rendered a harsh judgment, labeling him a "salon priest who eschews his duty to the fighting soldiers. Loves 'beautiful' masses in rear positions and favors spending time in the casino. Pretentious."[26] Did E. shirk the task of providing soldiers with spiritual and moral support because he found it too difficult or felt inadequate? Or was he more concerned with the material trappings of religion even in wartime? There is no testimony from E., but reports judged him as lacking decisively in pastoral skills. Therefore, the reports concluded, he was unfit for a service in which chaplains were required to be as mentally and spiritually tough as the soldiers engaged in physical battle.

Werthmann used these reports to form his own judgments about his chaplains. He also used them to make notes for a projected chaplaincy history that he intended to write after the war.[27] These notes suggest that, while Werthmann knew that his men collaborated ideologically with the regime to some degree (he set this example, after all), he would not tolerate a total embrace of the Nazi weltanschauung. He was especially hard on them, probably because of his own obsession with duty. He took his priestly vocation seriously and expected the same of those clergy under him. About Leonhard H., stationed with the Second Mountain Division, he wrote, "His geniality was not always sincere. His gestures were not always natural. . . . Others complained that he didn't say mass for Easter 1945 [April 1], when the division was deployed to Heilbronn."²⁸ Chaplain Paul D. presented countless ideological problems. He had the backing of the Nazi Party because he had been an open supporter of Hitler since 1932. The party had essentially forced the bishop of Berlin to accept him into his diocese, just as it later forced the field bishop to accept him in the chaplaincy. In 1943, D.'s early (temporary) retirement from the chaplaincy for health reasons was a blessing for Werthmann. But D. was not yet finished. He refused to recognize his retirement and was reinstated "due to angry hate mail that he addressed to Hitler and to Reinecke. He was uninhibited in the letters. He accused the field bishop as well as the OKH of sabotaging the work of the Führer."²⁹ Despite his demonstrated loyalty to the party, which has earned him Kevin Spicer's label "brown priest," whoever read his letters evidently did not take him seriously. Eventually D. ended up in the reserves, where he survived the war.³⁰

Another priest presented Werthmann with an even larger challenge over ideological allegiance to Nazism. Ordained in 1925, Joseph Thomann was involved with the Reichswehr chaplaincy and then the Wehrmacht chaplaincy. Werthmann recalled that in 1938 Thomann had a breakdown in Vienna. Instead of concentrating on his immediate spiritual duties, he had turned Austrian chaplains against each other and used his pulpit to attack both the Austrian and German bishops for their anti-Nazi attitudes, real and imagined. The apostolic nuncio in Germany, Cesare Orsenigo, ordered Rarkowski, as Thomann's superior, to prohibit Thomann from engaging in polemics and to confine himself to the pertinent pastoral tasks of an army chaplain. Perhaps anxious to avoid confrontation, Rarkowski "did not have the courage" to approach him. So Werthmann confronted Thomann, "who reacted to my remonstrance in a way that reflected his dubiety and his complete lack of self-awareness: he reproached me for refusing to give the 'German greeting' [the Heil Hitler] and attempted to use it against me. It's entirely possible that he denounced me at the time."³¹ Nothing happened to Werthmann, and Thomann continued to serve in the army (by 1942 he was a senior chaplain). The field vicar-general consistently categorized him as an exponent of Nazi ideology. It is difficult to avoid sharing Werthmann's conclusions. A prewar composition that Thomann wrote about the reorganization of pastoral care in the armed forces included phrases such as "Christianity is no opponent of Nazism; the voice of God in Christianity does not contradict His voice in our blood" and

> We hear this natural revelation of God today in what we call "the voice of blood" [die Stimme des Blutes]. The natural disposition of our people and our race is a gift of the Creator. It is not only a gift but also a duty. God has placed this knowledge before our eyes even more clearly today, in [National Socialism] . . . this is the command of the hour for the genuinely devout man: to follow the will of God.[32]

According to Werthmann's notes, Thomann represented a very small number of priests—one can number Rarkowski among them—who gave themselves over to Nazi racial ideology while simultaneously fusing it with their Catholic vocation.[33] Although his pamphlet concerned Werthmann, Thomann was not successful in transforming chaplains into ardent advocates of Nazism. He survived the war and returned to Germany in 1947 after two years in French captivity, eventually settling in the diocese of Rottenburg-Stuttgart.

By and large, Werthmann conceived of the priests mentioned above as disappointments and failures. They had strayed from their vocation, replacing their trust in Providence with addictions such as alcoholism, or they had embraced Nazism too fully, trading subservience to religious authority (God and the Field Bishop's Office) for devotion to the Führer and his movement. Overall, however, such priests who failed to meet the basic requirements for serving as a chaplain constituted a minority. As early as June 1945, Werthmann claimed that "the number of brothers [Mitbrüder] who collapsed during their service or who failed in their priestly conduct, and through this damaged the Catholic Church's reputation, is infinitesimal in comparison with those hundreds of chaplains who embraced their duty."[34] Other chaplains and priests serving in medical companies and hospitals had enough endurance to perform their services well, even when they were given to doubt—moments that occurred not infrequently, according to their wartime journals and postwar reminiscences. Expressions of defeatism were rare, given the murderous discipline that military commanders used to combat such sentiment. Perhaps the most blatantly defeatist comment came in chaplain Bernard S.'s diary. In early 1942, he wrote, "The war has become a giant process of self-destruction [after the invasion of the Soviet Union in June 1941 and the involvement of the United States in December 1941]."³⁵ Later, he went on to say that Stalingrad marked the point at which all confidence in a final victory was broken. All who "had their eyes and ears open knew it was the beginning of the end, though they didn't yet dare to speak aloud of it." At Stalingrad, he wrote, "238,000 German soldiers [were] killed in unimaginable martyrdom . . . [and the mere name of the city] not only alarmed soldiers along the entire front, but plunged them into a state of permanent angst over the possibility of a similar fate."³⁶ Such blunt writing, however accurately it reflected reality, was uncommon.

Seminarians, Faith, and Defeatism

Seminarians in the medical service, who were often younger than chaplains—sometimes by several years—were more prone to defeatism, as revealed in letters they wrote home that slipped past the censors. Moreover, the directors of seminaries expected their seminarians to correspond regularly while in the army, an opportunity that provided time and space to express deep frustrations. The seminarians explored here were all studying at the archdiocesan seminary in Freising, just outside of Munich, when the war broke out. The seminary director, Johann Westermayr, was a loyal correspondent, and many of his students wrote frequently and at length.³⁷ In his earlier letters, F. B. displayed a deep spirituality and patience. As the war continued, his mood noticeably changed. He succumbed to pessimism and blamed a lack of transparency for his agitation: "I have gone in circles, restlessly searching for clarity, but unable to find any. Often, if I ponder the two ways of understanding and look for the right one, in all honesty, I can't decide about either one. So then I decide randomly to go with one or the other. That it's such guesswork agitates me in the smoldering hopelessness of our own situation: What will become of us?"³⁸ A fellow seminarian was even more dejected, relating, "The disorientation of the spirit, and the hatred of the people, appears to grow stronger from day to day. . . . These days stimulate only death and corruption."³⁹ Fatalism was not specific to the devout soldiers of the Wehrmacht, but because of their beliefs they were vulnerable to it, especially when events turned against Germany. Not only was their country suffering defeat after disastrous defeat, but the God in whom they had placed their trust had apparently left them to wallow in the filth and misery of various fronts. Shortly before the Normandy invasion, A. F. wrote to Westermayr, "Fatalism is a stench that permeates the spirit of the time. The piety of the world can probably hold its own in times of affluence. But in the mud and nearness of death, in the trenches here, such piety becomes ludicrous and senseless."[40] In these cases, which represent a minority among seminarians from Freising, religious faith was clearly not helpful in their struggle to maintain optimism. Some actively tried to fight defeatism, such as B. E., who confessed,

> I often feel very downtrodden, depressed, and apathetic . . . an indomitable nostalgia [*Heimweh der Vergangenheit*] is made all the more stronger in that it pervades me, not merely from outside, but from the inside, surging into my heart. I *don't want*, even once, to fall victim to the general dourness that finds its repose in eating, drinking, sleeping, like an animated corpse.[41]

More often, priests and seminarians turned to religion to combat such crippling terror. They used spiritual beliefs to bolster their own courage and that of the soldiers around them. In a 1944 letter to Werthmann during Easter season, Paul Kaminski, a cleric in the medical corps, confided, "It's clear that we have more than a soldierly duty here. What the world thinks of us, lies on us here. The young soldiers are thankful for every word that brings them closer to clarity. Even the youngest soldier has not yet forgotten to pray."[42] It is unsurprising that men living in constant proximity to death would turn to religion. Priests and seminarians found strength and inspiration from their fellow soldiers who retained their faith and hungered for support. More than anything else, this convinced them that their presence was justifiable and indispensable. In the final weeks and days before his death at Stalingrad, Chaplain Gustav Raab confided to his family, "The more horrible it is, the deeper and firmer grows my trust in God. I believe, until the last instant, that God sustains my life."[43] One day later, he reflected on the grim thoughts that united him with the combat soldiers: "It cannot be that I will not see my home again. This thought occupies us hourly, daily. Every other need, deprivation, or exertion is secondary. It's a question of all or nothing. I order myself into God's hands and pray daily the last prayer of my life, to be ready at any instant. My last movement goes to God, that is certain."[44]

Religion did more for priests than simply strengthen their resolve to serve their fellow soldiers. For some priests, their faith helped them overcome the contradictions of serving an anti-Christian regime in a war defined by criminal behavior. Some of these men spoke of the profound doubts and depression that probably affected most soldiers at some point. They identified their faith in God as what kept them from giving in. In his postwar memoirs, Rudolf Unger remembered that he was particularly melancholic on All Souls' Day (2 November) while in Croatia, because he knew that priests in Germany would be saying three masses in honor of the solemn feast day. Unger, however, "wore the gray uniform, and was a soldier in a great war, as were millions of others. I could no longer exercise any priestly function, not even say a mass." He felt terribly alone and could only console himself with the thought that "my God lives, and this God is with me and in me... with this preparation, I fulfilled my duty, as hard and difficult as it sometimes was."[45] Many priests and seminarians were able to continue in the army, even to justify their lack of resistance to Nazism, by citing this faith in God. For some seminarians, it deepened their commitment to a vocational life. "I have learned so much," wrote A. B., "the love for my calling [to the priesthood] has grown clear only in these years. I have seen why the world today needs priests and I am ready to accept that, right now, I have to be a soldier and I have to wait."[46] In this sense, the war, and their participation in it, was a blessing for them.

A. H., another seminarian from Freising, also discovered that his army service led him to a more intimate understanding of his religious life because he was able to use his faith as an anchor for his fellow soldiers. He was "almost convinced that, by being a living example of 'Gaudete in Domino,' many comrades have been brought closer to the Christian religion than by countless words. My desire to study further, to prepare myself... to become a priest, is stronger than ever and grows each day, especially here in the army."[47] Chaplain Wilhelm K. shared a similar revelation in a sermon shortly before his own death: "Something resonates here, gripping those whose faith has suffered some trepidation in the hardness of the war and the battle for life. Now we know, comrades, what the Exemplar wants... 'His heart presides over every battle, to wrest your souls from death and nurture you in your hunger.' "⁴⁸ K. tempered the Bible passage to make it more relevant to the conditions of men in battle, as the original verse is addressed to the just and there is no direct reference to battle. But he took enough comfort from the readings to share them with his men. Chaplain Heinrich Müller was also conscious of how his example lent the soldiers guidance and support, citing reflections from a bishop's sermon: "Each chaplain must ponder how he will find that spiritual energy which is so vital for believers right now. It is the most difficult, most important creative [bildnerische] achievement to anchor the spirits, hearts, and wills of the faithful in the kingdom of God. It is done only with the help of God-given grace, so that the faithful are not wrenched from their spiritual community."⁴⁹

Observers also could see evidence of the priests' newfound spiritual strength and attachment to religious life. Werthmann viewed the experiences of young seminarians and priests that conscription forced into war as constructive by emphasizing the maturity that it gave them, "the mild, benevolent maturity of a fruitful harvest. . . . The steadfastness of a complete, aware man is within you, a man who is certain and secure, who possesses eternity."⁵⁰ The war became an expedient tool, preparing young men to be future priests. Here Werthmann conveniently overlooked its bleaker aspects and the reality that not all priests and seminarians who survived would be so optimistic about their experience. Nor did he acknowledge how closely his commentary echoed the Nazi position about the necessity of war and its maturing influence on those young men fighting it.

Sermons could raise the flagging spirits of troops. Especially at frontline seminars, priests emphasized finding the length, pitch, and subjects for sermons that would best meet the goal of bolstering morale. Chaplain Josef P.'s Christmastime sermon is one such example. The year of the sermon is unknown, but he delivered it after the invasion of the Soviet Union, thus, probably in 1941 or 1942, before the Wehrmacht suffered major defeats. P. acknowledged the grim world around the fighting men and offered a solace that, if grasped, would outlast any material or temporal consolation. He began rhetorically,

> Does God take the suffering away from the earth this night, or douse the fires of war? Will he guide those at the front back to their loved

ones waiting at home, will he give redemption to the dishonored, health to the wounded, will he send us victory and peace? No, comrades, none of this will happen. *The holy night is no fairy tale, no magical night;* in this night, hard reality remains.

He affirmed that those soldiers who felt the most disoriented were those who had abandoned belief in God and had no spiritual refuge. Such a man no longer had a permanent foothold in the world. It was not simple homesickness that caused morale to plummet in this situation, it was a "homesickness for God." How was one to solve it? P. admitted that the solution was not easy. It was a question of honest, lived faith:

> The smell of pine blows away, the lights go out, and you view tomorrow as doubly bleak. But he who celebrates this hour in the deepest, truest belief in Christmas, he takes with him a treasure, for the Christ Child will surely go with him. Wherever this Child lies within us, there lies a light, too. Even when all other lights go out, there is still peace in this bellicose world.[51]

Such sermons probably had a limited appeal. For chaplains in the army, their target audience was always their own men, and among them, only those who chose to attend divine services. Customarily, they spared little thought for foreign civilians, and prisoners of war entered their vision only peripherally unless one was a chaplain stationed at a prison.[52] OKH regulations restricting chaplains' interactions with foreign civilians and POWs reinforced this. Very little time was available for philosophizing about the deeper meaning of the war. Here, military command and spiritual authority met over a common goal: supporting the morale of the troops was the most important task of a chaplain.

Obedience, Nationalism, and the Idea of a Just War

Little direct evidence exists that priests—chaplains or otherwise—spent much time debating the war's justness during the war itself. One chaplain stressed the danger of writing anything, let alone speaking to others. Johann K. insisted that, with regard to philosophizing about bigger questions, "you didn't have much time, and you always had to be careful, because you never knew what the other men stood for."[53] Lorenz W. echoed this sentiment, confirming that discussions of the justness of war simply were not possible.[54] The presence of the NSFOs made priests very cautious about what they said. Wilhelm W. recalled that he entertained questions of a just war "with [only] this one priest, Tölner, with whom I could say anything. But on the whole, one really had to watch out. It was Christmas, the last year, and an NSFO came to our division . . . and he spoke with such polish that no one knew whether he was for Hitler or against him."[55] Only in a series of postwar interviews conducted with surviving veteran chaplains did they entertain the question of *bellum iustum*, or the justness of the war in which they were involved.

The theory of the right to war (*ius ad bellum*) and its parallel principle, just conduct in war (*ius in bello*), occupies an integral part of military ethics. The Christian churches have been deeply involved in its development since the writings of Augustine of Hippo, the fourth-century Church father.[56] Building on earlier theories of war by Cicero and the neo-Platonists, Augustine offered a conception of war intimately tied to divine command and state authority. A just war was a defensive war in which violence was a last resort to avenge injuries or regain what was wrongfully taken. Its ultimate aim was lasting peace. War was justly waged "when doing so constitute[d] the best available remedy for righting injustices."[57] Augustine also addressed the moral status of soldiers, the agents of the state who carried out its will, about which he was unequivocal. "In killing the enemy," he stated, "the soldier is an agent of the law; thus he merely fulfills a duty."[58] Even if the state sovereign giving the order is not in the right, or the state is not a just state, the soldier is excused from moral responsibility because a soldier's task is to obey.[59]

Augustine's theories about just war are clearly Christian-centered. For today's readers they offer ambiguous explanations and problematic reasoning. By definition, just wars are waged by virtuous men, that is, men who have a close relationship with God. This implies that wars waged by nonbelievers are inherently unjust, no matter the extent to which they honor the principles of just war in other ways.[60] Moreover, Augustine's argument leads to the discomfiting conclusion that all wars on earth are providentially just because God has allowed them to occur, even if the manner in which they unfold—waged by imperfect humans—

becomes unjust. Augustine argued, "For God's providence constantly uses war to correct and chasten the corrupt morals of mankind, as it also uses such afflictions to train men in a righteous and laudable way of life."[61] Was this the criterion that priests and seminarians used when they considered the justness of the cause for which they fought and the battles in which they were engaged? Or did they prefer to trust that a higher authority had control of the situation?

The Catholic just war doctrine had not changed radically from its Augustinian origins when the Second World War broke out.[62] However, Augustine was not the sole voice on the matter. In addition to papal writings up to and through the war years, the moral theology taught in seminary classrooms explicated the just war concept. For popes such as Pius X, Benedict XV, and Pius XI, who addressed morality and just war, self-defense was central to just cause. Thus war was morally justifiable if used as a shield and not a sword, if a nation was defending itself against an evil threatening to destroy Christian society.[63] In such a situation, the state's citizens had a moral obligation to render service on behalf of the community's common good. Unconditional, uncritical obedience to legitimate authority was not only encouraged, but also expected.[64] This interpretation of war was compatible with the nationalist proclivities of many Catholic Germans. Their priests and bishops wasted no opportunity to root out pacifism lurking in their flocks by stressing obedience, supplication, and a readiness for sacrifice in a national defensive war effort. Humility was the essential virtue of a Catholic soldier.[65] For priests and seminarians facing conscription, this also echoed their spiritual training. They had learned submission to God's will and readiness to provide pastoral care for Catholic souls even unto death, including death on the field of battle.

The rise of totalitarian regimes in Nazi Germany and Soviet Russia led Popes Pius XI and Pius XII to formulate unprecedented limitations on state authority, which delimited the just war concept. Pius XI acknowledged the rights of individual citizens vis-à-vis the state and the community, stressing in the 1937 papal encyclical *Mit brennender Sorge* that the needs of the individual and those of society were complementary, not antagonistic.[66] Six years earlier he had introduced the idea of "subsidiarity" to restrain the state, insisting that the state's direct involvement was limited to where it was absolutely vital. Social organizations were to take on tasks and responsibilities to prevent the consolidation of power in a large government.[67] Pius XII, who in his first six years as pontiff presided over the Second World War, took this as far as he dared without openly condemning any belligerent nation. He upheld the centuries-long tradition of papal neutrality since nearly all combatant countries featured Catholics among their populations. Pius was also anxious to serve as mediator in any potential negotiations. Nonetheless, in his 1942 Christmas message and repeated in his 1945 Christmas address, he asserted that one of the primary goals of the state was to assist individuals in the maintenance of moral order. War was justified only to preserve the common good.[68] Coercive force was permissible only to combat an evil that would threaten humanity's moral and spiritual development and its quest toward perfection. If such an evil did not exist, then the use of coercive force was wrong. This line of reasoning proved malleable enough that strong-minded Christians applied just war theory to Nazi Germany's "defensive" battle against the threatening godlessness of the Soviet Union. At the same time, the Nazi regime, which the pope never explicitly named, clearly met many of his descriptions, including the overreach of the state, the infringement on human rights, and the use of coercive force beyond the preservation of the common good.

Whether and to what extent, in the heat of battle, deprivation, and constant suffering and death, clergy in the Wehrmacht had the time to reflect on the justness of the war they were fighting is unknown. Their written testimony does not elucidate the degree to which these priests had been educated about the subject. While most priests and seminarians hinted at a basic familiarity with the topic, they spoke on the basis of their personal experience and reflections. All who addressed the question in postwar interviews or memoirs condemned the war as unjust, or at least unjustifiable. Yet it is remarkable how many qualified their condemnation. Martin Z. chose his words cautiously, avoiding saying explicitly that the war had not been just. Instead, he stated, "We found the war to be needless, there was no basis for it. Whether I went so far at the time as to say so, that the war into which we were driven was criminal. . . . I didn't go so far as to say that. But [it was] a terrible, wicked thing that simply shouldn't have been."[69] Even forty-five years after the fact, he could not assert that the war had been criminal. Josef P. was more comfortable in speaking directly, averring, "To me it was clear from the beginning that the war was not just. At the time I immersed myself in the schemes that Hitler had machinated about the war. And this bosh [*Gefasel*] about *Lebensraum*, brought about by the constrictions of the Versailles Treaty, I couldn't use it as an excuse to justify the war."[70] With similar conviction, Richard S. rendered his judgment of the war in notes for a postwar interview. He borrowed "the prophetic words" of a comrade, who declared, "This war was unjust from the beginning, it is calamity, and in the end it will bring downfall."[71] Alfons Mende was unequivocal as well, saying, "It was completely clear [that it was not a just war], it was clear from the outset. I was an opponent, though I never expressed myself. Everything was silent."[72] Some, like Karl S., found silence to be sufficient, as though the lack of articulation obviously indicated rejection: "In my sermons, I was merely silent about the regime. That was plain enough."[73]

Georg Paulus shared these conclusions, but he admitted that he said nothing at the time: "I never had the slightest illusion about it, this was an unjust war. And this point of view only got stronger over the course of my time in the army. But what use would it have been for me to be provocative about it? The most insignificant remark could cost one's life."[74] Friedrich D. echoed this helplessness and fear. He declared that it was a question he had asked himself constantly in order to justify his service. He also felt that the "simple soldier" was not qualified to decide whether the war was just. He then became ambivalent about the issue. He compared the Second World War with the Great War, both of which had "many roots," and after naming Hitler the chief aggressor [*Hauptmissetäter*], he argued that all the war's participants were equally guilty: "Who can say: who is guilty in war? In the end? Totally guilty? For there was the thing about the Versailles Treaty. That was a great injustice for the German people. [Using] that, Hitler regained some justice and courage for the Germans. Unfortunately in a bad way."[75] That priests made these statements might be shocking, or at least bewildering, if one expected them to condemn the war in its totality, especially long after the genocide perpetrated in the name of the German people came to light. However, these responses—the excuses of the futility in the face of criminality and of the impossibility of assigning guilt in times of war—are unique neither to German priests nor to war. Distinctions among Catholic chaplains, priests, seminarians, and other soldiers collapse at the point at which they all self-identified as German.

If no one among these clergy or clergy-in-training considered the war just, then why did they serve? Few, if any, questioned the justness of the war explicitly during the war years. Had they done so, they likely would have arrived at one of two understandings. One was that the war was necessary to right the wrongs inflicted by the Treaty of Versailles some twenty years earlier. The second was that it was a defensive war against the lethal forces of Bolshevism. They lacked genuine affection for or belief in the goals of the regime, but priests and seminarians still had every incentive to cooperate. The Vatican remained neutral, German spiritual and state leaders insisted the war was defensive and necessary, and they faced imprisonment and execution if they disobeyed the conscription order. Moreover, expressions of distaste for Nazism and rejection of its ideology came mostly in postwar memoirs or interviews, several decades after the end of the war.

The postwar interviews occurred several decades after the war. This was enough time for anyone who had harbored Nazi sympathies to change his mind about those sentiments. Priests in particular would have found themselves in sensitive situations. As figures of postwar moral authority, they would have been expected to have seen clearly the evil that Nazism represented and to denounce the war as unjust, especially after the turbulent debate about the "clean" Wehrmacht in German historiography.[76] But the paradox remains that they acknowledged an unjust war at the same time that they argued for the necessity of their service in that war.

Rudolf P. most fully embodies this contradiction in his wartime journals, which were later published as a book. As the catastrophe at Stalingrad unfolded, he wrote that soldiers constantly blamed God. He bridled with indignation at this charge and retorted that God had nothing to do with it. The inferno there had been created by men. He condemned those responsible for the losses at Stalingrad for their criminality and irresponsibility, and excused those who fought their wars, asserting, "The politicians' keywords are multifarious: freedom, living space, party. But it's always about power. Thus people go astray in the insanity of war. Our men at the front stopped fighting long ago for Hitler and the Nazis. Rather, they were convinced that they could protect their *Heimat*, their families, by what they were doing."[77] He affirmed that "our men," the simple soldiers, had no evil in their hearts. In fighting for their families and their homeland, P. suggested, they exculpated themselves from the moral and political ramifications of their actions.

Such exoneration may have worked similarly for priests and seminarians. They may have seen themselves as politically neutral without realizing that political neutrality was not possible in the Third Reich, not even within the ranks of the Wehrmacht. Martin S. knew that "through our activity in this strange place, we can give to the soldiers a piece of *Heimat*."[78] A word with no English equivalent, *Heimat* encapsulated the individual German's relationship with his community and homeland. The term expressed the feeling of an almost unbreakable bond with families back home. Drawn from childhood and predating Nazism, the term was synonymous with "Germany" and "Fatherland." It contrasted with the foreignness of "the outland" and "the front."[79] *Heimat* was a recurrent theme for chaplains. The word served as an emotion-inducing tool to which both soldiers and priests readily responded, regardless of how far physically they were separated from Germany. To preserve this bond, they willingly broke many rules. Josef P. responded affirmatively when a postwar interviewer suggested that chaplains, both Catholic and Protestant, served as a kind of hinge between homeland and soldiers:

> An effusive thanks was present in almost every letter [we received from civilians back home]. Repeatedly: we're praying for you and we'll send you packages. A giant congregation formed across the entire Reich. A congregation of men with whom one was connected intimately out of common concern for the young lads, out of common suffering. For the party, that was obviously anything but endearing. So then came new regulations: the chaplain can have nothing to do with family members [of soldiers], it's not part of his duties. But I continued anyway, and it went well.[80]

Werthmann was inclined to think in comparable terms about the meaning of the war and his own role. Such reflections are indicative of two things. The first is a faith deeply rooted in the Catholic understanding of suffering, in that even the most severe suffering has meaning. The second is a terrible self-centeredness, as though their authors were determined to affix some meaning to the war's devastation, regardless of the cost, who it neglected, or how it manipulated reality. Werthmann wrote,

> The war was a terrible burden, but it came from without like a thunderstorm and lashed us in the face. The suffering [that this brought] was liberating, uplifting, refreshing, and purifying. Its bitterness retrieved something of that great and deep and glorifying happiness that we see, so often unassuming, in the men who are severely tested and devastated and yet who carry on calmly and bravely.[81]

Werthmann also cited the "great Christian legacy" that chaplain participation in the war had preserved. Such a legacy served as a counterpoint to "the proclaimed eloquence of the party, embodied by the NSFO, and . . . the seductive power of ideological [weltanschaulicher] postulations."[82] A seminarian wrote to Cardinal von Faulhaber in Munich that the war experience had benefited him tremendously, claiming, "From this experience, we theology students have only drawn closer to our vocation. For this we can't thank God enough. So something good has come, even out of the horrible events of the war."[83] A focus on Nazism's enmity for Catholicism enabled Werthmann and the chaplains to find reasons for their behavior. Their ability to withstand the pressures and strains of war both physically and spiritually also encouraged such rationalizations. But these excuses also reveal an extraordinary narrow-mindedness, as if the only two contestants on the battlefield were party and Church.

Karl S., who above described his wartime silence as a protest against the regime, acknowledged the minor role that nationalism played. He elaborated, "Certainly I prayed for *Volk*, Führer and Fatherland every now and then, using our military hymnals—that was relatively bearable. But I couldn't risk any reproach because of my activities as a chaplain."[84] Other chaplains were more effusive about their attachment to Germany, their Fatherland. They learned to separate the Nazi regime from the army and the war. Richard S. explained in a postwar interview,

> Somehow or other, "Fatherland" is a value that's worth fighting for. "Fatherland" was not understood to be the same as the party. The two terms were distinct from each other. One could differentiate between them. And one could act on behalf of the Fatherland. It was a more encompassing concept, because by this word, you meant your home, your own family, your kinfolk, your livelihood, and everything like that [*und was alles*].[85]

While *Führer*, as a reference to Hitler, may not have resonated emotionally for priests and seminarians, *Volk*, Fatherland, and *Heimat* were older terms with deep cultural meaning with which most Germans, including Catholic clergy, identified positively.[86] One did not have to be a Nazi to be a German nationalist. Moreover, priests identified as both German and Catholic. They felt an obligation to defend their *Heimat*, *Volk*, and Fatherland with their lives just as urgently as they felt it their duty to attend to the spiritual needs of Wehrmacht soldiers. This dual obligation may even have increased amenability to the conscription order among clergy, if military service was for one's country and fellow Catholics, and not to the party that ran it.

Although most of these men distanced themselves from Nazism because of their religious principles, nationalist impulses could render their reasoning quite Nazi-like. This is shown in references they made to the values of blood, sacrifice, and greatness. Seminarian A. M. wrote, "The future of our beloved *Volk* and Fatherland must be secured through the blood of so many young warriors ... only that which is eked out through blood is truly valuable and augurs enduring prosperity. Maybe our people are destined yet for some kind of total greatness?"[87] While one must be careful not to overstate the affinities between Nazism and Catholicism, especially during the war years, even religious men were not immune to expressing radical nationalist sentiments.

Others saw the defense of home and Fatherland as a battle to preserve Christianity. The educational backgrounds of these men, their pride as Germans, and their conception of military service as a kind of crusade encouraged a fusion of nationalism and religious sentiment. Their religious leaders reinforced this fusion, producing a worldview in which Germandom and Christianity were inseparable and inherently superior to others they encountered on the battlefield:

> Our history is intimately tied to Christianity, *more than any other country or culture*.... Thus there is a self-evident duty in the "yes" we say to serving the German Fatherland. It is a holy duty at that, because this "yes" conforms to a genuine cultural mission [*Sendungsauftrag*].[88]

One front-line seminar in the East encouraged its chaplains to equate the fight for a terrestrial homeland with the fight for the eternal homeland of God. One lecture here came close to imbuing the Nazi keyword of *Lebensraum* with religious meaning. A lecture at a different seminar presented the fight for the Fatherland as a fight for Christ.[89] In a seminar lecture given in Warsaw, the senior chaplain paraphrased General Friedrich von Rabenau, insisting that soldiers needed an active relationship with God above all. Otherwise the war would lose its moral justification, and "without thinking toward the beyond, the soldier who stands daily in the face of death will not be able to cope."[90] One seminarian found confirmation of the "crusading" aspect of the war before the Germans even invaded the Soviet Union. He wrote to seminary director Westermayr from France in September 1940,

> I know that nowhere in the world are cathedrals and brothels standing so close together, that nowhere else are the gaps between classes so dire, that the most Christian country of all, France, has no grounds upon which to designate itself as the preserver of Christian culture. If somebody has to defend Christian culture, well, we're already doing that. German soldiers speak less about Christianity, but display more of it. We found smutty literature in the knapsacks of French soldiers, which really puts them in a bad light. Marshall Pétain himself appears to understand the roots of the French downfall: *Peu d'enfants* [Few children]![91]

Westermayr responded to another seminarian two years later, saying that he was "personally very nationalistically tuned, and oriented toward the Fatherland. I am proud that so many of our students are taking an active part in the decisive battle for the Fatherland."[92]

Vocational Conviction in the Wehrmacht's Ranks

Not all priests and seminarians understood their duty as a religious mission. Nor did they all find motivation by infusing their time in the

Wehrmacht with spiritual meaning. Some felt that the soldiers themselves made their work vital. They cited the camaraderie, sometimes quite strong, that emerged with men whom they otherwise might never have known.[93] Martin Z. never regretted his service as a chaplain for several reasons, explaining, "I learned how to approach different people in more sensitive ways, from simple soldiers to officers. I learned to work closely with Protestant colleagues. I became acquainted with other countries and peoples, and only thenceforth did I value much of what I brought with me from home."[94] Like most clerics, Josef K. disclaimed any military motivations. He emphasized that he had been conscripted as a medical orderly. He welcomed his promotion into the chaplaincy because there "at least I could offer the soldiers something on the basis of my vocation. I could write a book on my encounters with the wounded alone."[95] Other priests remembered the necessity of caution when speaking with other soldiers. Friedrich Dörr recalled that, despite having to be careful, the chaplain was in a natural position to be "a good conversationalist, with whom one could speak about the difficulties of the military situation or Hitler's regime.... If soldiers had revealed everything that their chaplain had said, I would have been hung dozens of times over. But they kept mum."[96]

Nor was it only chaplains who experienced such affirmation from other soldiers. As a priest, Benedict Häring was conscripted into the medical service in November 1939 and survived the war in this role. He stressed in his published postwar memoir, "It is hard to imagine two environments more diverse than that of the monastery major seminary where I had studied and taught for seven years and the rough environment of Hitler's army." Nonetheless he discovered quickly "a strong affinity between the priestly and the medical ministries" and felt he had an advantage over chaplains, who were constrained by "officialdom. In my activities as medical aide, I met the men in their daily needs and could minister to them in either of my capacities, as priest or as medical helper."[97] Yet others disagreed with Häring. One seminarian stated in a letter to Westermayr during the war, "Today this battle is more an inner battle, one that builds character and strengthens courage. In this way, time in the military is the best school for future officers of Christ."[98] Other seminarians found confirmation of their priestly vocation while serving in the military. As A. B. wrote, "I have seen how the world today needs priests, and I am calm, knowing that for now I must be a soldier and can wait until I achieve my aspiration."[99] J. H. was even more explicit, declaring, "My wish to continue studying to prepare myself for the greater vocation and become a priest is stronger than before. It grows each day, even here in the army."[100] Absent further personal information, it is difficult to ascertain what made Haring different from his colleagues: his age, the fact that he was already ordained, his personality, perhaps his specific wartime experiences. The divergence underscores the fact that the Wehrmacht was anything but a monolithic institution. Even the clergy had widely dissimilar interpretations of the war and their role in it.

When asked about their experiences concerning the influence of Nazi propaganda, seminarians and priests contested the extent to which Nazism penetrated the rank and file of the Wehrmacht. Their willingness to address the subject emerged only in postwar interviews. Of all the letters and reports perused in this book, only two remark on Nazism during the war itself. One was a seminarian, T. G. P., who was brave enough to allude, in rather convoluted fashion, to the Nazi worldview in late 1944:

> Even now, many comrades are having their eyes opened. They perceive that [this war] has nothing to do with the eternal paradise that was put on for them in better [prewar] days. [But] Christ's cross is more present in the sufferings of this time than the . . . muddled myth of blood and race.[101]

T. G. P.'s letter included a speculation that some soldiers who had abandoned the Church earlier now sought to return to the faith of their childhood, which "was once dear and valuable." But his feelings about Nazism are evident. Josef Perau was more oblique in his wartime journal. He was in Kiel on the fateful day of 1 May 1945 when news of Hitler's suicide swept through the ranks. He recalled, "A young lieutenant sprang up and declared, 'This is what we've been waiting for!' We quickly pushed him back because such expressions are still quite dangerous."[102]

Nazism, Atrocities, and the Wehrmacht

Rupert Ritzer represented both the naiveté of this viewpoint, about a Wehrmacht dissociated from Nazism, as well as the complications of asserting that the Wehrmacht was entirely Nazified. In December 1941, while preparing an old schoolroom for Christmas services, he discovered a giant swastika, which he quickly removed "so that our crucifix wasn't in accordance with the swastika." In January 1942, his next diary entry, he reported, "Guard Paul S. reported me to the company leader for removing the swastika in the school. [I was r]eported [then] to the company chief, who is well disposed toward me, so I got away with a warning. In normal cases, court-martial with death sentence."[103] Ritzer encountered the hard line of political allegiance to which many soldiers held—if not loyalty to Führer and Nazism, then loyalty to *Volk* and Fatherland—as well as considerable leniency when a higher-up overlooked his action. Ritzer recognized the rarity of this reaction, marveling that he had narrowly escaped execution. Whether he knew before removing the swastika of the likelihood of being reported is unknown. It is the only time he mentioned in his journal that he broke regulations.

Others retreated into naiveté, prejudice, and willful ignorance when confronted with the lethal living conditions for foreign populations in the East. Very few seminarians mentioned Jews explicitly in their letters. One exception was H. R., who witnessed an atrocity but, in translating it to Westermayr, displayed both a profound lack of comprehension of what he had witnessed and the devastating impact of dehumanization at the front: "The sniper war behind the front continues, in its most recent manifestation as a civil war between the Ukrainians and the Jews [!] . . . [The Jews] had committed egregious atrocities against the Ukrainians, who did wrong by apparently not wanting to join the Bolsheviks. The Jews had to exhume the mutilated bodies of the Ukrainians, and one witnessed a horror for which sanity cannot account. The revenge was fearsome, it became a virtual manhunt."[104] According to H. R.'s testimony, the German presence in the area had nothing to do with Ukrainian-Jewish relations or the "civil war" in which they were seemingly embroiled. He betrayed no emotional reaction to the brutality with which the Jews were treated.

Very few priests accepted that the army they worked in was complicit with the Nazi regime, especially the crimes perpetrated on the Eastern Front. To acknowledge this fact might have challenged their justifications for serving, for it would be tacit admission that they had also served Hitler and his Nazi Party. Josef Perau was the only one who wrote during the war about the collusion of the Wehrmacht in war crimes and atrocities. He deserves to be quoted from his published memoirs at length. Stationed in March 1944 in Rudobelka (Oktyabrsky, Belarus), he wrote:

> When one approaches the camp, one is presented with an image of horror. The entire field is saturated with the belongings of these people, which they can no longer carry. I was completely unprepared to face such terrible things. Through a fine drizzle I was returning, unsuspecting, to the main hospital as night fell. At first I felt the change in a peculiarly nauseating sound that I couldn't more closely identify until, at some distance, I detected the camp. The uninterrupted, muted keening of many voices rose from it to heaven. And then I saw, the body of an old man right in front of me, being towed off like a piece of meat. A cord had been tied around his legs. An old woman lay dead in the lane, fresh bullet hole in the forehead. I was instructed to continue by a member of the military police, who pointed out a pair of bundles covered in mud: dead children, over whom he had laid a pillow. Women, unable to carry their children further, had left them behind. But they were shot, as absolutely everyone here is "knocked off," because of sickness ... A medical officer to whom I feverishly wanted to report [the inhuman treatment and murder of foreign civilians] sent me away, saying, "Father, leave that to us. I myself shot a pair of helpless children for mercy's sake. Germany will become a civilized nation [*Kulturvolk*] again when the war is won." Very few talk like this in the regular armed forces. The soldiers who don't oppose these things on ethical grounds think, what will happen to us when we fall into captivity? What will happen to Germany if the war is lost? It's said that the SD carried out these actions, *but the troops are at least marginally involved.* Divine service in Portschje [*sic?*] had to be cancelled because the troops were occupied with "evacuating" civilians.... From some distance today I saw a general riding alongside the field of misery. In light of this, what's going on in higher military circles? In the blink of an eye I thought, I should step up to him and demand an accounting for it, in the name of God. But spirit alone wasn't sufficient, so I merely proclaimed my disgust openly in conversations.... This war is a horrific catastrophe for self-ruling humanism [*autonomen Humanismus*].[105]

What Perau witnessed obviously disturbed him: civilians and noncombatants killed or forced to live in conditions designed to hasten their deaths. But he blamed an abstract concept implying the absence of God rather than the very real individuals—his fellow countrymen—who were responsible. And though he condemned these actions in what were probably private conversations with individuals he trusted, he never complained to anyone beyond the lowly medical officer he approached. The horror, in addition to the knowledge that the army was "at least marginally" complicit, was not enough to induce him to stop serving or to register a formal protest with a superior officer.

The Crusade against Bolshevism

Some evidence suggests that, in the larger context of the war against the Soviet Union, chaplains, priests, and seminarians did not perceive the horrible acts committed to be atrocities as such but rather as necessary defensive measures against a lethal enemy. Since the Russian Revolution, the Catholic Church had reacted to the threat of communism and its Russian variant, Bolshevism, with fear and aggressive vigilance. The ideology's deep and open hostility to religion had been no secret since the mid-nineteenth century, when Marx wrote, "Religion is the sigh of the oppressed creature, the heart of a heartless world, just as it is the spirit of a spiritless situation. It is the *opium* of the people."[106] Lenin attacked religion in Russia after Russia had withdrawn from the First World War. The attack was motivated, in part, by the Orthodox Church's close ties to the tsarist regime and, in part, by the specific brand of Marxist revolution to which he was committed, necessitating the destruction of institutional religion. In short order, the government appropriated the physical structures of the church and either destroyed or put them to secular use. The regime imprisoned, exiled, or simply shot members of the clergy. Religiosity itself could not be eradicated, but it "disappear[ed] underground, or [was] diverted into shallower affective channels, and focused on false gods, the mightiest of whom gave socialism one omnipresent, pock-marked, smiling face."[107] No wonder, then, that Russians were so overjoyed to meet priests, albeit Catholic ones in German army uniforms, during the Second World War.

The German Catholic Church was in a particularly vulnerable position due to the twofold problem of the country's proximity to the Soviet Union and the strength of Germany's interwar Socialist and Communist parties. Church authorities responded quickly and vigorously with a campaign of denunciation and calls to resist the ideology. This definitive anti-Bolshevik attitude shared common ground with the Nazis. The Nazi Party had its own agenda concerning institutional religion, but the Church, from the pope down, was happy to cooperate with it as the lesser of two evils. A pastoral letter that the German bishops released a mere four days after the invasion of the Soviet Union relayed blessings to "our soldiers, your husbands, sons, and brothers in the field, who are performing unforgettable feats of heroic bravery and enduring profound stress. The war demands exertion and sacrifice from you all."[108] Again in December, after the Wehrmacht failed to claim decisive victory in the East and after the popular furor, unleashed when Münster Cardinal Clemens von Galen denounced the Aktion T-4 "euthanasia" program with a series of sermons, had ebbed, the bishops reaffirmed their stance on the war against the Soviet Union in a memorandum that read,

> With gratification we follow the battle against the power of Bolshevism, about which we German bishops have warned German Catholics and urged them to be alert in numerous pastoral letters between 1921 and 1936. The regime knows this. Because of her categorical rejection of it, the Church is still the strongest spiritual force with which to combat Bolshevism. The spiritual guidance exercised by her priests is the most effective defense in the battle against the teachings, principles and goals of Bolshevism.[109]

The Church in Germany had had its share of problems with the Nazi regime. But up to the end of 1941, at least, its leaders remained committed to accommodating Hitler's government on the home front. Church leaders displayed no reticence about assisting Hitler's armies actively in the fight against the much larger threat, Bolshevism.

Strikingly, the seminarians feverishly advocated the idea that Bolshevism needed to be crushed using all means necessary. This young, impressionable "social generation" was educated not necessarily to see Nazism as a danger to the Catholic Church but to identify Soviet communism as an enemy that could destroy Christian—and German—culture. Some expressed anguish over losing comrades in the battle "against the world enemy of Christianity and also of our German culture," while others keenly felt the obligation to fight: "As a German and a Christian I have to fight, and gladly, against Bolshevism and godlessness."[110] Their language underlines once more the extent to which Germany and Christianity constituted a single vital object worth dying for; one seminarian wrote, "As long as holy love glows within us, Bolshevism will never violate the soil of our homeland, and no one will discover us weak. Above all, our dead admonish us ceaselessly to never tire in the battle for Christ and homeland."[111] The responsibility to honor the sacrifice of fallen German soldiers by continuing the (hopeless) battle against monstrous Bolshevism was evident in F. H.'s declaration, "It is the greatest transgression of Bolshevism that so many German soldiers must sacrifice their lives in order to restore justice to victory."[112]

Among seminarians, the war in the East against Bolshevism was most frequently identified as a crusade ordained by God and for God's glory: "With each step that takes us further forward against Bolshevism, we work for God's greater honor."[113] Such statements showed how anti-Bolshevik propaganda, both Christian and Nazi, had permeated the seminary and how closely it was entwined with antisemitism. "Hopefully this bloody battle will soon find a good end," G. G. wrote to Westermayr, "and with it, Bolshevism will be extirpated once and for all. Otherwise, the many victims of this crusade against the world enemy would have died in vain. Indeed, it would be the greatest tragedy if the godlessness of the East led us to battle at the same time that religion was proscribed at home."[114] L. S. wrote from Melitopol in 1942, "Two worldviews will slug it out here in a battle of civilization; the civilization of the Christian world against the Judeo-Bolshevik will to destruction, the battle of the individual against collectivization."[115] Franz Kurz, not a seminarian but a devout soldier who wrote about his experiences to Cardinal von Faulhaber, described his conviction during the Russian campaign:

> The longer one is in Russia, the more one adopts the conviction that, in this place, one battles Satan and his helpers in this world. This

power must not only be fought, but totally destroyed. If the sacrifices are difficult to make and moroseness besets us, the idea remains that here we are charged with a holy task, with the preservation of the kingdom of Christ and of occidental culture.[116]

Another seminarian lamented that the war was not over, but he insisted with his next breath, "We are ready to make any sacrifice that is required of us. Bolshevism will be broken into pieces, and that is the only possibility! Only the war can overthrow this system."[117] To them as well as to the soldiers with whom they marched, the material conditions they encountered as they made their way into Russian territory proved that Bolshevism was the most destructive force in existence. "The impoverishment, the depletion is terrible," wrote seminarian J. M., "every village has a church [in Polish territory], but here [in Russia], such cannot be found anywhere, for even in our own quarters, it exists only as a ruin."[118] The two-pronged influence of Nazi propaganda and Church antipathy, which priests and seminarians reinforced, propelled devout soldiers to understand the war with the Soviet Union in this way. One soldier wrote to Cardinal von Faulhaber from the East in 1942, "There's no church here. That's the tragic lot of these people. God has been torn from their hearts. This is why so many German soldiers must lay down their lives, in order to help justice triumph."[119]

Another seminarian regretted that he was unable to better gauge Bolshevism's effects on the Russians themselves. Much of his experience of the Soviet Union, like that of many Germans, was limited to the open fields and evacuated villages, bereft of inhabitants, in which they took cover. The civilians he met presented a perplexing blend of astonishing elements: "What is contrary to us is nothing of the kind for them, because they live their lives in the depths, where antitheses unite everything."[120] Such remarks were condescending (bolstering notions of German cultural superiority) and tended to confirm preexisting anti-Russian prejudices. Others were conditioned by years of propaganda to see the Russians literally as human personifications of an ideology intent on destroying the Christian faith. Johann Lechner wrote from the Eastern Front,

World without God, world without morality, world of vengeance and avarice brings me ever nearer to God, in Whose love order has its origins.... Now, saved from the Soviet hell, we must fight on against a netherworld of brutish men who are possessed with the goal of tearing belief in God out of the hearts of men. But they will be completely destroyed. May the love of God always inspire me to remain a true, brave, and courageous fighter, true to the oath to battle for Führer, *Volk* and Fatherland.[121]

Not everyone witnessed such chaos and emptiness. Chapter 3 recounted the interactions of some men with Russian civilians and their admiration that religion had been preserved. H. O. was among them, writing to Westermayr, "I've found again and again holy cards and images of Christ in houses, and even on prisoners I've found religious cards that were undoubtedly of Russian origin. The religiosity of this people has not been completely eradicated."[122] Russia, then, proved to be a multifarious entity that confirmed some stereotypes and contradicted others. One thing remained clear: Bolshevism was a force that required destruction before it could obliterate faith in God. The German armies had come to do precisely that. In the hearts and minds of these young seminarians, and no doubt many priests and soldiers as well, other considerations were secondary. In this sense, they might have reasoned that the invasion of the Soviet Union was an Augustinian defensive war and, therefore, just.

* * *

Without doubt, the war, particularly on the Eastern Front, had a tremendous impact on how priests and seminarians viewed their vocation and religious faith as well as their responsibilities as soldiers and spiritual guides. Most men found ways to salvage something positive: noble self-sacrifice, a strengthening of vocational conviction, a satisfaction in seeing an unpleasant, arduous task through to the bitter end. Countless other soldiers surely followed the same path, preferring to categorize military service between 1939 and 1945 as a defense of *Heimat* and Fatherland, not necessarily of Nazism.[123] Nazi ideology was not an inspiring doctrine for many of these men at the beginning of the war. Certainly in the last years of the war, as the Wehrmacht suffered defeat after disastrous defeat, the homeland was physically devastated, and rumors of the murderous fates of the Jews, Soviet POWs, and countless civilians hardened into fact, faith in a higher moral authority could be infinitely more consoling.

Perhaps the alternatives to such rationalizations proved too overwhelming for them to accept. They were not prepared to believe that their presence had facilitated the crimes committed, under the guise of war, by the very soldiers who had need of them, nor admit that the only morally correct response to conscription was true martyrdom, a speedy trial ending in execution. They believed as Werthmann did. After the final defeat in 1945, he spoke to German youth as follows:

> Maybe it was a false offering for which [the soldiers] presented themselves, a false obedience, but their hearts were pure.... Many believed that it was for the Fatherland, and they didn't realize that it was for the party. But many didn't even believe this. Many knew that it was about something unjust and they hated that they were sent. But they believed in the soldierly duty to obey, and they obeyed.[124]

The intentions regarding pastoral care were good. But the consequences of focusing on intentions alone constituted a betrayal of one of Christianity's most famous imperatives, "Love thy neighbor as thyself." They shared with many lay German soldiers different motivations, including naiveté, indifference, prejudice, and fear. Such stimuli may explain their failure to act on behalf of their Jewish, Polish, or Russian, non-Catholic neighbors. Moreover, their spiritual and pastoral training in moral theology did not provide them with a language that called for them to defend non-Catholics to the same degree as Catholics. The example of their spiritual leaders, both on the front lines and at home, likewise failed to demonstrate that dissent, opposition, or outright resistance could be an option. The same moral theology that stressed the primacy of Catholic souls informed their behavior as well. These were priests and seminarians living in dark times, in extreme situations. Despite their vocation, they proved as fallible as the common man. They were also as patriotic as lay Germans and went to defend the Fatherland from an evil greater than anything German *Kultur* had faced before. This nationalist impulse proved as durable as any faith-based reasoning.

Their persistent postwar silence about the crimes of the Wehrmacht, which will be the subject of the conclusion, is a different matter. The vast majority of men who spoke after the war about their experiences participated in this silence. Their unflappable conviction that their service neither represented support for the regime nor enabled the atrocities the military perpetrated, and their inability, or refusal, to *understand* the full ramifications of this service is, in many ways, the most troubling aspect of their wartime roles.

5

THE GERMAN CATHOLIC CHURCH AND THE REALITY OF DEFEATED GERMANY

The story ends in 1945 with an unconditional surrender and Germany occupied by multiple foreign armies.

The conventional end of narratives of the Second World War in Europe is May 1945, when Admiral Karl Dönitz, Hitler's chosen successor, authorized the heads of the Wehrmacht to sign the Allied instruments of unconditional surrender. Thus, the war ended with the signing of that surrender on 8 May and with it, seemingly, Germany's fight. The reality on the ground in Germany, however, was much different. While the Third Reich may have crumbled and Wehrmacht soldiers may have put down their guns, fled their units, or been taken prisoner, the daily struggle for most Germans was far from over. Few would have agreed that May 1945 ushered in a true "postwar" period. It is more accurate to speak instead of an end-of-war period, a span of time that encompassed those weeks that witnessed the progressive end of the physical fighting, which took place with the announcement of unconditional surrender and the surrender of arms by the soldiers of the Wehrmacht (which did not occur everywhere at the same time); the arrival of Allied soldiers, which, like the tangible effects of unconditional surrender, was a staggered affair; the setting up of local Allied military administrations; and, for those Germans who had survived, the initial start of coming to terms with what had just occurred, even before they could begin to talk of reconstruction. This end-of-war period is often unhelpfully, and I believe incorrectly, lumped together with the postwar period; I focus here exclusively on the first several weeks of the former.[1]

The physical devastation of the country was owed primarily to the extensive area bombing campaign carried out by the Allies. Beginning in late 1941 and adopted more or less as official policy by early 1942, it continued unabated until the end of the war. The British Royal Air Force and the United States Army Air Force dropped some 2 million tons of bombs, leaving broad swathes of the German landscape, urban and rural, literally demolished. An estimated half a million German civilians were killed and entire cities were devastated.[2] Firestorms—massive conflagrations that spawned their own wind systems—broke out in Hamburg, Dresden, Kassel, Darmstadt, and other cities. The capital, Berlin, was a primary target of bombers from late 1943 to early 1944; when Allied targets shifted following the Normandy invasion that June, the respite for Berliners was short-lived. One year later, the Red Army threatened to take the city from the east, the Allied armies from the west. By the day of capitulation, Germany lay in ruins.

Nor was the desolation only physical. A huge political vacuum developed in advance of the German surrender. By 20 April 1945—Hitler's fifty-sixth birthday—the Red Army had all but encircled the German capital. On 29 April, the man who had led Germany into war six years earlier dictated his will and final political testament. In it, Hitler dismissed longtime Nazi stalwarts Hermann Göring and Heinrich Himmler for disloyalty and treason and appointed a new government to succeed him. He declared that he did not "wish to fall into the hands of enemies who, for the amusement of their whipped-up masses, will need a spectacle arranged by the Jews." The statement served to explain his forthcoming suicide alongside his longtime companion, Eva Braun, the following day.[3] It was not only the Führer who feared retribution from Germany's enemies. In Berlin alone in 1945, more than 7,000 people killed themselves in anticipation of the arrival of the Red Army and in the immediate aftermath of the Soviet occupation of the city. Suicides were also not uncommon outside the capital, though the rates were much lower than in Berlin and in other areas occupied by the Soviet Union.[4]

The arrival of foreign conquering armies fueled the pervasive chaos and despair: on 2 May, the red flag of the Soviet Union fluttered over the shell of the Reichstag. Later that day, the city's last defenders surrendered. The Red Army was the only occupying army in Berlin until early July, when Allied forces from the west finally arrived to take over their sections of the city. With Russians in eastern Germany and Americans, British, and French in western Germany, the enemies that Nazi propaganda had for years identified as intrinsically hostile to German interests occupied the entire country. The Russians, in particular, seemed to live up to German expectations that terror would ensue: unpredictable and volatile, Red Army soldiers could be kind to German children one moment and engage in random, wild, and murderous pillaging and raping the next. It was a veritable epidemic: by 1949, Soviet soldiers had raped as many as 2 million German women.[5]

The social devastation that this jumble of political chaos, military occupation, and physical ruination produced was overwhelming. With some 11 million German soldiers in prisoner-of-war camps around the world, virtually no family in Germany was untouched. Fathers, husbands, brothers, and sons were missing and not heard from for weeks, months, or years—or, in the most unfortunate of cases, were never heard from again. British and American army divisions liberated concentration camps on German soil in March and April 1945. The horrors found therein were so incredible that General Dwight D. Eisenhower, supreme commander of the Allied forces in Europe, forced himself to bear witness to every corner of Ohrdruf, a subcamp of Buchenwald near Weimar. The American authorities later ordered Weimar residents to walk five miles from the city to the camp to see for themselves what had occurred there. In the first years after the end of hostilities, almost 12 million former slave laborers and survivors of the concentration camps from across Europe mixed with another 12 million ethnic Germans fleeing retribution or expelled from countries in eastern and southeastern Europe.[6] Food and clothing were scarce and shelter was hard to come by, particularly in the bombed-out cities. Anguish over loved ones, soldiers, or civilians who had disappeared during the final weeks of the war was compounded by Germany's utterly final defeat, the challenges of daily survival in the reality that the defeat produced, and the contempt and hostility of the occupiers.

In many ways, Georg Werthmann epitomized the German home front experience of the war's final months. In private reflections and public statements he struggled both as a leader of Catholic priests and as a German national to negotiate the reality of defeated Germany. These were months of tumult, uncertainty, and displacement as bombs rained down from Allied planes and as foreign armies moved inexorably toward the German capital from all sides. The chaplaincy underwent its own upheaval. Rarkowski stepped down as field bishop in January 1945 due to ill health. Werthmann was his logical replacement. Accordingly, the nominal head of the OKW, Wilhelm Keitel, duly appointed him provisional field bishop, effective February 1945.[7] Keitel failed to consult the Holy See, either due to wartime exigencies or as a deliberate slight. Six weeks later, Werthmann fled Berlin, heading south and west toward Thuringia. By April 1945, he had made it to the medieval Bavarian town of Deggendorf. An American infantry division intercepted him there. The Americans interned him in the nearby Benedictine monastery at Niederalteich, just south of the town. Released at the end of July, he moved back to his old stomping grounds in Bamberg, where he took charge of pastoral care for prisoners of war.[8]

The civilian bishops were not much better off. They may have functioned publicly during the war as a monolith, but in the final months of hostilities communications were severely disrupted. Direct communication with Rome broke down in the winter of 1944–1945 and resumed, intermittently, only in the summer of 1945. The bishops had trouble communicating with each other as well, a problem exacerbated in the initial period of occupation as bishops under different occupying powers encountered difficulties contacting their brothers beyond zonal borders.[9] They also lost the formal leader of their group. The chairman of the conference, Adolf Cardinal Bertram of Breslau, had waited until his city was mostly evacuated, then retreated to his summer residence in Jauernig, Czechoslovakia (Javorník, Czech Republic), where he died at the age of eighty-six in July 1945. Josef Frings, archbishop of Cologne, quickly succeeded him, though communication remained spotty. Moreover, the bishops were consumed with the immediacy of their own ruined cities: few diocesan seats had escaped heavy damage and some cathedrals were almost entirely destroyed.

In the wake of not just Germany's second devastating military loss in less than three decades, but also the complete disintegration of the self-proclaimed "thousand year Reich," the victors looked skeptically at German religious authorities. It was by no means clear that the Allies could depend on the leadership of either the Protestant or the Catholic churches for support in inducing the German populace to accept responsibility for what had happened. On the home front, most Germans had been engaged in a battle of survival for months, if not years, stretching in some cases back to 1942 when the Allied bombing campaign began in earnest. Werthmann and his companions were fortunate to reach Bavaria before getting caught; their reception by Americans rather than Soviets was a comparative blessing, and the conditions of their internment were idyllic in contrast to what they had fled in Berlin. As a nation, Germans were reeling collectively, waking from one bad dream of privation and destitution into another of catastrophe and uncertainty.

What of the thousands of priests and seminarians in Wehrmacht uniforms, scattered across Europe, fighting for God, Führer, and Fatherland? How did they manage demobilization and reintegration, individually and within their communities? What characterized this transitional period from soldier to civilian, and in what ways were civilian bishops involved, in light of the total collapse of the German military and the government? Given that this was a period of intense upheaval and transition, these questions are difficult to answer. Werthmann tried to keep track of some of his men in uniform, and his correspondence provides some evidence for how these individuals navigated this tumultuous time. I answer some of these questions by assessing the initial experience of occupation as observed by German Catholic Church leaders. I also examine both the concerns of the bishops as they emerged from defeat and embraced their role as the authority figure in occupied Germany as well as the occupying authorities' perceptions of the German churches, particularly in the American zone. It was during these first crucial months following the end of the war in Europe that the bishops began collectively to comprehend the scope of the mass atrocities and wholesale genocide that had transpired. With that revelation came the destruction of traditional frameworks of understanding suffering and death. The bishops attempted to provide Germans with alternative methods of consolation and meaning in the face of personal and national disaster.

I also explore Werthmann's extensive collection of notes, which have been used throughout this book and were originally compiled in the immediate aftermath of his arrest in April 1945. These writings open a window into the matters that concerned him, themes and issues that other Church leaders likely shared. When examining Werthmann and the Church leadership closely, the idea of 1945 as either the end of the war or a true *Stunde Null* (zero hour) no longer seems appropriate. One can glimpse earnest endeavors to confront the recent Nazi past, endeavors that pressing new concerns, including dealing with the occupying authorities, ultimately overrode. However, one can also discern the need both to articulate a meaningful interpretation of ongoing suffering and misery and to confront the desire of Germans not simply to survive but to move forward.

American Perspectives on the Allies in Germany

To understand the reactions of the bishops and Werthmann to the situation at the end of the war, the stated priorities of the Allies are important. A closer (but necessarily brief) look at the impact of Allied occupation assists in our understanding of these clerics' responses to the arrival of the occupying authorities and the setting up of foreign military administrations. This section also elaborates on some of the causes of hardship, suffering, and misery across the defeated nation. Put simply, the policies that the Allies sought to implement in Germany did little to alleviate German anguish. These facts may also explain why Werthmann held the Americans (the Allies with whom he had the most contact during his internment in Bavaria) at arm's length, despite acknowledging that both the British and the Americans looked to the Church for help in maintaining order.

The Allies arrived in Germany with preconceptions of what they would find. These views, in turn, informed the behavior of the occupying troops, from the most senior regional commander to the lowliest foot soldier, as well as the rules the military tried to enforce. Before the formal capitulation, Allied troops moving into German territory were directed to trust no one, not even the German clergy, despite the signs of outward piety they might exhibit: "They [the Nazis] are masters of the art of guile and subterfuge. With the conquest of their armies in the field they will probably seek to continue their activities as an 'underground movement.' It is therefore possible to conceive that they would not hesitate to use the Church as one of their instruments. . . . ALL MUST BE TREATED WITH EQUAL SUSPICION."[10] An American soldier was even less equivocal. Julian Bach candidly concluded his published reminiscences in noting that the lingering nationalism and pro-Nazi sentiments, the political apathy and immaturity, the lack of moral responsibility, even the cheerlessness with which they greeted their own soldiers' homecomings made the Germans collectively seem "simply an immoral (or at best amoral) people in the most terrible sense of the word." He liked nothing about the country except the Autobahns and the Bavarian Alps.[11] One can only speculate whether Bach's views were representative, but his utterances suggest that the occupiers' hostility was not unusual, at least in the first few months.

One could hardly expect that Germans would jettison overnight the nationalist and racist attitudes that had permeated German culture under Nazi rule. Twelve years of intense social reorganization and an onslaught of propaganda in a variety of forms and from multiple angles had fueled radical nationalist sentiments and xenophobic, antisemitic prejudices. Nor does it seem quite fair to expect enthusiastic engagement with political matters in an atmosphere of physical devastation and social and cultural ruin, when the political sphere in Germany had effectively ceased to exist. This same atmosphere of devastation, combined with the unambiguous nature of defeat, no doubt contributed to the weariness and even dourness that returning German soldiers encountered, though this was by no means the only reaction they faced. Many observers commented on this weariness among Germans; it was not a manner reserved only for returning soldiers. Eugene Davidson remembered encountering Germans "dazed or sullen or spiritless . . . drained of energy and emotions," and usually bereft of fighting spirit: "rare traces of werewolves, no banzai charges, no last defense in the redoubt of the Bavarian mountains."[12] A second humiliating defeat in as many wars, this time with no doubt about the loss's finality, represented by the presence of foreign armies on German soil, sparked the weariness, apathy, and shock that Germans felt in mid-1945.

British and American soldiers' perspectives divulge a great deal about conditions in Germany at the end of the war. They complement and enrich the relatively scant written records from Germans, so consumed simply with surviving that they lacked the time or energy to write down the details of their daily struggles. They also reveal much about the impact on the Germans of the Allied troops, as they simultaneously provide a vividly detailed description of conditions in Germany. Bach described the country as existing in a "bicycle age," and because of high demand for the two-wheeled vehicles that needed no fuel, they could be bartered only at a steep cost. Thus, most Germans went about on foot.[13] Edward Peterson, a military intelligence sergeant stationed first in Berlin and then in Bavaria, recounted the curtailment of individual liberties that Germans living under American occupation endured: strict curfews, no mail or telephone communication, no meetings of more than five people, no access to outside books, newspapers, or magazines (at a time when the German press had all but ceased to function), and a prohibition on movies and theaters.[14] Because of the lack of resources, the black market thrived, especially in the large cities. The occupying forces benefited the most from this—Davidson remembered "one man [sending] home a dismantled motorcycle in three shipments"—but the market was simultaneously useful for the occupied, who could procure necessities otherwise unavailable.[15]

The existence of an operational black market was a symptom of a poorly functioning economy, a product of the strain of war and then of Allied occupation policy. This was particularly true in the American zone of occupation, where the draconian Morgenthau Plan seemed to find implementation in the form of JCS (Joint Chiefs of Staff) directive 1067 from May 1945 to mid-1947.[16] JCS 1067 covered all aspects of the occupation, including American military objectives, demilitarization, political activities, and economic reconstruction. The latter was to provide only enough for the needs of the occupying forces and "to prevent starvation or such disease and unrest as would endanger these forces." Attention was also given to denazification and reeducation, both firmly under American control. Finally, in a point that every American soldier who wrote about JCS 1067 griped about, the directive made clear that fraternization between the occupiers and the occupied was strictly forbidden. This mandated in no uncertain terms that the Germans were to be treated as a "defeated enemy nation."[17] In stark contrast to the British, French, and even the Russian zones, not even handshakes were permitted in the American zone.

Beyond the stringent control of the economy, these two pillars of JCS 1067—nonfraternization and denazification—produced the most tension between Allied occupiers and Germans, which Americans observed. The nonfraternization policy led to problems due to the massive disobedience of American soldiers, particularly with respect to socializing with German women.[18] Even the Americans were not blind to the fact that the Russians seemed to enjoy a better reputation among Germans than the Americans did: "As individuals the Russians were friendly to the Germans by comparison with the Americans; they shook hands, they offered the new German functionaries drinks and cigarettes, and they followed instructions to the letter." Indeed, the official American policy matched much more closely the French perspective of Germany and Germans, and the French program was unabashedly "almost entirely negative."[19] The Americans pursued denazification with extreme vigor and a harshness that far outstripped that of the other western Allies. Their program was ultimately rivaled statistically only by the Russians.[20] Germans had no rights, American observers noted, and any notion of habeas corpus did not apply to them. They were rounded up by the thousands and could be interned indefinitely, forbidden to communicate with their families. People could be arrested on the basis of an anonymous, unfounded denunciation or simply because they had violated one of the numerous Allied regulations. And errors, of course, were made: "Anti-Nazis might be arrested . . . but since the arrest officers were soldiers following orders . . . the accused could lie in jail for months ignorant of the charges brought against them."[21] Although at least one American insisted in his published memoirs that he felt the denazification process was not thorough enough, many others expressed some sympathy for the Germans.[22] If members of the Allied occupying forces were aware that their measures were severe, how then did the Germans react to the end-of-war period and the arrival of the Allied armies?

From Total War to Total Defeat

Nazism was broken, leaving a nation that had followed it into genocidal war bereft and shattered. The capitulation resulted in the permanent cessation of fighting, but not of hardship. In the war's immediate aftermath, Germans sought bishops and priests as sources of support, guidance, and, when church buildings were still standing, refuge. Many individual letters from the bishops report increased Sunday mass attendance, and other remarks indicate that many who had left the church in the 1930s—the so-called *Kirchenausgetretene*—were attempting to return. This resurgence in religiosity may not be surprising, given the larger context (just as increased religiosity among soldiers as the battlefront grew closer is not surprising). But it was sudden, and the bishops took it as evidence of a nation ripe for re-Christianization. Like Werthmann, they insisted on the centrality of the Church and of Christianity to any German recovery. They understood themselves to be examples of staunch resistance to the former regime, and, on occasion, they did not hesitate to depict Catholics, and the Catholic Church, as victims of Nazi policy. The bishops rarely acknowledged other victims (with the exception of priests in Dachau) and atrocities that the Wehrmacht or the SS had perpetrated, particularly against Jews. Of far greater concern for both the bishops and Werthmann was the notion of collective guilt. About this the Allies seemed adamant, using it to indict all Germans for the worst crimes of the Third Reich, especially the war and the horrors of the camps. It was in this context, by late spring 1945, before the western Allies had entrenched themselves in their share of divided Berlin, that Church leaders were constructing the framework they would operate within for the next several years: as partners of the Allies in rebuilding Germany, but as partners with a voice that they would use to defend their people. The question of collective guilt and the manner in which the Allies pursued denazification were two points that proved most contentious, although the destruction of their own cities and the arrival of the occupying forces consumed their most immediate attention.

Germany's bishops had lived through a devastating loss in 1918, but that wartime defeat left them ill-prepared for the nature of the loss in 1945. Some of their initial communications with each other after the capitulation laid out in stark detail the extent to which their home cities had been damaged. Archbishop Lorenz Jaeger of Paderborn wrote to the German nuncio, Cesare Orsenigo, about bomb attacks on his city on 17 January, 23 February, 10 March, 22 March, and 26 March. A final attack on 27 March accomplished the complete destruction of the inner city. Only houses in the outer city remained intact, and "all churches and chapels with the exceptions of both churches in the outer areas are completely destroyed or so badly hit that they are not usable for masses."[23] In September 1945 Jaeger wrote again, this time to Pope Pius XII, about the destruction in the final months of the war, the "indescribable chaos . . . the trains ran with great irregularity, the post and news came to a virtual standstill in mid-February. . . . All rail tracks were endangered, as were all human habitations lying close to the lines. A normal life was no longer possible."[24] Albert Stohr, bishop of Mainz, hinted at the mental and emotional wreckage when he wrote in his first postwar pastoral letter, "Today we have become so poor that there is no German position with which to negotiate with the victors for a peace. We are completely and without qualification in the hands of the victorious powers."[25] Writing from his archdiocesan seat in Freiburg, his fellow bishop Conrad Gröber was more explicit: "Hardly a single family within our diocese remains without significant loss of husbands or sons. Thus the awful war strode through the country like a merciless annihilator and signed house by house, soul by soul, with his bloodstained, murderous hands, and pressed out whole streams of tears."[26]

In mid-May 1945, Cardinal Michael von Faulhaber, archbishop of Munich and Freising, wrote a lengthy letter to Pope Pius XII, detailing his adventures as the hostilities ended. His own seat, the famous Frauenkirche cathedral in the heart of the city, had already sustained heavy damage in an air attack in 1944. On the last day of April, as the vanguard of American forces reached Munich, Faulhaber had taken refuge in the cellar of the chapel attached to the bishop's residence (*Bischofshof*), where his living quarters were located. American artillery scored a direct hit, shattering the chapel wall and crashing through the emergency exit of the cellar. "It was thanks to the mercy of the Lord," he wrote, "that the core of the bomb did not explode, otherwise all of us in the cellar, four meters away from the impact point and showered with stone and dust, would not have lived to see the light of day." He noted morosely that he would now have to repair his chapel for the fourth or fifth time.[27]

Werthmann, too, was not blind to the reality of the ruins beyond the Benedictine monastery. Since this was the second war of immense scale that he had experienced, he was more ready to discuss the post-1918 challenges to Germany that were resurfacing in comparison to 1945 than some of his confreres. He described how again German culture, "our humanity, our joy of the world and commitment to our people, our culture and our beauty, our education and our knowledge, our entire progress is imploded and gutted." He questioned, using the allegory of a spider web, whether to "tie together once more the brittle thread of our culture where it has been torn and continue to spin on, as we did before."[28] In one of the darkest sentences of his internment, he stated bitterly, "Have we not seen our gods die and the 'beautiful God' himself, whom we hold in the highest regard above all other idols . . . , have we not seen his corpse, ugly, stinking, and bestial, lying there already on the first day of the war?"[29] And in one of the harshest judgments in his reflections about the soldiers returning home, which he later contradicted with more hopeful appraisals, he lamented, "It would be a misapprehension of reality to assume that men coming home from the war were enriched religiously or became more believing and more pious."[30] Strikingly, Werthmann seems to have reversed this judgment when he wrote in October that year, in a second passage comparing the experience of the First World War with the Second, "[The 1939 generation] knew the war was a hard and nightmarish affair that was nevertheless necessary. But very quickly the men were aware of the necessity of a new or renewed moral order [Wertordnung], the necessity of a faith in something much greater and more real than that which their fathers had believed."[31] Echoing what other bishops and priests were stating, Werthmann was increasingly inclined to interpret the war—indeed, the entirety of the Third Reich—along traditional Christian lines of suffering and redemption. It had been a necessary period of cleansing and sacrifice so that a stronger Germany might emerge in its wake.

Necessity of Religion and the Church

Werthmann was convinced that Catholic priests uniquely possessed the skills and training to help others, and themselves, to survive that which still awaited them: defeat, occupation, humiliation, punishment. In a passage that moved from the war to the postwar period, Werthmann saw a crucial link between the war years and what would come later. By focusing on the longer term and referring to one of Catholicism's core articles of faith, namely the redemptive meaning of suffering, he was able to construe the actions of chaplains in a positive light: "No one may misconceive that, during the six years of epic struggle on all fronts of this conflagration, our chaplains cast spiritual seeds in service to their church, seeds whose growth flourishes in secret and that will bear fruit in their own time."[32] A few days earlier, he had been even more succinct about the role of men of God, claiming, "The chaos of the war and the postwar period can only be put in order by priests."[33] With this conviction, Werthmann could find strength and assurance in the idea that he and those who shared his vocation were still useful, even vitally so.

Most of the passages in which he reflected upon the war in positive terms were grounded in the belief that suffering could be cathartic and necessary. At the end of June, he was explicit:

> The war was a terrible suffering, but it came from outside, like a lightning storm that scourged our faces with its ice. In this way, this suffering is liberating, uplifting, refreshing, and purifying. In its acrimony it contains something of that great, deep, glorious happiness that we see in the men who were severely tested and stricken and bore it silently, bravely, gladly [gottfroh].[34]

One day later, in a reflection that might have served as the draft of an open letter to chaplains and priests in the Wehrmacht, he insisted that the war "has made you mature.... Your maturity is not the decay of the smug, super-saturated, disappointed, broken man, not the fatigue of the exhausted. A firm calm stands behind your countenance."[35] In couching the war experience in these terms, he was able to salvage something positive from the experience. It was not a period to be cast aside, written off, or ignored, but embraced as a time of testing and growth.

It lies beyond the scope of this survey to determine whether and to what extent his words convinced others of his view, or if even he himself truly believed them. Remarkably, the Catholic language of suffering he promoted was not that dissimilar to what the Nazi Party itself had employed during its tenure: suffering as purification, particularly suffering during war, was a theme used not infrequently, of which Werthmann doubtless was aware. Is it possible that the passages above demonstrate the man's loyalty to Nazism rather than his Catholicism? This question is hard to answer definitively, though with such passages, his Catholicism seems to have an edge: "The future of our *Volk* hangs on our suffering and death. . . . It must be a brave suffering, as you bore it, a restless dormancy that is storming on. . . . Intrepid faith! We will not conceive an unshrinking faith in eternal gods that we cannot yet see. Unshrinking faith is already required in order to possess the kingdom of God, and even more so as not to lose it, or to lose one's way to Him."[36]

If Werthmann was not a supporter of Nazism, he was still a nationalist. He felt strongly that, at least at the end of June 1945, Germany as a nation would recover. In Hegelian fashion, he ruminated, "The *Volk* in its life's core cannot be struck fatally by exterior force. . . . In this way, the *Volk* participate in the world ascendance of the spirit, which exterior force cannot debase in its personal majesty, its ethical greatness, and its eternal value."[37] He then became more prescriptive, opining on what was needed for Germans to once again become strong. He decided, "The good life, external worth and power, lucre and luxury [are not] salubrious for the German people. All that is great and spiritual and inspired by the soul will flourish more and more in a poor, laboriously working Germany." But it was not only that Germans had to suffer temporally to attain spiritual health. Werthmann went further and, rather ambiguously, addressed the relationship of Germans to others in the postwar era: "We have much to give to those who remain, this we still believe." It was precisely the act of giving that Werthmann identified as the key to his prescription, which sounded more Catholic than Nazi. A convinced Nazi could hardly write, "All veracious giving is selfless and does not offset ringing demands for remuneration." He identified "the moral good, the toiling love, the strong, representative suffering" and spurned the "cowardly enjoyment, avaricious piling up, vain and hollow swagger and flaunting."

Other clergy also underscored the necessity of religion in the post-Nazism era for the reconstruction of a strong Germany. Wilhelm Offenstein, a priest in Hildesheim writing to pastoral caregivers in his diocese, insisted, "The truth and law of Christ, which the Catholic Church alone announces unadulterated, is the fundament upon which the new construction of our *Volk* must be grounded in order to succeed and have stability." He stressed the importance of priests, claiming, "We have to imprint this truth on the *Volk*. Our people must receive an absolutely strong and solid confidence in the Church."[38] Lorenz Jaeger in Paderborn was even more blunt: "Never before has the world stood before such decisive alternatives: either forward with Christ or without him and against him further downward."[39] His confrere, Albert Stohr in Mainz, expressed similar sentiments, emphasizing Germany's thousand-year history intertwined with Christianity and the latter's integral role in the development and growth of German culture and moral character [*sittliche Wesen*]. He stressed, "German national life will be Christian or it will no longer be!"[40] This, then, was the dominant mode of the episcopate in the first months after the end of hostilities: an essential return to Christianity was the only way forward.

These bishops were uttering semi-public or public statements in the form of pastoral letters or circulars to the priests of their dioceses. Werthmann could afford to be less optimistic, as his notes were for himself alone. In June 1945 his emotions oscillated between glum pessimism about the postwar situation, and the Germans' ability to survive it, and cautious optimism. Though the bleaker passages of despair and hopelessness are few, there are parts in which the reader senses a profound depression, struggling to drown his hopeful resolve. In one lengthy paragraph, he questioned whether he and his fellow priests had the courage and strength to assume the tasks before them, tasks that "are tangled and intertwined, so that to me they can't be tackled individually, one after the other, nor can they be solved simultaneously."[41] Did priests have the fortitude to "heal all the wounds that the war has struck, restore all the domestic happiness that has been shattered, banish all the evil demons that have taken over the hearts of millions of men, the demons of the brutalization of our youth, the demons of dissatisfaction and bitterness, the greed of arrogance in men and women? Do we really have the strength to scoop out all the poison that has penetrated into the soul?"[42] Werthmann and the bishops saw that pastoral care was required now more than ever. The obligations of those chaplains and *Priestersoldaten* to give such care were far from finished. The situation was unprecedented: "Hardly any people have withstood so much in ruins before now as our own poor, humiliated people at the end of this war.... More important than the buildup of the debris pile surrounding us is the buildup of the broken spiritual values and the spiritual life, so badly damaged, of our people." For this reason, Werthmann recognized that "we priests are called to be in the front line." Despite this, he then asked a series of anxious questions:

> Will we understand the call of the hour? Will we be up to the difficult task?... Will we be understood? Will others have enough intuition and desire to empathize with our spiritual, intellectual, pastoral, priestly situation that has become so completely different? Will one be generous enough with us to grasp our peculiarity and make allowance for it? Will someone take us and our concerns, our often haunting problems seriously, will someone want to hear us at all? Will our desires regarding the further employment of pastoral care be fulfilled, or are they even capable of fulfillment? Will someone be patient with us and give us time to find ourselves again?[43]

Taken together, these sentiments illustrate the extent to which Werthmann was hesitant about the role and acceptance of priests in the postwar world. He was rarely pessimistic, but here the task of defining spiritual care and devotion in the wake of the Third Reich's downfall seemed to overwhelm him. Nor was his faith in the recovery of his fellow Germans boundless. Consumed with their own immediate needs, which often boiled down to simple survival, would Germans have the time or inclination to take on the weighty concerns of religion and spirituality? Or did Werthmann's fears go even deeper than this: had the experience of Nazism and another cataclysmic defeat in war somehow produced a fundamental rupture between Germans and their Catholic faith?

This passage, one of the longest in his notes, is dated to November 1945, well after his release from Niederaltaich. The urgency and emotion animating the questions suggest that the postwar atmosphere vis-à-vis priests who had served in the Wehrmacht was not always friendly or empathetic, and that the transition from wartime to postwar pastoral care was hardly seamless. During his internment, Werthmann had written prescriptively about what to expect. He had taken solace in his belief that life without religion was unbearable, and that the chaplains and *Priestersoldaten*, having survived six years of hellish animosity and brutalization, were ready to resist all attacks on religious life and pastoral care.[44] But the veterans had to do more than merely stand firm. He cautioned his priests to be "more respectful than before of people's feelings" because the German people "are agitated passionately, even pathologically, in multiple cases . . . their souls bleeding from countless wounds." The priest was a "merciful Samaritan" who had to act with caution and forethought, who, "even if he possesses truth and justice, should not hurl them against the wounded souls like a stone. Rather, he must try to understand with a gentle hand, with clemency and patience, waiting unwearyingly, liberally compliant, affectionately understanding, magnanimously exculpating and forgiving."[45] In this vision, priests were an essential element in the postwar period. They, not the Allied occupiers, were uniquely equipped to help Germans confront the legacy of the war and Nazism, to ask the difficult questions of themselves and others, and eventually to move on.

It was an immense, arduous, and thankless task. But even as Werthmann realized by the winter of 1945–1946 the great challenge faced by institutional religion, he nonetheless tried to find the inspiration to carry on and to exhort his brethren to do the same. That December, he included a quotation for his chaplaincy history from a letter written by chaplain Rudolf Schwertschlager:

> Given that it was my destiny to be funneled through all the hardship and to preserve my home, I see in this the duty to preserve the legacy of the dead at least in small spheres. Among our dear comrades there were no militarists, but rather men who were heavily afflicted with themselves, with the time, with God. . . . If the ongoing path now proves to be even more difficult, I'll find much strength in solidarity with these officers who are billeting with God.[46]

Like so many Germans in the end-of-war period, Schwertschlager and Werthmann deflected guilt about the recent past by focusing on those who were not Nazis, who had kept their distance or were motivated by other passions to fight and to die. It is deplorable, but not surprising, that this category of "innocents"—no militarists, no Nazis, only suffering Germans—was gradually expanded to take in a much larger segment of the military than could be justified. Such judgments fed the myth of the "clean Wehrmacht" that would take decades to dismantle.⁴⁷

The Church—and Chaplaincy—as Bulwark of Resistance

Nor was it just the Wehrmacht and its chaplaincy that elided the darker aspects of their Nazi past, including acquiescence, complicity, and participation in criminality and atrocity. The Church leadership also did not hesitate to glowingly assess its own behavior during the Third Reich, ignoring the cooperation it had consistently extended to the regime before and during the war. Hildesheim priest Wilhelm Offenstein declared: "In the midst of the raging storm of the past twelve years, the Church of Christ alone stood as the unshaken beacon in the dark night that sunk ever deeper around our *Volk*."⁴⁸ The Bavarian bishops were less poetic and more explicit, detailing examples of resistance on the part of the Church, from the pope to Catholic German laity. In their pastoral letter directed to Bavaria's lay Catholic population, they stated: "As you yourselves know, from the beginning the German bishops seriously warned of the heresies and wrong ways of National Socialism, and advised of the unlucky consequences that a struggle against faith, Christianity, and Church, against justice, freedom, and truth must bring with it . . . The greatest part of the Catholic people of Germany have suffered immensely beneath the fight against Christ, Faith and Church and against the rape of conscience, and have fervently desired the end of this religious war [*Glaubenskampf*] as much as they have desired the end of the war itself."⁴⁹ Archbishop Conrad Gröber of Freiburg also defended the German people and the Church, especially the bishops, against accusations that he found particularly unjust, including the charge that the bishops had not done enough to protest the crimes of the Nazis. In doing so, he underscored one of the (few) moments of timorous opposition: "The German bishops got wind of 'euthanasia,' of the 'assisted dying' that emptied mental asylums and hospitals. Already upon first acquaintance with this program, they raised vigorous protests and in all earnestness appealed to the consciences [*auf das Gewissen binden*] of the Catholic leaders of these institutions to stand up for the resident patients of their threatened communities. But every appeal was thrown into the wastebasket as irrelevant or filed away unanswered."[50] Gröber failed to clarify that the bishops never officially spoke out, as a cohesive whole, to condemn the T-4 Aktion. Instead, they relied on the sermons of one bishop, Clemens August von Galen in Münster, who delivered his remarks as an individual priest to his parishioners rather than a representative of the German episcopacy.[51]

As he explained to interviewer Georg Zimmer in April 1945, Werthmann remained convinced that Nazism would have destroyed the churches if Germany had won the war. He cited the indelible anti-Catholicism of Nazism's more radical proponents when he wrote, "For the radical wing of the party, the Catholic Church seemed to be the stumbling-block on the road to the Nazi empire's consummation. The Church was the adversary of the Nazi worldview and appeared to be nearly the only solid block of resistance." His characterization of the Church as a "solid block" in terms of resistance is problematic. No "solid block" of anything, let alone resistance, operated within the Catholic Church during the Third Reich. But it is also a perplexing statement. Werthmann elaborated neither on why he felt this way at that time nor how he reconciled this position with other statements, hinting at a more nuanced understanding of the reactions of individual priests and seminarians to Nazi policies.[52] What this note does reveal is a man who by no means had reached firm conclusions about what he had just experienced. Nor had he arrived at a clear assessment of the behavior of his superiors and the institution of which he was part.

Many of Werthmann's reflections about the impact of Nazism (and more specifically the Nazi Party) on German soldiers and clergy were supportive of the chaplains who had worked under him. He bitterly related the rapidity with which priests in the Wehrmacht became a target for criticism. He rejected the idea that the chaplaincy's existence had somehow complicated the overall struggle between the Catholic Church and the regime, arguing that this overlooked the support that chaplains had provided to the Church while in the military. According to Werthmann, such activities served as a bulwark for truth in the final years of the war, as the Nazi Leadership Office strategically deployed more of its propaganda-spouting officers in an attempt to bolster morale among the troops: "The chaplains were and remained a symbol of resistance in the eyes of the party, and if the NSFOs had already been as anchored in the military system of pastoral care in the first years of the war as they were in 1943 and particularly 1944, the light of the chaplaincy would have been blown out."[53] The chaplains and priests were able to find the resolve to persevere, Werthmann maintained, because "they possessed the truth. . . . How difficult it often was to justify their faith, to safeguard it in example, in practical confession, above all in grievous sacrifice and conflict underneath the bewildering influence of an unchristian, even anti-Christian, ideology that ruled the entire people."[54] The fortitude of the individual chaplain did not diminish the trauma of the war years and the spiritual and ethical dilemmas he had encountered during that time. On the contrary, Werthmann was aware that the war had been exceptionally difficult. For many priests in the military, it had challenged the meaning of their vocation and, indeed, their very existence, one "comprised of such horrors as the war, that had to survive such catastrophe, bought with so much suffering and blood and execration, that had to be developed and molded—what meaning did [all of] that have? All these questions, asked out of great need, straight from the heart, were not only posed to a priest in a soldier's uniform from outside of himself but soared menacingly from within."[55]

Atrocities, Jews, and Collective Guilt

On one subject, Werthmann was notably circumspect: the Allied notion of collective German guilt for the atrocities during the Nazi period. In contrast, the bishops spent a considerable amount of time and energy addressing this topic. They did not discuss the atrocities themselves in any detail. They made few explicit mentions of them in their correspondence, and when mention does appear, it is more often in internal communication with fellow priests, with each other, or with the pope than in writing meant for the public. For instance, Lorenz Jaeger prepared a draft petition on behalf of the West German bishops to Pope Pius XII (never made official due to a preemptive statement from the pope himself) that directly answered the much-asked question at the time: to what extent had Germans known about the horrors in the camps? His explanation was that most "thinking Germans [denkende Deutschen] assumed that appalling injustices occurred in the concentration camps. Concerning the Jews, there was practically a certainty. But it was profoundly difficult to learn authentic details."[56] He noted that foreign literature was not available to Germans during the war, and those who returned from the camps (he likely meant camps on German soil; the death camps in Poland released no inmates) stayed silent about their experiences out of fear of endangering themselves and their families. In fact, about many of the most horrific details—presumably death camps in the East—the Germans "learned only now for the first time, and to most people they appear to be hardly believable even today. The reports appear one-sided and at any rate incomplete."[57] While today such comments strain credulity, at the time the proliferation of stories about horrors in the East may well have led Germans to distrust such reports out of a sheer inability to accept what sounded incredible: the discovery of camps that Germans constructed for the sole purpose of murder. In this regard, differentiating between expressions of willful naiveté, genuine ignorance, and retrospective justifications can be an enterprise fraught with risk. The Bavarian bishops likewise asserted that the German people, "with few exceptions," had no knowledge of the inhumanities being perpetrated within the camps.[58] In a letter to one of his priests, Conrad Gröber alluded to "atrocities in France perpetrated by German soldiers, particularly by SS men."[59] Though the occupation of France was not nearly as brutal or lethal as was life on the Eastern Front, Gröber could have been referring to any number of incidents. Likely he meant the slaughter at Oradour-sur-Glane, a reprisal massacre of villagers in response to nearby partisan activity.[60]

The first collective pastoral letter issued by the German bishops following the war was released in late August 1945. It referenced both concentration camps and Jews, albeit in clumsy, obtuse language: "How it warms our hearts to recall that Catholics of all ranks and ages repeatedly embraced the opportunity to protect and defend national comrades of foreign tribes [*Volksgenosse fremden Stammes*], bestowing upon them Christian love. For such an act of love, some even perished in the concentration camps!" The letter went on to state, "Emotionally we remember all those who shared their meager daily bread with an innocent, persecuted non-Aryan, and had to be aware daily that an awful fate was prepared for them."[61] To the extent that such sentiment was true, it was the exception rather than the general rule. Nowhere in the letter does the word "Jew" even appear. Instead, they chose to concentrate exclusively on the actions of a few individual members of the Church—a small minority!—whose heroism rightly deserves to be lauded but should not obscure what the majority did (or did not do).

In fact, after the war, bishops were more likely to identify the Catholic Church than the Jews as the primary victim of the Nazi regime. Given the bishops' behavior over the preceding twelve years, the stance adopted by the Holy See, the mutual suspicion and mistrust between the regime and Church leaders, and the egregious anti-Catholicism of several high-ranking Nazis and the SS, many of them clearly felt victimized well in advance of the end of the war. Werthmann echoed this sentiment with his conviction that a wartime victory would have led to the obliteration of the churches in Germany. Bishop Joannes Baptista Sproll of Rottenburg described the regime as having waged a "battle against Christ and Christianity [and] broken the celebrated concordat with the Holy Father." It was first and foremost due to the grace of God that it had not realized its goal, "the elimination of Christianity in Germany and the annihilation of the Catholic Church."[62] The Bavarian bishops also lamented the experience of the majority of Germany's Catholics, who suffered unspeakably "under the battle against Christ, belief and church."[63] While the bishops, collectively and individually, employed various detailed descriptions of the physically ruined country that drew just short of claiming victim status in those passages, they implied that in 1945 the suffering of Germans merited attention and sympathy that outsiders failed to give. The regime was ultimately culpable, holding out empty promises, seducing and then betraying Germans.

To the bishops, a corollary of the premise that Germans had been victimized was a rejection of the notion of collective guilt. Indeed, Lorenz Jaeger's petition to Pius XII on behalf of the West German bishops concerned itself primarily with that question.[64] In no way did they wish to deny or excuse German guilt in toto; rather, they were concerned with qualification, and they expressed themselves once more in the language of suffering and victimization: "Millions among the German people have suffered inexpressibly beneath the disgrace of the infringements of these rights and, *perhaps with the exception of the Poles, have themselves been the primary sufferers* [Hauptleidtragende] *of these measures.*"⁶⁵ Toward the end of the petition, Jaeger conceded that what the Germans "were responsible for, they had effectively atoned for in the suffering of the war, whereby tens of thousands of innocents lost their lives, millions their belongings, their home and *Heimat*, in the most execrable anguish. The unavoidable consequences of the lost war will impose this atonement on them for a while longer." The implication of the foregoing is unambiguous: the Germans have suffered and are suffering enough. In the following months, Jaeger remained busy. In addition to a July 1945 letter addressed to the papal nuncio in Germany, in which he also mentioned the collective guilt question, he wrote to Pius XII in September to explain the dire situation in the British-occupied zone (his seat was in Paderborn). In this regard, he was distressed about the British process of denazification, which had removed the city's entire civil service apparatus, including schoolteachers. "The Germans were refugees and homeless in their own Fatherland," he noted morosely.⁶⁶

These sentiments echoed the bishops' first collective pastoral letter a month earlier, which had also bemoaned the blanket dismissal. It had declared, "It is a demand of justice that guilt always and everywhere be proven on a case-by-case basis, so that the innocent don't have to suffer with the guilty. We bishops have advocated this from the beginning, and for this we will advocate in the future." In that letter, the bishops had also emphasized, "Party membership often did not signify an inner agreement with the terrible deeds of the regime" and more implausibly, "many joined in ignorance of the goings-on and goals of the party, many were forced [to join], many with the good intention of preventing evil."⁶⁷ Gröber went still further. While initially conceding that Germany had brought the present misery upon itself, he then insisted, "No democratic Germany, no collective will of the people [*Volkswille*] is responsible for the calamitous plans and decisions [of the lost war]." The real culprit here was a Führer who ruled with absolute power, who threatened those who resisted him with death.⁶⁸

Werthmann on the Allies in Germany

Unlike his episcopal brethren, consumed with the urgency of taking charge in their respective dioceses, Werthmann spent the first few months after the end of the war essentially under house arrest. This left him plenty of time to reflect upon the past twelve years and the enormous challenges that the Church faced. For those dozen weeks, Werthmann agreed to remain in the vicinity of Niederalteich. The Benedictine monastery hosted him for the duration, along with the Protestant Reich field bishop, Franz Dohrmann, and Dohrmann's field vicar-general, Friedrich Münchmeyer. Not long after the Benedictines took them in, the three most senior chaplains of the defeated German military gave a joint interview to Gregor Zimmer, a German-speaking journalist accompanying the American forces. Werthmann kept an undated copy for his files. The interviewer noted that all three still wore their Wehrmacht uniforms, indistinguishable from other soldiers' uniforms but for the violet badges on collar and overcoat. In fact, the Americans who captured them initially assumed they were arresting army officers.[69] At the beginning of the interview, Werthmann forcefully asserted, "I know that if Germany had won this war, the entire Church in Germany would have been dissolved, with the exception of the party faction *Deutsche Christen* [German Christians], and that all clergymen, both Catholic and Protestant, would have been liquidated. I have documentary proof of this."[70] His companions expressed similar sentiments, maintaining that they knew the war was lost as soon as it began, that the Nazis sinned against God and man, and that it was time for Germany to come clean. Perhaps swept up in the mood, or affected by the romantic setting of the gardens of a baroque cathedral in late spring, Zimmer ended his report: "If the church in Germany can help the Allies convince the German nation that it is useless to put all the blame on others—thus exonerating themselves—then perhaps—just perhaps—there is some hope for Germany."

Werthmann's description of the American soldiers who captured him revealed them to be frankly curious, for the most part respectful, but also capable of asking earnest, pointed questions about the role of the churches during the Third Reich. This dialogue took place as Allied divisions rolled eastward across Germany, encountering concentration camps and atrocities along the way. Werthmann did not encounter any Allied clergymen, though he knew of the policy of nonfraternization, remarking that it did not apply to a German woman identified as a spy.[71] The policy of nonfraternization, set in place as early as September 1944, was reiterated in a March 1945 circular addressed to American chaplains, who were directed to help enforce the policy. It then was subsequently enacted as formal policy in JSC 1067 one month later. While relations between the occupiers and the occupied were to be correct and respectful, intimacy and familiarity were forbidden in the interests of military order and future world peace. Though "religion in the purest sense transcends national boundaries and embraces all peoples," the Supreme Allied Commander still felt it was vital to maintain a clear demarcation between the Allied chaplains and their services and those of German clergy.[72]

That the Allies were not completely averse to German religious activity served to help the reestablishment of the churches as a significant moral authority in the postwar public sphere. For example, British chaplains were anxious to take advantage of the situation in order to help rehabilitate the Protestant churches. A report made on 5 July 1945 observed that the potential existed for the "resurgence of the Christian Church in Germany" and that British chaplains should try to exploit this. In mid-July, a second report composed by the British Royal Air Force Chaplains' Department began with the line, "Special opportunities of encouraging the Christian Church in Germany are presenting themselves to the R.A.Ch.D."[73] It proposed that, because British chaplains could not be completely disinterested in church affairs as reconstruction proceeded, a revision be made to the strict policy of nonfraternization. It also asked that a modified questionnaire be used to determine the religious suitability of clergy who had served in the Wehrmacht. While the report specifically concerned Protestant clergymen, its language (also in related documents) was sufficiently ambiguous, most often employing the nondistinctive "the churches" to reference their subject, that one may assume the changes applied to Catholic clergymen as well.

During this period, Allied observers continued to hold grave concerns about the disposition of German priests they encountered in their parishes, but their attitudes were not inflexible. One report about a sermon in an unnamed Catholic parish in Iserlohn, southeast of Dortmund, commented that it "stressed the national phase too much, rather forgetting that the Church is first and foremost Catholic. . . . There was no reference to humility, penitence (whether individual or national), charity, carrying the cross, or imitating our Lord Jesus Christ" and on the whole, it was "theologically unsound and certainly not proof of good spiritual direction." Still, by the autumn of 1945, at least one British staff chaplain spoke in favor of the churches' standing. He described a renewed interest in religion among Germans and the friendliness of pastors toward occupying forces. "The Churches are unquestionably the strongest institution left in Germany," he pointed out, "and enjoy a prestige and confidence among the German people such as has not existed, probably, since the Reformation. . . . Hounded by the Nazi state from without, and weakened by treachery and divisions from within, they have nevertheless shown themselves capable of purging their own number, and of rising to a new unity of purpose."[74]

Werthmann knew that the Americans were similarly disposed toward the Catholic Church, though by mid-June he was already sounding a note of caution: "It's obvious, and everyone knows, that the American military authority has taken up a friendly attitude to the Catholic Church, sometimes in brusque contradistinction to its attitude to the German population." While he appreciated the liberty to speak and work freely after twelve years of repression, the dual American approach, of friendliness toward priests and animosity toward Germans, was more than awkward; it was a quandary. He warned his fellow priests against presenting Americans as "liberators" in their sermons and conversations, underscoring the nature of their interactions with the German people. "Whether the Allies are our 'liberators' in the true sense of the word . . . , for the present, this should in no way be presumed," he continued.[75]

But it was not merely the Americans and their posture vis-à-vis the Germans that drew Werthmann's criticism. He was discomfited by a trend he observed among his brethren, clerics who were strategically currying favor with the occupying power by distancing themselves publicly from Nazism and in the process estranging their flocks. He felt there were limits to such statements at a time when priests needed to establish a relationship of trust with the German population and simultaneously keep the Allies at a distance:

> It is absolutely insupportable if, for example, a priest knows of nothing better to do than, on the first Sunday after the capitulation of the German Wehrmacht, to get into his pulpit and turn the following

phrase, "Nazism and its representatives ascended from the cloaca, and are now sunk back into it." *Cui bono* (to whose benefit)? What do such formulations have to do with the pulpit in a house of God?

Such a priest risked nothing of himself, he asserted, but could inflict extensive mental damage on others. He referenced the "hundreds of thousands of Germans today who are undergoing a *Götterdämmerung* without equal with the collapse of Nazism . . . [whose] entire world has caved in, and they are standing back in a debris field of shattered hope." Now was not the time to strike out at them, Werthmann insisted. Such attacks could only increase their doubt as they wavered in uncertainty and weakness. While he spoke specifically of one priest, he knew that the case was not anomalous. He was cognizant of the "many priests who in the last weeks cannot get enough of homiletic effusions of a political nature. Many of them give the impression that they are in haste to make up for having failed to speak politically from the pulpit over the past twelve years." The only way to discuss Nazism from the pulpit as the "unspeakable calamity that it was" was to focus on contemporary religious errors, examining them and displaying them "conclusively as the root of all the evil that has befallen us." In this, Werthmann was consistent in his worldview. The rejection of, or at least distancing from, Christian tradition and teaching was primarily responsible for the rise and fall of Nazism.

In search of a solution, he turned his attention back to the problem of the Americans. He categorically rejected the stance that the occupiers reportedly took, the assumption that "it was sometimes bad for the churches and cloisters, the priests and religious orders over the last twelve years, while things were great for the rest of the people. That persuades no one because it's absolutely unsound." The proper answer lay in the work of Christian charity. This alone was capable of moderating such arguments and differences of opinion, and it had to be preserved at any cost. As priests, Werthmann insisted, "We must 'become all things for all people' [*Allen alles*] and charity must provide for this." The priests he was addressing would have understood his allusion to Paul's letter to the Corinthians, which examines the obligations and rights of an apostle preaching the Gospel.[76] In Germany's end-of-war climate, it was not hard for these men to imagine themselves as missionary apostles, seeking to bring those around them back to God.

But it was not just the Americans who the priests had to watch. Werthmann confessed that on occasion, he served as a witness to Allied examinations of Germans during what eventually became the standard denazification process: arrest of an individual based on a denunciation or accusation, followed by interrogation. He reported that he was "aghast" to discover that the accused "were not only told what accusation had been made against them . . . but also *who* had leveled the charge. In this context, the names of local Catholics priests and priests from the neighboring villages were given, among others. It is understandable on a basic human level [*menschlich begreiflich*] that these Germans were shattered to discover that even their village priests were among their accusers." Werthmann was firm about the evil that this practice caused. He insisted that too much was at risk if individual clerics cooperated "excessively" with the Allies or became too implicated in an element of reconstruction that included the obliteration of Nazism. Priests were not to be "consigliores" (Werthmann used the Latin *"Consiliarii"*) to the occupying authorities.

As a result of making themselves available to the Allied powers, who were in turn keen to take advantage of any help they could get on the ground in Germany, Church leaders such as Werthmann and the bishops would come to play an integral role in Germany's reconstruction beyond the end-of-war period. In their public and private correspondence, they stressed repeatedly that priests were to avoid any lengthy sermons or discourses of a political nature. How strictly this was adhered to is a difficult question to answer. Certainly many bishops were, like Werthmann, already weighing in by May 1945 with their disapproval of mass arrests of former Nazi Party members, part of the early Allied approach to denazification.[77] They viewed this, as many Germans did, as misguided and overly harsh. Their opposition was instrumental in winding the process down in the following years before it had been completed. In any case, even if priests and bishops refrained from engaging in politics, the churches became important focal points of social, cultural, and spiritual authority. Given that the western Allies were slow to permit Germans to resume independent political activity, it was natural that Germans looked to their clergy for guidance and support in this realm as well. They did so even if that guidance was unofficial and indirect, even if all they sought from their spiritual leaders were cues on how to interact with the occupying powers.[78]

The Internment of Werthmann

Much of what Werthmann knew of the Americans, and by extension the Allies, came from his firsthand experience when they captured him at the end of April. His detailed report regarding the first few days of his internment is both representative of the chaos and confusion most Germans faced in those days and exceptional in that he experienced his arrest as a leader in the German military. The report is also noteworthy because it was among the first set of notes he wrote to himself at the beginning of his internment, with "Monday, 30 April 1945" handwritten at the top of the page.[79] His report contains observations about the Americans who arrested him; the treatment he received along with his chaplain colleagues, Dohrmann and Münchmeyer; and his fellow German soldiers and citizens. Moreover, the reader gets the sense that Werthmann, uncharacteristically, had not yet processed the situation. The writing is full of restrained emotion, from dread uncertainty and defensiveness to genuine curiosity and (ultimately) palpable relief.

The report opens dramatically. Werthmann and his Protestant companions had already taken refuge at the monastery in Niederalteich when they were found. "Dohrmann was sitting and reading innocently in the garden at about eleven in the morning when an American soldier materialized before him and pointed a pistol into his chest," Werthmann explained. The "Yankees" were searching for two deserting soldiers, presumably from their own army, when they arrived at the monastery. Along with the inhabitants of the neighboring village of Hengersberg between the ages of seventeen and sixty, the Americans took the three chaplains to a collection point. There they were given "preferential treatment," likely because the Americans supposed that the violet badges on their uniforms indicated officer status (it is not clear from Werthmann's notes when the Americans realized they were chaplains and not officers). From Hengersberg, they were taken to the company commander's headquarters a few miles away. As they sat waiting to be questioned, Werthmann watched his captors "coming and going, working nonchalantly. What we understood about the Wild West was visible in this room, the world of the American soldier. The large table in the middle of the parlor was strewn with motley cans, keys, boxes and leftovers from provisions. We've likely never seen something so grungy and neglected. The soldiers sat or stood around, curious but without any malice."

Eventually a major approached and informed them through an interpreter that, not far from where they were camped, an SS unit had gruesomely executed sixteen Russian POWs, shooting them in the ankles and, when they could no longer run, bludgeoning them. Werthmann recalled, "[The major's] rage colored his face and his speech. When Dohrmann uttered something to the effect that the German Wehrmacht had nothing to do with such things, the major brusquely returned that SS men were also German soldiers." They were taken to view the bodies, an episode that Werthmann acknowledged "affected us greatly."

They then met with a German-speaking intelligence officer who attempted to converse with them in such a way as to avoid the impression of a formal interrogation. The "conversation" centered on the mentality of the German people. The questions and statements he posed included, verbatim from Werthmann's report:

1. How does it happen that in the houses here one finds so often a crucifix hanging on the wall next to a picture of Hitler?
2. The German people are complicit in so many horrible things that have happened in Germany because they never tried to cast off the horrible regime, but rather they tolerated it.
3. German priests, too, have incurred a heavy guilt since they employed neither their positions nor their pulpits to fearlessly castigate the regime. If they had done this, things would have been different.
4. Why didn't parents protest the recruitment of their sons into the Waffen-SS?
5. The German people have a slavish obedience and answer "yes" to every order, without considering the moral integrity of the order.
6. In the future, as in the past, the German youth will idolize Hitler and will consider him a choirboy if the foundations of the current catastrophe are not sought. Everything possible will be offered as an explanation for Hitler's downfall, above all the treason of the German generals and the enemy air terror, but never one's own individual failure.

7. Did Hitler actually leave the Church? Was it possible that he received the Last Rites?

The officer, a chemistry student who had studied in Switzerland, was direct and unyielding. He demonstrated a firm understanding of what was at stake for the German people in terms of collective responsibility for war and genocide. Indeed, some of his questions continue to resonate more than sixty years after they were first posed. For Werthmann, they represented an "American mentality," but he conceded that the queries were not easily answered.

The Americans then left the Germans to decide what to do with them, and Werthmann passed the time trying to discover the details of the campaign raging around them. He was ignored when he asked if Passau had fallen. In a neighboring room, he could see German soldiers being questioned, and their information passed on via telephone. He noticed a seated woman whom Dohrmann identified as a spy. Werthmann gave a brief description—"she flirted and reported"—then noted sardonically that she got along well with "the Yankees." The rigid prohibition that forbade American soldiers from speaking with Germans clearly did not apply to her.

It was not until the next day, 1 May, that the Americans informed the Germans that they were to remain in Niederalteich. The news reduced Dohrmann to tears of relief. Werthmann's reaction was more ambivalent: "But I know what this news means for myself." He did not elaborate in his notes on what he meant by this, but it did not take him long to find a way to fill his time.

Werthmann's Notes

Defeat and occupation pose two methodological obstacles for the historian intent on following these men into the end-of-war period. First, few of them had the time or inclination to express themselves about their experiences, orally or in writing. Second, in the end-of-war chaos, documentary evidence was destroyed, both accidentally and deliberately. The retrospectives and memoirs that do exist were often composed decades later, when emotional and temporal distance made it easier for these men reflect upon their experiences with some degree of detachment and perspective. This makes the historian's attempt to approach the mentality and emotional disposition of these men—to get into their heads, as it were—a particular methodological challenge.

Yet one underutilized source proves an exception. Georg Werthmann wrote extensively about his experiences in the chaplaincy and not only during his internment at Niederalteich in the spring of 1945. These notes continued into the years and decades that followed, until the late 1960s. These observations, jotted down shorthand or typewritten as brief remarks or personal reflections, were meant to aid him in the ambitious project of writing a history of the military chaplaincy from 1935 to 1945. He called it *"Geschichte der Feldseelsorge"* (History of the Military Chaplaincy). He put aside the project because of his postwar responsibilities with pastoral care and the subsequent assistance he provided to the Bundeswehr to construct a new military chaplaincy in the 1950s. He later abandoned the project completely when he felt himself too old to write.[80] Though he ordered his personal journal from the Nazi period destroyed upon his death (one can only imagine what insights into his personality and his understanding of the situation this would have offered), the extensive and thorough notes he made for his history of the chaplaincy have survived nearly intact. From this trove of information, one can discern something of Werthmann's hopes and ideas and his struggles and triumphs. It forms an autobiographical sketch of a man who had a deep and abiding commitment to his vocation and his military duty. He quickly distanced himself from the Nazi regime and its leadership in the war's aftermath (like most Germans). The notes reveal the climate that he was operating in in mid-1945: the political upheaval, the social devastation and uncertainty, and the challenges confronting Germans about their recent collective past.

It is problematic that these observations were made post facto—he began his writing as a prisoner of the Allied forces, with the full knowledge that the Third Reich was disintegrating before his eyes along with, literally, entire German cities. Undoubtedly, this affected his understanding of his own experiences from the previous twelve years. It explains certain passages of uncharacteristic melancholia in his writings about the future of Germany. And it necessitates that the historian approach Werthmann's notes with caution, paying full attention in particular to the external factors that influenced his mind-set. It is unsurprising that he was intensely critical of Nazism and the regime's leadership, at a time when most Germans were abandoning their support, ardent or otherwise, for the regime. That he avoided commenting on Germany's vanquishers, even the Soviet Union, is less predictable.

But even if we cannot accept his statements at face value, neither can we afford to ignore them. However untrustworthy or biased, these materials are evidence of the tremendous ideological flux that the end of the war and the beginnings of the occupation caused, both for the Catholic German priests and seminarians serving in the Wehrmacht and for lay Germans in general. They also reveal a great deal about the note-writer, as a priest who felt keenly the spiritual needs of the men around him; a man driven by a sense of his own self-importance and self-value; a German devastated by the collapse of the Third Reich and the physical destruction of his Fatherland; a Catholic clinging desperately to his faith for solace and support.

After the interrogation, Werthmann returned to the monastery to begin writing prolifically about his experience in the chaplaincy. It seems that this was a form of therapy. Between 12 May and 29 December 1945, he produced more than 100 separate reflections on various topics, some only a paragraph long, others taking up several pages.[81] Between 1946 and 1968 he produced another half-dozen reflections, two of which are especially lengthy. The end of June 1945 was most productive, with twenty-seven reflections penned in the last week alone. He continued to write, though at a less feverish pace, with another thirty-nine entries emerging over the next three and a half weeks. Five of these came on 26 July, the day before his release from internment. The topics were varied, though the previous ten years in which he served as one of the leaders of the Catholic military chaplaincy clearly inspired most of the choices. The majority of his reflections concerned pastoral care in the field and the regulations governing its exercise during the war. Other subjects that preoccupied him were the Nazi Party (especially the Chancellery) and its anti-Catholicism; the purpose of chaplaincies and the difficulties chaplains experienced during the war (a subject he separated from his comments about general pastoral care); and the purpose, legitimacy, and meaning of the war. He wrote of the end-of-war atmosphere and the challenges it posed to priests and the Church, and he reflected on the nature of state-Church relations, both what they should be and what they had become during the Hitler era. He also singled out several individuals for more specific commentary, including his superiors, Franz Justus Rarkowski, Karl Edelmann, and Hermann Reinecke, as well as several chaplains. Most of the reflections are moderate in tone, displaying a man striving to maintain a neutral analytical eye, though occasionally the mask slips and raw emotions surface. This occurs in particular during his discussion of the end-of-war devastation of German culture and the party's attacks on the Church.

Nazism, the Party, and the War

During his internment, Werthmann did not dwell at length on Hitler or the specifics of Nazi ideology. Instead he offered exculpatory condemnations of a more general nature: for example, "a meticulous plan, probably composed well in advance, underlay the anticlerical politics of Nazism" or "the Nazi Party anxiously avoided giving clear expression to their fundamental anticlericalism. Many measures of an anti-Church nature were launched under misleading declarations."[82] He also catalogued the abuses of the regime on the home front, "the abolition of cloisters and schools, the seizure of church property, the deportation of priests to Dachau, the prohibition of pastoral letters, the blocking of the distribution of written religious material, including catechisms and songbooks." These actions, he said, affected the chaplains on the frontlines.[83]

Werthmann was adamant that Nazism's defeat was rooted in its attacks on the Catholic Church. It was not the invasion of the Allied armies from the west that spelled the regime's end, and certainly not the Red Army from the east, but rather, an internal struggle of its own making that doomed the movement. In one striking reflection, he lamented what he perceived to be a lost opportunity on Nazism's part to find a way to rejuvenate Germany spiritually and to make peace with the churches. But because "the radicalism of the party carried the day over the moderate orientation, above all concerning the solution of religious problems," this was not possible. The "hateful clique of church reformers and ideological fanatics" ensured that "the conditions of a peaceful coexistence between Christian and anti-Christian circles in Germany" were never realized. "Instead," he opined, "people have become bitter, chagrined, detached and, thanks to the Reich, more estranged than ever."[84] In this analysis, Werthmann kept good company with other Germans across the intellectual and political spectrum who gravely misunderstood Nazism as either a force that could be controlled or a force whose "radicals" ruined its potential for good.[85] Werthmann also found it difficult to understand his own relationship to Nazism after its disintegration. That he made the above comment after Nazism's downfall suggests at the very least that he was struggling to accept his own naiveté (or willful blindness) on this issue.

Nor was the struggle finished. Werthmann was not foolish enough to believe that a clear path lay ahead for Germany and its priests. Yet he was obstinate in his conviction that they would play an important role in the end-of-war world as the nation grappled with the record of the last twelve years and confronted all that had happened. "As Christians and priests," he mused, "we stand alone now more than ever as the only undeviating representatives of superhuman norms and eternal values, and it can be that a raging storm of antagonism and hate is rising up, a storm that will shake our very foundations more than what lies behind us."[86] While he was wrong to depict all Catholic priests as stalwart symbols of Catholic values, faithfully living by these principles, Werthmann correctly assessed the chaos of the end-of-war period, the antipathy that all Germans had to confront, and the feeling that Germany had to start over, from a zero hour, or *Stunde Null*.

The Chaplaincy

The theme that most consumed Werthmann's attention during his internment was the chaplaincy. This is predictable since he began to jot down his thoughts with the express purpose of producing a history of that institution under the Third Reich. He returned repeatedly to the organization he helped construct and the men who worked within its framework as well as those who operated discreetly alongside it. The wealth of information he left to the Field Bishop's Office, which now forms a collection that bears his name, is the largest source of evidence concerning the chaplaincy during those years. He did not shy away from examining his own role, and he was both laudatory and critical, penning reflections that were alternately descriptive and interpretive. That he emerged as a major figure in the reconstruction of the West German

Bundeswehr's chaplaincy in the mid-1950s shows that he remained convinced that pastoral care was necessary for fighting men. No matter how compromised chaplains became, or how fiercely the organization was criticized, its benefits ultimately outweighed its drawbacks.

Werthmann set out a brief history of military chaplaincies in the western world, likely to legitimize the Wehrmacht's chaplaincy as an institution. He began in antiquity, citing the Edict of Milan in 313, the decree responsible for making tolerance of Christianity in the Roman Empire official and that also established a system of pastoral care for soldiers in the army. This history continued until the Council of Germany in 742, when a missionary-archbishop named Boniface originated the idea of an organized military chaplaincy for use in times of war.[87] Boniface laid down rules, including the prohibition on clerics bearing weapons and the requirement that spiritual advisors accompany nobles at war ("one or two bishops as well as a palace priest [*Pfalzpriester*]"). Later popes approved of the chaplaincy, though they protested against military service for priests. It was not until the emergence of modern, standing armies in Europe (a development that Werthmann located in the seventeenth century) that a more formally regulated chaplaincy became a necessity.[88]

This tradition of pastoral care mattered to Werthmann because it reminded his putative readers that the idea of a military chaplaincy predated Nazism. Accordingly, long-observed conventions were in place that the Nazi Party simply could not eradicate, at least not quickly and not without endangering its relationship with the military's leadership. The party tried to interfere with soldiers attending mass by granting furlough on Sundays or assigning work that made attendance difficult. But, Werthmann underscored, the "barracks hours were very well attended, and masses were arranged once per month for each unit."[89] Those Nazis interested in frustrating the activities of the chaplains and their leaders, however, found other means to do so. They included surveillance of the field bishop's pastoral letters, which Rarkowski tried to issue regularly during the war. Another was curtailment of pastoral activity as punishment for transgressions. A third was the frequent issuance of new lists of regulations and guidelines.

Moreover, in Werthmann's mind, the concordat itself excused Nazi control of the chaplaincy. The concordat guaranteed the existence of pastoral care for Catholics in the military, a basic foundation for the chaplaincy that would continue so long as its regulations were not violated. For this reason, "the field bishop had no right to throw in the towel of his own accord." Even if, according to his conscience, he was called to make judgments about the legitimacy of the state and its organs as an individual, Werthmann was unyielding that as the field bishop, the head of the Catholic chaplaincy, to expose himself to such options would lead to "subjectivism [and] a general insecurity" with fatal consequences.[90] In other words, the field bishop worked to achieve a higher aim, which compromised his ability to think or act of his own volition. Doing so risked endangering the entire enterprise and possibly implicating others who may have shared his view.

In Werthmann's view, this higher purpose also justified the lack of dissent, opposition, or open insurrection among the Church hierarchy, from the pope down to each individual chaplain. He insisted that the pope never gave up "on lamenting the war and admonishing for peace" throughout the six long years of the conflict. Nor could he pass judgment on an individual nation because he had to avoid estranging large segments of the European Church. Since Catholic priests found themselves on all sides of the fight, and each "had the right to understand that his side of the war was justified, it was therefore that priest's moral, Christian duty to stand at the disposal of his people, to help and to serve." Even if these men decided that "their war was immoral, this did not entitle them as private individuals in the army to intrude on the legitimate government of their state and to preach insurrection against the leadership of the people."[91] Again, Werthmann returned to the broader societal objective of the chaplaincy and to the biblical exhortation to obey the authority of a legitimate state. To Werthmann, it was unthinkable to question the state's legitimacy as a whole, even if he had qualms about certain individuals. This logic displays the same thinking that branded the conspirators of the 20 July bomb plot that nearly assassinated Hitler as traitors of the highest level and not merely by hardened anti-Nazis.[92]

Whether leading Nazis were aware of this self-imposed obedience on the part of Catholic priests is ultimately irrelevant. If they did know, they proceeded as if they could not rely on that obedience. Their attempts to control the system of pastoral care in the military extended even to the chaplain's uniform, the most obvious manifestation of his station. Chaplaincy ranks were given no easily recognizable characteristics, no epaulettes or other insignia. What did the lack of identifiable rank connote in a social institution governed by just that? If ranking imparts authority, then its absence might have enabled potential harassers to act on their hostility with less hesitation. It also might have made it more difficult for soldiers seeking pastoral care to identify their chaplains. Yet Werthmann insisted that the lack of insignia could benefit chaplains. Limiting the uniform distinction to bands of color on the collar constituted "evidence that the chaplain was neither soldier nor officer nor civil servant, but a priest, and as such couldn't somehow be schematically inserted into the military rank and file." He also had to work consciously to make others, from the common soldier to the field marshal, aware that he was present as a chaplain. Moreover, epaulettes and other insignia conferred an automatic hierarchical status on the individual wearing them and, consequently, a power relationship between himself and the soldier with whom he interacted. Without this insignia, the chaplain had to rely on his own internal authority and comportment. Those chaplains with "inferiority complexes" found the "occasional humiliation" difficult to manage. But for the one whose belief in himself and his mission was less faltering, "such [episodes] could only [reinforce] his belief in the singularity and greatness of the task given to him."[93]

Werthmann interpreted the exemption of the chaplaincy and the field bishop from German ecclesiastical oversight as necessary for his work. A bishop responsible to both military and civilian authorities would be too compromised, he insisted. Moreover, the confidentiality of military affairs that emerged within the sphere of pastoral care could be called into question if the field bishop was also a civilian authority. The field bishop was "independent, subservient to no German bishop, not a participant in the Fulda Conference, and directly responsible to the Holy See."[94] The problem with this interpretation was that the field bishop's independence existed on paper only. Practically speaking, Rarkowski, and Werthmann as well, operated within all sorts of constraints, both hidden and obvious. Nor was he responsible directly to the pope, though this was a concordat term. It is not clear that Rarkowski and Pius XII ever met, and throughout the war, the Field Bishop's Office and the papacy virtually never corresponded.[95] Moreover, the field bishop was jointly responsible, not just to the pope, but also to Hitler, the head of the German government. The appointment of Werthmann as provisional field bishop showed that it was Hitler, via Keitel, who was really the field bishop's superior.

Party Control of the Chaplaincy

It is evident that the entity that Werthmann called the "Party" or the "Chancellery" achieved a great deal of success in controlling the Church within the military during the war.[96] Despite Werthmann's attempts to make the opposite case, the available evidence indicates that these men, bent on curbing or even eliminating the influence of chaplains and priests in the military, came closer to realizing this goal than did their Nazi Party counterparts dealing with civilian bishops and clergymen. The field bishop was weak and easily controlled. His second-in-command showed no signs of open resistance or dissent. The chaplains could be restrained via a series of decrees that some individual army leaders complained about but never formally protested. The chaplaincy was being gradually but actively eroded when in October 1942 the OKW mandated that no more chaplains would be recruited. Strict regulations controlled the *Priestersoldaten*, and by 1944 the OKW was taking steps to reduce their numbers under arms. It is difficult to construe any of these developments positively for the chaplaincy. Taken together, they created a stifling atmosphere.

Though he consistently worked to depict his chaplains as occupying positions of strength, brimming with devotion and exercising all possible autonomy within the chaplaincy, Werthmann minced no words in retrospectively describing their enemies' reach and their attempts to minimize the chaplaincy's efficacy. To him, the Nazis were insidious and omnipresent, "ready to strike and criticize the chaplaincy, when and if offered the means to do so." The party was so good at employing procedural machinations to inhibit and undermine pastoral care that it was impossible to obtain an overall view of its effects on priests.[97] "We chaplains got the feeling that above all we were tolerated," Werthmann reflected several months after his internment ended, and "sooner or later Nazism was going to abolish the chaplaincy completely."[98] He detailed painstakingly what he viewed as a multistep strategy, a "meticulous plan, probably put together long in advance," that undergirded the "anticlerical politics of Nazism." These efforts included the constriction of pastoral care activities to the practice of religion and the characterization of religious soldiers as "confessionally constrained" in an attempt to outlaw chaplains. When this failed, the "starving out [Aushungerung]" of the chaplaincy began via the prohibition of new appointments in October 1942 and continued with the liquidation of religious literature in the Wehrmacht.[99]

In spite of these challenges (or perhaps because of them), Werthmann aggrandized the role of the chaplain to heroic proportions. In a passage quoting Nietzsche—"A hero is someone who serves so great a thing that his own self does not enter the picture"—he insisted that the chaplain forswore his own health and life for the sake of the mission to serve others. No soldier would ever "get the impression that his pastor is more certain, or that he's better off."[100] The chaplain was the caretaker of "a great Christian legacy among soldiers of war," a "holy inheritance," preserving the religious life of Christian soldiers "in the face of the proclaimed eloquence of the party, embodied by the NSFO, and in the face of the seductive power of ideological postulations."[101] He did not minimize the wartime difficulties that chaplains encountered, asking rhetorically, "How could they please everyone?" The party wanted to entrap chaplains, the bishops at home wanted them to be reserved and passive, the OKH wanted to use them to eliminate church-state tensions by focusing exclusively on loyalty to *Volk* and Fatherland, and the officers wanted them to be aides in leading the troops. Yet "in many cases the soldier looked up to his division chaplain in the silent hope of seeing in him a secret ally in his own rejection of the political system."[102] This last comment suggests a willful distortion of reality on Werthmann's part and a certain readiness to see an opponent of Nazism, or at least of the dictatorship, in every soldier. Did he also misrepresent the impact of the chaplain on the rank and file? Given the contemporaneous evidence highlighting other voices attesting to the influence of chaplains, this does not seem to be the case. Rather, this was one more effort made by Werthmann to deliberately distance himself, and those with whom he served, from the regime and its crimes in the end-of-war period.

The *Priestersoldaten*

A second issue over which Werthmann obsessed in his notes, an issue of great contestation in which the Nazi Party's interests clearly trumped those of the chaplaincy, concerned the "priest-soldiers," or *Priestersoldaten*. Very little study has been conducted of them. This imprecise term encompassed several categories of men, either in religious life or intending to enter it, who were conscripted after war broke out but who did not serve in the chaplaincy. *Priestersoldaten* included Catholic priests (whether attached to a diocese or religious order); nonordained religious brothers; and aspirants to the priesthood (both seminarians and advanced theology students intending to enter the seminary). Reasons for excluding them from the chaplaincy differed, ranging from party animosity toward an expanding chaplaincy to the fact that priests serving outside the chaplaincy could not administer the sacraments. Though in an army of millions they were very scarce, estimates putting their number at more than 11,000 prove they were not insignificant.[103] According to Werthmann's own notes, the highest number of Catholic chaplains ever to serve at one time was 410, in the summer of 1942.[104] In other words, priests serving outside the chaplaincy far outnumbered those serving within it. Because they were not formally part of the chaplaincy, its rules did not govern their conduct. Moreover, as Werthmann made clear, a demand for more chaplains came from the chaplaincy leadership as well as from soldiers and officers who asked for pastoral care. In the eyes of the party, therefore, the *Priestersoldaten* constituted a threat that required control.

Werthmann conceded that no one kept statistics about the *Priestersoldaten* and their exact contribution to pastoral care, but he felt (perhaps unsurprisingly) that it was substantial: "Despite the comparatively small number of chaplains, the greatest possible number of units were provided with masses and, most importantly, the greatest possible number of dying soldiers received the last sacrament in hospitals [because of these priests]." These men, "who selflessly and altruistically placed themselves at the service of the chaplaincy, are owed a special thanks."[105] Initially, in a sweeping 1940 prohibition, the OKW officially forbade them from saying masses for troops after the authorities became aware of the activity. Later, the OKH supplemented this decree with a contradictory directive, valid only for the army (not for the air force or navy) that provided a loophole: *Priestersoldaten* were required to obtain a complicated series of permissions involving the relevant chaplain (likely the divisional chaplain, though Werthmann does not clarify this) and the issuance of an indult, or special permission, from the appropriate local (civilian) bishop and notarized by Rarkowski as field bishop. What was painstakingly transparent was that the use of such a priest was supposed to be temporary, and it was to be allowed only if the relevant permissions had been obtained. But the loophole existed.[106]

In his notes, Werthmann indicated that the loophole was exploited as often as possible owing to the lack of chaplains and because, for their part, the *Priestersoldaten* resented the proscription on administering pastoral care. It is impossible to say how often this happened, how many priests received the permissions, and how many did not bother with the permissions and, with the help of a sympathetic chaplain, operated covertly anyway. Evidence that Werthmann kept suggests that military authorities enforced the policy as consistently as possible. It is not clear what happened to those priests caught breaking the rules.

The OKW and the Party Chancellery remained apprehensive enough about this group (especially the ordained priests) to issue directives imposing increasingly severe limits on their activities as the war progressed. One ordinance tried to ban the *Priestersoldaten* from saying mass privately, that is, without a congregation of troops. Werthmann seemed particularly incensed about this directive, recalling that it "was absolutely not easy to convince Wehrmacht authorities that there was a difference between private and public masses, and that the Wehrmacht had no right to forbid *Priestersoldaten* from saying private masses." Eventually the OKW released a modification that permitted such masses but "only in the individual's free time, and other civilians or members of the Wehrmacht cannot participate."[107] In June 1944, the OKW took an even more drastic step, releasing from active service all Roman Catholic priests, brothers, deacons, and candidates for the priesthood ("those studying Roman Catholic theology") who had advanced into the officer corps of the reserve.[108] Though, again, no hard statistics are available about how many men this move affected, at a time when the military needed fresh bodies desperately it seems like a foolishly self-destructive decree. Taken together, such antagonistic behavior on the part of the Nazi leadership makes it more difficult to dismiss Werthmann's claim that the churches would have been destroyed had the war culminated in a German victory.

Werthmann even insinuated that this hostility had something to do with the removal of Brauchitsch, commander of the army, in late 1941. He reported Edelmann's disclosure of a conversation with Wilhelm Keitel, leader of the OKW, who apparently said, "Field Marshal von Brauchitsch is gone. He held the view that a Christian army is essential. The Führer holds the view that each [soldier] should be spiritual in his own way."[109] If Keitel accurately captured Hitler's view, then this was a radical departure from the professions of respect for religion that the Führer uttered when the concordat was signed in 1933. Such sentiments would also have given those anti-Catholic Nazis in Hitler's inner circle freer rein to act upon their hostility.

* * *

After the fighting ended in May 1945, hardship and suffering defined daily life for most Germans for many more months. The physical reality of the country compounded the privation of its citizens: cities of rubble, disrupted communications, and a humiliating occupation. The Catholic cathedrals in Dresden, Munich, Hildesheim, Würzburg, Münster, Berlin, Mainz, and elsewhere were either heavily damaged or totally destroyed. Like all Germans, the Catholic bishops awaited news about the fate of family and loved ones while trying to process the resounding German defeat. They said masses and administered the sacraments as often as they could in the bombed-out, blackened husks of their churches, masses that were extraordinarily well attended judging by photos and observers' reports. And they dealt with foreign troops in their streets and their homes, troops that brought to the forefront the incontrovertible truth about the atrocities that the Nazis perpetrated in the name of the German *Volk*. Auschwitz may not yet have become the standard signifier of genocidal terror, but the opened gates of the German camps that the advancing Allies liberated released more than enough horror with which the Germans were compelled to deal.

Given this context, it is disappointing but perhaps unsurprising that Germans en masse, their spiritual leaders included, failed to understand what they had just survived: the nature of the Nazi dictatorship, which had preached national revival through the lens of a biological-racial worldview that necessitated war, ethnic cleansing, and genocide. Indeed, we expect too much to think they might have apprehended the full extent of Nazism in the immediate wake of a cataclysm that shattered political systems, families, armies, and even the traditional frameworks for understanding what philosophers have long considered staples of the human condition itself: suffering, persecution, death. Catholic clergy were no more equipped than lay Germans to come to terms with the unprecedented chaos and anguish that the Nazi regime had unleashed. Whether we consider a bishop caring for his diocese or a seminarian making his way on foot back to his home town, no amount of education, training, or even faith could have prepared them to process (to our satisfaction or theirs) sites of mass shooting and systematized murder such as Auschwitz and Babi Yar, Lidice and Treblinka, Mauthausen and Belzec. What had been attempted in these places had never before been attempted and was, simply, unthinkable. Tellingly, this particular word is one that postwar scholars continued to employ even decades after 1945. Given this, that Catholic bishops lacked not only the language but also even the mental and emotional framework to comprehend and process what they had undergone is hardly surprising.[110]

To acknowledge this reality is not to excuse their conduct, permit apologetics, or suggest that the manner in which they chose to make sense of their recent past was acceptable. The language they employed and the justifications they resorted to were often wrongheaded, insensitive, and offensive, but they were not irrational. In trying to understand better what compelled men such as Werthmann, Stohr, Jaeger, and Gröber to think, write, and say what they did is an exercise in empathy, but not exculpation.

Based on Werthmann's voluminous notes alone, it becomes clear to the historian that the man who essentially ran the military chaplaincy remains an enigma. He was certainly an ardent German nationalist who loved his country and his fellow Germans, but he was also a dedicated priest whose devotion to the chaplaincy and his fellow clerics is undeniable. He did not conceive of the end of the war as the end of trials and tribulations for himself and his brethren or for Germany. In fact, he was convinced that the Germans who survived into the postwar world of physical and spiritual devastation on an unimaginable scale could navigate that world only with the help of priests and the Christian faith. Whatever else the war and Nazism had visited upon the priests who had served in the Wehrmacht, at a minimum they had experienced privation and warfare, which they shared with all Germans. This common experience provided an essential basis for recovery and rebuilding.

Beyond these conclusions, however, Werthmann is difficult to characterize. Many of his reflections are written in language that sounds both Catholic and Nazi. While some passages indicate that his mindset remained predominantly Catholic, others suggest that he did not oppose Nazism as adamantly as his retrospective criticism might indicate. He found ways to work within the party's framework. He never openly protested its policies, even when they undermined the chaplaincy. He thought highly of Karl Edelmann, a career soldier who worked in the OKH and who clearly valued pastoral care, but who was ultimately faithful to his superiors in the military and keen to keep the chaplaincy under their control. Werthmann stayed at his post to the bitter end, defended the men serving in the Wehrmacht, and continued to wear the military uniform until after Allied forces captured him.

Unlike his contemporaries, Werthmann left us with an abundance of written evidence (even if he failed to mention anything about atrocities or death camps). With bishops, chaplains, and priests, far less evidence is available to go on, and certainly very little personal reflection of the same depth and breadth as Werthmann's notes. Trying to explain the silence in the written record, particularly with respect to the genocide of the Jews, is no easy task; resisting the urge to rush to judgment or misread silence are significant challenges that this book will address in the conclusion. Yet these challenges are not impossible to overcome. Scholars increasingly devote attention to theorizing silence and providing interpretive frameworks through which silence can be better understood. Silence itself is a form of communication, a social activity, and a tacit collective enterprise between those who might speak and those who might hear.[111] It bears emphasis that the bishops and Werthmann were not totally silent; they did speak about the recent past and about Nazism. That they had no words for the sufferings of the regime's true victims testifies on one level to their obsession with their own suffering. Their fixation reflected not only the genuine hardships facing their country and their people, but also their own inability to confront the emerging knowledge of the anguish and murder that the war (one that they had willingly supported) had brought—and Germany's responsibility for those crimes.[112]

Is Werthmann's perspective representative of the spiritual leaders of Germany or the majority of Germans themselves? Werthmann's notes admit of no easy answer. He lived through the death throes of the Nazi regime, total defeat in war, and complete political and social disintegration. He witnessed the emergence of a postwar Germany, its identity in flux, its people divided among four occupying powers, its leaders fled or dead. At this critical juncture the Catholic Church's leaders stepped forward, compelled by the suffering of the German people and encouraged by the Allies who sought their help. They tried to shepherd their flocks back to a state of normalcy as defined by Christian doctrine and dogma. Werthmann, too, felt a keen sense of responsibility to those who had been under his care in the military and who were now attempting to find their way back to civil (and civilized) life. For them, he could do little during his internment, but he played a pivotal role after his release in the same way that bishops and priests were appealed to for guidance, succor, help, and support.

But Werthmann also exemplified common German attempts to navigate the turbulent wake of the Third Reich: a deliberate distancing from the Nazi regime and the conviction that soldiers, and Germans generally, were not culpable of the crimes in the concentration camps and knew nothing of Auschwitz. Catholics, in particular, revised the recent past to give the Church the gloss of unwavering resistance and opposition to the regime. The bishops fixated on Christian Germans at the expense of those peoples whom Nazi policies most grievously harmed, especially the Jews. Werthmann himself used this kind of language, as did perhaps most Germans. As German scholar Ulrich Helbach reminds us, "the bishops were also part of the people," and therefore prone to the same anxieties, the same despair, the same defensiveness and coping strategies, however shortsighted they proved.[113] Like his episcopal brethren, Werthmann never displayed hesitation or regret over having missed a historic opportunity to acknowledge loudly and unambiguously the primary victims of the Nazi regime—the Jews—and the complicity of broader German society, including the Church, in enabling their victimization. But it was an opportunity missed for reasons that are readily apparent.

At the end of the war, Catholic German clergy were disillusioned and devoid of resources. Although priests were quickly consumed with the immediate task of gaining the confidence of and carving out a sphere of agency with the occupying authorities, they were also attempting to confront and comprehend the recent past, albeit with varying degrees of success. If one accepts Werthmann's efforts as typical in this regard, these confrontations with the past were generally more exculpatory than self-critical. Given the context, however—a second catastrophic war ending in defeat, the apparent victory of Bolshevism, the material obliteration of German cities—and knowing that Germany had brought all of this upon itself, from a psychological standpoint, perhaps Germans were incapable of doing more.

CONCLUSION

APPROXIMATELY 17 million men wore the Wehrmacht uniform during the Second World War, most of whom were conscripted. Of these, more than 17,000 of them self-identified as Catholics who were either ordained priests or in the process of becoming priests. Numerically they constituted but a small subset of a larger cohort of German boys and men who transitioned at some point during the war.[1] However, the small number of these men belies their significance. Taken as a whole, their example attests to the continued relevance of traditional expressions of belief—especially the Christian religion—even in the Nazified army of the Third Reich. They felt that the men with whom they served, both soldiers and officers, needed them because of their open spirituality. Nazi ideology, with its central tenets of biological racism and *Lebensraum*, could not justify the war or their role in it, something they felt that they shared with other soldiers. As catastrophic defeats subsumed initial German victories, their religion and their vocation took on increasing significance. By the day of capitulation, with the regime shattered and the country devastated, these men, like the priests and bishops who had remained on the home front, could rightly claim that their religious faith had outlasted Nazism itself.

Even in a world defined rigidly by total war and Nazism, in which individuals subordinated themselves to the needs of the community, personal agency and independence were still possible. This was true for those serving in a tightly controlled military machine. Priests and seminarians in the Wehrmacht show this definitively. In doing so, they complicate two conventional explanations of behavior during the Third Reich: first, that the majority of Catholic clergy passively accommodated, and only very rarely resisted, the regime's policies; second, that soldiers by and large served in Hitler's army out of ideological conviction, particularly as the war dragged on.[2] In this regard, their collective experience reaffirms Thomas Kühne's work on comradeship and the desire to sustain a sense of belonging, even within the genocidal community that Wehrmacht soldiers and SS men comprised.[3] In other words, while there were certainly ignoble reasons (peer pressure, cowardice, fear, to name a few) for soldiers to continue fighting a criminal war and incentives to participate in atrocities, there were also positive reinforcements for involvement. For men such as Werthmann, the chaplains, and priests and seminarians in uniform, this positive reinforcement was founded on the spiritual needs of soldiers, needs that did not dissipate when Hitler came to power or when the war began.[4] As did many Germans, both Catholic and Protestant, believing and nonbelieving, they actively and willfully understood the war effort, and their own role in it, to be part of a mission for the greater good. Whereas other Germans may have interpreted the "greater good" in purely nationalist, political (i.e., secular) terms (the reversal of the humiliations of the Treaty of Versailles, the reestablishment of Germany as a great power), the men who are the subjects of this book stand apart from those who held these interpretations because of the vocational aspect of their military service. The religious terminology they employed to articulate the "greater good," which highlighted the need for pastoral care for the soldiers and the acquisition of skills to become an effective priest, also set them apart. Many Catholic priests and priests-in-training believed that the war could not be won without them, just as a future Germany without Christianity was likewise unthinkable (as was the idea, after 1941, of a communist victory).

This conviction was so powerful and so deep-rooted that it continued to inform the justifications of many of these men four decades after the German capitulation. A series of interviews given in 1990 and 1991 confirm this. Following the thirty-year anniversary of the appointment of the Bundeswehr's first military bishop, in late 1986 the director of the archives of the Catholic Military Bishop's Office in Berlin sent out a general letter to all surviving priest-veterans of the Wehrmacht. He requested any documentation regarding their military service that they still possessed. Several of the approximately 140 still-living veterans agreed to be interviewed at the archives about serving in the Wehrmacht. The interviews would be used to make a documentary film about pastoral care during the Second World War. Karl-Heinz Peschke, a journalist who had worked for the Vatican organ *Osservatore Romano*, Radio Vatican, and several German Catholic newspapers, conducted the interviews. Their testimony was also compiled and edited into a narrative volume of short stories and reflections. The interview questions they were posed disappear in this book.[5] But the interview transcripts are housed at the archives, complete with interviewer questions and interjections and the interviewee's unedited answers.

The questions ranged from general queries about wartime experience to specific probes about situations and the individual's emotional responses. Unsurprisingly, Peschke asked the men about their interactions with other officers and soldiers, their views on Nazism and whether their service had helped the regime, and their knowledge, or lack thereof, of atrocities in extermination camps. Most interviews mentioned the NSFO, the Nazi political commissar unleashed in the Wehrmacht in the last two years of the war. Most interviewees reflected seriously, often at length, about the war's justness. And yet, very few willingly admitted to the influence of Nazism in the Wehrmacht. Indeed, a couple of them reacted defensively, and even angrily, to the idea.[6]

What follows is a cursory examination of some of these responses, focusing on the themes of the atrocities, a "Nazi Wehrmacht," and the near universal (and counterintuitive) claim of no regrets for having served. These answers are striking because, in addition to the men's religious conviction about their duty to their fellow soldiers—a form of comradeship, a commitment to community, and a manifestation of their vocational aspiration—the essential ingredient of nationalism remains evident. These men were deeply German.

Atrocities

Few chaplains, priests, or seminarians serving in the Wehrmacht acknowledged the atrocities they witnessed or heard about, against Jews and non-Jews, contemporaneously. It was only years after the war, when they wrote memoirs or gave interviews, that they addressed the subject. Despite the intervening decades, the veterans—all of them still priests—divulged what they had known about the crimes perpetrated both on German soil and in the East. More than a few steadfastly maintained that they knew nothing, even those who had served on the Eastern Front (most of them did at one point). "I was never a witness to any atrocities or massacres," insisted Karl S., "nor knew anything of deportations of Jews or concentration camps. Only after the war did I learn of them. Soldiers hardly spoke of such things, they probably didn't know much about it. I only heard about the priests in Dachau after the war, too, but very soon after."[7] Franz E. likewise said, "I knew nothing of the Jews, absolutely nothing. But there was Dachau, that I knew about, and I knew that there were priests in there. . . . But of the stories of the Jews [*Judengeschichten*] I knew nothing."[8]

Other priests admitted to hearing rumors, but claimed to be unable to distinguish between what was true and what was not. They tended to treat isolated instances as anomalies, refusing to believe that they were emblematic of something more systematic. In this manner they echo the sentiments of the bishops at home and even of Werthmann, who carefully qualified their reactions to news of atrocities with claims of ignorance and the inability to distinguish between fact and rumor. Alois K. had learned of "this thing in Katin [*sic*]," he said when asked if he had witnessed any massacres, referring to the massacre of Polish officers by Soviet soldiers.[9] "But in Stalino [Donetsk, Ukraine]," he went on, "they had done away with the Jews there. There we were even more outdoors, for there was an old mine. And there, allegedly, the Jews were all shot and thrown into the pit. So, that was the only thing that I picked up on . . . [about concentration camps and persecution of the Jews] we hardly heard anything."[10]

Josef P., who published his wartime journals about his time as a medical orderly and, later, chaplain, explained, "At the time I was in a small Polish city that was full of Jews, all of whom wore the Jewish star. But the systematic extermination had not yet begun. . . . I never witnessed atrocities against Jews or civilian populations. I only heard about it after the war." He recalled, "Someone explained to me that SS troops had thrown Jewish children into the air and picked them off. But those were stories—I never witnessed it. I didn't know if it was true."[11] But in his provocative published journal, he mentioned several times seeing Jews wearing the yellow star in the streets and being packed into ghettoes. He must have concluded that there was some truth to the "rumors" because in 1943, when stationed in Krasny (Russia), not far from the site of the Katyn massacre, he wrote in quiet despair, "What gruesome secrets are hidden in Russia's silent expanse! I think of the mass grave at Roslawl [Russia], the droves of Jews that we've seen in the Polish cities and who in the meantime have been killed. What should we expect when the blood of an Abel screams loudly from the earth?"[12]

Others witnessed the ghettoes but were unsure what to make of them. As Christians, they claim to have recoiled at the sight. But as part of the German army, no individual priest issued a formal protest. Joseph H. never saw Jews murdered, but he witnessed "a horrific suffering when I twice crossed through the Warsaw ghetto. There I saw suffering. That affected one at the most profound inner level. I was speechless that such a thing could be possible. We also once drove past a smaller ghetto in Poland, and we stood at the fences there . . . the bodies already ravenous and emaciated."[13] He alluded to helping the inhabitants clandestinely whenever possible, but he never spoke of it to others or questioned his superiors. Did he understand it as an unfortunate consequence of the war? As something disconnected from the persecutions of German Jews before 1939 or the antisemitic propaganda of the Nazi Party since 1933? On this level, priests' reactions reflect a spectrum of possibilities available to other soldiers: evasion, astonishment, disapproval, apathy, but generally no indication of revulsion, reproach, or indignation about the treatment of another human being. No evidence exists that they greeted the crimes with enthusiasm, as some soldiers did, or that they participated in them directly. Nor is there evidence that they reflected on the meaning of their inaction.

Other testimonies, however, suggest that there were too many rumors during the war for contemporaries to ignore them completely. Several priests learned of the atrocities from eyewitnesses. Chaplain Otto F. was stationed with units working not far from the SS and "Gestapo-people . . . who were killing Jews." He remembered that one man "really said to me, 'Father, do you know, what we're doing here is the biggest disgrace [*Schweinerei*] in the world. Once the war is over, may God grant that it ends, then they'll hang all of us.' He said that, verbatim."[14]

Franz E., who claimed to know only of Dachau's horrors before the war ended, admitted hearing troubling news from Holland, where he was stationed up to the end of 1940 before he transferred to northern Germany and Scandinavia. While in the Hague he met both Edith Stein, a German-Jewish convert, philosopher, and Carmelite nun, as well as Archbishop Jan de Jong. Only after 1944, when "everything was at an end for Holland," did he hear about the pastoral letter that de Jong and the other Dutch bishops circulated "for the benefit of the Jews. Then on the next day all the Jews [of Holland] had been immediately rounded up, among them Edith Stein."[15] Martin Z. received disturbing information in August 1944 from a Polish priest in Galicia (a region in eastern Europe that straddles modern Ukraine and Hungary): "He then explained to us about Auschwitz. . . . Before this I knew nothing. . . . He said, 'When the war is over, we'll go on a pilgrimage and mourn our dead.' He gave no information how many, or anything. But he said it, and I took notice. During transport we went by it . . . there were large fields and people working in them. It must have been in the vicinity of Auschwitz."[16] He did not elaborate on what else the priest told him, or about the workers he had seen. Nor did he opine on why a Catholic priest considered Auschwitz the death site of "our dead," in light of the fact that the vast majority of its victims were killed because they were Jewish.[17] But he clearly identified the experience as the first time he learned of the extermination camp.

A minority of priests had more direct experiences than merely hearing rumors. The events remained disturbing for them decades later. At the time, however, they were not traumatic enough to merit interfering with or questioning orders. These men encountered the massacres during or immediately after their perpetration. Wilhelm R. was in the Crimea, "where there were 6,000 Jews. They had been shot into an anti-tank ditch, children had also been seized by the legs and struck dead with stones. They were Jews."[18] Later, a Jewish doctor approached him; she had been temporarily spared, "perhaps because she was needed. She said to me, 'I know that I'll get it soon, a curse hangs over our people, its blood is over us and over our children.' She was recaptured at Jalta [sic] and shot."[19] R. did not say how he had learned of her fate. He explained in the interview that he approached a commander of his medical transport unit and told him that he was scared, that they had to atone for what they were doing, and that the officer was "nice" and "likable." This seems to be the extent of R.'s reaction. While stationed in Thessalonica, Lorenz W. lived on the fourth floor of an apartment building that, in the front, housed German officers and in the back a Jewish family. On the morning that the city's Jews were deported, a young woman of the Jewish family asked him to try to spare her grandmother, who had bad asthma. His response is not clearly explained, but he recalled seeing them "suddenly in the city with their bed sheets and all of their worldly goods now removed [from their home] . . . and [when] I returned, the apartment was empty. They were gone. What could one do? Nothing! One was powerless."[20]

In garbled postwar testimony, Kunibert P. claimed to have been in Rutnia [sic—Ruthenia?] when he

> was near a shooting [*war ich lediglich einmal bei einer Erschießung dabei*], completely voluntary . . . [the SS, who were already in the area] shot Jews. There was a collection point, and the Jews there had grown lousy, and in fact [it had happened in spite of] the typhus inoculation and others. . . . Then the SS came, and outside was an anti-tank ditch, and there they were taken out and were shot. I went out as well, in order to see more closely . . . it was ghastly, this I can say, these shootings . . . they shot the people, first they had to strip and they collected the fabric for [re-]use . . . and I saw young girls who hugged each other, and were shot embracing each other. And on another day, there were trails of blood in the snow from those who had been only half-shot, and who had crawled out again and got maybe 500 meters and then froze and bled to death. They had simply been shot [into the ditch] and left lying in there, half-living, half-dead. And those who were not yet dead were then smothered by those lying on top of them. This was the shooting of Jews that I experienced by the SS [*die ich da mitgemacht habe bei der SS*].[21]

Like W. and countless others, P. did not confront those doing the shooting. They remained nameless except for allusions to the SS.

Assessing these reactions satisfactorily is a methodological challenge. Should this testimony be accepted at face value? If not, how does one determine its veracity in the absence of confirmatory evidence? To this conundrum, there is no definitive solution. What is certain is that at least a small minority of priests knew of atrocities during the war, told of them by soldiers who had seen or participated in them. The others profess ignorance, either genuine or willful. Given what contemporary scholarship holds about the reality of the war in the Soviet Union, and that most of these men were stationed on the Eastern Front at some point between 1941 and 1945, it is highly improbable (but not impossible) that they had heard nothing of mass shootings and death camps before the end of the war. Regardless of what they knew, what they dismissed as rumor, and what they accepted as wartime collateral damage, the effect was the same: no voice raised dissent to official Wehrmacht policy.

Defending the Wehrmacht

In the Wehrmacht, these men were not simply priests or priests-in-training who happened to be outfitted in a uniform. They were also soldiers. Questioning an order, let alone disobeying one, was a dangerous, even lethal proposition. It is therefore unsurprising that insubordination occurred infrequently. Instead, in the postwar interviews they focused on the reason they had donned a uniform: soldiers and officers. Given this behavior, the few veterans (both former chaplains and *Priestersoldaten*) who spoke on the subject were defensive about the army of which they had been part. To this end, they distinguished it from the regime, Nazi Party ideology, and politics in general, even after historians had revealed the extent to which the Wehrmacht was complicit with Nazism. Since most interviews were conducted in 1990, the traveling Wehrmacht exhibit, which for the first time forced Germans to confront publicly the complicity of the Wehrmacht in war crimes and genocide during the Second World War, had not yet taken place. The discussion of Wehrmacht atrocities was largely confined to scholarly texts and individual stories.[22] It is not clear how many, if any, of these men saw the Wehrmacht exhibit, and if they did, whether it changed their views of the soldiers with whom they fought. Unfortunately very few of these men are still alive, and none well enough physically to be interviewed for this book. So their testimony remains a snapshot of a moment in time, at the beginning of the 1990s. It is representative of the pervasive popular opinion in Germany that the Wehrmacht (and by extension its chaplaincy) had been "clean," not guilty of genocide, just before that opinion was shattered beyond repair.

According to these veterans, the Wehrmacht was "a world apart. It was shaped by old traditions and soldierly reasoning, it was apolitical," and National Socialist tendencies had no effect.[23] Kunibert P. declared, "I have to say, our Wehrmacht, or at least the division I was in, was anything but Nazi." When his interviewer responded, "I hear this repeatedly," he reiterated, "Anything but Nazi."[24] Otto F. explained the lack of resistance within the army as part of the "soldierly sphere," and that "it was abhorrent to us, to defect, to desert." He decisively condemned Nazism—"the Nazi worldview, just like the communist one, is repugnant to me," and "we served an unethical regime, that was clear to everyone, the Nazis were criminals"—but he also adamantly maintained, "I've already said, I was gladly a soldier, but we were never Nazis."[25] Josef Buslay even targeted the historiography of the 1980s and 1990s that challenged the image of an apolitical, "clean" Wehrmacht: "That was no Nazi Wehrmacht. Today things are simply warped and presented indiscriminately. The majority of men wanted nothing to do with Hitler, Goebbels, Göring, and the rest of them. Most were also— at least I can say this about the Catholics—cemented in their beliefs."[26] This testimony indicated two parallel beliefs in the minds of many surviving veterans: the first, that one could make apolitical decisions even in the highly politicized environment of the Wehrmacht; the second, that one could divorce military service from Nazism. These beliefs reinforced the stance many had taken in the late 1940s, one rooted deeply in their psyche, that the Catholic Church, from its leadership to its most humble layperson, had been a bastion of resistance. This conviction had penetrated into the army through its Catholic soldiers. Therefore, one could serve in the military and simultaneously reject the tenets of Nazism.

Georg Werthmann commented on this point during his 1945 internment. He did not waver from the belief that officers were generally supportive of pastoral care in the army. In fact, so many seemed to accommodate his efforts and those of Bishop Rarkowski that "a quiet hope crowded into me, that Nazism would suddenly be overcome and toppled by the military." He lamented that such hope proved delusional: "The opportunity to forge a career, glancing sideways at epaulettes, the 'sore throat' [*Halsschmerz*, an allusion to the Knight's Cross of the Iron Cross], clouded their view of the actual welfare of the Fatherland."[27]

But eliminating opportunism did not necessarily create a more pious officer corps or military. In fact, Werthmann had written explicitly a few weeks earlier about the extent of Nazism's penetration into the military: "The 'Heil Hitler' was performed in the army. Nazi training and the NSFO were the alpha and omega of the Wehrmacht. The German army, whose pride and duty was always to protect the *Heimat* and to serve the *Volk*, was dead. The Wehrmacht was nothing more than a party organization, reshaped as "Nazistic" to pressure the soldiers uniformly into the hands of the party with the most radical instruments of power. [This was so that they would] fight on, if only to protract the end of the Nazi Party."[28]

Werthmann composed his observations in the end-of-war period, before the narrative of the "clean Wehrmacht" had emerged but as Nazism's evils were being exposed to the world. As part of the chaplaincy, holding the equivalent rank of major general as acting field bishop, Werthmann was a member of the Wehrmacht's officer corps, which he described as "Nazistic" and "nothing more than a party organization." As astute as he was in his end-of-war reflections, it must have occurred to him in writing those words that he implicated himself in the process, at least indirectly. It is one of the most critical expressions uttered about the Wehrmacht at the end of the war, not just by Werthmann but by anyone involved in the military.

How does one reconcile these two incongruous interpretations of the Wehrmacht? Either the Wehrmacht was a instrument of the Nazi Party's objectives or it was not. Generalizations about its ideological makeup are difficult to make, since more than 17 million individuals served in its ranks. Perhaps it was possible for some priests to avoid any serious Nazis in uniform during the war. But the interviews with the veterans took place nearly five decades after the end of the war. These men had a vested interest in holding to the concept of a "clean Wehrmacht." They clung to the narrative that West Germany had adopted wholeheartedly after the war, namely that the Nazis and the SS were the villains and the Wehrmacht had held out against their tyranny and evil. This neat bifurcation enabled veterans, including priests, and Germans in general to salvage something out of the total disaster that was the Third Reich.

No Regrets

Questions about the Wehrmacht and its relationship to Nazism generated queries about whom the priests had served in the military: the regime, the Church, or a third party. This question also involved issues of hindsight and regret. When pressed after the war whether he had served the regime or the church, Martin Z. answered, "I wanted always to serve the church. I believe that my service went in this direction."[29] A seminarian in the medical corps wrote to Werthmann in 1943, "You become better acquainted with a country and its people and individual men than in peacetime. Then we aren't so packed in with each other, a motley group forced together. And you get further when you join in, even to the smallest degree."[30] Egon S. explained that pastoral care was an integral part of any army, and that he never regretted his service in the Wehrmacht. It was not for the sake of the regime that priests went to war, he argued, but for the soldiers in uniform who were putting their lives in danger. As Josef H. claimed and most chaplains would have agreed, "I never served the regime, only my Church, and even more so the men [in the army]."[31] Chaplains would always be essential to armed forces, "for the military will always be a group that stands for itself, that has difficult tasks and therefore requires guidance for its conscience."[32] H. insisted that he went for the sake of the men, to attend them in their final hours, to help them with their struggles and stand by them in death. When nothing else could be done, he was there "to be able to bend the rules for him [*oder ihm dann auch nur die Augen zudrücken kann*]."[33]

Friedrich Dörr acknowledged the complexities in saying yes to wartime service: "This was of course in certain ways a service to Adolf Hitler, but for our part, we didn't think of it this way. The men should [be allowed to] maintain their faith in God, and despite all the difficulties through which they were living, find a foothold and remain unwavering [on their path]."[34] Wilhelm W. also reflected on the nature of his service and its meaning:

> I served the Church. A side effect of this was, in effect, to render a service to the state, but I had to hazard the consequences. I believe fundamentally in helping soldiers, in serving them, in preserving the

Church and to that final end serving the glory of God, and I believe that this was a serious matter. The other part of it included a cooperation that one simply couldn't repudiate. Incidentally, the same problem exists regarding the [denazification] advisory offices. I don't know if you know about this? It's also said that, because this advisory body issues clean bills of health, it is possibly guilty. But how far does the guilt extend . . . ? That, then, is the question.[35]

W. clearly had no answers to his own question. Otherwise he was unwilling to push himself to consider them. By invoking the advisory bodies that issued certificates of denazification (these allowed individuals to be rehabilitated after the war), he intended to point out the inherent difficulties of multiple allegiances. This was a real dilemma over which he reflected, maybe even agonized. Of the many priests who looked back on their wartime service decades later, he was one of few who acknowledged that, as a group, chaplains' actions had had an important, in some ways negative, effect on the overall war effort.

Most, like Lorenz W., tried to avoid the question altogether by claiming the obvious:

I must say, these questions [about whether I served the church or the state], they've emerged in postwar discussions. . . . The theory of criticism came out first with Adorno's Frankfurt School, before it didn't exist. Before it was more a mind-set, which wasn't really theoretically reflective. . . . So, have you served more the state or . . . that is really self-conscious conceptual terminology [*Begriffssprache*].[36]

W.'s response evades the problem of having served a criminal regime through military service. While he and most other priests gave testimony in the postwar period, they refused to reflect on the nature of their service and how it contributed to the war effort beyond the spiritual support that they knew it provided for soldiers. Alternatively, some veterans declared that there was only one right choice, and that was to sacrifice one's moral and political qualms with respect to Nazism and work solely for the men: "The [importance of the] work with badly wounded men became unquestionably clear to me," Josef P. stated. "We had to use this freedom, this opportunity, that was given to us. If we had rejected the opportunity to be in Hitler's army, then we would have consigned countless Christian soldiers to a desolate death. . . . I have no doubt; that, for me, this was the right thing to do."[37] When pressed whether politics played a role in making this decision, P. insisted, "No, never. Everyone knew that. [Being political] made no sense, because it would have unnecessarily endangered us.... For us, a Europe ruled by Hitler was a horrific vision.... One could only wish that the end might come soon, eventually through a putsch carried out by higher military men, and the damage contained as much as possible."[38] Such reasoning led priests like P. to believe that abandoning Christian soldiers to brutal war because they disagreed with the regime was contrary to their calling. If they claimed refuge in apolitical statements or declarations of rejection—"We never agreed with Hitler or the Nazis"—then participating in the war that these powers waged was sanctioned.

Two other important contexts for these comments are worth noting. The first is that the regime had designed the terms of the 1933 concordat explicitly to depoliticize Catholic clergy. To preach from the pulpit about nonreligious issues or to hold meetings about the regime's policies would have violated the concordat's terms, which the clergy were careful not to do. This behavior continued into the ranks of the Wehrmacht, underscoring the belief that acting or speaking politically was dangerous. Second, some of these priests may have understood that the regime's criminality and war should have met with protest or resistance, perhaps even a refusal of the conscription order. But such an action would left conscripted Catholics with one less spiritual guardian in a life-or-death environment. The consciousness of the dire need for pastoral care must have weighed heavily. This outweighed any impulse to take a principled stand against a regime that did not tolerate dissent. When a priest can literally see before him a phalanx of Catholics asking for spiritual guidance in the midst of a battle of annihilation, the idea of abandoning his training and ignoring that plea for guidance was morally irresponsible.

One veteran chaplain's response encapsulates the dilemma that most priests and seminarians anxiously avoided contemplating, which this book has tried to explore: "Naturally, one wondered repeatedly if this was a just war ... on the one hand, as a Christian, one couldn't endorse the regime, couldn't support it. But *on the other hand, we did this indirectly, by emboldening the soldiers.* Doubt often came over me: should I continue doing this or not? And if I thought about the soldiers themselves, I could do nothing but continue."[39] D. may have been one of the few who verbalized the inner conflict that many of his colleagues shared. He is also representative of the choice that they all eventually made. They could not abandon their men, even if that meant aiding and abetting a hostile regime or enabling the murder of innocent civilians. Like all good Catholics following the example of their elders, they were no different from the bishops on the home front or the field bishop of the chaplaincy and his vicar-general. In short, they did not perceive that other options were available to them. The one priest who declined to serve upon being drafted was Franz Reinisch, an Austrian Pallottine priest. He rejected conscription because he refused to recognize the authority of the Nazi regime. In this he clearly acted according to his own sense of right and wrong rather than the example of his spiritual leaders. For this, he was executed.[40]

Faith, Hindsight, and the Problem of Memory

None of these men justified the war. But none of them refused to serve. How, then, did priests and seminarians come to serve—willingly, even enthusiastically—in an army that was perpetrating an unjust war? In their own words, they found no contradiction between acknowledging an unjust war and arguing for the service they provided within that war. The fighting men needed them, and so they went. As Germans, it was their duty to defend *Heimat* and Fatherland. As Catholic priests, they were obliged to provide spiritual nourishment for men in combat. No conflict between nationalism and religion existed; both worked together to reinforce their actions and behavior during the war and their ex post facto justifications for it. It is easy to forget or overlook, as Chancellor Otto von Bismarck did in his nineteenth-century Kulturkampf, that Catholic priests were also German, and, like him, to assume that the loyalty of any Catholic lay ultimately with Rome. However, this was not the case for the majority of Catholics in Germany, both in Bismarck's time (when Catholics resisted state persecution but did not flee Germany and did not convert to Protestantism) and under Hitler. Catholics in Germany could look to a tradition of negotiating religious and national loyalties. Hard-pressed to choose between God and Caesar, Catholic clergy often chose Caesar, even if they rationalized that choice using the language of faith.

Because they were German *and* Catholic, the reasons for these men to serve voluntarily in the Wehrmacht are readily apparent. To expect resistance to the conscription order is understandable in hindsight. However, at the time such refusal would have required tamping down nationalist compulsions and ignoring their seminary training. Their options were more complex than the seemingly simple moral imperative to stand up to anti-Catholic hostility and criminality. Indeed, the dichotomy of silence and opposition is ultimately misleading. In the face of injustice and suffering, the most common response is conformity, complicity, silence. Hence the heroism of those few who do speak out. However, Catholic priests and seminarians, even the bishops and Werthmann, never understood themselves as silent. Their official record is filled with words, and one can only imagine the unofficial record, what was said conversationally or in private.

The aims of this book are not merely to caution against the dangers of ahistorical judgments, to better understand the complexity of human motives, and to attempt to account for so-called silences in the evidentiary record. It also seeks to grapple with the problem of memory, which weighs heavily both in Werthmann's end-of-war notes about events from years earlier, as well as in the published postwar diaries and daybooks of chaplains and the interviews of veterans in the 1990s. Forty-five years is a long time that is bound to produce gaps in memory, especially concerning traumatic events. These interviews demonstrate three things: first, it is important to note that the subjects were willing to speak, even if they could find nothing to say on some topics. To this end, it is imperative to try to understand why language failed or why not speaking was preferable to doing so. Second, interviews show that the passage of time had not diminished the subjects' commitment to service. They continued to stress that their reason for going to war had been to support other soldiers spiritually. Finally, the interviews suggest that the inability of priests and seminarians to confront the darkest aspects of their service was reflective of the general lack of serious self-examination and contrition within other social institutions, notably the German military and the Catholic Church. Only in the 1990s did intense, sustained, and very public discussions take place in Germany about the crimes of the Wehrmacht during the Second World War.[41] We still await a mea culpa of similar magnitude from the Catholic Church with regards to its role in centuries of anti-Jewish and antisemitic discrimination and persecution.[42]

Is it reasonable to expect otherwise from these men, given the parameters of their lives, the overlapping circles of loyalty and devotion to family, Fatherland, Church, and Christ? We may be dissatisfied with their explanations, but they stand as evidence of a long-term, unflinching dedication that did not change in the intervening decades. To comprehend these motivations in an empathetic way is not to exculpate their lack of protest over atrocities or war crimes. Nor does it obscure the fact, which a few acknowledged postwar, that in their capacity as spiritual guides and boosters of morale in the Wehrmacht, they were also enablers of the crimes that did occur. To understand the historical reasons for this behavior is not to excuse it.

Between 1933 and 1945, the seminarians, priests, and chaplains whom I have followed tended, with few exceptions, to mirror the example of Georg Werthmann: they accommodated Nazism. They did so not only under compulsion, but also because they truly believed that giving themselves to their country and their soldiers was a sacred obligation, stitched into the fabric of their vocation and their identity as Germans. Years of negotiation between higher Church officials, both in the Vatican and in Germany, and the Nazi regime presented a model of acceptable behavior that they could cite. The Catholic episcopate condemned the strident racism of the regime even before Nazism came to power, and many bishops and priests expressed concern about the hostility of some of its members toward organized religion. But as few as a dozen Catholics felt strongly enough about these obstacles to refuse their cooperation during the war. The rest fell somewhere between understanding Nazism as the lesser of two evils and understanding Nazism as essential for the defense of German Christendom. Nazi-led Germany in 1933 was infinitely preferable to communist victory in Europe. Additionally, this dilemma was a burden unique to Germany. Other largely Catholic countries, including France and Poland, could not be depended on to defeat Bolshevism. The Nazi war machine overrunning these countries in 1939 and 1940 must have settled any doubts about this. The invasions and defeat of these Catholic countries by an aggressive Wehrmacht elicited no commentary, and no evidence of sympathy, from their religious brethren in Germany.

Moreover, like Werthmann, these priests and seminarians saw that the salvation of Catholic German souls was more important than questioning the ideological, social, cultural, and military policies of the ruling party. Like the larger Church of which they were part, they tended to think about the temporal sphere in terms of the next life—*das Jenseits*, or the hereafter—and how to ensure that the maximum number of Catholics gained it. Confrontation with the Nazis was tantamount to abandoning those Catholic souls when they most needed spiritual aid. Their compromise with Nazism was, therefore, essential. To demand otherwise would be asking these priests and seminarians to go against their religious authorities and God. It would be asking Catholics to reject centuries of tradition. It would be asking Germans to betray not only their government, but also their country and fellow German citizens.

Not everyone compromised. Others could and did resist, and they paid for it with their lives. Choosing to collaborate with the lesser evil was still choosing evil.[43] Moreover, by focusing so exclusively on Catholics, these priests refused to aid those who most needed help between 1933 and 1945, particularly the Jews. Ingrained anti-Jewish sentiment, antisemitism, and feelings of fear, helplessness in the face of authority, and apathy no doubt constituted part of the reaction of clergy in the army to Nazi ideology before and during the war. But this does not explain it entirely.[44]

In the end, the problem was not a question of resisting evil or protesting wrongdoing, but one of (Catholic) souls and service to the Fatherland. Five decades later, those souls and the nationalist enterprise, which they understood as distinct from Nazism, remained the priest-veterans' justification for going to war as well as the basis for their total lack of regret about their experience. Such fierce dedication should be admirable in such circumstances. But it is not what these men did and said that strikes most deeply into the reader's consciousness. It is what they failed to do, neglected to say, and proved incapable of facing: that to accommodate or compromise with a racist, genocidal regime was antithetical to everything their faith stood for. The story of these men raises new questions about the nature of collaboration and resistance, the construction of morality and theology, and the limitations of religious men and women under the Third Reich.

APPENDIX 1

German Church Provinces, Dioceses, and Bishops in the Third Reich

The list below excludes Austrian and Sudetenland dioceses added to the Greater German Reich in 1938.

Church Province Bamberg
Archdiocese: Bamberg—Jakobus von Hauck
Eichstätt—Konrad von Preysing to 1935; Michael Rackl from 1935
Speyer—Ludwig Sebastian
Würzburg—Matthias Ehrenfried

Church Province Breslau
Archdiocese: Breslau—Cardinal Adolf Bertram
Berlin—Christian Schreiber to 1935; Konrad von Preysing from 1935
Ermland—Maximilian Kaller
Prelature: Schneidemühl—Franz Hartz

Church Province Cologne
Archdiocese: Cologne—Cardinal Karl Joseph Schulte to 1942; Josef Frings from 1942
Aachen—Joseph Vogt to 1937; Johannes Joseph van der Velden from 1943. (Aachen administered by auxiliary bishop Hermann Sträter from 1938 to 1943.)
Limberg—Antonius Hilfrich
Münster—Clemens August von Galen
Osnabrück—Wilhelm Berning
Trier—Franz Rudolf Bornewasser

Church Province Freiburg
Archdiocese: Freiburg—Conrad Gröber
Mainz—Ludwig Maria Hugo
Rottenburg—Johannes Baptista Sproll

Church Province Munich and Freising
Archdiocese: Munich—Cardinal Michael von Faulhaber
Augsburg—Joseph Kumpfmüller
Passau—Sigismund von Ow Felldorf to 1936; Simon Konrad Landersdorfer from 1936
Regensburg—Michael Buchberger

Church Province Paderborn
Archdiocese: Paderborn—Caspar Klein to 1942; Lorenz Jaeger after 1942
Fulda—Joseph Damian Schmitt to 1939; Johann B. Dietz from 1939
Hildesheim—Nikolas Bares to 1934; Joseph Machens from 1934

Exempt Diocese of Meissen—Petrus Legge

Vicariates-general Branitz and Glatz

APPENDIX 2

April 1944 Overview of Catholic Priests, Members of Religious Orders, Seminarians, and Theologians in Military Service for Greater Germany (Including Austria and the Sudetenland)

From the notes of Georg Werthmann; numbers valid for 1 January 1944.

CALLED INTO MILITARY SERVICE

Total number of Catholic priests beforehand (app.)	134,000
Of whom:	
(a) Catholic diocesan priests: 27,000	
(b) Catholic order priests 7,000	
Total number called into military service	6,218
Of whom:	
(a) Diocesan priests: 3,909	
(b) Order priests: 2,309	
Theology students (including those tonsured) called into military service	6,439
Of whom:	
(a) Those preparing to become diocesan priests: 4,387	
(b) Those preparing to become order priests: 2,052	
Lay brothers and religious [*Ordensleute*] called into military service	4,237
Order novitiates called into military service	872
Grand total*	17,776

* Statistics and totals are presented as they appear in the original document.

CASUALTIES

Accurate statistics of priests, seminarians, etc. who have fallen, are wounded, missing, or taken captive not possible due to destruction by hostile elements [*Feindeinwirkung*] or loss of corresponding documentation.

According to the statistics of 1 May 1943:

Fallen priests	316
Of whom	
(a) Diocesań priests: 187	
(b) Order priests: 129	
Theology students (including tonsured)	893
Of whom	
(a) Diocesan: 622	
(b) Order: 271	
Lay brothers	388
Order novitiates	121
Total	**1,718**
Missing priests	216
Of whom	
(a) Diocesan priests: 138	
(b) Order priests: 178	
Theology students (including tonsured)	250
Of whom	
(a) Diocesan: 159	
(b) Order: 91	
Lay brothers	127
Order novitiates	43
Total	**636**

Wounded priests	499
Of whom	
(a) Diocesan priests: 257	
(b) Order priests: 242	
Theology students (including tonsured)	1,214
Of whom	
(a) Diocesan: 779	
(b) Order: 435	
Lay brothers	557
Order novitiates	133
Total	**2,403**
Disabled [*arbeitsunfähig*] priests	33
Of whom	
(a) Diocesan priests: 23	
(b) Order priests: 10	
Theology students (including tonsured)	40
Of whom	
(a) Diocesan: 28	
(b) Order: 12	
Lay brothers	24
Order novitiates	3
Total	**100**

APPENDIX 3

Chaplain Rankings and Equivalents

The following, in ascending order, were the chaplain ranking equivalencies, although chaplains did not wear identifiable officer insignia.

Hospital chaplain (no ranking)
    (Lazarettpfarrer, Lazarettgeistliche)

Army chaplain—major *(Majore)*
    (Divisionspfarrer/geistliche, Korpspfarrer/geistliche, Armeepfarrer/ Geistliche)

Army senior chaplain—lieutenant colonel *(Oberstleutnant)*
    (Armeeoberpfarrer/geistliche, Heeresgruppenpfarrer)

Defense force deacon—colonel *(Oberst)*
    (Wehrmachtdekan)

The field bishop's rank was equivalent to a major general *(Generalmajor)*.

NOTES

ABBREVIATIONS

BA-MA   Bundesarchiv-Militärarchiv, Freiburg im Breisgau

EAB   Erzbistumsarchiv Berlin

EAM   Erzbistumsarchiv Munich and Freising

KMBA   Catholic Military Bishop's Office *(Katholische Militärbischofsamt)*

NARA   National Archives and Records Administration, College Park, Maryland

SW   Georg Werthmann Collection (at the KMBA), Berlin

INTRODUCTION

1. This estimation is taken from Hans Jürgen Brandt and the Katholisches Militärbischofsamt, eds., *Priester in Uniform: Seelsorger, Ordensleute und Theologen als Soldaten im Zweiten Weltkrieg* (Augsburg: Pattloch, 1994), 11. Brandt cites as his source for the exact number, 17,353, the military archives in Freiburg; it includes conscripted priests, seminarians, theology students, and members of religious orders from across the Greater German Reich in 1939, including Austria and the Sudetenland.
2. This was Franz Reinisch, an Austrian Pallottine priest. His story is recounted in the Conclusion.
3. Throughout this book I will use the term *Church*, with a capital letter, to refer to the Catholic Church specifically. The term *church*, lowercase, will refer more generally to Christianity or to issues common to both Catholicism and Protestantism.

4. This approach is very much at the heart of John Connelly's most recent book, *From Enemy to Brother: The Revolution in Catholic Teaching on the Jews, 1933–1965* (Cambridge, MA: Harvard University Press, 2012); quote from 9.
5. See Alon Confino, *The Nation as a Local Metaphor: Württemberg, Imperial Germany, and National Memory, 1871–1918* (Chapel Hill: University of North Carolina Press, 1997), and Helmut Walser Smith, *German Nationalism and Religious Conflict: Culture, Ideology, Politics, 1870–1914* (Princeton, NJ: Princeton University Press, 1995).
6. Because no single authoritative source exists on service statistics for the Wehrmacht during the Second World War, the total known number of German soldiers who wore the Wehrmacht uniform will never be exact. Rüdiger Overmans's *Deutsche militärische Verlüste im Zweiten Weltkrieg* (Munich: R. Oldenbourg, 1999) is the most frequently cited source for statistics. Sönke Neitzel and Harald Welzer estimate that Wehrmacht strength in September 1939 stood at about 2.6 million men; up to another 17 million were conscripted during the war. See Neitzel and Welzer, *Soldaten: On Fighting, Killing, and Dying* (New York: Alfred A. Knopf, 2012), 35. Hans-Erich Volkmann and Thomas Kühne echo the statistic of roughly 17 million soldiers. See Volkmann, "Zur Verantwortlichkeit der Wehrmacht," in *Die Wehrmacht: Mythos und Realität* (Munich: R. Oldenbourg Verlag, 1999); Kühne, *Kameradschaft: Die Soldaten des nationalsozialistischen Krieges und das 20. Jahrhundert* (Göttingen: Vandenhoeck & Ruprecht, 2006), 11.
7. Critics in the first group also often cite German Catholics' general acquiescence to, and occasional enthusiastic support of, Hitler's regime in their censure.
8. The most important studies of Catholic clergy under Nazism are Thomas Breuer, *Verordneter Wandel? Der Widerstreit zwischen nationalsozialistischem Herrschaftsanspruch und traditionaler Lebenswelt im Erzbistum Bamberg* (Mainz: Matthias-Grünewald-Verlag, 1992); Ulrich von Hehl, *Priester unter Hitlers Terror: Eine biographische und statistische Erhebung* (Paderborn: F. Schöningh, 1996); Kevin P. Spicer, *Resisting the Third Reich: The Catholic Clergy in Hitler's Berlin* (DeKalb: Northern Illinois University Press, 2004); Spicer, *Hitler's Priests: Catholic Clergy and National Socialism* (DeKalb: Northern Illinois University Press, 2008); Thomas Forstner, *Priester in Zeiten des Umbruchs: Identität und Lebenswelt des katholischen Pfarrklerus in Oberbayern, 1918–1945* (Göttingen: Vandenhoeck & Ruprecht, 2014). Recognition must also be given to Manfred Messerschmidt, whose two articles, both in the journal *Militärgeschichtliche Mitteilungen* in the late 1960s, were the first to treat Catholic chaplains in Nazi Germany as a historical subject: "Aspekte der Militärseelsorgepolitik in nationalsozialistischer Zeit" (1968) and "Zur Militärseelsorgepolitik im Zweiten Weltkrieg" (1969).
9. Currently, the most important works on the German chaplaincy of the Second World War are Doris L. Bergen, "Between God and Hitler: German Military Chaplains and the Crimes of the Wehrmacht," in Omer Bartov and Phyllis Mack, eds., *In God's Name: Genocide and Religion in the Twen-*

tieth Century (New York: Berghahn Books, 2001); Dagmar Pöpping, "Die Wehrmachtseelsorge im Zweiten Weltkrieg: Rolle und Selbstverständnis von Kriegs- und Wehrmachtpfarrern im Ostkrieg, 1941–1945," in Manfred Gailus and Armin Nolzen, eds., *Zerstrittene "Volksgemeinschaft": Glaube, Konfession, und Religion im Nationalsozialismus* (Göttingen: Vandenhoeck & Ruprecht, 2011); Johannes Güsgen, *Die Katholische Militärseelsorge in Deutschland zwischen 1920 und 1945: Ihre Praxis und Entwicklung in der Reichswehr der Weimarer Republik und der Wehrmacht des nationalsozialistischen Deutschlands unter besonderer Berücksichtigung ihrer Rolle bei den Reichskonkordatsverhandlungen* (Cologne: Böhlau, 1989); Thomas Breuer, *Dem Führer gehorsam: Wie die deutschen Katholiken von ihrer Kirche zum Kriegsdienst verpflichtet wurden: Dokumente* (Oberursel: Publik-Forum, 1989); Hans Jürgen Brandt and the Katholisches Militärbischofsamt, eds., *Christen im Krieg: Katholische Soldaten, Ärtze, und Krankenschwestern im Zweiten Weltkrieg* (Munich: Pattloch, 2001); Hans Jürgen Brandt and the Katholisches Militärbischofsamt, eds., *Priester in Uniform*; Katholisches Militärbischofsamt, ed., *Mensch, was wollt ihr denen sagen? Katholische Feldseelsorge im Zweiten Weltkrieg* (Augsburg: Pattloch Verlag, 1991); Heinrich Missalla, *Für Gott, Führer und Vaterland: Die Verstrickung der katholischen Seelsorge in Hitlers Krieg* (Munich: Kösel, 1999); Antonia Leugers, *Jesuiten in Hitlers Wehrmacht: Kriegslegitimation und Kriegserfahrung* (Paderborn: Schöningh, 2009).

10. Bruno Cabanes's concept of *sortie de guerre*, literally "exit from war," which I have translated as end-of-war period, distinguishes the period from the true *post*war era that follows. It will be more fully explored in Chapter 5 and the Conclusion. His original concept of the end-of-war period is introduced in *La victoire endeuillée: La sortie de guerre des soldats français, 1918–1920* (Paris: Seuil, 2004), 10–12.
11. Alon Confino, "A World without Jews: Interpreting the Holocaust," in *German History* 27/4 (2009): 547.
12. This was Michael von Faulhaber, who served as *Feldpropst* until 1917, when he was named cardinal and appointed archbishop of the diocese of Munich and Freising.
13. As quoted in Missalla, *Für Gott, Führer und Vaterland*, 209.
14. Further study awaits of Werthmann's postwar activities, in particular his role in reconstructing a military chaplaincy for the Bundeswehr in the 1950s. This story is too big to be told within the confines of this book, whose subject is not focused exclusively on this one man.
15. Both the subdiaconate and the terms of the secret appendix will be explored at greater length in Chapter 2.
16. The office and its archive were located in Bonn until 2000.
17. There exists only one, unpublished, biography of Werthmann, at the KMBA. It remains unpublished because of discrepancies in some of the factual details of the manuscript that were never revised. See Klaus-Bernward Springer, "'Ein guter und getreuer Knecht': Georg Werthmann (1898–1980), Generalvikar der Militärseelsorge im Dritten Reich und in der Bundeswehr" (Bonn, 1999). Werthmann is mentioned briefly in other works, including

those referenced above by Breuer, Güsgen, Messerschmidt, and Missalla. See also Gordon C. Zahn, *German Catholics and Hitler's Wars: A Study in Social Control* (New York: Sheed and Ward, 1962). Monica Sinderhauf's unpublished article on the resources of the archive where she works (the KMBA) also provides important details about Werthmann's career. Finally, Werthmann is fairly prominent in Georg May's work on pastoral care. See May, *Interkonfessionalismus in der deutschen Militärseelsorge von 1933 bis 1945* (Amsterdam: B. R. Grüner, 1978).

18. Bergen, "Between God and Hitler," 134.
19. Michael Phayer, *The Catholic Church and the Holocaust, 1930–1965* (Bloomington: Indiana University Press, 2000), 72.

1. CATHOLIC BISHOPS AND CATHOLIC YOUTH IN GERMANY AFTER THE GREAT WAR

1. Various pastoral letters dated 17 December 1918, 20 December 1918, 8 January 1919, and 22 August 1919, reprinted in Heinz Hürten, ed., *Akten deutscher Bischöfe über die Lage der Kirche, 1918–1933, Bd I (1918–1925)* (Paderborn: Schöningh, 2007), 32–43, 47–50, 98–103. This document collection will be referred to as *Akten DB*, followed by the relevant editor and volume number. A note: Throughout this book, all translations from German and French are my own unless otherwise noted. I have included the original German for particularly difficult, tricky, or ambiguous phrases.
2. Pastoral letter of Fulda Conference of Bishops, 22 August 1919, in *Akten DB I*, 102. The term will be explained below.
3. Antonia Leugers, *Gegen eine Mauer bischöflichen Schweigens: Der Ausschuß für Ordensangelegenheiten und seine Widerstandskonzeption 1941 bis 1945* (Frankfurt am Main: Verlag Josef Knecht, 1996), 14.
4. Hereafter referred to as nuncio, using the ecclesiastical title by which papal ambassadors stationed in countries with formal diplomatic relations with the Vatican are addressed.
5. Heinz Hürten, *Deutsche Katholiken, 1918–1945* (Paderborn: F. Schöningh, 1992), 63. Hürten states that the percentage of Germany's Catholic population dropped from 37 percent to 34 percent. There were twenty-five dioceses divided among six church provinces.
6. The diocese of Meissen was created in 1921 and placed directly under the jurisdiction of the pope and not a bishop. Meissen and its bishop were thus exempt and not included in the territory-based administration of the German church provinces. Leugers explains this in *Gegen eine Mauer*, 58–60.
7. The power structure of the Roman Catholic Church is centered on the bishop of Rome, whose jurisdiction extends over the College of Bishops (all bishops in communion with him). The College is further divided into separate conferences usually based on national boundaries. Each conference is divided into church provinces, with each province containing one archdiocese and a number of smaller (suffragan) dioceses. In this manner, the hierarchical chain of command stretching between pope and priest is clearly delineated. In Nazi Germany, that chain of command was considerably truncated, as political and diplomatic exigencies made communication be-

tween the Vatican and Germany difficult. While the bishops followed the pope's lead, they often formulated their own reactions to Nazi policy. Thus the bishops were both the authority to which Catholic Germans (clerical and lay) turned for guidance and the model of behavior that religious men and women were invited to imitate.

8. Leugers gives an excellent overview of the German episcopate between 1933 and 1939 in *Gegen eine Mauer*, 61–68. She includes several useful statistics, such as that 83 percent of the episcopate had studied theology at the university level and one-third had spent semesters in Rome; 66 percent were ordained bishops between 1906 and 1933; and 56 percent were born between 1860 and 1879. For a more general analysis of the Catholic bishops in Germany, see Karl-Joseph Hummel, "Die deutsche Bischöfe: Seelsorge und Politik," in Karl-Joseph Hummel and Michael Kißener, eds., *Die Katholiken und das Dritte Reich: Kontroversen und Debatten* (Paderborn: Ferdinand Schöningh, 2009), 101–124.
9. Mary Fulbrook, *Dissonant Lives: Generations and Violence through the German Dictatorships* (Oxford: Oxford University Press, 2011), 99.
10. Gerhard Rempel, *Hitler's Children: The Hitler Youth and the SS* (Chapel Hill: University of North Carolina Press, 1988), 59.
11. Fulbrook, *Dissonant Lives*, 7. The German pioneer of the study of generations is sociologist Karl Mannheim; see his "Das Problem der Generationen," *Kölner Vierteljahreshefte für Soziologie* 7/2 (1928): 157–184. Other studies based on the concept of generations include Walter Jaide, *Generationen eines Jahrhunderts: Wechsel der Jugendgenerationen im Jahrhunderttrend; zur Sozialgeschichte der Jugend in Deutschland, 1871–1985* (Opladen: Leske-Budrich, 1988); Mark Roseman, ed., *Generations in Conflict: Youth Revolt and Generation Formation in Germany, 1770–1968* (Cambridge, UK: Cambridge University Press, 1995); Jürgen Reulecke, *Generationalität und Lebensgeschichte im 20. Jahrhundert* (Munich: Oldenbourg, 2003); Ulrike Jureit and Michael Wildt, eds., *Generationen: Zur Relevanz eines wissenschaftlichen Grundbegriffs* (Hamburg: Hamburger Edition, 2005).
12. Fulbrook, *Dissonant Lives*, 54–55.
13. Fulda Conference of Bishops, pastoral letter of 22 August 1919, in *Akten DB I* (Hürten), 102.
14. Ronald J. Ross, *The Failure of Bismarck's Kulturkampf: Catholicism and State Power in Imperial Germany, 1871–1887* (Washington, DC: Catholic University of America Press, 1998), 5.
15. Ellen Lovell Evans, *The German Center Party, 1870–1933: A Study in Political Catholicism* (Carbondale: Southern Illinois University Press, 1981), 76. Margaret Lavinia Anderson, *Windthorst: A Political Biography* (Oxford: Clarendon Press, 1981), 178.
16. For more of this argument, see Ross, *Failure of Bismarck's Kulturkampf*, and Michael B. Gross, *The War against Catholicism: Liberalism and the Anti-Catholic Imagination in Nineteenth-Century Germany* (Ann Arbor: University of Michigan Press, 2004).
17. Ross, *Failure of Bismarck's Kulturkampf*, 136–142. Vandalism included the destruction of fences, walls, trees, and gardens and the smearing of

excrement on house walls. All are related in Ross, *Failure of Bismarck's Kulturkampf*, in addition to further details about passive resistance.
18. Gross, *War against Catholicism*, 222.
19. Evans, *German Center Party*, 92. The May Laws were not officially repealed for decades.
20. Jeffrey T. Zalar references Thomas Nipperdey in pointing out that interconfessional animosity was "one of the fundamental everyday and vital facts" of life in Imperial Germany, as important "as gender and class." Zalar, "Knowledge and Nationalism in Imperial Germany: A Cultural History of the Association of Saint Charles Borromeo, 1890–1914," unpublished dissertation (Georgetown University, 2002).
21. As Helmut Walser Smith states, "German Catholics could feel themselves both German and Catholic, but their Catholicism—despite the best efforts of Catholic polemicists—did not make them somehow more German." Smith, *German Nationalism and Religious Conflict: Culture, Ideology, Politics, 1870–1914* (Princeton, NJ: Princeton University Press, 1995), 68.
22. Evans, *German Center Party*, 93. Thomas Nipperdey describes it as an organization of the masses, particularly the middle strata, with members totaling 60,000 in 1891, 295,000 in 1905, and 470,000 in 1911. Nipperdey, *Religion im Umbruch: Deutschland, 1870–1918* (Munich: C. H. Beck, 1988), 81. Today, it remains one of Germany's largest and most prominent Protestant organizations.
23. Two excellent sources on this are Ronald J. Ross, *Beleaguered Tower: The Dilemma of Political Catholicism in Wilhelmine Germany* (Notre Dame, IN: University of Notre Dame Press, 1976), and Wilfried Loth, *Katholiken im Kaiserreich: Der politische Katholizismus in der Krise des wilhelminischen Deutschlands* (Düsseldorf: Droste Verlag, 1984). Ross attributes the discord in political Catholicism to regional variations, as the rivalry between Cologne and Berlin became more contentious in the two decades prior to the First World War. Loth, on the other hand, locates the tension primarily in a plurality of interests within diverse social groups. Both historians concentrate on the upper levels of political Catholicism, namely the Center's leadership and Church authorities.
24. Evans, *German Center Party*, 108.
25. Johannes Schauff, *Die deutschen Katholiken und die Zentrumspartei: Eine politisch-statistische Untersuchung der Reichstagswahlen seit 1871* (Cologne: J. P. Bachem, 1928), 74 (especially the table).
26. Schauff's statistics show that between 1898 and 1912, the Catholic vote in Germany rose from 28.1 percent to 30.6 percent of the voting population; in contrast, those Catholics who voted for the Center fell from 68.3 percent in 1903 to 54.6 percent in 1912. Schauff, *Die deutschen Katholiken*, 74. Nipperdey estimates that the Center enjoyed the support of about 90 percent of practicing Catholics at the peak of its popularity in the mid-1870s and somewhere around 60 percent at its nadir in 1912. Nipperdey, *Religion im Umbruch*, 23.
27. *Akten DB I* (Hürten), pastoral letter, 20 December 1918, 39.
28. Ibid.

29. Ibid., letter to Prussian state assembly, 14 October 1919, 116.
30. Pope Leo XIII, *Quod Apostolici Muneris*, 28 December 1878. All referenced papal encyclicals are accessible on the Vatican's official website, at http://www.vatican.va/offices/papal_docs_list.html (last accessed 9 April 2014).
31. Pope Leo XIII, *Rerum Novarum*, 15 May 1891.
32. Pope Benedict XV, *Ad Beatissimi Apostolorum*, 1 November 1914.
33. Peter Godman, *Hitler and the Vatican: Inside the Secret Archives That Reveal the New Story of the Nazis and the Church* (New York: Free Press, 2004), 99.
34. The first explicit mention of a crusade of prayers comes in a letter from Pope Pius XI to Cardinal Basilio Pompili, vicar of Rome, 2 February 1930, http://www.vatican.va/holy_father/pius_xi/letters/documents/hf_p-xi_lett_19300202_ci-commuovono_it.html (last accessed 9 April 2014). My thanks to Sebastian Rosato for help with translating this document.
35. *Akten DB II* (Hürten), "Report on Bolshevism," based on the protocol for the annual Fulda Conference of Bishops meeting, 6 August 1930, 1070–1071.
36. EAM Faulhaber 2013/3. The title of the second edition changed to "Storm over Russia." See also Andrea Kamp and Peter Jahn, *Unsere Russen, Unsere Deutschen—Bilder vom Anderen: 1800 bis 2000* (Berlin: Links-Verlag, 2007).
37. EAM Faulhaber 2013/3, emphasis added.
38. Ibid., "Der Antichrist auf dem Marsche," in *Wiener Kirchenblatt*, 19 January 1930.
39. Ibid., "Bolschewismus und Kultur," in *Umschau*, February 1930.
40. Ibid., "Die Religionsverfolgung in Russland," in *Münchener katholische Kirchenzeitung*, 11 March 1930.
41. All newspaper articles cited this paragraph in EAM Faulhaber 2013/1 and 2013/2, and included the following newspapers: *Wiener Kirchenblatt, Die Fränkische Wochenzeitung, Aus Welt und Kirche, Der Bayerischer Kurier, Die Deutsche Zeitung Berlin, Die Neue Zeitung, Die Kölner Volkszeitung*.
42. EAM Faulhaber 2013/2, 23 February 1930.
43. EAM Faulhaber 2013/2, 13 and 14 February 1930.
44. Lawrence D. Walker, *Hitler Youth and Catholic Youth, 1933–1936: A Study in Totalitarian Conquest* (Washington, DC: Catholic University of America Press, 1971), 4.
45. Peter Stachura, *The German Youth Movement, 1900–1945* (New York: St. Martin's Press, 1981), 21.
46. Ibid., 45–46.
47. Walter Laqueur, *Young Germany: A History of the German Youth Movement* (New York: Basic Books, 1962), xi.
48. Stachura, *German Youth*, 17.
49. Walker, *Hitler Youth*, 26. Walker's study of the Catholic and Nazi youth movements, though dated (some membership statistics are inaccurate), is still useful. He gives a brief overview of several other Catholic groups, 23–26. Two additional sources on the competition between Catholic and

Nazi youth groups are Laqueur, *Young Germany*, 162–164, and Stachura, *German Youth*, chapter 3.
50. Ulrich Linse, "Bernhard Grzimek," in Barbara Daldrup Stambolis, ed., *Jugendbewegt geprägt: Essays zu autobiographischen Texten von Werner Heisenberg, Robert Jungk, und vielen anderen (Formen der Erinnerung)* (Göttingen: Vandenhoeck & Ruprecht, 2013), 308–309. For a detailed history of the Quickborn movement, see Johannes Binkowski, *Jugend als Wegbereiter: Der Quickborn von 1909 bis 1945* (Stuttgart: K. Theiss, 1981).
51. Walker, *Hitler Youth*, 28–29.
52. Rempel, *Hitler's Children*, 267. The Nazi youth groups included the HJ, the Bund deutscher Mädel (Association of German Girls), the Jungmädelgruppen (Young Girls Groups), the Jungvolk (Young Folk), the Nationalsozialistischer Schülerbund (Nazi Pupils League), and the Nationalsozialistische Deutscher Studentenbund (Nazi Students League).
53. Rempel, *Hitler's Children*, 266.
54. See Derek Hastings, *Catholicism and the Roots of Nazism: Religious Identity and National Socialism* (Oxford: Oxford University Press, 2010), esp. chapter 4.
55. See Schauff's figures in *Die deutschen Katholiken* as well as Thomas Childers, *The Nazi Voter: The Social Foundations of Fascism in Germany, 1919–1933* (Chapel Hill: University of North Carolina Press, 1983), 113, 189, 261.
56. *Akten DB II* (Hürten), Mayer to the Munich ordinariate, 24 December 1929, 998–999. Emphasis added. Mayer remained concerned about the compatibility of Nazism and Catholicism, publishing an article in November 1930 in the Munich weekly *Allgemeine Rundschau* titled, "Can a Catholic Be a Nazi?" See EAM Faulhaber 8045/2.
57. John Connelly's most recent book provides an important analysis of Catholic racism in the 1920s and 1930s in Europe. He finds that centuries of racism required a "revolution in a church that claimed to be unchanging" and that during that period, Catholic Germans, including clergy, were more comfortable with racist language and attitudes than has previously been thought. See Connelly, *From Enemy to Brother: The Revolution in Catholic Teaching on the Jews, 1933–1965* (Cambridge, MA: Harvard University Press, 2012).
58. *Akten DB II* (Hürten), Faulhaber to the Congregation of the Council, 25 January 1930, 1002–1004.
59. The German bishops were sensitive to the 1864 *Syllabus of Errors* that Pope Pius IX had released, which condemned the freedom of religion and declared liberalism and Catholicism to be incompatible. They also took issue with Pius IX's doctrine of papal infallibility in 1870, which declared the pope incapable of error in matters of faith and morals when speaking *ex cathedra*. Many Catholic leaders, including bishops, had campaigned for Catholic rights "under the liberal banner of religious freedom" in the preceding decades, and the decrees from Rome seemed like a backhanded slap. For more information see Gross, *War against Catholicism*, 118. No less a figure than Wilhelm Emmanuel von Ketteler, bishop of Mainz and one of the most pop-

ular leaders of the time, joined Catholic politician Ludwig Windthorst in voicing opposition, particularly to papal infallibility. Later, he and other bishops would again align with Windthorst in an attempt to rebuff the attempts of Pope Leo XIII to interfere in German politics in the 1880s. See Anderson, *Windthorst,* 121, 127, 219–220, 335–358.
60. Leugers, *Gegen eine Mauer,* 14–15.
61. This is exemplified by their condemnation of the ideas in Alfred Rosenberg's text, *Mythus des 20. Jahrhunderts.* Published in 1930 by the Nazi Party's self-appointed ideologue, the book rejected traditional Christianity in favor of a paganistic, highly racialized "positive Christianity." Dominick Burkard, *Häresie und Mythus des 20. Jahrhunderts: Rosenbergs nationalsozialistische Weltanschauung vor dem Tribunal der Römischen Inquisition* (Paderborn: Schöningh, 2005), esp. 41–52.
62. Emma Fattorini has rightly observed that the intersection at which Nazi antisemitism met with the Church's centuries-old anti-Judaism had very blurred boundaries, and at some points were virtually indistinguishable, although the essentially racist aspect of Nazi antisemitism was rarely adopted by Catholics. See Fattorini, *Hitler, Mussolini and the Vatican: Pope Pius XI and the Speech That Was Never Made,* translated by Carl Ipsen (Malden, MA: Polity, 2011), 108–111. John Connelly's book is also vital reading on the issue of Catholic racism and antisemitism in the 1930s and 1940s in Europe; see Connelly, *From Enemy to Brother.* For a powerful argument against retaining the scholarly distinction between antisemitism and (religious) anti-Judaism, given in consideration of German Protestants but worth applying to the larger Christian context, see Susannah Heschel, "Historiography of Antisemitism versus Anti-Judaism: A Response to Robert Morgan," *Journal for the Study of the New Testament* 33/3 (Summer 2011): 257–279.
63. It is often incorrectly claimed that the 1933 concordat was the first international recognition of Hitler's government. In fact, two agreements preceded it that are often overlooked because of their relatively modest impact on international affairs: the renewal of the German-Soviet "Friendship Treaty" in May 1933 (initially signed in 1926) and the Four-Power pact signed with Great Britain, France, and Italy on 15 June 1933. See Dieter Albrecht, "Der Heilige Stuhl und das Dritte Reich," in Klaus Gotto and Konrad Repgen, eds., *Kirche, Katholiken, und Nationalsozialismus* (Mainz: Matthias-Grünewald Verlag, 1980), 36.
64. See John Zeender, "Introduction," in Frank J. Coppa, ed., *Controversial Concordats: The Vatican's Relations with Napoleon, Mussolini and Hitler* (Washington, DC: Catholic University Press of America, 1999).
65. As related in William Roberts, "Napoleon, the 1801 Concordat, and Its Consequences," in *Controversial Concordats.* The other concordats include agreements with Switzerland (1845), Spain (1851), Austria (1855), Portugal (1866), and Colombia (1918).
66. Peter C. Kent, *The Pope and the Duce: The International Impact of the Lateran Agreements* (New York: St. Martin's Press, 1981), 1–10. See also the newest study on this topic: Fattorini, *Hitler, Mussolini, and the Vatican.*

67. Georg Denzler and Volker Fabricius, *Christen und Nationalsozialisten: Darstellung und Dokumente; mit einem Exkurs, Kirche im Sozialismus* (Frankfurt am Main: Fischer Taschenbuch Verlag, 1993), 29. This is the one-volume edition.
68. Frank J. Coppa, "Mussolini and the Concordat of 1929," in *Controversial Concordats*, 81–84.
69. Letter from Pacelli to Archbishop Cardinal Bertram, 30 July 1920, as quoted in Ludwig Volk, *Das Reichskonkordat vom 20. Juli 1933: Von den Ansätzen in der Weimarer Republik bis zur Ratifizierung am 10. September 1933* (Mainz: Matthias-Grünewald-Verlag, 1972), 7.
70. Hürten, *Deutsche Katholiken*, 101; Evans, *German Center Party*, 317.
71. Hürten, *Deutsche Katholiken*, 108.
72. See Dieter Golombek, *Die politische Vorgeschichte des Preussen-Konkordats, 1929* (Mainz: Grünewald, 1970).
73. Hürten, *Deutsche Katholiken*, 105.
74. Ibid., 110.
75. Only Preysing in Berlin corresponded more often with Pacelli.
76. Susanne Plück, *Das Badische Konkordat vom 12. Oktober 1932* (Mainz: Matthias-Grünewald-Verlag, 1984).
77. Volk, *Das Reichskonkordat*, 95–116.
78. How negotiations for a concordat were started has been a matter of some historiographical debate. For a recent overview of the concordat and the postwar debates about it, see Carsten Kretschmann, "Eine Partie für Pacelli? Die Scholder-Repgen Debatte," in Thomas Brechenmacher, ed., *Das Reichskonkordat 1933* (Paderborn: Schöningh, 2007). See also Guenter Lewy, *The Catholic Church and Nazi Germany* (New York: McGraw-Hill, 1964), 63–71; Volk, *Das Reichskonkordat*, 90–104; Evans, *German Center Party*, 394; Hürten, *Deutsche Katholiken*, 233–234.
79. As quoted in Lewy, *Catholic Church and Nazi Germany*, 34.
80. *Akten DB I* (Stasiewski), Bertram to Hitler, 16 April 1933 (Hitler's response dated 28 April 1933), 60–64.
81. Ibid., Conference minutes of representatives of the Church provinces, by Negwers, 25–26 April 1933, 89.
82. Ibid., Faulhaber to the Minister of State of Bavaria, 5 July 1933, 257, 259.
83. Ibid., Faulhaber to Hitler, 24 July 1933, 271.
84. Bertram, as quoted in Hürten, *Deutsche Katholiken*, 246. In his thank-you note, Bertram made no mention of the controversial compulsory sterilization law (the *Gesetz für Verhütung erbkranken Nachwuchses*), which the regime passed in the same session, and the corresponding Genetic Health Court (*Erbgesundheitsgericht*) that it established, though the law would later receive much episcopal opprobrium.
85. Volk, full copy of the *Reichskonkordat* including supplements and the secret appendix concerning the conscription of priests, in *Das Reichskonkordat*, 234–244.
86. Evans describes the theory of the "horse trade" in *German Center Party*, 392–394. The signing of the concordat on 20 July had followed the formal dissolution of the Center by sixteen days. For an important volume of es-

says regarding newly released archival records and recent historiography about the dissolution of the Center Party and the signing of the concordat, which determines that there is no proof of this "horse trade," see also Brechenmacher, *Das Reichskonkordat 1933*.
87. Hürten, *Deutsche Katholiken*, 241.
88. *Gleichschaltung*, literally coordination or "making the same," was how the Nazis successfully established extensive control over German society. They did so between 1933 and 1937 by creating organizations with compulsory membership, such as youth groups and unions, and either amalgamating or abolishing all non-Nazi organizations and institutions. Two authorities of the period disagree about the celebration of thanksgiving services in the aftermath of the concordat's signing: Guenter Lewy insists that all dioceses offered one, but Ludwig Volk maintains that only the nuncio, Orsenigo, and the archbishop of Bamberg, Jakobus von Hauck, did. Other bishops and priests offered a "Te Deum," a hymn traditionally used in thanksgiving for a special blessing. See Joseph A. Biesinger, "The Reich Concordat of 1933: The Church Struggle against Nazi Germany," in *Controversial Concordats*, 142, n. 68. For more on the Catholic response to the concordat, see Lewy, *Catholic Church and Nazi Germany*, 100–112.
89. Volk, *Das Reichskonkordat*, 250–251.
90. KMBA SW/1008 VII (1), speech, 2 June 1945.
91. Kretschmann, "Eine Partie für Pacelli?" in Brechenmacher, ed., *Das Reichskonkordat 1933*, 18. See also Konrad Repgen, "P. Robert Leiber SJ, der Kronzeuge für die vatikanische Politik beim Reichskonkordat 1933," in the same volume, 25–36.
92. Thomas Brechenmacher, "Reichskonkordatakten und Nuntiaturberichte: Wie ergiebig sind die neu freigegebenen Quellen des Vatikanischen Geheimsarchivs?" in Brechenmacher, ed., *Das Reichskonkordat 1933*, 145.
93. Both quoted in Hürten, *Deutsche Katholiken*, 245.
94. As quoted in *The Persecution of the Catholic Church in the Third Reich: Facts and Documents Translated from the German* (London: Catholic Book Club, 1942), 89.
95. Rempel, *Hitler's Children*, 59.
96. Walker, *Hitler Youth*, 106–117.
97. Arno Klönne, *Jugend im Dritten Reich: Die Hitler-Jugend und ihre Gegner* (Düsseldorf: Diederichs, 1982), 194–197.
98. The tale of the regime's gradual dismantlement of the concordat is told in great detail in *Persecution of the Catholic Church*, particularly Part 2. It relies chiefly on decrees and laws, newspaper accounts, and bishops' sermons. Statistics regarding periodicals are taken from Lewy, *Catholic Church and Nazi Germany*, 148. An authoritative overview of the dismantling of the Catholic press is given in Karl Aloys Altmeyer, *Katholische Presse unter NS-Diktatur: Die katholischen Zeitungen und Zeitschiften Deutschlands in den Jahren 1933 bis 1945: Dokumentation* (Berlin: Morus-Verlag, 1962).
99. John S. Conway, *The Nazi Persecution of the Churches, 1933–1945* (New York: Basic Books, 1968), 79, 115.
100. Lewy, *Catholic Church and Nazi Germany*, 156.

101. The first trials that historian Hans Günter Hockerts considers part of the assault on the morality of priests—referred to in German as the *Sittlichkeitsprozesse*—began in 1935, when in separate cases two Franciscan friars in the Rhineland were accused of homosexual acts. The majority of trials occurred between May and August 1936 in Koblenz, and April to July 1937 in Koblenz and Bonn. They targeted clergymen from friars to priests of various orders. See Hockerts, *Die Sittlichkeitsprozesse gegen katholische Ordensangehörige und Priester, 1936/1937: Eine Studie zur nationalsozialistischen Herrschaftstechnik und zum Kirchenkampf* (Mainz: Matthias-Grünewald-Verlag, 1971), 4, 34–35.

102. Anselm Reichhold, *Die deutsche katholische Kirche zur Zeit des Nationalsozialismus, 1933–1945* (St. Ottilien: EOS Verlag, 1992), 92, 94. Pastoral letter, 24 December 1936. Emphasis added.

103. Leugers gives a fascinating study of the personalities of Bertram and Preysing. See *Gegen eine Mauer*, 19–54. For further reading on these two bishops, see Sascha Hinkel, *Adolf Kardinal Bertram: Kirchenpolitik im Kaiserreich und der Weimarer Republic* (Paderborn: Schöningh, 2010), whose solid analysis unfortunately ends in 1933; Stephan Adam, *Die Auseinandersetzung des Bischofs Konrad von Preysing mit dem Nationalsozialismus in den Jahren 1933–1945* (St. Ottilien: EOS Verlag, 1996); Walter Adolph, *Kardinal Preysing und Zwei Diktaturen: Sein Widerstand gegen die totalitäre Macht* (Berlin: Morus, 1971).

104. See *Akten DB* IV (Volk), pastoral letter of the German bishops, 19 August 1936, 555–564. Biblical reference from Acts of the Apostles 5:29.

105. Spicer does not detail how many this was. See Kevin P. Spicer, *Hitler's Priests: Catholic Clergy and National Socialism* (DeKalb: Northern Illinois University Press, 2008), 29–30.

106. See EAM 3055 (1): Gustav Staebe, "Große Sorgen in Fulda," in *Mainfränkische Zeitung*, 26/27 September 1936, and Bishop Matthias Ehrenfried's response, "Hirtenwort betr. Pressangriffe," in *Würzburger Diözesan-Blatt*, 14 October 1936.

107. The Vatican issued this encyclical, *Divini Redemptoris*, on 19 March 1937. For the full English text, see http://www.vatican.va/holy_father/pius_xi/en cyclicals/documents/hf_p-xi_enc_19031937_divini-redemptoris_en.html (last accessed 9 April 2014).

108. Fattorini, *Hitler, Mussolini, and the Vatican*, 88.

109. Reichhold, *Die deutsche katholische Kirche*, 83–87.

110. For example, see EAM 3055 (1), "Wer lügt, Herr Kardinal?" in *Das Schwarze Korps*, 20 February 1936. The Gestapo assaulted Faulhaber's place of work so often that he and his assistants regularly culled his personal correspondence and destroyed any letters that could potentially bring trouble. My thanks to Susan Kornacker, former archivist at EAM, for bringing this to my attention.

111. In one more example, the Gestapo took into "protective custody" Munich priest Rupert Mayer for half a year, after which he ended up in Sachsenhausen concentration camp. He was released in 1938 only because the Nazis feared that his death would make him a public martyr; he had spoken out

actively against the anti-Church policies of the regime. For more information, see Otto Gritschneder, *Ich predige weiter: Pater Rupert Mayer und das Dritte Reich; eine Dokumentation* (Rosenheim: Rosenheimer Verlagshaus, 1987). See also a powerful sermon delivered by his archbishop, Faulhaber, in the wake of his arrest, 4 July 1937, as printed in Hubert Gruber, *Katholische Kirche und Nationalsozialismus, 1930–1945: Ein Bericht in Quellen* (Paderborn: Ferdinand Schöningh, 2006), 348–353.

112. Dagmar Herzog, "Theology of Betrayal," *Tikkun* 16/3 (May/June 2001): 70.
113. Robert P. Ericksen and Susannah Heschel, "Introduction," in Robert P. Ericksen and Susannah Heschel, eds., *Betrayal: German Churches and the Holocaust* (Minneapolis: Fortress Press, 1999), 9–12.
114. Dagmar Herzog, *Sex after Fascism: Memory and Morality in Twentieth-Century Germany* (Princeton, NJ: Princeton University Press, 2005), 46.
115. "Anweisung des Erzbischofs von München und Freising, Michael Kardinal v. Faulhaber, an den Klerus seiner Erzdiözese über das Verhalten zum Nationalsozialismus (Auszug)," 5 April 1933, in Gruber, *Katholische Kirche*, 50.
116. "Hirtenbrief der deutsche Bischöfe (Auszug)," 3 June 1933, in Gruber, *Katholische Kirche*, 83.
117. EAM 3055 (1), Pope Pius XI, from a speech at the opening of the Vatican world exhibition, as quoted in Dr. Edmund Freiherr Raitz v. Frentz, "Vatikan und kommunistische Weltgefahr," in *Die Schönere Zeit*, XI. Jahrgang, June 21, 1934 (original undated). Emphasis in original.
118. Ibid., Dr. Weißthanner, erzbisch. Sekretär, "Das Bündnisangebot der Kommunisten an dem Katholizismus," in *Münchener Beobachter*, 31 July 1935.
119. Encyclicals are letters written by the pope to the entire Church, usually focusing on matters of doctrine, discipline, pastoral concern, or occasions of commemoration. They are usually written in Latin. This is the only German-language encyclical, a deliberate decision that Germans, both Catholic and non-Catholic, would have noticed. For the original German encyclical, see *Acta Apostolicae Sedis* 39 (1937), 145–167. All translations are my own.
120. Fattorini, *Hitler, Mussolini, and the Vatican*, esp. 115–121.
121. "Accusatory" is Fattorini's adjective. See ibid., 118.
122. Rudolf Voderholzer, "Die Enzyklika 'Mit brennender Sorge,'" in Thomas Forstner et al., eds., *Kardinal Michael von Faulhaber, 1869–1952* (Munich: Danuvia Druckhaus Neuburg GMBH, 2002), 315–316.
123. Fattorini, *Hitler, Mussolini, and the Vatican*, 121.
124. *Mit brennender Sorge*, section 6.
125. Ibid., section 14.
126. Among those who defend the encyclical are Dieter Albrecht, "Das Heilige Stuhl und das Dritte Reich," in Gotto and Repgen, *Kirche, Katholiken und Nationalsozialismus*, 42–43; Hürten, *Deutsche Katholiken*, 371–379; and Michael Phayer, *The Catholic Church and the Holocaust, 1930–1965* (Bloomington: Indiana University Press, 2000), 18. Phayer labels the encyclical as "anti-racist." Those who have labeled it apologetic or ineffective are John Cornwell, *Hitler's Pope: The Secret History of Pius XII* (New York:

Viking 1999), 183–184; Daniel J. Goldhagen, *A Moral Reckoning: The Role of the Catholic Church in the Holocaust and Its Unfulfilled Duty of Repair* (New York: Alfred A. Knopf, 2002), 46–47; Lewy, *Catholic Church and Nazi Germany*, 158–159.

127. Numbers varied as to how many clergy members were implicated in these trials, largely because Nazi propaganda inflated the numbers considerably. State statistics from the end of November 1937 placed the number of condemned priests at 242, with another 955 cases pending. Some 7,000 convictions had been handed down against Catholic clergy since 1933. The bishops disputed these numbers and cited in June 1937 that only twenty-one diocesan priests and one order-priest had been convicted out of fifty-seven total brought to trial, rendering a ratio of clergy affected by the trials to be about one priest per 500 in Germany. See *Persecution of the Catholic Church*, 304–307; Hockerts, *Die Sittlichkeitsprozesse*, 167.

128. Klönne, *Hitler-Jugend*, 188.

129. Law on the Hitler Youth, 1 December 1936, as posted on the document website of the German Historical Institute: German History in Documents and Images, http://germanhistorydocs.ghi-dc.org/sub_document.cfm?document_id=1564&language=german (last accessed 9 April 2014).

130. Heike Kreutzer, *Das Reichskirchenministerium im Gefüge der nationalsozialistischen Herrschaft* (Düsseldorf: Droste Verlag, 2000), 230–234; Conway, *Nazi Persecution*, 166–172; Lewy, *Catholic Church and Nazi Germany*, 158.

131. Rempel, *Hitler's Children*, 4. Rempel's text, the best on this subject, substantiates the complex connections between the SS and the HJ from 1933 to the end of the war. He proves that the two, in tandem, worked to produce a superior fighting force for the Third Reich that would lay the groundwork for the future "Aryan" master race. Schirach and Himmler were devoted to using the HJ as a means of militarizing young Germans and eliminating opposition to Nazi ideology.

132. Preysing's memorandum, 17 October 1937, in *Akten DB IV* (Volk), 356–361.

133. NARA T-175, roll 577, frame 951, report, 2 August 1937.

134. Ibid., roll 1612, frames 165–166. The surveillance was constant: the Gestapo arrested co-leader Father Konrad Engel in September 1935 and held him in detention until February 1936, when his trial began; the court sentenced him to six months in prison for slandering the state (breaking the *Heimtückegesetz*). The *Regierungspräsident* imposed a prohibition on him from 1939 to 1945, with the result that he earned no salary [*Gehaltssperre*]. Less is known with certainty about the other leader, General Vicar Dr. von Meuers, although the Gestapo did search his office and his home in November 1938 and April 1943, and in June 1943 they interrogated him. See Ulrich von Hehl, ed., *Priester unter Hitlers Terror: Eine biographische und statistische Erhebung*, 2nd ed. (Mainz: Matthias-Grünewald-Verlag, 1985), 1302–1303 for Engel and 1353–1354 for von Meuers.

135. Ibid., roll 410, frames 2933987–88, reports dated 30 October and 15 November 1938. Emphasis in original. Franz Bungarten endured more than thirty complaints, reports, interrogations, and warnings from the Gestapo during the Third Reich, which he would outlive. See *Priester unter Hitlers Terror*, 1291.

136. The best recent study of *Kristallnacht* based on eyewitness accounts is Alan E. Steinweis, *Kristallnacht 1938* (Cambridge, MA: Belknap Press of Harvard University Press, 2009).
137. Walker, *Hitler Youth*, 146.
138. Wilhelm Damberg scrutinizes the sources that demonstrate this attitude in "Kriegserfahrung und Kriegstheologie, 1939–1945," *Theologische Quartalschrift* 182 (2002): 323–324.
139. As quoted in Lewy, *Catholic Church and Nazi Germany*, 226.
140. Alexander B. Rossino, *Hitler Strikes Poland: Blitzkrieg, Ideology, and Atrocity* (Lawrence: University Press of Kansas, 2003), 25, 205. This is echoed in Michael Phayer's study of Pope Pius XII. See Phayer, *Pius XII, the Holocaust, and the Cold War* (Bloomington: Indiana University Press, 2008), 23.
141. Statistics about Polish clergy taken from Lewy, *Catholic Church and Nazi Germany*, 227. See also Jochen Böhler, *Auftakt zum Vernichtungskrieg: Die Wehrmacht in Polen 1939* (Frankfurt am Main: Fischer Taschenbuch Verlag, 2006).
142. Statistics taken from *Nazism, 1919–1945: A Documentary Reader*, Vol. 3, edited by Jeremy Noakes and Geoffrey Pridham (Exeter, UK: University of Exeter Press, 1998), 956.
143. In March 1939, following Germany's violation of the September 1938 Munich Agreement with the invasion of what remained of independent Czechoslovakia, Britain and France had pledged to guarantee the territorial integrity of Poland—they would declare war on Germany if Germany invaded Poland. Thus there was no doubt of the Allied reaction should Germany take down its eastern neighbor. If some bishops did decipher the Molotov-Ribbentrop Pact as a time-buying measure (I have not found evidence of this, though I have also not searched exhaustively through the private papers of the bishops in the individual archives; it is not unreasonable to speculate that some of the more astute bishops could have figured this out), it is one more example of episcopal myopia, for they could also have viewed the 1933 concordat in this light. Pacelli basically acknowledges this interpretation in his remarks to the British chargé d'affaires, Ivone Kirkpatrick, relayed above.
144. For more information on this, see Robert Zurek, "Die Haltung der katholischen Kirche in Deutschland gegenüber den polnischen Katholiken im Zweiten Weltkrieg," *Inter Finitimos* 3 (2005): 11–51.
145. Manfred Messerschmidt speaks of this wartime *"Burgfrieden"* called for by Hitler as not entirely serious, which in any case changed nothing: officially the existence and rights of the churches were confirmed, but in the various provinces the "small war [*Kleinkrieg*] against priests, church organizations and the ecclesial press progressed speedily." Messerschmidt, "Zur Militärseelsorgepolitik im Zweiten Weltkrieg," *Militärgeschichtliche Mitteilungen* 1 (1969): 49–50.
146. Pius XII, *Summi Pontificatus* (On the Unity of Human Society), 20 October 1939, http://www.vatican.va/holy_father/pius_xii/encyclicals/documents/hf_p-xii_enc_20101939_summi-pontificatus_en.html (last accessed 9 April 2014). According to Phayer, the Poles never forgave Pius XII for failing to

condemn the German invasion or the atrocities perpetrated against clergy in its aftermath. *Pius XII, the Holocaust, and the Cold War,* 1–2.
147. Letter from Pius XII to Bishop von Preysing, 12 June 1940, in Pierre Blet, Angelo Martini, and Burkhart Schneider, eds., *Actes et documents du Saint Siège relatifs à la seconde guerre mondiale II: Lettres de Pie XII aux évêques allemands, 1939–1944* (Vatican City: Liberia Editrice Vaticana, 1966), 143–144.
148. Leugers, *Gegen ein Mauer,* 84–102.
149. See KMBA 1051/IX, copy of manuscript by Rudolf Absolon, "Wehrgesetz und Wehrdienst, 1935–1945: Das Personalwesen in der Wehrmacht," as published by Harald Boldt Verlag (Boppard am Rhein, 1960). Antonia Leugers gives a full account of the Jesuits' service in, and expulsion from, the Wehrmacht, including a copy of Keitel's expulsion decree dated 31 May 1941, in *Jesuiten im Hitlers Wehrmacht.*
150. Salutation of the German bishops to Pius XII, 24 June 1941, in *Akten DB V* (Volk), 455.
151. KMBA 997/VII, excerpt from memorandum of the German bishops concerning the situation of the Catholic Church in Germany, 10 December 1941.
152. Pastoral letter of the Bavarian episcopate, 12 August 1941, in Ludwig Volk, ed., *Akten Kardinal Michael von Faulhabers, 1917–1945,* Vol. 2 (Mainz: Matthias-Grünewald Verlag, 1975), 784–785. This document collection will be referred to as *Akten KMF,* followed by the relevant volume number.
153. Sermon by Bishop von Galen, 3 August 1941, in *Akten DB V* (Volk), 500–501.
154. Lewy, *Catholic Church and Nazi Germany,* 234.
155. Schewick in Gotto and Repgen, eds., *Kirche, Katholiken und Nationalsozialismus,* 98.
156. Letter from Faulhaber to Alois Wurm, 8 April 1933, as printed in Gruber, *Katholische Kirche,* 55. Emphasis added.
157. Protocol for the Inaugural Session of the Relief Committee for Catholic Non-Aryans in *Akten DB II* (Stasiewski), 129–136. See also Supplement 14 to the Fulda Conference's 1937 annual meeting, "Emigration Help for Catholic Non-Aryans," 26 August 1937, in *Akten DB IV* (Volk), 326–329. It is not clear how many people these associations helped, or how much money they raised, before they were shut down, but it was not insignificant. In mid-1937, the general secretary of the St. Raphael Society, Max Grösser, traveled to New York asking for help for 2,500 people. An estimated contribution of $200,000 (USD) from various German and American agencies was sought, but there is no indication that the funds were raised, or how many of the 2,500 arrived in the United States. See ibid., 326–327. Grösser made a report one year later expressing dissatisfaction with the success rate of the Relief Committee, stating that only 221 out of 967 applicants for aid that year had been helped. He was also concerned that the committee was facing a potential boom in applicants following the *Anschluss* with Austria, with its approximately 180,000 "Catholic non-Aryans." See Grösser's report, 31 March 1938, in ibid., 441.

158. The St. Raphael Society had been founded in 1871 by Peter Paul Cahensly, initially to help Catholic German immigrants trying to settle in the United States. It was named for St. Raphael, patron saint of travelers and lost souls. After 1935, it worked in tandem with the committee to focus on aiding Jewish emigration, until the regime shut the society down in 1941.
159. Protocol of the Fulda Conference of Bishops' annual meeting, August 1939, in ibid., 709.
160. The best account of Sommer's work and Preysing's involvement is in Jana Leichsenring, *Die katholische Kirche und "ihre Juden": Das "Hilfswerk beim bischöflichen Ordinariat Berlins," 1938–1945* (Berlin: Metropol, 2007). See also Heinrich Herzberg, *Dienst am Höheren Gesetz: Dr. Margarete Sommer und das "Hilfswerk beim bischöflichen Ordinariat Berlin* (Berlin: Servi, 2000); Stephan Adam, *Die Auseinandersetzung des Bischofs Konrad von Preysing mit dem Nationalsozialismus in den Jahren 1933–1945* (St. Ottilien: EOS Verlag, 1996); Walter Adolph, *Kardinal Preysing und zwei Diktaturen: Sein Widerstand gegen die totalitäre Macht* (Berlin: Morus-Verlag, 1971).
161. Report by Sommer, before 14 February 1942, in *Akten DB V* (Volk), 677.
162. Draft, petition of the German episcopate, 22/23 August 1943, in *Akten DB VI* (Volk), 220–221.
163. Bertram's file notes, after 24 August 1943, in ibid., 215–216. Also ibid., letter from Bertram to Hans Lammers (head of the Reich Chancellery), Hermann Muhs (minister responsible for church questions), and Joseph Goebbels (propaganda minister), 3 March 1943, 23–25.
164. EAM 8431, copy of letter written by Faulhaber, 13 November 1941.
165. Ibid., draft of letter unsigned but included in sheath of drafts of letters written by Faulhaber, Easter 1943.
166. Father Dr. Philipp Haeuser was one of the foremost examples of priests who loudly and publicly trumpeted his support for Nazism. He offered comparisons of Hitler and Christ and tirades against "the Jew, [who] is now definitely master of the world [and who] through his cleverness, his ruthless, his—almost exemplary—determination and tenacity has bound almost all nations and governments to slavish obedience." As quoted in Kevin P. Spicer, "Working for the Führer: Father Dr. Philipp Haeuser and the Third Reich," in Spicer, ed., *Antisemitism, Christian Ambivalence and the Holocaust* (Bloomington: Indiana University Press, 2007), 110–114.
167. Lewy, *Catholic Church and Nazi Germany*, 253.
168. This is Georg May's interpretation in *Interkonfessionalismus in der deutschen Militärseelsorge von 1933 bis 1945* (Amsterdam: B. R. Grüner, 1978), 12. Heinz Hürten shares this interpretation in " 'Endlösung' für den Katholizismus? Das nationalsozialistische Regime und seine Zukunftspläne gegenüber die Kirche" in *Stimmen der Zeit* 203 (1985): 534–546. Both take a largely apologist position in view of the Catholic Church under Nazi Germany.
169. Richard Steigmann-Gall, *The Holy Reich: Nazi Conceptions of Christianity* (New York: Cambridge University Press, 2003), 259. From Steigmann-Gall's work, it is not clear how many, if any, clerical Nazi Party members were

expelled, or even how many there were at the time. Spicer's work numbers 138 "brown priests" in total, including fifty-three card-carrying members of the Nazi Party. He lists three priests withdrawing from the party after joining it (one changed his mind and returned to the party); a fourth, Werner Kreth, was expelled, perhaps due to homosexual activity, and later sentenced to twelve years in prison. A far higher number of priests ended up leaving the Church (and their vocations) rather than abandon Nazism. See Spicer, *Hitler's Priests*, 239–300 (Appendix 2).

170. Nor can the historiography be adequately cited in a single endnote. The most recent valuable analyses, which I have used throughout this chapter, are Michael Phayer, *Pius XII, the Holocaust, and the Cold War*, and Emma Fattorini, *Hitler, Mussolini, and the Vatican*. The first scholar to gain access to the recently opened archives for the Supreme Congregation of the Holy Office (now known as the Congregation for the Doctrine of the Faith, which pronounces judgments on matters of faith and morals), Peter Godman's text is also worth reading: *Hitler and the Vatican: Inside the Secret Archives That Reveal the New Story of the Nazis and the Church* (New York: Free Press, 2004). Finally, Thomas Brechenmacher offers a useful overview of the historiography, from one end of the spectrum to the other, in "Der Papst und der Zweite Weltkrieg," in Hummel and Kißener, eds., *Die Katholiken und das Dritte Reich*, 179–195.

2. PASTORAL CARE IN THE WEHRMACHT

1. See the Introduction, n. 6, for more about sources on estimating Wehrmacht statistics.
2. The Nazi censuses of 1933 and 1939 are problematic and controversial. Their explicitly nefarious purpose was to aid in the creation of a Jewish registry. For a study of the censuses, which also has its problems, see Götz Aly and Karl Heinz Roth, *The Nazi Census: Identification and Control in the Third Reich* (Philadelphia: Temple University Press, 2004).
3. The distinction between a seminarian and a student of theology in Germany in 1930 is difficult to make. The former began as the latter when he applied to become a candidate for the priesthood via formal application to the regional bishop. This application required, among other things, a certificate of eligibility for university entrance from a humanistic *Gymnasium* and a sealed pastoral letter of reference attesting to the individual's moral, physical, and familial character. In the early twentieth century, state universities remained in charge of education for all Germans, including Catholics entering the priesthood, since there was no Catholic university. These theological faculties offered required courses in philosophy, languages, and theology that future seminarians would take, in addition to other university requirements. The seminary was the location of pastoral training, where one learned how to be a priest (that is, administer the sacraments) and deal with the needs of the laity. Not all students of theology went on to become seminarians and then priests, but all priests had at one point been a theology student at a university. For more information on priestly training and the history of the evolution of the seminary, see A. Bea, S.J., "The Apos-

tolic Constitution Deus Scientiarum Dominus: Its Origin and Spirit," *Theological Studies* 4/1 (1943); Paul Seibel, *Priester: Ausbildung und Verfolgung* (Frankfurt am Main: Haag + Herchen, 1994); Karl Hillenbrand and Rudolf Weigand, eds., *Mit der Kirche auf dem Weg: 400 Jahre Priesterseminar Würzburg, 1589–1989* (Würzburg: Echter, 1989). Many thanks to Kevin Spicer for puzzling through this with me.

4. Patrick J. Houlihan's book about Catholics serving in the German and Austrian militaries during the First World War is forthcoming with Cambridge University Press. See also Patrick Houlihan, "Imperial Frameworks of Religion: Catholic Military Chaplains of Germany and Austria-Hungary during the First World War," *First World War Studies* 3/2 (2012): 165–182.

5. Blomberg was forced to resign when he refused to divorce his wife after she was accused (falsely) of prostitution; Fritsch was accused of homosexuality and dismissed. Heinrich Himmler and Hermann Göring engineered both scandals. Beck resigned after repeatedly advising Hitler against aggressive action against Czechoslovakia, which Beck believed would result in a premature war that Germany would lose.

6. Thomas Kühne, *Belonging and Genocide: Hitler's Community, 1918–1945* (New Haven, CT: Yale University Press, 2010), 5, 83. See also Kühne, *Kameradschaft: Die Soldaten des nationalsozialistischen Krieges und das 20. Jahrhundert* (Göttingen: Vandenhoeck & Ruprecht, 2006).

7. Volk, *Das Reichskonkordat*, 240.

8. The "exemption" status indicates that a person or institution is excluded from the jurisdiction of an inferior ecclesiastical authority and placed under that of a higher power. In the case of the German military chaplaincy, its members were directly responsible to the field bishop, who, in turn, was directly responsible to the pope (otherwise bishops are responsible to the metropolitan archbishop). Because of the field bishop's exempt status (he was not an ecclesiastical authority), the chaplaincy automatically carried exempt status as well. Exemption is historically common for military chaplaincies and their religious leaders in order to place them under the jurisdiction of the pope and to acknowledge secular jurisdiction (in the cases of Prussia and Austria, the respective emperors, and in the case of Nazi Germany, the government).

9. Georg May, *Interkonfessionalismus in der deutschen Militärseelsorge von 1933 bis 1945* (Amsterdam: B. R. Grüner, 1978), 75.

10. Volk, *Das Reichskonkordat*, 44–58, esp. 48. The official title was *Reichsfeldbischof*, which is sometimes translated as "military bishop." In German, however, a qualitative distinction is made between a *Militärbischof*—military bishop—and a *Feldbischof*. The *Feldbischof*, or field bishop, strongly emphasizes that the man will lead the military chaplaincy physically in a time of war: he will be present in the theaters of war (*Kriegsschauplätze*). A military bishop may perform the same role, but he may not necessarily be employed at the battlefront. Such is currently the case in the German Bundeswehr, an army envisioned since 1956 as a defensive unit, one that employs a military (as opposed to a field) bishop. My thanks to Dr. Monica

Sinderhauf, director of the archive of the Catholic Military Bishop in Berlin, for underscoring this difference.

11. BA-MA RH 12 II/5, Nr. 503/36, copy without author or date, though likely pre-1939 and drafted by Rarkowski, titled "Katholische militärkirchliche Dienstordnung für die Wehrmacht." Cutting off all contact between military chaplains and civilian church authorities in the first half of the war was one of Martin Bormann's primary goals, which later most of the upper Nazi Party apparatus shared. According to one historian, Bormann was the most dedicated opponent of the churches throughout the war. Manfred Messerschmidt, "Zur Militärseelsorgepolitik im Zweiten Weltkrieg," *Militärgeschichtliche Mitteilungen* 1 (1969): 50–56.

12. In Catholic terminology of the time, a cleric was any individual who received tonsure (the act of shaving part of the top of the head), indicating his intention to enter the priesthood. This step, sometimes taken in high school, included both seminarians as well as students of theology. A minor cleric completed the requisite studies, which usually took four years and involved studying philosophy and theology, and then he was ordained a subdeacon, the highest order of minor clergy. The next step was the diaconate, the lowest level of major clergy, though a deacon was still not fully ordained. Those ordained beyond the level of subdeacon were ineligible for armed service, but those below it were. In sum, the stages of ordination from tonsure to priesthood were: student of theology or seminarian (including the minor orders of porter, exorcist, acolyte, and lector), subdeacon, deacon, priest. Many thanks to Kevin Spicer for elaborating on the ordination process. For a complete copy of the secret appendix to the *Reichskonkordat*, see Ludwig Volk, *Das Reichskonkordat vom 20. Juli 1933* (Mainz: Matthias-Grünewald-Verlag, 1972), 244.

13. As relayed in Güsgen, *Die katholische Militärseelsorge*, 244–246. In diplomatic circles, the Vatican was derided for its "tacit consent to German rearmament" after Pacelli confirmed the existence of the secret appendix to François Charles-Roux, French ambassador to the Vatican. He was forced to do so by an article in the French paper *L'écho de Paris* about the appendix on 17 August 1933, buried on page 3, which the more significant daily *Le temps* ran verbatim the next day (also buried, on page 2; Güsgen incorrectly cites the date as 21 August 1933). Neither paper cited a source beyond "a well-informed political correspondent," probably Pacelli himself, who sought to head off further reports about the appendix by describing it as "a list of a few detailed regulations of secondary importance, concerning the employment of chaplains [*ecclésiastiques en champagne*]." See "Le concordat allemand comporte-t-il une clause secrète sur les aumôniers militaires en temps de guerre?" in *L'écho de Paris*, 17 August 1933, and "L'enseignement de l'histoire," in *Le temps*, 18 August 1933, both at http://gallica.bnf.fr/ (last accessed 9 April 2014). Evidently Charles-Roux then confided his frustrations to his British colleague, Ivone Kirkpatrick, who informed the British foreign minister, John Simon, of the affair. Simon felt that it would be only a matter of time before the secrecy of the appendix unraveled. However, he was wrong—it remained a closely guarded secret, at

least within Germany, until 1939. The reception (or even the awareness) in Germany of the two French news reports about the appendix is unknown.

14. In 1113, a papal bull officially recognized the Order of Malta—sometimes called the Knights of Malta—as the Knights Hospitallers. The same bull conferred on them exempt status: they could elect their own superiors without interference from religious or secular authorities. They were charged with caring for pilgrims in the Holy Land regardless of religion or race. They served in the Crusades, caring for the sick and wounded, until they were forced to flee, first to Rhodes in 1310, then to Malta in 1530, and finally to Rome, where they settled after being forced to leave Malta by Napoleon's armies in 1798. After 1530, the order pledged to remain neutral in any war between Christian nations. Information taken from the Order of Malta's English-language website, http://www.orderofmalta.int/?lang=en (last accessed 7 September 2014). See also H. J. A. Sire, *The Knights of Malta* (New Haven, CT: Yale University Press, 1994).

15. *Biographisches Lexikon*, lvii–lxi.

16. Ibid., lxiv.

17. Part V (Articles 159–213) of the Treaty of Versailles deals with the limitations put on the German military. See http://avalon.law.yale.edu/imt/partv.asp (last accessed 3 April 2012).

18. The key term "acting" indicates that the head of the chaplaincy retained the rank of field vicar-general. This is true for both Schwamborn and Rarkowski up to 1936. The position of field provost remained vacant until then because the bishops and the Ministry of Defense could agree neither on the jurisdiction of the chaplaincy nor on whether the field provost and his chaplains were subordinate to the Church (what the bishops desired—a nonexempt chaplaincy) or to the state (what the Ministry of Defense wanted, based on the Prussian model of an exempt chaplaincy). The pope and the Foreign Ministry (*Auswärtiges Amt*) were also involved in this debate. Johannes Güsgen provides the best overview of the *Reichswehr* chaplaincy's history during the Weimar Republic and its political entanglements involving the pope, the German bishops, and the state in attempting to reach a formal agreement about the rights of Germany's Catholics. See Güsgen, *Die katholische Militärseelsorge in Deutschland zwischen 1920–1945* (Cologne: Böhlau, 1989), esp. 45–122.

19. Güsgen, *Katholische Militärseelsorge in Deutschland*, 301–311. Güsgen gives the Protestant-Catholic ratio in the Reichswehr in 1932 at 3.26:1, slightly larger than the overall Protestant-Catholic ratio in Germany, at about 2:1 (290). See also Heinrich Missalla, *Für Volk und Vaterland: Die kirchliche Kriegshilfe im Zweiten Weltkrieg* (Königstein: Athenäum Verlag, 1978), 56; *Biographisches Lexikon*, 637.

20. "Aus dem Protokoll der Konferenz der Diözesanvertreter in Berlin vom 25. und 26. April 1933," in Hans Müller, ed., *Katholische Kirche und Nationalsozialismus* (Munich: Deutscher Taschenbuch Verlag, 1965), 130. Bishop Wilhelm Berning of Osnabrück, who had visited Hitler on the afternoon of 26 April, reported on the conversation with observations of Hitler's reactions. He noted that the discussion was "cordial and to the point" (127).

21. *Akten KMF Bd. II*, Faulhaber's report on a conversation with Hitler, 5 November 1936, 184–194.
22. KMBA 1008/VII (Nr. 1), from Werthmann's notes, 7 June 1946. See also *Biographisches Lexikon*, 637. Heinrich Missalla produced a short analytical biography of Rarkowski that included the texts of many pastoral letters and circulars. See Missalla, *Wie der Krieg zur Schule Gottes wurde: Hitlers Feldbischof Rarkowski; eine notwendige Erinnerung* (Oberursel: Publik-Forum, 1997).
23. Information taken from an unpublished biographical sketch of Georg Werthmann at the KMBA in Berlin. See Klaus-Bernward Springer, "'Ein guter und getreuer Knecht': Georg Werthmann (1898–1980), Generalvikar der Militärseelsorge im Dritten Reich und in der Bundeswehr" (1999), 52. Gordon C. Zahn suggests that this family connection was integral to his later appointment as field bishop, which occurred "over the objections of the majority of the German hierarchy." See Zahn, *German Catholics and Hitler's Wars: A Study in Social Control* (New York: Sheed & Ward, 1962), 149.
24. KMBA 1008/VII (Nr. 1), from Werthmann's notes, 7 June 1946. He did not, however, officially assume the position of field provost (the head chaplain of the Reichswehr chaplaincy); rather, his title was *Beauftragter*, or authorized representative, until 1936.
25. Guenter Lewy, *The Catholic Church and Nazi Germany* (New York: McGraw-Hill, 1965), 12.
26. Lewy, *Catholic Church and Nazi Germany*, 237. Manfred Messerschmidt relates similar details in "Aspekte der Militärseelsorgepolitik in nationalsozialistischer Zeit," *Militärgeschichtliche Mitteilungen* 1 (1968): 81.
27. The Marist Fathers, or Society of Mary (Societas Mariae), is a clerical congregation founded in 1816 by Jean Claude Courveille and Jean Claude Colin in Lyon, France, and recognized by the pope in 1836. Their self-appointed primary task is comprehensive pastoral work, and their daily routine and spirituality is modeled on the Virgin Mary, from whom the congregation takes its name. Not to be confused with the Marianists, who carry the same post-nominals (S. M.), a slightly larger congregation founded in 1817 by William Joseph Chaminade.
28. Biographical information taken from *Biographisches Lexikon*, Franz Justus Rarkowski, 637.
29. KMBA SW 1008/VII (Nr. 1), letter from Schwamborn, 11 August 1933.
30. Ibid., letter from Semler (no other identifying information given), 17 August 1933.
31. Ibid., letter from Rarkowski, 16 August 1933. He explained that he eventually ended up in Berlin and immediately applied to his superior, Joeppen, to be sent back into the field.
32. Ibid., letter from Reichswehrminister Groener, 29 April 1930.
33. In the copy of a letter written in Rarkowski's defense in 1933, its writer, identified only as Semler, reveals that Schwamborn had been "for decades [*seit Jahrzehnten*]" an unambiguous opponent of Rarkowski. It does not say why, though it also mentions that Rarkowski "didn't complete the *Abitur*, but has been lawfully dispensated by the Prussian minister of education

from the preparatory training requirements stipulated for tenure in a spiritual office." Nor is there any information in Rarkowksi's files about how he came to use false titles at Schwamborn's insistence. See ibid., letter from Semler, 17 August 1933.

34. Ibid., letter from Rarkowski, 16 August 1933.
35. Ibid., letter from Groener, 29 April 1930.
36. Missalla, *Wie der Krieg*, 19.
37. KMBA 1008/VII (Nr. 1), Pastoral letter, Easter 1937. The passage from *Mein Kampf* to which he is referring reads, "But in the forefront of military training will stand what has to be regarded as the highest merit of the old army: in this school the boy must be transformed into a man; in this school he must not only learn to obey, but must thereby acquire a basis for commanding later." Adolf Hitler, *Mein Kampf*, translated by Ralph Manheim, reprinted edition (London: Pimlico, 1998), 376.
38. KMBA 1009/VII (Nr. 1), Pastoral letter, 2 September 1939.
39. *Biographisches Lexikon*, 637–38.
40. Lewy, *Catholic Church and Nazi Germany*, 237.
41. This was (and still is) a title given to bishops who did not have residential sees—titular sees were those dioceses of the ancient church that later fell into "infidel" (i.e., Muslim) hands, most of which are located in modern Africa and the Middle East.
42. Monica Sinderhauf, "Katholische Wehrmachtseelsorge im Krieg: Quellen und Forschungen zu Franz Justus Rarkowski und Georg Werthmann," in Karl-Joseph Hummel and Christoph Kösters, eds., *Kirchen im Krieg: Europa, 1939–1945* (Paderborn: Schöningh, 2007), 283.
43. KMBA SW 1008/VII Nr. 1, written observations made by Werthmann, 2 July 1945. Pfister's biographical information taken from Hans Jürgen Brandt and the Katholisches Militärbischofsamt, eds., *Priester in Uniform: Seelsorger, Ordensleute und Theologen als Soldaten im Zweiten Weltkrieg* (Augsburg: Pattloch Verlag, 1994), 133. Pfister likely relayed the information to Werthmann in a conversation at the end of June 1945, during which time he had returned to his monastery at Niederaltaich—the same one where Werthmann was interned.
44. KMBA SW/III 310, Akte Otto F., interview, 25 April 1990. Most of the personal files I used in the military bishop's office archives, and all of the seminarians' letters I used in the Munich archdiocesan archive, fall under the protection of a *Sperrfrist*, or blocking period. Normally this lasts thirty years following the individual's death date, but for diocesan archives this stretches to forty years, and it applies to all the seminarians (some of whom died during the war). The archivists asked that I keep these files anonymous to protect the personal rights of the individuals named. Therefore, with chaplains, I have used only the individual's first name and last initial; with seminarians, I have used initials only.
45. For Kunibert P., KMBA SW 627/III, interview undated; for Schmitt, KMBA SW 750/III, interview undated.
46. KMBA SW 947/III, interview, 14 June 1990. See also Messerschmidt, "Aspekte der Militärseelsorgepolitik," 82.

47. KMBA SW 1008/VII, Nr. 1, written observations entitled "Katholische Feldbischof der Wehrmacht Rarkowski," 14 May 1945.
48. Ibid.
49. As the years passed and Werthmann became involved with setting up a chaplaincy for West Germany's newly established Bundeswehr, his criticism of Rarkowski became even more pointed: "Rarkowski had too little spiritual capacity, too little nerve, too little genuine experience, too little activity, and too much fragility," and "The Catholic field bishop Rarkowski thought much too patriotically in the traditional sense, was far too much convinced of the necessary cooperation of 'two authorities,' the temporal and the spiritual, to be able to consider whether the defeat of the 'Third Reich' was indeed be the only way . . . to return to Germans their freedom." First remark from 10 April 1952, the second from 31 July 1968; both from KMBA SW 1008/VII, Nr 1.
50. Güsgen, "Die Bedeutung der katholischen Militärseelsorge in Deutschland von 1933 bis 1945," in Rolf-Dieter Müller and Hans Erich Volkmann, eds., *Die Wehrmacht: Mythos und Realität* (Munich: Oldenbourg, 1999), 516.
51. Gordon C. Zahn, *German Catholics and Hitler's Wars: A Study in Social Control* (New York: Sheed & Ward, 1962), 145.
52. In early historiography on the subject, see Lewy, *Catholic Church and Nazi Germany*, 236–242; Messerschmidt, "Aspekte der Militärseelsorge," 81–82; Zahn, *German Catholics*, 143–172; Thomas Breuer, *Dem Führer gehorsam: Wie die deutschen Katholiken von ihrer Kirche zum Kriegsdienst verpflichtet wurde; Dokumente* (Oberursel: Publik-Forum, 1989), 7; Heinrich Missalla, *Für Volk und Vaterland*, 73–82, and Missalla, *Wie der Krieg*, both of which include lengthy excerpts of Rarkowski's pastoral letters. For a more recent but no less critical assessment, see Johannes Güsgen, "Die Bedeutung der katholischen Militärseelsorge in Deutschland von 1933–1945," 512–517.
53. Missalla, *Für Volk und Vaterland*, 90.
54. Hans Jürgen Brandt, "Introduction," in Katholisches Militärbischofsamt, ed., *Mensch, was wollt Ihr denen sagen? Katholische Feldseelsorge im Zweiten Weltkrieg* (Augsburg: Pattloch Verlag, 1991), 15.
55. All biographical information of Werthmann is taken from *Biographisches Lexikon*, 896–898, unless otherwise noted.
56. Springer, "'Ein guter und getreuer Knecht,'" unpublished manuscript, available at KMBA. The Iron Cross is the equivalent roughly of the American Silver Star.
57. Missalla, *Für Volk und Vaterland*, 72–73.
58. See Monica Sinderhauf, "Katholische Wehrmachtseelsorge," in *Kirchen im Krieg*, 278–281.
59. Springer suggests that Hauck did this to protect Werthmann from the Gestapo, who had searched Werthmann's apartment "because of his attitude toward National Socialism." Transferring him into the Wehrmacht chaplaincy presented an opportunity for the archbishop to take him out of the Gestapo's firing line (*aus der Schlußlinie nehmen*). Springer, "'Ein guter und getreuer Knecht,'" 45–46. He was not the only priest to find security in the ranks of the chaplaincy. Johann Schmutz insisted that his

bishop, Conrad Gröber in Freiburg, also sent him to the chaplaincy for his protection. As related in Dagmar Pöpping, "Die Wehrmachtseelsorge im Zweiten Weltkrieg: Rolle und Selbtsverständnis von Kriegs- und Wehrmachtpfarrern im Ostkrieg, 1941–1945," in Manfred Gailus and Armin Nolzen, eds., *Zertrittene "Volksgemeinschaft": Glaube, Konfession und Religion im Nationalsozialismus* (Göttingen: Vandenhoeck & Ruprecht, 2011), 269.

60. Related in Missalla, *Für Volk und Vaterland*, 72–73. Missalla's source is Werthmann himself, with whom he had several conversations in the 1970s. The two were on personal terms.
61. May, *Interkonfessionalismus*, 132. According to one source, Werthmann was not expecting such an appointment and was "completely astonished" by it. Springer, "'Ein guter und getreuer Knecht,'" 63.
62. The title was *Päpstlicher Hausprälat*, now referred to as *Päpstlicher Ehrenkaplan*, or chaplain of honor.
63. Werthmann's reports to Rarkowski about these trips are found at BA-MA RH 15 Nr. 280, dated 9 July 1943, 27 March 1944, 5 May 1944, and 25 June 1944, respectively.
64. KMBA SW 1009/VII Nr.1, letter, 29 January 1945. Keitel emphasized the temporariness of the assignment by ordering Werthmann to sign "provisional" ahead of his title in every communication he made.
65. Ibid., copy of report from HQ, 26th Infantry Division, 1 May 1945.
66. KMBA SW 310/III, Otto F., interview, 25 April 1990.
67. KMBA SW 723/III, Richard S., interview, 21 March 1990.
68. KMBA SW 750/III, Egon Schmitt, undated interview.
69. KMBA SW 635/III, Joseph P., Nr. 12, Bd. 1, undated notes.
70. The term is Omer Bartov's, from *Hitler's Army: Soldiers, Nazis, and War in the Third Reich* (New York: Oxford University Press, 1992).
71. As quoted in Güsgen, "Die Bedeutung der Katholischen Militärseelsorge," in *Die Wehrmacht*, 518.
72. The OKH consisted of five departments, one of which was the General Army Office (Allgemeine Heeresamt).
73. As summarized in Springer, "'Ein guter und getreuer Knecht,'" 105.
74. "Approved Regulations, Which Pertain to the Spiritual Care of Catholic Soldiers in the German Army," published 15 September 1935 in *Acta Apostolicae Sedis* 27 (1935): 367–373. Vatican Secretary of State Eugenio Pacelli signed the regulations and, given his involvement with the 1933 concordat, likely played a role in their drafting. The preamble explained that the German government accepted the rules that followed. The "Sacred Congregation," also known as the Congregation for the Doctrine of Faith, also recognized them, though there is no indication whether that office played a supervisory or a more active role (i.e., had a direct hand) in their construction.
75. Pöpping, "Die Wehrmachtseelsorge," 267–268.
76. See, as an example, KMBA SW 797/III, Akten Bernhard Schwarz.
77. BA-MA RH 12 II/5, Nr. 503/36, letter to OKH, 5 January 1937.
78. Ibid. The brochure was entitled "Soldier, War, and Death" and published by the Ludendorff Verlag.

79. The original German is *"staatpolitische Schulung."* *Staatpolitisch*, translated literally as "state-political," can mean either national or ideological. Under the Third Reich these two terms became virtually interchangeable. I have chosen to use "ideological" throughout this work to reflect more accurately the type of training that both soldiers and Nazi Party members experienced, training that propagated various elements of the Nazi worldview.
80. BA-MA 12 II/5, Nr 503/36, "Katholische militärkirchliche Dienstordnung für die Wehrmacht vom . . . (no date or signature, but the army and chaplaincy leadership likely coauthored it, according to the content and the language employed).
81. Ibid.
82. KMBA SW 1006/VI, AHA/Ag/S, Nr 2838/39, "Merkblatt über die Feldseelsorge," 21 August 1939.
83. Güsgen, "Die Bedeutung der katholischen Militärseelsorge," 519.
84. KMBA SW 1006/VI, "Merkblatt über die Feldseelsorge," 21 August 1939. All direct quotes are taken from here.
85. Ibid.
86. This is specific neither to the period nor to Germany. Sociologist Gordon C. Zahn conducted interviews with former and active RAF chaplains in the 1960s and determined that the chaplains' dual role as officer and priest was well balanced, and that if ever tension existed between the two, the tension was often resolved in favor of the military (officer) role. See Zahn, *The Military Chaplaincy: A Study of Role Tension in the Royal Air Force* (Toronto: University of Toronto Press, 1969), 32. Duff Crerar's history of the Canadian military chaplaincy and its pre-1914 evolution also points out that the chaplaincy was treated, and viewed itself, as a military department. This was one motivation for keeping military and civilian church services separate. See Crerar, *Padres in No Man's Land: Canadian Chaplains and the Great War* (Montreal: McGill-Queen's University Press, 1995), 16–18.
87. KMBA SW 1003/VI, 3 July 1945.
88. KMBA SW 1002/VI, 28 May 1945. Christian Streit offers a brief biography of Reinecke, the "little Keitel," in Gerd R. Ueberschär, ed., *Hitlers militärische Elite* (Darmstadt: Primus Verlag, 1998), 203–209, though he makes no mention of Reinecke's strident hostility to the churches.
89. Ibid., 1 June 1945.
90. KMBA SW 1019/VII, 1 October 1943 (copy).
91. BA-MA RH 15/282, "Wesen und Aufgabe der Feldseelsorge," signed by Edelmann, undated (likely written sometime in mid-1941, given the date references within the text and the lack of any direct mention of, or allusion to, the war in the East with the Soviet Union).
92. Ibid.
93. Bartov, *Hitler's Army*, 118. According to Bartov, many soldiers' letters directly quoted in the text include the use of religious and political (Nazi) rhetoric, often side by side: "May God allow the German people to find now the peace of mind and strength which would make it into the instrument needed by the Führer to protect the West from ruin, for what the Asiatic hordes will not destroy will be annihilated by Jewish hatred and revenge"

(169); "The Lord must see and help us once more out of this predicament" (written in August 1944; 170); "A thousand-year Reich is going to the grave ... God will help us ... No one in the world is more blessed than our *Volk*, which even today sends its roots deep into the earth" (this last from a theologian; 174).

94. More research is needed about the use of nondenominational services in time of war. Edelmann did not invent the idea of a nondenominational service within the military (other armies used them during the Second World War, and they were also used during the First World War), but they were not championed to the same extent that Edelmann's office promoted them.
95. Pöpping, "Die Wehrmachtseelsorge," 260.
96. BA-MA RH 15/282. Quotes from the following two paragraphs are from this source.
97. The 1917 Code of Canon Law, the Catholic Church's extensive system of laws and legal principles, explicitly forbade Catholics to attend non-Catholic services. The very few exceptions mentioned did not include military service, and it was made clear that even within the exceptions, the Catholic was merely an observer, not an active participant (canon 1258). This canon was rooted in the contemporary antagonism Catholics felt toward Protestants, and Catholic fears that Protestants would never cease their attempts to evangelize Catholics or question the pope's authority. The 1983 Code of Canon Law, which generally reflects an increased orientation toward ecumenism on the part of the Catholic Church, relaxed some of these prohibitions. However, many strictures still remain, such as canon 844, which limits Catholic priests to administering the sacraments only to Catholics and Catholics to receiving the sacraments only from Catholic priests, and canon 908, which forbids Catholic priests from concelebrating a mass with a priest from a rite "not in full communion with the Catholic Church." The 1983 Code of Canon Law is found in English at http://www.vatican.va/archive/ENG1104/_INDEX.HTM (last accessed 13 June 2014). The 1917 Code is online in Latin at http://www.catho.org/9.php?d=fo (last accessed 13 June 2014) and in English translation in print, curated by Edward N. Peters, *The 1917 or Pio-Benedictine Code of Canon Law* (San Francisco: Ignatius Press, 2001).
98. KMBA SW 1006/VI, 31 v/mob. AHA/Ag/S (I), Nr 51/40 g, 13 February 1940.
99. For a detailed account of Catholic religious materials available to soldiers during the war, see Missalla, *Für Volk und Vaterland*, esp. 103–189.
100. KMBA SW 1006/VI, 31 v/mob. AHA/Ag/S (I), Nr 51/40 g, 13 February 1940.
101. Antonia Leugers, *Jesuiten im Hitlers Wehrmacht: Kriegslegitimation und Kriegserfahrung* (Paderborn: Ferdinand Schöningh, 2009), 110, 115.
102. Ibid., 189.
103. Ibid., 114.
104. The definitive biography of Bormann is still Peter Longerich, *Hitlers Stellvertreter: Führung der Partei und Kontrolle des Staatsapparates durch den Stab Hess und die Partei-Kanzlei Bormann* (Munich: K.G. Saur, 1992).
105. KMBA SW 1006/VI, "Richtlinien für die Durchführung der Feldseelsorge," OKW Az v AWA/J (Ia) Nr 4100/42, from 24 May 1942. All the following direct quotations are taken from here.

106. For Werthmann's reflections, see KMBA SW 1006/VI, 1 June, 28 June, and 17 July 1945.
107. The most recent biography of Bormann using newly discovered documents is Volker Koop, *Martin Bormann: Hitlers Vollstrecker* (Cologne: Böhlau, 2012).
108. KMBA SW 1006/VI, "Richtlinien für die Durchführung der Feldseelsorge," 24 May 1942.
109. See KMBA 77/I 12, OKW decree, 6 August 1941.
110. KMBA SW 84/I 14, Rarkowski's letter, 7 October 1941, the General Staff's response, 24 October 1941. Both reference the following decree: OKW Nr 4798/41 und 4798/41 II.Ang., 10 September 1941.
111. This is a suggestion proffered by Omer Bartov.
112. A copy of this communication from the head of the secret police to the OKH is contained in the same file as the exchange of letters about the prohibition on using churches in Russian territory. Werthmann had preserved both, and it is telling that Heydrich's message is dated 1 November 1941, a mere week after the General Staff's last response to the field bishops. Further quotations in this paragraph are taken from KMBA SW 111/III, copy of letter (secret) to OKH, signed by Heydrich.
113. KMBA SW 1006/VI, 1 June 1945.
114. This was also true for the home front, where other historians have shown that the Nazis held religion at a distance, even when different groups—the *Deutsche Christen*, for example—agitated for a closer relationship with the Nazi movement. See Doris L. Bergen, *Twisted Cross: The German Christian Movement in the Third Reich* (Chapel Hill: University of North Carolina Press, 1996), and Richard Steigmann-Gall, *The Holy Reich: Nazi Conceptions of Christianity, 1919–1945* (Cambridge, UK: Cambridge University Press, 2003).
115. Pöpping makes the observation about the unexpected increase in chaplains' autonomy, in "Die Wehrmachtseelsorge," 260.
116. KMBA SW 1006/VI, 28 June 1945.
117. Ibid., 31 v/mob. AHA/Ag/S (I), Nr 51/40g, 13 February 1940. The exact wording is, "Die Teilnahme an Gottesdiensten und anderen seelsorglichen Veranstaltungen ist auch im Feldheer eine freiwillige Angelegenheit des einzelnen Soldaten. Dieser Grundsatz kommt auch in Ziff. 7 des "Merkblattes über FSS" zum Ausdruck. Durch den dort erwähnten Befehl des Truppenführers wird nur die Frage geregelt, ob und wann ein Gottesdienst stattfindet. Die Teilnahme wird nicht befohlen." ("Participation in holy services and other pastoral care activities is a voluntary opportunity for individual soldiers in the army. This policy is expressed in paragraph 7 of the Bulletin. The noted command of troop leaders regulates only whether and when a holy service might occur. Participation [as such] will not be ordered.")
118. One report of the infraction was given by a chaplain stationed in France; see KMBA SW 743/III, activity report, December 1942.
119. KMBA SW 1006/VI, 17 July 1945.
120. KMBA SW 152/III 8, OKH decree, February 1942.

121. Werthmann cites the October 1942 decree that announced the termination of new chaplains in the army as also ending plans for the continuation of seminars on a broad scale past 1942. See KMBA SW 958/III, *Geschichte der Feldseelsorge*, 20 June 1945.
122. KMBA SW 152/III 8, February 1942.
123. Ibid., handwritten reflection by Werthmann, 15 June 1944.
124. KMBA SW 997/VI, OKH decree (secret), 10 October 1942.
125. See KMBA SW 1002/VI, letter signed by both Dohrmann and Rarkowski, 9 March 1943. Nineteen Catholic and fifteen Protestant chaplains were lost at Stalingrad, either through death or imprisonment, when the Sixth Army surrendered.
126. BA-MA 15 280, 9 July 1943. Of all Hitler's field marshals, Küchler remains one of the most enigmatic. His career in the military demonstrates his capability of standing up to men like Himmler and Hitler, but he picked and chose his battles. After the war he was charged with war crimes at one of the Nuremberg military tribunals and sentenced to twenty years, of which he served less than five before his 1952 release. See John McCannon, "Generalfeldmarschall Georg von Küchler," in Ueberschär, ed., *Hitlers militärische Elite*, 138–139.
127. BA-MA 15 280, report, 27 March 1944. Kurt Haseloff was a decorated general whose known antipathy for Nazism led to his forced retirement in the summer of 1944, after the failed assassination attempt on Hitler.
128. The seminal study of the National Socialist Leadership Office continues to be Arne W. G. Zoepf, *Wehrmacht zwischen Tradition und Ideologie: Der NS-Führungsoffizier im Zweiten Weltkrieg* (Frankfurt am Main: P. Lang, 1988). Zoepf provides an overview of the operation that concentrates on the political entanglements created between the Nazi Party and Wehrmacht officers. See also Waldemar Besson, "Zur Geschichte des nationalsozialistischen Führungsoffiziers (NSFO)," *Vierteljahrshefte für Zeitgeschichte* 9/1 (January 1961): 76–116, and Volker Berghahn, "NSDAP und 'Geistige Führung' der Wehrmacht, 1939–1945," *Vierteljahrshefte für Zeitgeschichte* 17 (1969): 7–71. More recent literature that deals briefly with the NSFOs includes Frank Vossler, *Propaganda in die eigene Truppe: Die Truppenbetreuung in der Wehrmacht* (Paderborn: F. Schöningh, 2005), and Jürgen Förster, *Die Wehrmacht im NS-Staat: Eine strukturgeschichtliche Analyse* (Munich: R. Oldenbourg, 2007). From now on, these propaganda officers will be referred to by their more common German acronym, NSFO (*Nationalsozialistische Führungsoffizier*).
129. Zoepf, *Wehrmacht zwischen Tradition*, 12.
130. Gerhard L. Weinberg, "Adolf Hitler und der NS-Führungsoffizier," *Vierteljahrshefte für Zeitgeschichte* 12 (October 1964): 443–456, quote from 446. Weinberg includes the complete transcript of the January 1944 meeting. The other Wehrmacht officers were Lieutenant-General Rudolf Schmundt, Major-General Walter Scherff, and Lieutenant-Colonel Heinrich Borgmann.
131. Zoepf, *Wehrmacht zwischen Tradition*, 81. Bormann failed due to resistance across the Wehrmacht leadership level, including from Keitel and Himmler, his archrival.

132. Weinberg, "Adolf Hitler," 446.
133. This is Zoepf's argument, *Wehrmacht zwischen Tradition*, 373.
134. BA-MA RW 6/587, "Tagung unter Leitung des Chefs des NSF/OKW, Gen.d.Inf. Reinecke," no date but likely early 1944.
135. NARA T312, roll 630, fr 8257066, 28 March 1944. Emphasis in original.
136. Ibid., fr 8257068, 28 March 1944.
137. Ibid., fr 8257081, 28 February 1944. Emphasis in original.
138. KMBA SW 148/III 5, 9 June 1945.
139. Ibid., 5, 28 September 1945. Berghahn and Zoepf's scholarship confirms Werthmann's suspicions about the NSFO's purpose and activities.
140. BA-MA RH 15/280, p. 219, report, 25 June 1944.
141. KMBA SW 1052/IX, OKH secret decree, 25 August 1944, referencing an earlier decree from 11 June 1944.
142. This happened according to the concordat's appendix, which stated that all students studying philosophy and theology, and all seminarians, were free from military service and its attendant exercises except in the case of general mobilization. In October 1939, not long after the fall of Poland, the OKW clarified that all seminarians and students of theology preparing for the priesthood who had not yet been ordained to the subdiaconate [i.e., those considered to be minor clerics] were eligible for full military service "if they cannot be used in the medical service." See KMBA SW 1052/IX, copy of copy, OKW Berlin, Bericht betr. Heranziehung von römisch-katholischen Geistlichen und Theologiestudierenden zum aktiven Wehrdienst (geheim; nur zum vertraulichen Gebrauch), 14 October 1939.
143. KMBA SW 1006/VI, 3 July 1945.
144. KMBA SW 1052/IX, no date given. The *Volkssturm* was a kind of people's militia, formed within Germany in the last months of the war and composed primarily of very young and very old men as well as women and girls. Its purpose was to defend the Reich against invading armies. While Werthmann did not discuss how many men these decrees may have affected, or how broadly "ecclesiastical office" was defined, the fact that the decrees were promulgated at all is further evidence of the drive to eliminate religious influence in the military.
145. Weidemann revealed this fascinating information in conversation with Werthmann on 25 July 1944, a mere five days after the attempted assassination of Hitler, when Weidemann's life was in great danger. Evidently Werthmann told no one of Weidemann's involvement at the time, which would itself have been seen as a crime deserving execution if he had been discovered. See KMBA SW 1019 SW/VII, notes.
146. KMBA SW 1052/IX, written 31 May–28 September 1945. Emphasis added.
147. Ibid.
148. As quoted in Missalla, *Wie der Krieg*, 41.
149. Ibid., 42–43.
150. Ibid., 67.
151. Ibid., 100. Rarkowski's last pastoral letter was his New Year's greeting in 1944; the Advent pastoral letter from December 1944 is a copy of 1943, abbreviated by Werthmann, who had already informally assumed the responsibilities of the field bishop due to Rarkowski's illness.

152. Missalla, *Für Volk und Vaterland*, 57. Missalla's source is Werthmann. See also Katholische Militärbischofsamt and Hans Jürgen Brandt, *Christen im Krieg: Katholische Soldaten, Ärzte und Krankenschwestern im Zweiten Weltkrieg* (Augsburg: Pattloch, 2001), 17. There were an additional 215 part-time chaplains in March 1939, that is, priests who were formally part of civilian dioceses but who could be used as military chaplains in special cases. It is not clear how many of these 215 men eventually became part of the chaplaincy.
153. Numbers taken from Wilhelm Deist, *Militär, Staat und Gesellschaft: Studien zur preussisch-deutschen Militärgeschichte* (Munich: R. Oldenbourg, 1991), 326–333, and Jost Dülffer, "Vom Bündnispartner zum Erfüllungsgehilfen im totalen Krieg: Militär und Gesellschaft in Deutschland, 1933–1945," in Wolfgang Michalka, ed., *Der Zweite Weltkrieg: Analysen, Grundzüge, Forschungsbilanz* (Munich: Piper, 1989), 289.
154. As with most modern armies, the organization of the Wehrmacht in terms of numbers fluctuated depending on wartime exigencies. Generally speaking, an army consisted of between 60,000 and 100,000 men; an army group comprised two or more adjacent armies that shared a headquarters.
155. KMBA SW 84/I 14, 22 April 1952. One year later, in a more formal report, Werthmann gave slightly higher figures: 561 Catholic chaplains served during the war, with the highest number at one time reached in the summer of 1942, with 410. Seventy-two chaplains were active at the outbreak of the war, and sixty-four were killed in action. There is no explanation for the discrepancy. KMBA SW 997/VI, 5 July 1953. These numbers are contradicted by Georg May, whose work on interdenominational cooperation in the chaplaincy during the Third Reich offers the following figures, which for the Catholic side seem inflated: 673 Catholic chaplains active between 1935 and 1945, and 428 Protestant chaplains active during the war years (1939–1945). He claimed to be using "research completed up to 15 February 1964" at the KMBA, which at that time was in Bonn and lacked most of Werthmann's personal documents. See May, *Interkonfessionalismus*, 495. Even now, there is no consensus among historians about how many chaplains might have served during the war. Please see Appendix 2 for an overview of Werthmann's statistics.
156. KMBA SW 148/III (Nr. 5), 19 January 1952.
157. KMBA SW 1052/IX, series of reflections from 1 June 1945. See Appendix 2 for more information about the statistics and the individuals it included.
158. KMBA SW 997/VI, 15 May 1945.
159. Ibid., 31 May 1945.
160. Ibid., 30 June 1945.
161. These include the Bavarian Jesuit priest Rupert Mayer, who was one of the few Catholics who spoke loudly and clearly against Nazism from the beginning; the well-known Protestant theologians Martin Niemöller and Dietrich Bonhoeffer (who was hanged for his role in the July 1944 assassination attempt); and seven Austrian priests who refused to be conscripted, six of whom were executed as a consequence.
162. The interview was conducted with Werthmann, Dohrmann, and Münchmeyer together, by Gregor Zimmer, presumably with the American infantry

division that interned them in Niederalteich. Copies were made in English and German. See KMBA SW 1009/VII (Nr. 1), no date given.

163. Jochen Böhler, *Auftakt zum Vernichtungskrieg: Die Wehrmacht in Polen 1939* (Frankfurt am Main: Fischer Taschenbuch Verlag, 2006); Alexander B. Rossino, "Destructive Impulses: German Soldiers and the Conquest of Poland," *Holocaust and Genocide Studies* 11/3 (December 1997): 351–365; Rossino, *Hitler Strikes Poland: Blitzkrieg, Ideology, and Atrocity* (Lawrence: University Press of Kansas, 2003).

3. PRIESTS AND SEMINARIANS IN THE WEHRMACHT

1. This indicates that the "secret appendix" detailing general mobilization and its effects for priests was, in fact, kept secret until 1939. See, for example, KMBA SW 632–633/III, Nachlass Rudolf P., undated interview.
2. See Hans Jürgen Brandt, ed., *Priester in Uniform: Seelsorger, Ordensleute, und Theologen als Soldaten im Zweiten Weltkrieg* (Augsburg: Pattloch, 1994), 9.
3. Chaplains were technically part of the officer corps, so the lack of epaulettes was significant. Please see Appendix 3 for a list. See also Katholische Militärbischofsamt and Hans Jürgen Brandt, eds., *Christen im Krieg: Katholische Soldaten, Ärzte und Krankenschwestern im Zweiten Weltkrieg* (Augsburg: Pattloch Verlag, 2001), 23.
4. See Manfred Messerschmidt and Wolfram Wette, *Was damals Recht war: NS-Militär- und Strafjustiz im Vernichtungskrieg* (Essen: Klartext, 1996). Messerschmidt and Wette found that roughly 300 "conscientious objectors" were executed during the war by military tribunals, almost the same number as those executed for the same crime, civilian and military, between 1907 and 1932. See p. 76. A growing literature treats the subject of Wehrmacht justice and soldiers' crimes. See for example Fietje Ausländer, Norbert Haase and Gerhard Paul, eds., *Die anderen Soldaten: Wehrkraftzersetzung, Gerhorsamsverweigerung und Fahnenflucht im Zweiten Weltkrieg* (Frankfurt am Main: Fischer Taschenbuch Verlag, 1995); Magnus Koch, *Fahnenfluchten: Deserteure der Wehrmacht im Zweiten Weltkrieg; Lebenswege und Entscheidungen* (Paderborn: Schönigh, 2008); Manfred Messerschmidt, *Die Wehrmachtjustiz, 1933–1945* (Paderborn: Schöningh, 2005); Manfred Messerschmidt and Fritz Wüllner, *Die Wehrmachtjustiz im Dienst des Nationalsozialismus: Zerstörung einer Legende* (Baden-Baden: Nomos, 1987). For Austrian deserters of the Wehrmacht, see Maria Fritsche, *Entziehungen: Österreichische Deserteure und Selbstverstümmler in der deutschen Wehrmacht* (Vienna: Böhlau, 2004).
5. Gordon C. Zahn conducted a study more than forty years ago that found only seven Catholics in the Greater German Reich—Germany and Austria after the 1938 *Anschluss*—who could be considered conscientious objectors. These were Franz Reinisch; Josef Fleischer; Franz Jägerstätter (an Austrian peasant beatified by Pope Benedict XVI in June 2007); Josef Mayr-Nusser, the Catholic Action leader in Austria; and three men associated with the religious community *Christkönigsgesellschaft*: Max Josef Metzger, Brother Maurus, and Brother Michael. See Zahn, *German Catholics and Hitler's*

Wars: A Study in Social Control (New York: Sheen & Ward, 1962), 55. Heinrich Missalla contradicts some of these names, pointing to unresolved discrepancies in more recent German-language historiography. He includes Michael Lerpscher, Josef Ruf, Ernst Volkmann, and Richard Reitsamer as conscientious objectors. On one thing they seem to agree: Josef Fleischer, from Freiburg, was the only survivor. Missalla, *Für Gott, Führer, und Vaterland: Die Verstrickung der katholischen Seelsorge in Hitlers Krieg* (Munich: Kösel, 1999), 228, n. 41.

6. KMBA SW 1052/IX, "Übersicht" by Werthmann, April 1944. The number breaks down as follows: 6,218 priests (3,909 diocesan priests and 2,309 order priests); 6,439 students studying theology, including clerics (i.e., those who had received tonsure but had not yet been fully ordained; presumably this includes seminarians); 4,237 lay brothers; and 872 order novices. The lay brothers and novices were eligible for full military service as were any theology students and seminarians who were not ordained to the subdiaconate before their conscription.

   This number is different from that cited in the introduction, fn. 1: Hans Jürgen Brandt relied on Freiburg's military archives, and his statistics include the period 1939–1943 (Werthmann's statistics are dated to April 1944). I have been unable to ascertain which number is more accurate. It is possible that both are correct, and that Werthmann's higher number includes those seminarians and theology students who became eligible for military service between 1943 and April 1944. Please refer to Appendix 2 for further statistical information.

7. See KMBA SW 1055/IX 4, Abschrift (geheim) der Oberbefehlshaber des Heeres, 13 February 1940, third provision, and KMBA SW 1055/IX 4, "Heranziehung von Soldaten zur Feldseelsorge," excerpt from 1 April 1943.

8. I borrow the term from Brandt, *Priester in Uniform*, 7, who in turn borrowed it from Georg Wagner. There is no perfect term for this group of men, either in English or in German. *Priestersoldaten*, literally "priest-soldiers," implies that the individuals were all priests, whereas I am also including in this group seminarians who had not yet been ordained as priests. However, I have chosen to use it to be able to refer to this group more simply.

9. KMBA SW 1052/IX, draft entitled "Stellungnahme zu der Frage der Militärpflicht der Kleriker," by Georg Werthmann, 19 January 1952.

10. KMBA SW 767/III 12 (Bd 9), Akten Johann G. S., handwritten letters from R. L., 26 August 1941 and 3rd Sunday of Advent (mid- to late December) 1941.

11. Ibid., letter from B. Hebel, 10 October 1941.

12. Ibid., letter from H. Barthl, 18 June 1942.

13. KMBA SW 750/III, Akte Egon Schmitt, activity report, 17 March 1941.

14. KMBA SW 447/III, Akte Dietrich H., activity report, 1 January–31 March 1944, undated.

15. KMBA SW 1006/VI, pastoral care report, 1 January–30 June 1945, undated. Himmler created the *Volksgrenadierdivisionen* in 1944 in response to the Allied invasion of Normandy and heavy losses in the East. These units were de facto not part of the Wehrmacht but rather the SS Leadership Office, along

the same lines as the Waffen-SS. As per the order that no new chaplains would be placed in the armed forces after 1943, they were not provided with chaplains.
16. KMBA SW 543/III, Akte Hubert L., undated postwar interview.
17. KMBA SW 441/III, Akte Joseph H., postwar interview, 22 June 1990.
18. KMBA SW 632, 633/III, Akten Peifer, manuscript, 105-106. This was later published as *Den Menschen ein Angebot: Erinnerungen eines Seelsorges* (Cologne: Styria, 1993). All subsequent quotes will reference the manuscript contained in the Nachlass.
19. Brandt, *Priester in Uniform*, 80, 82.
20. KMBA SW 293/III, Akte Franz M.E., interview, 2 July 1990. *Pfaffe* is a German term that was originally designed to differentiate between priest and monk (*Monch*). Since the Reformation, it has been regarded as a pejorative term, especially in spoken language.
21. KMBA SW 324/III, Akte Wilhelm F., evaluation, 20 August 1945.
22. KMBA SW 1050/IX, letter, 13 October 1943.
23. Ibid., letter, 21 November 1943.
24. Ibid., "Besser in Tuchfühlung bleiben," newspaper excerpt, early 1960s (no other identifying information).
25. KMBA SW 767/III 12 (Bd. 9), Akten Johann G. S., letter, 16 October 1941.
26. KMBA SW 386/III, Akte Johann A. H., Werthmann's reflections, 29 February 1944.
27. Ibid., letter to Werthmann from H., 15 January 1954, as well as undated notes entitled "Verhaftung und Haft als Kriegspfarrer," by H.
28. The wording of the charges is H.'s own description, given retrospectively. See ibid., letter to Werthmann from H., 15 January 1954.
29. KMBA SW 386/III, Akte Johann A. H., letter from Adalbert Dähn, paymaster and chief of office, 5 May 1944. The other letters are contained in this file as well.
30. KMBA SW 1053/IX 2, report, 25 August 1943.
31. KMBA SW 236/III, Akte Erich B., Werthmann's notes, 25 August 1943.
32. KMBA SW 1050/IX, postcard, 20 January 1944.
33. Ibid., letter, 9 November 1944.
34. Ibid., letter, 15 October 1943, written by Moser, a *Sanitätgefreiter*. No other information given.
35. Ibid., "Meine Kriegserlebnisse," Rudolf Unger, 22 January 1968. Unger dedicated these unpublished memoirs to Georg Werthmann.
36. KMBA SW 310/III, Akte Otto F., interview, 3 July 1979. It is clear that he was speaking about *Volksgrenadierdivisionen*, not *Volksdivisionen* (see note 15, above). For the impact of the 1941 demobilization of Jesuits, see Antonia Leugers, *Jesuiten im Hitlers Wehrmacht: Kriegslegitimation und Kriegserfahrung* (Paderborn: Schöningh, 2009).
37. KMBA SW 1050/IX, letter, 3 December 1942.
38. EAM, Kardinal-Faulhaber Archiv, 6796/2, letter, 26 December 1942.
39. KMBA SW 947/III, Akte Martin Z., interview, 14 June 1990.
40. Matthew 16:19.
41. John 20:22-23.

42. For an excellent overview of the development of auricular confession, see chapter 1 in John Mahoney, *The Making of Moral Theology: A Study of the Roman Catholic Tradition* (Oxford: Oxford University Press, 1987).
43. As related in Mahoney, *The Making of Moral Theology*, 26. These four orders are singled out because of their global reach and significance, to underscore the importance that the sacrament of Penance took on in the post-Reformation age.
44. For more on the evolution of moral manuals, see the preface in James F. Keenan, *A History of Catholic Moral Theology in the Twentieth Century: From Confessing Sins to Liberating Consciences* (New York: Continuum, 2010).
45. As laid down in Canons 983 and 1388, 1983 Code of Canon Law.
46. In any case, such intervention would have resulted in the arrest of the confessing soldier, not because he had committed certain actions but because he had reported them to someone else. My thanks to Omer Bartov for pointing this out.
47. Richard Breitman, *The Architect of Genocide: Himmler and the Final Solution* (New York: Alfred A. Knopf, 1991), 35. See also Peter Longerich, *Heinrich Himmler: Biographie* (Munich: Siedler, 2008).
48. Breitman, *Architect of Genocide*, 15. One needs look no further than the pages of the popular SS circular *Das Schwarze Korps*. The paper ran frequent articles slandering the pope and individual German bishops, particularly Cardinal von Faulhaber, archbishop of Munich, and the Church in general. See, for example, EAM Kardinal-Faulhaber Archiv, 3055/I and II; "Wer lügt, Herr Kardinal?" *Das Schwarze Korps*, 20 February 1936; "Und dazu schweigt der Papst!" *Das Schwarze Korps*, 13 August 1936; "Schwarzer Dolchstoß," *Das Schwarze Korps*, 25 February 1937.
49. KMBA SW 631/III, Akte Georg Paulus, interview, 15 May 1990.
50. KMBA SW 750/III, Akte Egon Schmitt, activity report, 17 March 1941. The SS-*Totenkopfdivisionen*, or Death's Head units (so called for the skull-and-bones insignia on their uniforms), were a division of the *Waffen-SS* whose members were formerly guards in concentration camps. They participated in war crimes on multiple fronts. See Charles W. Sydnor, *Soldiers of Destruction: The SS Death's Head Division, 1933–1945* (Princeton, NJ: Princeton University Press, 1977).
51. KMBA SW 192/III, Akte Erich A. B., *Geschichte der Feldseelsorge*, 25 June 1945.
52. KMBA SW 324/III, Akte Wilhelm F., *Geschichte der Feldseelsorge*, 6 September 1945.
53. KMBA SW 551/III, Akte Theodor L., unpublished *Tagebuch*.
54. KMBA SW 810/III, Akte Josef Seitz, photocopy of letter written by Martin Maller regarding Seitz's wartime activities, sent to the archives following his death in 1964. Undated.
55. See Doris L. Bergen, "Between God and Hitler: German Military Chaplains and the Crimes of the Third Reich," in Omer Bartov and Phyllis Mack, eds., *In God's Name: Genocide and Religion in the Twentieth Century* (New York: Berghahn), 123–138; and Missalla, *Für Gott, Führer, und Vaterland*,

209. Both Missalla and Breuer are very critical of the leadership of the bishops and Rarkowski, whom they view as instrumental in inducing priests and seminarians to embrace their service to the regime. For Breuer, see, Breuer, ed., *Dem Führer gehorsam: Wie die deutschen . . . Dokumente* (Oberursel: Publik-Forum, 1989), 3–7.
56. KMBA SW 441/III, Akte Joseph H., interview, 22 June 1990.
57. Ibid., interview, 22 June 1990.
58. KMBA SW 811, 812/III, Akten Martin S., letter, 15 June 1942.
59. The only book-length study of the NSFO is Arne W. G. Zoepf, *Wehrmacht zwischen Tradition und Ideologie: Der NS-Führungsoffizier im Zweiten Weltkrieg* (Frankfurt am Main: P. Lang, 1989); quotes from 54, 89. See also Volker Berghahn, "NSDAP und 'geistige Führung' der Wehrmacht, 1939–1945," *Vierteljahreshefte für Zeitgeschichte* 17 (1969); Frank Vossler, *Propaganda in die eigene Truppe: Die Truppenbetreuung in der Wehrmacht, 1939–1945* (Paderborn F. Schöningh, 2005).
60. KMBA SW 944/III, Akte Wilhelm W., interview, 20 June 1990.
61. KMBA SW 947/III, Akte Martin Z., interview, 14 June 1990.
62. BA-MA RH 15 280, Georg Werthmann, "Bericht über die Dienstreise nach Prag und Holoubkau," 5 May 1944.
63. KMBA SW 465/III, Akte Johann E. K., interview undated.
64. KMBA SW 621/III, Akte Joseph Ohseforth, report to the military vicar-general, 7 June 1979. Since Hitler did not promulgate the decree establishing the National Socialist Leadership Office under Reinecke until December 1943, Ohseforth likely confused his dates.
65. KMBA SW 723/III, Akten Richard S., interview, part I, 21 March 1990.
66. KMBA SW 510/III, Akte Alois K., interview, 1 June 1990.
67. KMBA SW 635/III, Akten Josef P., undated postwar dictation.
68. My thanks for Dr. Monica Sinderhauf for refining this distinction for me.
69. As detailed in NARA T312 roll 118 frame 7648807, experience report, signed by Chaplain Kauder, 25 October 1940.
70. KMBA SW 750/III, Akte Egon Schmitt, activity report, 2 December 1940.
71. Ibid., pastoral care report, 29 January 1942.
72. Omer Bartov also notes this increase in religiosity as soldiers drew closer to battlefields. See *Hitler's Army: Soldiers, Nazis and War in the Third Reich* (New York: Oxford University Press, 1992), esp. chapter 4.
73. NARA T312 roll 419, frame 7995362, activity report, 12 April 1942 (chaplain's signed name not legible). Another chaplain, Leopold Ellner, wrote virtually the same thing: "I try to bring to soldiers the most beautiful piece of *Heimat* through divine services. We always think about how, in the same hour each Sunday, our loved ones at home are standing around the altar like we are, and that we are all deeply bound together through God." EAM, Faulhaber Archiv 6796/1, letter to von Faulhaber from Ellner, 14 July 1942.
74. NARA T312 roll 177 frames 7715690 and 7715695, activity report, 9 October 1942, signed by Rincke.
75. KMBA SW 724/III, Akten Richard S., pastoral care report, 6 October 1942.
76. Ibid., pastoral care report, 3 July 1944.
77. Ibid., pastoral care report, 5 January 1945.

78. KMBA SW 317/III, Akte Johannes F., pastoral care report, 5 April 1942.
79. Ibid., pastoral care report, 8 January 1942.
80. Ibid., pastoral care report, 3 July 1942.
81. Ibid., pastoral care report, 31 [sic] September 1944. Materialism can have a double meaning: in the Nazi sense, it equates with Bolshevism, capitalism, and Jews; the conservative Catholic definition identifies it in opposition to spiritualism which, through its emphasis on the material, intrinsically denies the existence of God. Earlier popes had condemned materialism as one of the chief errors of modernity.
82. KMBA SW 1055/IX, pastoral care report, Siegfried Döring, 1944 [3rd quarter].
83. KMBA SW 743/III, Akte Alfred Schmidt, activity report, December 1942.
84. KMBA SW 447/III, Akte Dietrich H., activity report for first quarter of 1944.
85. NARA T312 roll 177 frame 7715692, activity report, 9 October 1942.
86. BA-MA RH 15 280, "Bericht über die Dienstreise nach Krakau, 15–17 March 1944" (dated 27 March 1944).
87. NARA T312 roll 419 frame 7995346-49, activity report, 20 January 1942.
88. KMBA SW 1052/IX, remarks on the concordat appendix by Georg Werthmann, 1 June 1945.
89. KMBA SW 543/III, Akte Hubert L., undated postwar interview.
90. KMBA SW 688/III, Akte Wilhelm Ritthaler, undated postwar interview, and 750/III, Akte Egon Schmitt, undated postwar interview.
91. KMBA SW 293/III, Akte Franz M. E., postwar interview, 2 July 1990.
92. KMBA SW 632, 633/III, Akten Rudolf Peifer, manuscript.
93. KMBA SW 518/III, Akte Karl Ernst Kuhn, *Geschichte der Feldseelsorge* (Werthmann), 9 June 1945.
94. NARA T312 roll 419, frames 7995355-56, "Bericht über Kampfhandlung," addressed to Rarkowski, 9 January 1942. Satzger led a colorful life during the Third Reich. Beginning in 1935 and until he was conscripted, Satzger served as diocesan youth chaplain in Kaufbeuren in southern Bavaria, where the Gestapo interrogated him thirty times, gave him fifteen warnings, and subjected his house to eight raids. How he managed to clear the screening that all candidates for the chaplaincy were put through, meant to weed out potentially unreliable priests, is not clear. See Hans Jürgen Brandt, Peter Häger, Karl Hengst, and Katholisches Militärbischofsamt, eds., *Biographisches Lexikon der katholischen Militärseelsorge Deutschlands, 1848 bis 1945* (Paderborn: Bonifatius, 2002), 685.
95. KMBA SW 518/III, Akte Kuhn, *Geschichte der Feldseelsorge*, 13 August 1945. The priest who relayed the information about Kuhn to Werthmann was Metzner, first name not given, who also served in the 384th infantry division in North Africa.
96. Ibid., 5 July 1945.
97. Ibid., 12 September 1940.
98. Ibid., 20 February 1943.
99. KMBA SW 1055/IX 4, OKW decree (copy), 10 August 1944.
100. A rich historiography exists about letter-writing and its significance during the war, between German soldiers and their family and friends, and the value of and the problems in using these letters as historical documents.

See, for example, Ortwin Buchbender and Reinhold Sterz, *Das andere Gesicht des Krieges: Deutsche Feldpostbriefe, 1939–1945* (Munich: C. H. Beck, 1983); Klaus Latzel, *Deutsche Soldaten—nationalsozialistische Krieg? Kriegserlebnis, Kriegserfahrung, 1939–1945* (Paderborn: Schöningh, 1998); Karl-Theodor Schleicher and Heinrich Walle, eds., *Aus Feldpostbriefen junger Christen, 1939–1945: Ein Beitrag zur Geschichte der Katholischen Jugend im Felde* (Stuttgart: Steinert, 2005); Jens Ebert, Thomas Jander, and Veit Didczuneit, eds., *Schreiben im Krieg—Schreiben vom Krieg: Feldpost im Zeitalter der Weltkriege* (Essen: Klartext, 2011).

101. KMBA SW 597/III, Akte Heinrich Müller, letter, 19 September 1943.
102. KMBA SW 811, 812/III, Akten Martin S., letter from Amalie Moser, 15 February 1942.
103. KMBA SW 632, 633/III, Akten Rudolf P., letter from Agnes Tauber Fürth, 1 September 1941.
104. Ibid., letter from Anna Feck, 21 October 1941.
105. KMBA SW 635/III, Akten Josef P., letters from Frau Krunz begin 5 March 1943 and end 19 December 1943.
106. Bartov, *Hitler's Army*, 95–96. Bartov argues that soldiers became more violent but that this violence was not the reason for increased executions. Harsher disciplinary measures were taken to hold together an army that was disintegrating *because* of the violence involved in criminal orders being issued. See also Manfred Messerschmidt and Wolfram Wette, *Was damals Recht war*.
107. As contained in KMBA "Zusammenfassung der allen im Felde stehenden Wehrmachtgeistlichen und Kriegspfarrern zu Beginn und während des Krieges erteilten besonderen kirchlichen Vollmachten unter Berücksichtigung der hierzu gegebenen kirchenrechtlichen, moraltheologischen und pastoralen Weisungen." This essential collection of rules was simply referred to as "the Compendium [*die Zusammenfassung*]" by Werthmann and Rarkowski. It was released in three editions (1941, 1942, and 1944), updating the changes in OKW and OKH regulations.
108. EAB V/69-6, Nachlass Georg F., various letters.
109. *Biographisches Lexikon*, 808. See also Ludovic Lécuru, *L'abbé Stock: Sentinelle de la paix* (Paris: Técqui, 2003); Erich Kock, *Abbé Franz Stock: Priester zwischen den Fronten* (Mainz: M. Grünewald Verlag, 1996); Karl Heinz Kloidt, *Chartres 1945: Seminar hinter Stacheldraht; Eine Dokumentation* (Freiburg: Herder, 1988).
110. For Loevenich: KMBA SW 551/III, Akte Loevenich, "Erinnerungen des Grauens" by Hermann Josef Riesop in *Frechener* (postwar; undated), and Loevenich's "Erzählung vor der Kamera in Köln" (transcript), 24 March 1962. For Paul Steinert: KMBA SW 883/III, Akte Steinert, "Franziskus von Fresnes," *Hessische Jugend* 6/7 (June/July 1954).
111. KMBA SW 767/III 12 (Bd. 9), Akte Anton Ullrich, circular attached to letter, 17 October 1941.
112. EAM 6796/1, June 1942.
113. NARA T312 roll 177 frame 7715690, activity report, 4. Armee, 9 October 1942, signed by Rincke.
114. KMBA SW 627/III, Akte Kunibert P., undated postwar interview.

115. EAM Priesterseminar Freising, seminarian J. K., 9 August 1941.
116. A rich literature exists on German conceptions of Russians, Slavs, and "the East," delineating how these prejudices developed over decades, in many ways predating Nazism. See especially Hans-Erich Volkmann, ed., *Das Russlandbild im Dritten Reich* (Cologne: Böhlau, 1994); Vejas G. Liulevicius, *War Land on the Eastern Front: Culture, Identity, and German Occupation in World War I* (New York: Cambridge University Press, 2000); Gerd Koenen, *Der Russland-Komplex: Die Deutschen und der Osten, 1900–1945* (Munich: Beck, 2005); Johannes Hürter, *Hitlers Heerführer: Die deutschen Oberbefehlshaber im Krieg gegen die Sowjetunion, 1941/42* (Munich: R. Oldenbourg Verlag, 2007); Andrea Kamp and Peter Jahn, *Unsere Russen—unsere Deutschen: Bilder vom Anderen, 1800 bis 2000* (Berlin: Links, 2007); and more recently, Annemarie Sammartino, *The Impossible Border: Germany and the East, 1914–1922* (Ithaca, NY: Cornell University Press, 2010).
117. KMBA SW 293/III, Akte Franz M. E., interview, 2 July 1990.
118. KMBA SW 310/III, Akte Otto F., interview, 3 July 1990.
119. KMBA SW 1050/IX, Unger, "Meine Kriegserlebnisse," 18.
120. KMBA SW 632, 633/III, Akte Peifer, manuscript, 130–131. In the same passage, Peifer reveals that he administered as a priest to Polish civilians with full awareness that he was doing something illegal that bore consequences. He remained undiscovered.
121. Bernhard Häring, *Embattled Witness: Memories of a Time of War* (New York: Seabury Press, 1976), 20–21. Häring's memoir is written in English. He does not state explicitly that he baptized the boy, though no other conclusion can be drawn from the circumstances. Häring was very active after the war, teaching moral theology in Rome and holding visiting professorships at Yale University and Union Theological Seminary in New York.
122. Rudolf Ritzer, "Priesterrock und Uniform: 2,028 Tage als Sanitäter im II. Weltkrieg unter dem Schutz der Vorsehung; Tagesbuchaufzeichnungen vom 5.12.1939 bis 24.6.1945." Privately published manuscript taken directly from his wartime journals, with no publication date (but after 1987).
123. KMBA SW 881/III, Akten Josef Vennemann, "Dokumentation zur Militärseelsorge im 2. Weltkrieg," 7–8. For an excellent study of the Nazi conquest of Ukraine and how its occupying administration was set up, see Wendy Lower, *Nazi Empire-Building and the Holocaust in Ukraine* (Chapel Hill: University of North Carolina Press, 2005).
124. Alexander B. Rossino, *Hitler Strikes Poland: Blitzkrieg, Ideology and Atrocity* (Lawrence: University Press of Kansas, 2003), esp. chapter 1. Rossino clearly establishes the fact that the SS frequently targeted Polish priests and clerics for execution during the invasion of Poland. See also Jochen Böhler, *Auftakt zum Vernichtungskrieg: Die Wehrmacht in Polen, 1939* (Frankfurt am Main: Fischer Taschenbuch Verlag, 2006).
125. KMBA SW 881/III, Akten Vennemann, "Dokumentation zur Militärseelsorge im 2. Weltkrieg," 7–8.
126. KMBA SW 280, Akte Friedrich D., and 510/III, Akte Alois K., interviews, 5 June 1990 and 1 June 1990, respectively.
127. EAM Priesterseminar Freising, seminarian G. W., 23 September 1941.

128. EAM Priesterseminar Freising, seminarian W. H., 6 November 1941.
129. EAM Priesterseminar Freising, seminarian W. M., 2 July 1944.
130. KMBA SW 1050/IX, Unger, "Meine Kriegserlebnisse," 6, 29; also KMBA SW 543/III, Akte Wilhelm L., postwar interview, undated.
131. EAM Priesterseminar Freising, seminarian A. A., 8 August 1941.
132. EAM Priesterseminar Freising, seminarian S. E., 1 September 1941.
133. KMBA SW 280/III, Akte Friedrich D., interview, 5 June 1990.
134. KMBA SW 901/III, Akte Wassong, *Tagebuch*, Band II. Perhaps not coincidentally, this was also Hitler's birthday.
135. KMBA SW 580/III, Akte Menke, *Kriegstagebuch*, 11 November 1944. The diary in this file was not the original but a copy created mostly likely after the war, hand-written by Menke himself. It is not clear how much, if anything, he altered.
136. Ibid., 17 November 1944. In a 1966 addendum, Menke remarked that during a 1961 visit to Venice, he learned from the former monsignor, now Patriarch Urbani, that Sister Cressin was still alive.
137. Saul Friedländer, *The Years of Extermination: Nazi Germany and the Jews, 1939–1945* (New York: HarperCollins, 2007), 561. Raul Hilberg gives the higher number of 9,000 Italian Jews killed during the Holocaust; see Hilberg, *The Destruction of the European Jews*, Vol. 3, 3rd ed. (New Haven, CT: Yale University Press, 2003), 1321.
138. KMBA SW 840/III, Akte Stelzenberger, 19 October 1941, 97–98. It is possible that the date is not accurate, since the next two excerpts followed this in sequence but are dated earlier. Stelzenberger survived the war and taught moral theology at the University of Tübingen.
139. Ibid., 17 October 1941, 100. The diary has been recopied posthumously with notes made by another unnamed priest, who took care to keep his contextual remarks separate from the narrative of the diaries.
140. Ibid., 100–101.
141. Ibid., 13 February 1942, 107.
142. Biographical information taken from *Biographisches Lexikon*, 804–805.
143. Doris L. Bergen and Saul Friedländer wrote about the case independently and almost simultaneously. See Friedländer, "The Wehrmacht, German Society, and Knowledge of the Mass Extermination of the Jews," in Omer Bartov, Atina Grossmann, and Mary Nolan, eds., *Crimes of War: Guilt and Denial in the Twentieth Century* (New York: New Press, 2002), 17–30; Bergen, "Between God and Hitler," 123–138.
144. Ernst Tewes, "Seelsorger bei den Soldaten, 1940–1945: Aufzeichnungen und Erinnerungen," in Georg Schwaiger, ed., *Das Erzbistum München und Freising in der Zeit der nationalsozialistischen Herrschaft*, Vol. 2 (Munich: Schnell & Steiner, 1984), 251.
145. See "Statement by C.-in-C. Sixth Army, Field Marshal von Reichenau, 26 August 1941," in Ernst Klee, Willi Dressen, and Volker Riess, *"The Good Old Days": The Holocaust as Seen by Its Perpetrators and Bystanders* (New York: Free Press, 1991), 152–153. Reichenau confirmed that he "ascertained in principle that once begun, the action was conducted in an appropriate manner." This can mean only one thing, that the women and children were killed.

146. For general information about the postwar activities of Tewes, see KMBA SW 863/III, "Korrespondentenbericht 303," in *Katholische Nachrichten Agentur*, 4 December 1993, p. 2; Werthmann's comments are included in the same file, *Geschichte der Feldseelsorge*, 13 June 1946. The 1968 trial in question is Landgericht Darmstadt, which prosecuted former members of *Einsatzkommando 4a* (part of *Einsatzgruppe C*), a unit involved in the Babi Yar massacre of 1941.
147. KMBA SW 578/III, Akte Alfons Mende, interview, 2 June 1990.
148. For Heinrich Niewind's remarkable story, see the following from KMBA SW 1050/IX: "Der Retter Velesmes," *Katholische Nachrichten-Agentur* 7, 11 January 1965; "Er will kein Held sein," *Bildgott* (?), 17 January 1965; "Französisches Dorf ehrt deutschen Priester," *Die Welt—Ausgabe B* (Berlin, Westsektor), September 1965; untitled article from *Bremer Nachrichten*, 28 September 1965; untitled article from *Rheinischer Merkur*, 8 October 1965. See also KMBA SW 1054/IX, "Retter eines französischen Dorfes ermittelt," *Militärseelsorge VII (Katholische Nachrichten-Agentur)*, undated.
149. This is John Connelly's argument in *From Enemy to Brother: The Revolution in Catholic Teaching on the Jews, 1933–1965* (Cambridge, MA: Harvard University Press, 2012), esp. 68.
150. Christopher R. Browning, *Ordinary Men: Reserve Police Battalion 101 and the Final Solution in Poland* (New York: Harper Perennial, 1998), esp. chapter 18.
151. Thomas Kühne speaks at length of (the myth of) *Kameradschaft*—what I would translate as "brotherhood"—within the German military. This *Kameradschaft* relied on feelings of community and solidarity to the point of creating a "grand brotherhood" of criminality that embraced even those soldiers who did not want to be complicit. His argument resonates strongly with my own, although he is speaking more generally about the average German soldier, not specifically about Catholic clergy. See Kühne, *Kameradschaft: Die Soldaten des nationalsozialistischen Krieges und das 20. Jahrhundert* (Göttingen: Vandenhoeck & Ruprecht, 2006), and Kühne, *Belonging and Genocide: Hitler's Community, 1918–1945* (New Haven, CT: Yale University Press, 2010).
152. *Biographisches Lexikon*, xvi.
153. Ralph W. Mathisen, "Emperors, Priests and Bishops: Military Chaplains in the Roman Empire," and Michael McCormick, "The Liturgy of War from Antiquity to the Crusades," both in Doris L. Bergen, ed., *The Sword of the Lord: Military Chaplains from the First to the Twenty-first Century* (Notre Dame, IN: University of Notre Dame Press, 2004).
154. This observation is made by Missalla, *Für Gott, Führer und Vaterland*, 172, and by Jörg Seiler, "Kameradschaft als Widerstand? Der Bamberger Regens Johann Schmitt und priesterliche Identität im Krieg," in Franz Brendle and Anton Schindling, eds., *Geistliche im Krieg* (Münster: Aschendorff, 2009), 323, 342.
155. KMBA SW 1009/VII (Nr. 1), copy of Gregor Zimmer interview (English version); undated.
156. The text of the infamous *Kommissarbefehl*, or Commissar Order, can be found online courtesy of the Deutsches Historisches Museum: http://www

.dhm.de/lemo/html/dokumente/kommissarbefehl/index.html (last accessed 3 April 2014). Felix Römer's recent study of it in the context of the war in the East is invaluable: Römer, *Der Kommissarbefehl: Wehrmacht und NS-Verbrechen an der Ostfront, 1941/42* (Paderborn: Schöningh, 2008).
157. Bartov, *Hitler's Army*, 182.

4. RELIGION, NATIONALISM, AND WHY PRIESTS WENT TO WAR

1. Kathleen M. Comerford, "Italian Tridentine Diocesan Seminaries: A Historiographical Study," *Sixteenth Century Journal* 29/4 (1998): 999–1000.
2. In addition to Comerford, "Italian Tridentine Diocesan Seminaries," 1000–1001, see Klaus Ganzer, "Das Trienter Konzil und die Errichtung von Priesterseminarien," in Karl Hillenbrand and Rudolf Weigand, eds., *Mit der Kirche auf dem Weg: 400 Jahre Priesterseminar Würzburg, 1589–1989* (Würzburg: Echter, 1989), 11–24.
3. Perhaps this helps to explain the lack of a general study of seminary training in Germany. Most that do exist are specific to a diocese. The most useful texts utilized for this project are Paul Seibel, *Priester: Ausbildung und Verfolgung* (Frankfurt am Main: Haag + Herchen, 1994); Hillenbrand and Weigand, *Mit der Kirche auf dem Weg*; Thomas Schulte-Umberg, *Profession und Charisma: Herkunft und Ausbildung des Klerus im Bistum Münster, 1776–1940* (Paderborn: Schöningh, 1999); Erwin Gatz, ed., *Wie Priester leben und arbeiten: Quellen zur Lebenskultur und Arbeitswelt des deutschen Seelsorgeklerus seit dem Ende des 18. Jahrhunderts* (Regensburg: Schnell + Steiner, 2011). Also quite useful is a study of theological faculties in Germany under Nazism: Dominik Burkard and Wolfgang Weiss, eds., *Katholische Theologie im Nationalsozialismus* (Würzburg: Echter, 2007).
4. See Rudolf Weigand in *Mit der Kirche auf dem Weg*, 19–20.
5. Schulte-Umberg, *Profession und Charisma*, 436.
6. Ibid., 437–438. The German term *Konvikt* can be translated as seminary, boarding school, or finishing school. I have chosen to retain the closest Roman Catholic equivalency, namely seminary. Readers should bear in mind that in Germany, even today, two different types of seminaries cover two different but essential parts of the priestly vocation: spiritual and intellectual education, completed in theological seminaries, and practical, pastoral, and liturgical training, undertaken in clerical seminaries.
7. As quoted in Seibel, *Priester*, 19.
8. Schulte-Umberg, *Profession und Charisma*, 477.
9. I cannot give Guardini his due credit in this short space for the degree to which his intellectual and theological thought influenced twentieth-century reforms in the Catholic Church. This is particularly with respect to the liturgy and his elucidation of challenges facing the Church in modern times. Among his most famous texts still widely read are *Vom Geist der Liturgie* (1917) and *Der Herr: Betrachtungen über die Person und das Leben Jesu Christi* (1951). The standard German-language biography of Guardini is Hanna-Barbara Gerl-Falkovitz, *Romano Guardini, 1885–1968* (Mainz: Matthias-Grünewald-Verlag, 1985). See also Robert Krieg, *Romano Guar-*

dini: A Precursor of Vatican II (Notre Dame, IN: University of Notre Dame Press, 1997), and Robert Krieg, *Catholic Theologians in Nazi Germany* (New York: Continuum, 2004), 107–130.
10. Schulte-Umberg, *Profession und Charisma*, 446.
11. For more on these developments, see John Mahoney, *The Making of Moral Theology* (Oxford: Clarendon, 1987), chapter 1; John F. Keenan, *A History of Catholic Moral Theology in the Twentieth Century* (London: Continuum, 2010), chapter 2. The concept of the lay person as wounded, ignorant, untrustworthy, and incapable of knowing right from wrong without the guidance of a priest-confessor is rooted in Augustinian theology. It was not seriously challenged until the twentieth century and not reformed officially until the Second Vatican Council in the 1960s.
12. Keenan gives the best overview of the development of moral manuals between the twelfth and twentieth centuries in the preface and first two chapters of *History of Moral Theology*.
13. 1 Corinthians 12:12. The entire passage concerning the "one body with many members" runs from verse 12 to verse 31.
14. *Mystici Corporis Christi*, paragraphs 2, 4, 73, 106, 107, http://www.vatican.va/holy_father/pius_xii/encyclicals/documents/hf_p-xii_enc_29061943_mystici-corporis-christi_en.html (last accessed 21 March 2014).
15. Wilhelm Damberg gives an excellent analysis of this in "Kriegserfahrung und Kriegstheologie 1939–1945," *Theologische Quartalschrift* 182 (2002): 321–341.
16. Omer Bartov talks about the rise in drunkenness among army soldiers and officers, even before the critical invasion of the Soviet Union. See Bartov, *Hitler's Army: Soldiers, Nazis and War in the Third Reich* (New York: Oxford University Press, 1992), esp. chapter 3. It seems that, ultimately, alcohol was more or less permitted as an anesthetic for those involved in mass killing operations on the Eastern Front. Commanders also distributed it as the reward for a "job well done." Christopher Browning discusses the use of alcohol by Reserve Police Battalion 101 throughout their killing campaign in the East in *Ordinary Men: Reserve Police Battalion 101 and the Final Solution in Poland* (New York: HarperCollins, 1998).
17. KMBA SW 154/III, *Geschichte der Feldseelsorge*, 22 June 1945.
18. KMBA SW 756/III, Akte Franz Schmitz, "Beurteiling durch Wehrmachtoberpfarrer Kuhn," A.O.K. 6, 30 October 1945.
19. KMBA SW 756/III, Akte Schmitz, *Geschichte der Feldseelsorge*, 12 May 1945. Unfortunately, Werthmann does not include Schmitz's "defeatist" remarks.
20. Ibid.
21. All information taken from KMBA SW 329/III, Akte Johannes F., reports dated 15 June 1944, 14 July 1944, 10 August 1944. It is not clear from the documentation why he was called a conman.
22. KMBA SW 492/III, Akte Franz K., Werthmann's note dated 25 May 1947.
23. KMBA SW 304/III, Akte Franz E., report from Wehrmachtdekan Kostorz, 1 May 1944.
24. Ibid., report from Stabsarzt Hornekamp, 21 April 1944.

25. Hans Jürgen Brandt, Peter Häger, Karl Hengst, and Katholisches Militärbischofsamt, eds., *Biographisches Lexikon der katholischen Militärseelsorge Deutschlands 1848 bis 1945* (Paderborn: Bonifatius, 2002), 182.
26. KMBA SW 287/III, Akte Ludwig E., report from Wehrmachtpfarrer Weis, 376th infantry division, undated.
27. This project of Werthmann is the focus of Chapter 5.
28. KMBA SW 430/III, Akte Leonhard H., *Geschichte der Feldseelsorge,* 4 March 1946 and 27 June 1945.
29. KMBA SW 283/III, Akte Paul Drossert, *Geschichte der Feldseelsorge,* 1 July 1945.
30. Kevin P. Spicer lists D. in his appendix as one of the brown priests, Catholic priests who ardently and actively promoted National Socialism. Spicer, *Hitler's Priests: Catholic Clergy and National Socialism* (DeKalb: Northern Illinois University Press, 2008), 246. Additional biographical information taken from *Biographisches Lexikon,* 160.
31. KMBA SW 154/III (10), undated postwar notes made by Werthmann, likely for his *Geschichte der Feldseelsorge.*
32. Ibid., Wehrmachtdekan Thomann, "Die organistorische Neuordnung der Wehrmachtseelsorge in ihrer Bedeutung für den Wehrmachtpfarrer," undated but written between July and August 1938, 5, 7–8. (This was the only period of time during which Thomann held the position of defense force deacon, the highest level of chaplain in the chaplaincy.) Biographical information taken from *Biographisches Lexikon,* 834.
33. See Spicer, *Hitler's Priests,* for an invaluable examination of these men. Rarkowski is included in the book's appendix, whereas Thomann is not.
34. KMBA SW 152/III, letter from Werthmann addressed to all archbishoprics and bishoprics of Germany, June 1945. Werthmann was still interned at this point at the monastery in Niederalteich.
35. KMBA SW 744/III, Akte Bernhard S., copy of war diary forwarded to archives in 1978, passage undated.
36. Ibid.,' diary entry between 5 July and 18 October 1943.
37. With very few exceptions, Westermayr's responses to his students' letters are unfortunately not held at the archdiocesan archives. What follows is a one-sided conversation highlighting the seminarians' impressions of the war without the benefit of Westermayr's replies.
38. EAM Faulhaber-Archiv Priesterseminar Freising, 1939–1945: F. B., letter, Königsberg, 10 December 1943. The Freising seminary is one of the largest and most famous in Germany, located just outside Munich in the heart of Catholic Bavaria.
39. EAM-FA Priesterseminar Freising: A. A., letter, 19 December 1942. It is not clear to which people he was referring; presumably he meant the foreign populations he was encountering in the East.
40. Ibid., A. F., letter, 16 April 1944.
41. Ibid., B. E., letter, Halle, 22 June 1940. Emphasis in original.
42. KMBA SW 1050/IX, letter, 30 April 1944.
43. KMBA SW 670/III, Akte Gustav Raab, letter, 18 January 1943.
44. Ibid., letter, 19 January 1943.

45. KMBA SW 1050/IX, copy, "Meine Kriegserlebnisse," Richard Unger, 22 January 1968.
46. EAM-FA Priesterseminar Freising: A. B., letter, Straßburg, 16 November 1944.
47. Ibid., A. H., letter, North Europe, 28 April 1943. "Gaudete in Domino" translates literally to the imperative, "rejoice in the Lord." It is taken from Paul's letter to the Philippians, 3:1. The paragraph is an appeal to all-encompassing confidence in Christ.
48. KMBA SW 489/III, Akte Wilhelm K., sermon, 18 June 1944. The biblical quote is the introit (opening passage of a mass) for the feast of the Sacred Heart of Jesus. The full quotation is: "The thoughts of His Heart are from generation to generation: to deliver their souls from death, and feed them in famine." Psalms 32: 1, 11.
49. KMBA SW 597/III, Akte Heinrich Müller, letter, 17 February 1943. Müller was likely quoting Joseph Damian Schmitt, bishop of Fulda, Müller's home diocese.
50. KMBA SW 150/III, *Geschichte der Feldseelsorge*, 27 June 1945.
51. KMBA SW 635/III, Akten Josef P., Christmas sermon, undated. Emphasis in original.
52. Chaplains could be assigned to care for prisoners held in western and southern occupied territories, such as Abbé Franz Stock who worked in Fresnes, just outside of Paris (see Chapter 3). Chaplains were also assigned to care for German soldiers charged with breaches of discipline; this included visiting the condemned regularly, administering the sacraments, accompanying them to the execution site, and in many cases corresponding with the family after military authorities had informed them of their loved one's death. See KMBA SW 145, Zusammenfassung (2nd edition), 53–55. I found no evidence of chaplains administering to foreign POWs on the Eastern Front.
53. KMBA SW 465/III, Akte Johann E. K., undated postwar interview.
54. KMBA SW 943/III, Akte Lorenz W., interview, 24 August 1990.
55. KMBA SW 944/III, Akte Wilhelm W., interview, 20 June 1990.
56. Many of Augustine's just war theories are outlined in his *Reply to Faustus the Manichaean* and in *The City of God*. For modern reflection on Augustine's theories, see John Mark Mattox, *Saint Augustine and the Theory of Just War* (London: Continuum, 2006); Terry Nardin, ed., *The Ethics of War and Peace: Religious and Secular Perspectives* (Princeton, NJ: Princeton University Press, 1996); Brian M. Kane, *Just War and the Common Good: Jus ad Bellum Principles in Twentieth Century Papal Thought* (San Francisco: Catholic Scholars Press, 1997); Henrik Syse and Gregory M. Reichberg, eds., *Ethics, Nationalism, and Just War: Medieval and Contemporary Perspectives* (Washington, DC: Catholic University Press of America, 2007); Michael Walzer, *Just and Unjust Wars: A Moral Argument with Historical Illustrations*, 3rd ed. (New York: Basic Books, 2006). In the early modern era, following the mid-seventeenth century Peace of Westphalia, the parallel development of international relations, natural law, and international law contributed to just war theory. I focus exclusively on the Catholic theological

contributions to the concept since this would have been prominent in seminary classrooms. For an American perspective on this subject, see Lawrence P. Rockwood, *Walking Away from Nuremberg: Just War and the Doctrine of Command Responsibility* (Amherst: University of Massachusetts Press, 2007), esp. chapter 1.

57. Mattox, *Saint Augustine*, 51.
58. Ibid., 61.
59. The International Military Tribunal at Nuremberg, and later the UN General Assembly, recognized that individual soldiers could be held legally accountable for executing orders contravening international law. See Rockwood, *Walking Away from Nuremberg*, 75–79.
60. See Henrik Syse, "Augustine and Just War: Between Virtues and Duties" in *Ethics, Nationalism, and Just War*.
61. As quoted by Gerson Moreno-Riaño, "Reflections on Medieval Just War Theories," in *Ethics, Nationalism, and Just War*, 134.
62. Wilhelm Damberg provides a persuasive overview of the relatively static theological interpretations of just war in "Krieg, Theologie und Kriegserfahrung," in Karl J. Hummel and Christoph Kösters, eds., *Kirchen in Krieg: Europa, 1939–1945* (Paderborn: Schöningh, 2006), 203–204.
63. Kane, *Just War and the Common Good*, 16.
64. Ibid., 111.
65. Damberg, "Kriegserfahrung und Kriegstheologie," 323. Damberg also makes this observation in "Krieg, Theologie und Krieserfahrung," 208–209.
66. Kane, *Just War and the Common Good*, 114. Paragraph 30 of the encyclical makes this point: "Man as a person possesses rights he holds from God, and which any collectivity must protect against denial, suppression or neglect. To overlook this truth is to forget that the real common good ultimately takes its measure from man's nature, which balances personal rights and social obligations."
67. Pius XI, *Quadragesimo anno*, 15 May 1931, paragraphs 79–80, http://www.vatican.va/holy_father/pius_xi/encyclicals/documents/hf_p-xi_enc_19310515_quadragesimo-anno_en.html (last accessed 21 March 2014).
68. Kane, *Just War and the Common Good*, 121–124. Pius XII's Christmas messages are available in the original Italian on the Vatican website at http://www.va/holy_father/pius_xii/speeches/index.htm (last accessed 9 April 2014).
69. KMBA SW 947/III, Akte Martin Z., interview, 14 June 1990.
70. KMBA SW 635/III, Akte Josef P., undated postwar dictation.
71. KMBA SW 723/III, Akte Richard S., "Konzept für ein Interview," 26 January 1990.
72. KMBA SW 578/III, Akte Mende, interview, 2 June 1990.
73. KMBA SW 784/III, Akte Karl S., postwar interview, undated.
74. KMBA SW 631/III, Akten Georg Paulus, interview, 15 May 1990.
75. KMBA SW 280/III, Akte Friedrich D., interview, 5 June 1990.
76. The seminal texts that successfully dismantled the idea of a "clean" Wehrmacht, confirming its complicity in the atrocities committed on the Eastern Front, include Manfred Messerschmidt, *Die Wehrmacht im NS-Staat: Zeit der Indoktrination* (Hamburg: R. V. Decker, 1969); Christian

Streit, *Keine Kameraden: Die Wehrmacht und die sowjetischen Kriegsgefangenen, 1941–1945* (Stuttgart: Deutsche Verlags-Anstalt, 1978); Omer Bartov, *Hitler's Army: Soldiers, Nazis, and War in the Third Reich* (New York: Oxford University Press, 1992); and Hamburger Institut für Sozialforschung, ed., *The German Army and Genocide: Crimes against War Prisoners, Jews, and Other Civilians in the East, 1939–1944* (New York: New Press, 1999).
77. KMBA SW 633/III, Akte Rudolf P., manuscript, 173–174.
78. KMBA SW 811/III, Akte Martin S., pastoral care report, 1 October 1941.
79. Klaus Latzel's scrutiny of terms such as *Vaterland, Deutschland, Heimat,* and *Reich,* and their appearance in soldiers' letters during the war, is especially useful here. See Latzel, *Deutsche Soldaten—nationalsozialistischer Krieg? Kriegserlebnis, Kriegserfahrung, 1939–1945* (Paderborn: Schöningh, 1999), 303–307.
80. KMBA SW 635/III, Akten Josef P., interview with Perau in *Katholische Nachrichten-Agentur*, 1 September 1989.
81. KMBA SW 1053/IX, *Geschichte der Feldseelsorge*, 26 June 1945. One might also notice how similar this is to fascist and Nazi language, namely that temporary suffering and misery were necessary for the realization of an eternal, purified existence.
82. KMBA SW 150/III, *Geschichte der Feldseelsorge*, 19 July 1945.
83. EAM-FA 6797, Letters to Faulhaber, this from Thomas Gobitz-Pfeifer, 4 January 1944.
84. KMBA SW 784/III, Akte Karl S., postwar interview, undated.
85. KMBA SW 723/III, Akte Richard S., postwar interview, 1st part, 21 March 1990.
86. This is an overextension in Missalla's argument as presented in Heinrich Missalla, *Für Gott, Führer und Vaterland: Die Verstrickung der katholischen Seelsorge in Hitlers Krieg* (Oberursel: Publik-Forum, 1999). His contention that priests acted equally for Hitler as they did for other Germans and the Fatherland is not demonstrated in the documents I discuss here.
87. EAM Priesterseminar Freising: A. M., 16 August 1941.
88. Ibid.: A. F., 21 August 1943. Emphasis added.
89. KMBA SW 152/III (8), front-line seminar in Charkow, 16–17 April 1942, and Deutsch-Brod (now Havlickuv, Czech Republic), 22 September 1944.
90. Ibid., experience report, Warsaw, 14–15 April 1942. Friedrich von Rabenau, a general of the artillery, was an ardent anti-Nazi Protestant until 1942, when his open antipathy forced him into premature retirement. Though he never officially joined the Resistance, he had connections to the Kreisau Circle, and he was arrested in the aftermath of the July 1944 assassination attempt. He was one of the last inmates executed at the Flossenburg concentration camp, without being charged or tried, in April 1945. Rabenau surfaces briefly in the following texts: Manfred Messerschmidt, *Die Wehrmacht im NS-Staat: Zeit der Indoktrination*, 281; Shelley Baranowski, *The Confessing Church, Conservative Elites, and the Nazi State* (Lewiston, NY: Edwin Mellen Press, 1986), 38–39.
91. EAM-FA Priesterseminar Freising: H. R., France, 8 September 1940. Reiter is clearly referring to Philippe Pétain's famous radio appeal to the French on 20 June 1940, shortly before the French-German armistice was signed,

in which he announced France's defeat. Pétain declared, "We are less strong than we were twenty-two years ago, and we also had fewer friends. Too few children, too few weapons, too few allies: these are the causes of our defeat." Jean-Claude Barbas, ed., *Discours aux français, 17 juin 1940–20 août 1944* (Paris: Éditions Albin Michel, 1989), 60.

92. Ibid.: Regens Johann Westermayr's response to M. F., 29 September 1942.
93. This very closely echoes Thomas Kühne's findings about camaraderie and the sense of belonging that may have made it easier for soldiers to participate in mass killing. See Thomas Kühne, *Belonging and Genocide: Hitler's Community, 1918–1945* (New Haven, CT: Yale University Press, 2010).
94. KMBA SW 947/III, Akte Martin Z., interview, 14 June 1990.
95. KMBA SW 467/III, Akte Josef K., copy of written postwar notes, undated.
96. Dörr, "Wenn ich gehe, wird mein Platz nicht mehr besetzt," in Katholisches Militärbischofsamt, ed., *Mensch, was wollt Ihr denen sagen? Katholische Feldseelsorger im Zweiten Weltkrieg* (Augsburg: Pattloch Verlag, 1991), 154.
97. Bernard Häring, *Embattled Witness: Memories of a Time of War* (New York: Seabury Press, 1976), 41, 9, 13.
98. EAM Priesterseminar Freising, A. N., 26 October 1941.
99. Ibid., A. B., 16 November 1944.
100. Ibid., J. H., 17 September 1942.
101. Ibid., T. G. P., letter, far north, 20 November 1944. The original reads: "Viele Kameraden sind eben jetzt die Augen aufgegangen und sie merken, dass es nichts ist mit dem Paradies auf Eden, das man ihnen in besseren Tagen vorgegaukelt hatte und dass das Kreuz Christi den Leiden dieser Zeit näherliegt als das Pochen auf die eigene Kraft und ein verschwammener Mythos und Blut und Rasse."
102. Josef Perau, *Priester im Heere Hitlers: Erinnerungen 1941–1945* (Essen: Ludgerus Verlag, 1962), 1 May 1945, 48. He could have added the incident when he was editing his book for publication, but its timing suggests that he might have felt safe enough to record it right after it happened.
103. Rupert Ritzer, "Priesterrock und Uniform: 2,028 Tage als Sanitäter im II. Weltkrieg unter em Schutz der Gottlichen Vorsehung," manuscript published privately after 1987, entries for 20 December 1941 and 5 January 1942, while Ritzer was stationed in Russia.
104. EAM Priesterseminar Freising, H. R., 5 July 1941.
105. Perau, *Priester im Heeres Hitlers*, 15 March 1944, 159–161. Emphasis added. It is unclear to which camp he is referring, and he does not elaborate with respect to whom he was speaking when he declared his disgust about the activities he witnessed.
106. Karl Marx, "Contribution to the Critique of Hegel's Philosophy of Right," as reprinted in Karl Marx and Friedrich Engels, *On Religion*, introduction by Reinhold Niebuhr (Chico, CA: Scholars Press, 1964), 42 (initially printed in *Deutsch-Französische Jahrbücher*, 1844). Emphasis in original. Early papal responses to socialism and communism, notably from Pius IX (r. 1846–1878), condemned the ideologies for their "misuse" of words such as liberty and equality. Papal views paralleled those of conservatives in abhorring these ideologies and their effect on the working masses, namely in urging them to violent revolution threatening loss of property and status.

107. Michael Burleigh, *Sacred Causes: The Clash of Religion and Politics, from the Great War to the War on Terror* (New York: HarperCollins, 2007), 40–41.
108. "Hirtenwort des deutschen Episkopats" (Fulda, 26 June 1941), in Ludwig Volk, ed., *Akten deutscher Bischöfe über die Lage der Kirche, 1933–1945,* Bd. V (Mainz: Matthias-Grünewald-Verlag, 1968–1985), 463.
109. KMBA SW 997/VI, copy of "Denkschrift der deutschen Bischöfe," 10 December 1941. See also *Akten deutscher Bischöfe* (Volk) "Denkschrift der deutschen Bischöfe an die Reichsregierung" (Breslau), 10 December 1941, 651–658.
110. EAM Priesterseminar Freising, J. R., 31 March 1942, and J. H. R., 27 August 1944.
111. Ibid., H. A., 4 January 1944.
112. Ibid., F. H., 15 April 1942.
113. Ibid., F. H., 27 February 1942.
114. Ibid., G. G., Strassröd, 28 July 1941.
115. Ibid., L. S., Melitopol, 7 February 1942.
116. EAM-FA 6796/3, letter (copy) from Franz Kurz, 3 March 1942.
117. EAM Priesterseminar Freising, H. R., Soviet Russia, 5 July 1941.
118. Ibid., J. M., 23 July 1941.
119. EAM-FA 6796/3, letter (copy), 15 April 1942.
120. EAM-FA Priesterseminar Freising, W. M., 2 July 1944.
121. EAM 6796/3, letter (copy) from Lechner to Cardinal von Faulhaber, 17 January 1942.
122. EAM-FA Priesterseminar Freising, H. O., southeast, 11 August 1941.
123. Both Klaus Latzel and John Connelly point out that even before 1933, such terms—in German, *Heimat, Vaterland, Volk, Reich*—were infused with ultra-nationalist and racial connotations. Between 1933 and 1945 the words were nearly impossible to extricate from their use by Nazi ideology and propaganda. See Klaus Latzel, *Deutsche Soldaten—nationalsozialistischen Krieg?* 303–307; John Connelly, *From Enemy to Brother: The Revolution in Catholic Teaching on the Jews, 1933–1965* (Cambridge, MA: Harvard University Press, 2012), 68–78.
124. KMBA SW 1053/IX, excerpt from speech given in 1945 by Ernst Wischert in Georg Werthmann, notes, "Fronterlebnis und Reichsgottesarbeit: Der Inhalt des Fronterlebnisses," 26 June 1946. According to the same set of notes by Werthmann, Wischert was interned in Buchenwald, where he lost his faith in God. In spite of this, "what he has written about the German soldiers is remarkable."

5. THE GERMAN CATHOLIC CHURCH AND THE REALITY OF DEFEATED GERMANY

1. Bruno Cabanes explores the concept of the *sortie de guerre* (literally, "exit from war"), which I have translated as the end-of-war period, in the context of French soldiers and demobilization at the end of the First World War. See *La victoire endeuillée: La sortie de guerre des soldats français, 1918–1920* (Paris: Seuil, 2004), esp. 10–12.
2. See Overmans as cited in chapter 2, fn 1.

3. As quoted in Ian Kershaw, *The End: The Defiance and Destruction of Hitler's Germany, 1944–1945* (London: Penguin, 2011), 356.
4. See Christian Goeschel, "Suicide at the End of the Third Reich," *Journal of Contemporary History* 41/1 (2006): 153–173, esp. 162, for statistics. See also Christian Goeschel, *Suicide in Nazi Germany* (Oxford: Oxford University Press, 2009).
5. We will never know this statistic with any degree of accuracy. See Norman Naimark, *The Russians in Germany: A History of the Soviet Zone of Occupation, 1945–1949* (Cambridge, MA: Harvard University Press, 1995), 132–133.
6. Statistics from Frank Biess, *Homecomings: Returning POWs and the Legacies of Defeat in Postwar Germany* (Princeton, NJ: Princeton University Press, 2006), 44.
7. KMBA SW 1009/VII (Nr.1), copy of order from OKW commander, 29 January 1945. Werthmann may have been acting as the head of the chaplaincy a full year earlier; in his first postwar letter to the civilian bishops, he stated that Rarkowksi has been absent from his post in Berlin due to sickness from January 1944. See letter from Georg Werthmann to all diocesan ordinaries, June 1945, in Ulrich Helbach, ed., *Akten deutscher Bischöfe seit 1945: Westliche Besatzungszonen, 1945–1947* (Paderborn: Ferdinand Schöningh, 2012), 112.
8. KMBA SW 1009/VII (Nr 1), copy of U.S. 26th Infantry Division HQ report, 1 May 1945, and entry for "Werthmann, Georg" in Brandt and Jäger, eds., *Biographisches Lexikon der katholischen Militärseelsorge Deutschlands, 1848–1945*, 897. In a puzzling statement that Werthmann gave to his captors on 3 May 1945, he identified Pope Pius XII as the person responsible for his appointment as acting field bishop, not Keitel.
9. As relayed by Ulrich Helbach in the introduction to *Akten DB I* (Helbach), 17–19.
10. John S. Conway Collection, housed at Regent College, University of British Columbia, Vancouver, Canada, file with LC call number BR856.3 G48 1997 (File 1), "Reports on non-fraternization," undated but likely March 1945. Emphasis in original.
11. Julian S. Bach Jr., *America's Germany: An Account of the Occupation* (New York: Random House, 1946), 254, 264.
12. Eugene Davidson, *The Death and Life of Germany: An Account of the American Occupation of Germany* (New York: Alfred A. Knopf, 1959), 48–49.
13. Bach, *America's Germany*, 15–16.
14. Edward N. Peterson, *The American Occupation of Germany: Retreat to Victory* (Detroit: Wayne State University Press, 1978), 157. For an excellent overview of Berlin's experience of occupation, see Grossmann, *Jews, Germans, and Allies*, chapter 1.
15. Davidson, *Death and Life of Germany*, 84–85.
16. The Morgenthau Plan, devised by Secretary of the Treasury Henry Morgenthau Jr., was designed to prevent Germany from ever again becoming an industrial power. Even contemporaries regarded it as punitive and vengeful

and therefore hotly contested it as potential policy. JCS 1067 was not the Morgenthau Plan, as senior military commanders added changes and adjustments to make the former distinctive, but the rigid, vindictive tone of both documents invites instant comparison.
17. "Directive to the Commander in Chief of the U.S. Occupation Forces (JSC 1067), April 1945," in United States Department of State, *Germany 1947–1949: The Story in Documents* (Washington, DC: U.S. Government Printing Office, 1950), 22–28.
18. Grossmann, *Jews, Germans, and Allies*, 71–77. Peterson estimated that as many as 94,000 "illegal occupation babies" had been born out of sexual relations between American soldiers and German women, including from rape. Peterson, *American Occupation of Germany*, 155.
19. Davidson, *Death and Life of Germany*, 73, 82.
20. Statistics, however, are especially tricky in relation to denazification proceedings, and not only in the Soviet zone. Davidson, *Death and Life of Germany*, 128, compares numbers for the western Allies and comes up with 2,296 Germans tried by the British for "Nazi or militaristic activities," 17,353 by the French, 18,328 by the Russians, and 169,282 by the Americans (citing W. Friedman as quoted by Harold Zink). Peterson, *American Occupation of Germany*, 145, writing later, gives numbers for a smaller span of time, up to the end of 1946: 19,880 interned by the French; 64,000 by the British; 67,000 by the Russians; well beyond 100,000 by the Americans. He cites Alfred Grossner. Gareth Pritchard, citing M. Dennis, more recently offered the figure of 520,000 dismissed from their posts in the Soviet zone by the end of 1945, "more than the three other occupational powers put together." Pritchard, *The Making of the GDR, 1945–53* (Manchester, UK: Manchester University Press, 2000), 84.
21. Davidson, *Death and Life of Germany*, 86–87.
22. The less sympathetic American is Julian Bach. See his memoirs, *America's Germany*, esp. 169–187.
23. *Akten DB I* (Helbach), letter from Jaeger to Orsenigo, 26 July 1945, 192.
24. Ibid., letter from Jaeger to Pius XII, 29 September 1945, 266.
25. Albert Stohr, pastoral letter, 29 June 1945, in Wolfgang Löhr, ed., *Dokumente deutscher Bischöfe: Hirtenbriefe und Ansprachen zu Gesellschaft und Politik, 1945–1949*, 2nd ed. (Würzburg: Echter, 1986), 33.
26. Conrad Gröber, first postwar pastoral letter, 21 September 1945, in ibid., 47.
27. *Akten KMF*, letter from Faulhaber to Pius XII, 17 May 1945, 1060. In a later pastoral directive to the diocesan clergy, Faulhaber mentioned that in Munich alone, forty-three churches had been so badly damaged that they could not be used for masses. *Akten KMF*, Faulhaber, pastoral directive, after 18 June 1945: 1068.
28. KMBA SW 150/III (Nr 6), 26 June 1945.
29. Ibid.
30. KMBA SW 1053/IX (Nr 2), 30 June 1945.
31. Ibid., 18 October 1945.
32. KMBA SW 1009/VII (Nr 1), 17 July 1945.
33. KMBA SW 150/III (Nr 6), 13 July 1945.

34. Ibid., 26 June 1945.
35. Ibid., 27 June 1945.
36. Ibid., 30 June 1945.
37. Ibid., 28 June 1945. All quotes in this paragraph are from this passage.
38. *Akten DB I* (Helbach), Offenstein's pastoral instructions, 16 June 1945, 128.
39. Ibid., Jaeger's report on the situation in the British zone, 29 September 1945, 273.
40. Stohr's pastoral letter, 29 June 1945, in Löhr, ed., *Dokumente deutscher Bischöfe*, 37. The German reads, "*Deutsches Volksleben wird christlich sein oder es wird nicht mehr sein!*" Emphasis in original.
41. KMBA SW 150/III (Nr 7), 26 June 1945.
42. Ibid.
43. Ibid., 6 November 1945.
44. Ibid., 27 June 1945.
45. KMBA SW 997/VI, 30 June 1945. Nor was Werthmann anomalous in cautioning priests in this manner. A few bishops explicitly discouraged their clergy from engaging in any kind of activity that could be construed as political. See the following from Löhr, ed., *Dokumente deutscher Bischöfe*: Gröber to diocesan clergy, 21 June 1945, 18; Buchberger to diocesan clergy, 25 June 1945, 27; and from *Akten DB I* (Helbach): Notes by Archbishop Josef Frings of Cologne about the West German Bishops' Conference, 15 May 1945, 99; pastoral instructions of Bishop Johann Baptist Dietz of Fulda, 19 September 1945, 238, n. 1.
46. KMBA SW 1053/IX (Nr 2), 29 December 1945.
47. The chaplaincy, an intrinsic part of that Wehrmacht, at least in the self-conception of its leaders, has not faced the same rigorous scrutiny since Werthmann, in those first three months after the German surrender, attempted on his own to evaluate its effectiveness and importance.
48. *Akten DB I* (Helbach), Offenstein's pastoral instructions, 16 June 1945, 128.
49. Bavarian bishops' first postwar pastoral letter, 28 June 1945, in Löhr, ed., *Dokumente deutscher Bischöfe*, 30–31.
50. Gröber's pastoral letter concerning accusations against the German people, 21 September 1945, in Löhr, ed., *Dokumente deutscher Bischöfe*, 50–51.
51. For more on this episode, see Beth A. Griech-Polelle, *Bishop von Galen: German Catholicism and National Socialism* (New Haven, CT: Yale University Press, 2002), esp. chapter 4.
52. KMBA SW 1002, 18 July 1945.
53. KMBA SW 1008/VII, 18 July 1945.
54. KMBA SW 1053/VII, 26 June 1945.
55. KMBA SW 150/III (Nr 6), 26 July 1945.
56. *Akten DB I* (Helbach), draft petition by Lorenz Jaeger, before or on 5 June 1945, 117.
57. Ibid.
58. Bavarian bishops' first postwar pastoral letter, 28 June 1945, in Löhr, ed., *Dokumente deutscher Bischöfe*, 31.
59. *Akten DB I* (Helbach), letter to Father Leo Rager, 21 June 1945, 135.
60. Sarah Farmer, *Martyred Village: Commemorating the 1944 Massacre at Oradour-sur-Glane* (Berkeley: University of California Press, 2000).

61. German bishops' first collective pastoral letters, 23 August 1945, in Löhr, ed., *Dokumente deutscher Bischöfe*, 41.
62. Sproll's first pastoral letter after returning from exile to his diocese, 24 June 1945, in ibid., 23.
63. Bavarian bishops' first pastoral letter, 28 June 1945, in Löhr, ed., *Dokumente deutscher Bischöfe*, 31.
64. *Akten DB I* (Helbach), petition, 5 June 1945, 115–120.
65. Ibid., 116. Emphasis added.
66. Ibid., letter from Jaeger to Pius XII, 29 September 1945, 269.
67. Löhr, ed., *Dokumente deutscher Bischöfe*, German bishops' first collective pastoral letter, 23 August 1945, 42.
68. Ibid., Gröber's pastoral letter, 21 September 1945, 48.
69. KMBA SW 1009/VII (Nr 1), interview with Gregor Zimmer, undated typewritten copy. The direct quotations in the rest of this paragraph are from this source. It is not clear how long it took for the Americans to realize that (1) the Germans they had arrested were not officers, and (2) their prisoners were in fact the heads of the Catholic and Protestant chaplaincies. Presumably Dohrmann and Werthmann would have volunteered this information relatively quickly, seeing no advantage in hiding it.
70. Ibid., interview with Gregor Zimmer.
71. Atina Grossmann provides a nuanced analysis of the experience of "gendered defeat," remarking in particular on the complicated nature of fraternization that German women experienced (and the ramifications of the reactions of German men to those experiences), in *Jews, Germans, and Allies: Close Encounters in Occupied Germany* (Princeton, NJ: Princeton University Press, 2007), esp. chapter 2, 48–87.
72. Conway Collection, BR856.3 G48 1997 (file 2), "Relations of (Allied) Chaplains to Christians in Germany (March 1945)."
73. Ibid., first report: "Subject: Relations of R.A.Ch.D. to German Church and Wehrmacht Chaplains," 5 July 1945; second report: "Screening of Wehrmacht Chaplains (July 1945)."
74. Ibid., report on Iserlohn parish, unsigned, appended to "Attitude of the Churches, 19 June 1945; (File 3) second report, "Relations with the German Churches (secret)," addressed to the Chaplain-General in London, 19 September 1945.
75. KMBA SW 997/VI, 18 June 1945. All quotations from the next three paragraphs are from this document. All emphases in original.
76. The reference is to a passage from 1 Corinthians 9. The full passage reads, "Though I am free and belong to no one, I have made myself a slave to everyone, to win as many as possible. To the Jews I became like a Jew, to win the Jews. To those under the law I became like one under the law (though I myself am not under the law), so as to win those under the law. To those not having the law I became like one not having the law (though I am not free from God's law but am under Christ's law), so as to win those not having the law. To the weak I became weak, to win the weak. I have made myself all things to all people so that by all possible means I might save at least some."
77. See, for example, *Akten KMF* II, Faulhaber's letter to Pope Pius XII, 17 May 1945, in which he laments that the occupying authorities had rounded up

members of the Nazi Party en masse without trying to determine who had really been an ardent National Socialist (1062), and a later complaint in a pastoral directive, delivered after 18 June 1945, that the Allied military government was continuing to fail to make any distinction between the guilty and the innocent when it came to meting out justice (1068).

78. Again, this would become important especially for denazification proceedings, as the western Allied forces treated the testimony of a priest or bishop on behalf of an arrested German as almost impeachable. Werthmann and many bishops and priests were entreated to testify in this manner. Werthmann evidently did so for Karl Edelmann. While I was unable to obtain information pertaining to Edelmann's denazification file, a copy of an *Eidestattliche Versicherung* (Affirmation in Lieu of Oath), signed by Werthmann, is available in Edelmann's file in the KMBA archives. In this testimony, Werthmann explicitly testifies that Edelmann "belonged to that circle of officers that internally rejected the politics of violence of the Nazi regime." Further evidence in the file reveals that Edelmann was kept in prison until 1947. Werthmann intervened on his behalf again in 1949 to help him secure a job in Düsseldorf. The two corresponded for the rest of Edelmann's life (he died in 1971), though not regularly. See KMBA SW 1019/VII (3c), Der Amtsgruppenchef 1943–1971. Faulhaber also involved himself in the denazification process; an example of what this process looked like, and the cardinal's contribution, can be found in EAM 8555: Rehabilitierungseingabe, Herr Professor Georg Keidel. Faulhaber's own conduct in early June 1945 is an example of how denazification necessarily became political: despite his entreaty to his priests that they not involve themselves in political activities, on 9 June 1945 he wrote to the American military regime on behalf of the former Slovakian president Josef Tiso, also a Catholic priest, who had fled from the Red Army through Austria and took refuge in Bavaria. Faulhaber pleaded that Tiso remain in Altötting for his internment and be treated well by his captors because he was responsible for "keeping religious life alive in his country despite grave difficulties." Under Tiso, Slovakia was also the first German ally to agree to the deportation of Jews, and he ultimately oversaw the deportation of more than 70,000 Jews, of whom 60,000 were murdered. The American authorities decided against Faulhaber's petition and in October 1945 turned Tiso over to a reconstituted Czechoslovakia. In 1947 he was condemned by a Czechoslovak court for treason and collaboration with Nazism, and he was executed in Bratislava. For the text of Faulhaber's petition, see *Akten KMF II*, 1069, fn. 1.

79. The extant document is based on notes he wrote in his daybook, according to the document's title. The revised version, which I am using, is dated 3 June 1945. See KMBA SW 1008/VII (Nr 1), "Bericht über die Internierung des Feldgeneralvikars Werthmann nach Tagebuchaufzeichnungen." All the following quotations are taken from this document.

80. Thanks to Dr. Monica Sinderhauf at the KMBA for bringing this to my attention.

81. These reflections in and of themselves are not without their problems for the historian. The notes are a combination of typewritten and handwritten shorthand, the latter of which only he could decipher. Some of these are available at the KMBA, regretfully not decipherable. The typewritten comments often have multiple copies and occasionally repeat themselves.
82. KMBA SW 147/III, 8 July 1945, and KMBA SW 997/VI, 3 June 1945.
83. KMBA SW 148/III (Nr 5), 3 July 1945.
84. Ibid., undated reflection.
85. On this point, Werthmann invites comparison with Martin Heidegger, whose famous "Nazi turn" was illustrated by his May 1933 address espousing the view that Germany's future was bound to the Führer. Heidegger later distanced himself from the Nazi Party, but he never resigned his membership. Dominick LaCapra, among others, has suggested that Nazism was more central to Heidegger's philosophy than the philosopher himself was ready to admit. See Dominick LaCapra, "Heidegger's Nazi Turn," in *Representing the Holocaust: History, Theory, Trauma* (Ithaca, NY: Cornell University Press, 1996), 137–168.
86. KMBA SW 148/III (Nr 5), 30 June 1945.
87. Saint Boniface is known as the apostle of the Germans and is the patron saint of Germany.
88. KMBA SW 1008/VII (Nr 1), 12 July 1945. Werthmann might have been referring to the professional army of James II of England, created in 1685, though Charles VII of France had deployed one more than two hundred years earlier.
89. Ibid.
90. KMBA SW 1008/VII (Nr 1), 11 June 1945.
91. Ibid., 30 June 1945.
92. See Michael Walzer, *Just and Unjust Wars: A Moral Argument with Historical Illustrations* (New York: Basic Books, 2006), 34–41.
93. KMBA SW 146/III (Nr 5), 23 June 1945.
94. Ibid., 4 July 1945.
95. Whatever correspondence might have occurred between the two, beyond the pope's general addresses to "the German bishops," which technically included Rarkowski, it has yet to be unearthed.
96. The Chancellery was the name of the party's head office, which can refer to any number of important men involved in running it, including Bormann, Reinecke, and Himmler.
97. KMBA SW 146/III (Nr 5), 9 June 1945.
98. Ibid., 28 September 1945.
99. KMBA SW 147/III, 8 July 1945.
100. KMBA SW 150/III (Nr 7), 19 December 1945.
101. Ibid., 19 July 1945.
102. KMBA SW 1008/VII (Nr 1), 30 June 1945.
103. Werthmann's estimate is 11,548 as of January 1944, and includes Catholic candidates for the priesthood (*Priesteramtskandidaten*), lay brothers, and order novitiates. Candidates for the priesthood include both seminarians, that is, those students enrolled in seminaries with the explicit goal of entering holy orders, as well as theology students, whose inclusion

renders the concept much more difficult to grasp firmly. Please refer to Appendix 2.
104. This is Werthmann's statistic; he did not elaborate in his notes on how he arrived at it. KMBA SW 997/VI, "Stand der Wehrmacht- und Feldseelsorge im Zweiten Weltkrieg, 1939–1945," 5 July 1953.
105. KMBA SW 147/III, 4 July 1945.
106. KMBA SW 1053/IX (Nr 2), 12 July 1945. See also KMBA SW 147/III, two entries for 4 July 1945.
107. KMBA SW 1003/VI, copy of orders issued by OKW/AWA/J (Ia) printed in "H Dv 22/I Pol. Handbuch Teil I vom 1.4.1943," 18 March 1940 and 28 July 1940. Werthmann's reflection is in KMBA SW 1053/IX (Nr 2), 5 July 1945.
108. KMBA SW 1051/IX, copy of secret OKH order, 25 August 1944, explaining OKW decision, 11 June 1944. The decision is attributed to "the head of OKW," Wilhelm Keitel, no friend of Catholic priests in the military.
109. KMBA SW 1006/VI, 1 April 1946.
110. Just a sampling of scholarly texts within the past twenty-five years describing the Holocaust as "unthinkable," sometimes explicitly in the title, include Roger S. Gottlieb, *Thinking the Unthinkable: Meanings of the Holocaust* (Paulist Press, 1990); Carol Rittner and John K. Roth, eds., *From the Unthinkable to the Unavoidable: American Christian and Jewish Scholars Encounter the Holocaust* (Westport, CT: Greenwood Press, 1997); Inga Clendinnen, *Reading the Holocaust* (Cambridge, UK: Cambridge University Press, 2002). Brown University's student group Holocaust Initiative (HIBU) hosts an annual series entitled "Surviving the Unthinkable," aimed at improving Holocaust education using survivor narratives.
111. A most useful volume of essays on this topic is Efrat Ben-Ze'ev, Ruth Ginio, and Jay Winter, eds., *Shadows of War: A Social History of Silence in the Twentieth Century* (Cambridge, UK: Cambridge University Press, 2010). See especially the two introductory essays by Jay Winter and Eviatar Zerubavel.
112. Svenja Goltermann's essay in the above volume explores this idea in connection to Wehrmacht veterans and their psychiatric files between the end of the war and the early 1960s. See Goltermann, "On Silence, Madness and Lassitude: Negotiating the Past in Post-war West Germany," in *Shadows of War*, 91–112.
113. *Akten DB I* (Helbach), 19.

CONCLUSION

1. Rüdiger Overmanns, as cited in Karl-Theodor Schleicher and Heinrich Walle, eds., *Aus Feldpostbriefen junger Christen, 1939–1945: Ein Beitrag zur Geschichte der katholischen Jugend im Felde* (Munich: Franz Steiner Verlag, 2005), 25.
2. Omer Bartov makes this argument powerfully in *Hitler's Army: Soldiers, Nazis, and War in the Third Reich* (New York: Oxford University Press, 1992).
3. Thomas Kühne, *Kameradschaft: Die Soldaten des nationalsozialistischen Krieges und das 20. Jahrhundert* (Göttingen: Vandenhoeck & Ruprecht, 2006), and Thomas Kühne, *Belonging and Genocide: Hitler's Community, 1918–1945* (New Haven, CT: Yale University Press, 2010).

4. Because it lies beyond the scope of my argument, this study has not exhausted the spectrum of possibilities accounting for why men (and sometimes women) are capable of perpetrating extraordinary evil or of standing by silently while others do so. One of the most comprehensive analyses of the subject is James Waller, *Becoming Evil: How Ordinary People Commit Genocide and Mass Killing* (New York: Oxford University Press, 2002).
5. The volume in question is Katholische Militärbischofsamt, ed., *Mensch, was wollt ihr denen sagen? Katholische Feldseelsorge im Zweiten Weltkrieg* (Augsburg: Pattloch Verlag, 1991). The afterword by Heinz-Gerhard Justenhoven gives the statistic of 140 veterans still alive in 1990, not including surviving Austrian chaplains. Twenty-eight responded to the questionnaire or were interviewed and twenty-six made it into the edited volume. Ibid., 197, and Katholische Militärbischofsamt and Hans Jürgen Brandt, eds., *Christen im Krieg: Katholische Soldaten, Ärzte und Krankenschwestern im Zweiten Weltkrieg* (Augsburg: Pattloch Verlag, 2001), 360–363. Most of those interviewed in 1990 are still protected by a *Sperrfrist* that prevents me from using full names. Accordingly, first names and a last initial have been used in reference to the interviews.
6. These negative reactions closely reflect some of the Wehrmacht veterans' reactions to the Hamburg Institute for Social Research's traveling Wehrmacht exhibit, which documented Wehrmacht soldiers participating in war crimes during the Second World War. The original exhibition was open in Germany from 1995 to 1999. A revised version, put together after inaccurate photo captioning was corrected, went on display from 2001 to 2004. Its website is still active: http://www.verbrechen-der-wehrmacht.de/docs/aktuell/aktuell.htm (last accessed on 1 April 2014.)
7. KMBA SW 784/III, Akte Karl S., undated interview.
8. KMBA SW 293/III, Akte Franz E., interview, 2 July 1990.
9. See Gerd Kaiser, *Katyn: Das Staatsverbrechen—Das Staatsgeheimnis* (Berlin: Aufbau Taschenbuch Verlag, 2002), esp. 156–182.
10. KMBA SW 510/III, Akte Alois K., interview, 1 June 1990.
11. KMBA SW 635/III, Akten Josef P., undated dictation, 3.
12. Ibid. I used an early manuscript (not the final version) of the published book. Entry for 5 September 1943, 132. The book is published as Josef Perau, *Priester im Heere Hitlers: Erinnerungen, 1940–1945* (Essen: Ludgerus-Verlag, 1962).
13. KMBA SW 441/III, Akte Joseph H., interview, 22 June 1990.
14. KMBA SW 310/III, Akte Otto F., interview, 25 April 1990 (first part).
15. KMBA SW 293/III, Akte Franz E., interview, 2 July 1990. In 1998, Pope John Paul II canonized Edith Stein as Saint Teresa Benedicta of the Cross, which was her monastic name, but she is commonly referred to as Saint Edith Stein. For more information on Stein, who was a student of Edmund Husserl and only the second woman in German history to earn a doctorate in philosophy, the comprehensive collection of essays edited by Joyce Avrech Berkman is indispensable: *Contemplating Edith Stein* (Notre Dame, IN: University of Notre Dame Press, 2006).
16. KMBA SW 947/III, Akte Martin Z., interview, 14 June 1990.

17. Jonathan Huener discusses the Polish tendency to view Auschwitz as "their" camp. See Huener, *Auschwitz, Poland, and the Politics of Commemoration, 1945–1979* (Athens: Ohio University Press, 2003).
18. KMBA SW 688/III, Akte Wilhelm R., interview undated.
19. Ibid.
20. KMBA SW 943/III, Akte Lorenz W., interview, 24 August 1990.
21. KMBA SW 627/III, Akte Kunibert P., interview undated.
22. The seminal texts that discuss the myth of the "clean Wehrmacht" are cited in Chapter 4, n. 76.
23. Fangohr, "Herr Pfarrer, die kriegen mich nicht tot!," in *Mensch, was wollt Ihr denen sagen?*, 91.
24. KMBA SW 627/III, Akte Kunibert P., interview, undated.
25. KMBA SW 310/III, Akte Otto F., interview, 25 April 1990 (Part II).
26. Buslay, "Au revoir, mes garçons, au revoir," in *Mensch, was wollt Ihr denen sagen?*, 49.
27. KMBA SW 1006/IX, "Geschichte der Feldseelsorge," 28 September 1945. Soldiers in the army used the cynical jargon "*Halsschmerz,*" "afflicted with throat trouble" or "having an itchy neck" or "sore throat," to refer to glory-seeking officers willing to do anything, including risk their own lives or those of their troops, to win a Knight's Cross. This military decoration was worn at the throat, unlike the Iron Cross, which was worn on the breast. The Iron Cross dates to the beginning of the nineteenth century. The Knight's Cross, a grade of the Iron Cross that the Nazis created, was the highest military decoration in Nazi Germany; it recognized outstanding battlefield bravery or leadership.
28. KMBA SW 1002/IX, "Geschichte der Feldseelsorge," 20 August 1945.
29. KMBA SW 947/III, Akte Martin Z., interview, 14 June 1990.
30. KMBA SW 1050/IX, letter to Werthmann from Xaver Haimerl, 25 October 1943.
31. Hoser, "Ich habe mir nie den Sieg gewünscht," in *Mensch, was wollt Ihr denen sagen?*, 166.
32. KMBA SW 750/III, Akte Egon S., postwar interview, undated.
33. KMBA SW 441/III, Akte Joseph H., postwar interview, 22 June 1990. The German expression also means "to turn a blind eye," which H. might have used cryptically to refer to excusing crimes that he felt powerless or afraid to stop. In the context of the paragraph, I have interpreted it as rule-bending.
34. Dörr, "Wenn ich gehe, wird mein Platz nicht mehr besetzt," in *Mensch, was wollt Ihr denen sagen?*, 153.
35. KMBA SW 944/III, Akte Wilhlem W., interview, 20 June 1990. The passage in its original German is vague, so I include here the last three sentences: "Es ist übrigens das selbe Problem, was heute ansteht mit den Beratungsstellen. Ich weiß nicht, ob Sie das wissen? Da wird auch gesagt, weil diese Beratungsstelle so einen Schein ausstellt, deswegen ist sie unter Umständen schuldig. Aber wieviel ist sie schuldig?" The "Schein" in question seems to be a reference to the *Persilschein*, or certificate of denazification, that was used to rehabilitate former Nazis or Nazi collaborators after 1945.

36. KMBA SW 943/III, Akte Lorenz W., interview, 24 August 1990.
37. KMBA SW 643/III, Akten Josef P., interview in *Katholische Nachrichten-Agentur*, from the series "Wehrmachtseelsorge im II. Weltkrieg," 1 September 1989.
38. Ibid.
39. Dörr, "Wenn ich gehe, wird mein Platz nicht mehr besetzt," in *Mensch, was wollt Ihr denen sagen?*, 157. Emphasis added.
40. On 15 April 1942, Reinisch reported for duty one day later than his mobilization papers had ordered. The staff sergeant who received him noted that his behavior suggested his indifference to military service, to which Reinisch responded, "I would attach importance to it if I were serving another regime." The sergeant promptly arrested him, and Reinisch was taken to Berlin to stand trial, where he refused to recognize the authority of the Nazi state and would not perform the oath of loyalty. The court sentenced him to death, and he was executed on 21 August 1942. See also Heinrich Kreutzberg, *Franz Reinisch: Ein Martyrer unserer Zeit* (Limburg: Lahn Verlag, 1952), and Wojciech Kordas, *Mut zum Widerstand: Die Verweigerung des Fahneneids von P. Franz Reinisch als prophetischer Protest* (St. Ottilien: EOS-Verlag, 2002).
41. A comprehensive overview of the exhibit can be found in the published catalogue: Hannes Heer and Klaus Nauman, eds., *Vernichtungskrieg: Verbrechen der Wehrmacht, 1941–1944* (Hamburg: Hamburger Edition, 1995).
42. John Connelly gives a thorough overview of the shortcomings of the Church's soul-searching with regards to antisemitism and the Holocaust in *From Enemy to Brother: The Revolution in Catholic Teaching on the Jews, 1933–1965* (Cambridge, MA: Harvard University Press, 2012). In 1998, Pope John Paul II formally apologized for the Church's failure to challenge the Nazi regime openly during the Holocaust in the document "We Remember: A Reflection on the Shoah," http://www.vatican.va/roman_curia/pontifical_councils/chrstuni/documents/rc_pc_chrstuni_doc_16031998_shoah_en.html (last accessed on 13 September 2014). The apology was unprecedented and represents an important point in Catholic-Jewish relations. However, many critics have stressed its inadequacies, especially as it does not take unequivocal responsibility for Church teachings that encouraged anti-Jewish sentiment and antisemitism.
43. Hannah Arendt, "Personal Responsibility under Dictatorship," in *The Listener*, 6 August 1964.
44. Three excellent treatments of Catholicism and antisemitism in modern Germany are Olaf Blaschke, *Katholizismus und Antisemitismus im deutschen Kaiserreich* (Göttingen: Vandenhoeck & Ruprecht, 1997); Kevin P. Spicer, ed., *Antisemitism, Christian Ambivalence, and the Holocaust* (Bloomington: Indiana University Press, 2007); and Connelly, *From Enemy to Brother*.

ACKNOWLEDGMENTS

My *Doktorvater*, Omer Bartov, has provided invaluable support throughout my intellectual development. From him, I have learned how to be a historian and a scholar. He is an extraordinary individual who continues to inspire me, and I am grateful for his mentorship and his friendship. At Brown University I benefited from interactions with an amazing group of scholars and scholars-in-training: Tom Gleason, Carolyn Dean, Joan Richards, Amy Remensnyder, Mary Gluck, David Kertzer, Chris Barthel, Adam Webster, Lauren Jones, Jennifer Wilz, Gabriel Rosenberg, and Julia Timpe have been important sources of encouragement, advice, and companionship at different times and in different ways.

John Munro, Alisa Webb, Geoff Hamm, Greg Kozak, Jeffrey Beglaw, Karen Routledge, Trevor Smith, Paige Raibmon, Don Grayston, Nadine Roth, and the late Bill Cleveland were central to my development as a young historian at Simon Fraser University. Martin Kitchen is one of the primary reasons I became interested in finding answers to the tougher questions in German history. He has taught me the importance, and the art, of telling a riveting narrative. He remains an inspiration and a dear friend.

In addition to reading chapters, many colleagues and friends have talked with me through some of the especially challenging issues that my research confronts. Without the insight and encouragement of Dagmar Herzog, Sebastian Rosato, John Deak, Jim Turner, Denise Della Rossa, Bob Krieg, Bob Sullivan, Brad Gregory, and Kevin Spicer, CSC, it would have been much more difficult to navigate these stormy waters.

Other colleagues took the time to read all or a portion of this manuscript in the midst of busy professional and personal lives and to provide generous feedback. Many thanks to Deborah Cohen, Doris Bergen, Mark Noll, Alex Martin, Semion Lyandres, Mikolaj Kunicki, Martina Cucchiara, Tom Kselman, Tobias Boes, Julia Douthwaite, and Lesley Walker, and to all those faculty and students at the University of Notre Dame who stayed late one winter evening to hear about a shattered Germany in May 1945.

For their aid and support in my professional development, and for their willingness to converse about dark subjects such as Nazism and genocide, I must thank John McGreevy, Patrick Griffin, Karen Graubart, John van Engen, Thomas Noble, Margaret Meserve, Paul Ocobock, Jon Coleman, Raully Donahue, John Conway, Wendy Lower, Margaret Anderson, John Mearsheimer, Bob Ericksen, Wilhelm Damberg, Alex Alvarez, Antonia Leugers, and Katharina von Kellenbach.

I am indebted to Thomas Devaney and Sebastian Rosato for their aid in translations from Italian and Latin. Denise Della Rossa and John Deak were always ready to help me refine the English translation of particularly tricky German passages. For accuracy in details related to Catholic doctrine and dogma, I must thank Gary Chamberlain, CSC, Kevin Spicer, and Bob Sullivan.

Archives in Europe, the United States, and Canada were important sources of documentation and information, without which this book would not exist. To the archivists and staffs at the Katholische Militärbishofsamt (Berlin), in particular Monica Sinderhauf and Julia Guske; the Erzbistumsarchiv München und Freising, in particular Thomas Forstner, Susan Kornacker, and Guido Treffler; the Erzbistumsarchiv Berlin, in particular Gotthard Klein; the Bundesarchiv-Militärarchiv Freiburg; the National Archives and Records Administration (Washington, DC); the Militärgeschichtliche Forschungsamt (Potsdam); the United States Holocaust Memorial Museum; and the John S. Conway Archive at Regent College, at the University of British Columbia (Vancouver, Canada), I am very grateful.

For financial support in pursuit of my research and writing over the past six years, I must thank the American Council on Germany for the Richard M. Hunt Fellowship; the Office of Research at the University of Notre Dame; the Institute for Scholarship in the Liberal Arts and the Nanovic Institute for European Studies, also at the University of Notre Dame.

The participants and lecturers of the Holocaust Educational Foundation's 2011 Summer Institute, and the participants of the U.S. Holocaust Memorial Museum's 2012 Seminar for Seminary and Religious Faculty, especially seminar leaders Bob Ericksen and Vicki Barnett, provided me with food for thought about the relationship between religion and Nazism. It was a privilege to be part of both of these important intellectual seminars.

Two anonymous readers for Harvard University Press wrote very detailed and constructive reviews of the manuscript. I much appreciated their suggestions for revision and hope they will be pleased with how this story has evolved.

I would not have completed this book without the unswerving love and support of close friends and family. Ivy, Aabid, Scott, Eddie, Wylie, Gina, Chrissi, and Tine have numbered among my biggest fans and dearest friends for many years and have kept me grounded when I felt overwhelmed by the demands of my work. Whether it was a patient ear or a glass of wine that was needed, they have always been there. My siblings, Alison and David, and my parents, Don and Margaret, have taught me generosity, selflessness, humility, and patience. They all know far more now than they ever wanted to about the Nazis and genocide. Our Sunday dinner conversations have contributed in no small way to my intellectual formation, even if they have been unaware of it. It is to my parents, who made it possible for me to become what I am, that this book is dedicated.

My daughter, Helena, arrived toward the end of this process. She has brought me endless joy and happiness. Her smiles give me renewed determination to find the answers to all the unanswerable questions that she will someday ask.

Finally, I must acknowledge the role played by Dionysios (Dino) Rossi. I hope this book exceeds the expectations that he built up when he read "that essay" about the Warsaw Ghetto Uprising that I left accidentally on a computer at school. At the time he was merely an inquisitive classmate; fourteen years later, he is my copy editor and critic, my devil's advocate, my partner-in-crime, my husband, my best friend. I could not have gotten here without you.

INDEX

Anschluss, 15, 41, 51, 280n157, 296n5
anti-Catholicism: Kulturkampf, 20; Nazi, 28, 30, 36, 39–42, 49–50, 52, 66, 78, 81, 96, 109, 210, 213, 224, 234; in the military, 61, 86, 103, 113, 125
anticlericalism, 33, 80, 100, 113, 225, 231
antisemitism: Nazi, 7, 28–29, 31, 51, 109, 198, 243; Catholic, 45, 57, 60, 150, 254–255, 273n62; in the seminary, 187
Auschwitz, 148, 149, 150, 234, 235, 237, 244, 322n17
authority, 159, 160, 173, 229, 252, 255; moral, 8, 176, 190, 216; state/secular, 13, 20, 57, 161, 172, 173, 228; episcopal, 16, 29; spiritual, 37, 45, 63, 83, 121, 166, 171, 196, 219; legitimate, 42, 160, 173; field bishop's, 84–85, 229; military, 92, 94, 217
Axmann, Artur, 28

Babi Yar massacre, 235, 305n146
Bach, Julian, 198, 199
baptism, 57, 59, 143
"barbed wire" theological seminary, 140
Bavarian People's Party (BVP; Bayerische Volkspartei), 33, 79
Beck, Ludwig, 66, 283n5
Belzec, 235
Benedict XV, 23, 173
Berning, Wilhelm, 285n20
Bertram, Adolf, 31, 36, 42, 47–48, 54–55, 59, 81, 195

Betreuung, 64–65, 129
bishop. *See* episcopate
Bismarck, Otto von, 4, 18, 19, 20, 61, 129, 252
Blomberg, Werner von, 66, 283n5
Bolshevism: papal condemnations of, 14, 23–25; compared with Nazism, 28, 60, 109; episcopal condemnations of, 30, 42, 43, 44, 46, 53, 55–56, 62; as motivation for military service, 91, 99, 110, 151, 154, 155, 156, 176, 254; encounters with, 141, 142, 145; crusade against, 185–189, 238. *See also* Judeo-Bolshevism
Bonaparte, Napoleon, 32
Boniface, 227, 319n87
Bormann, Martin: anti-Catholicism of, 81, 96, 97, 103, 104, 284n11; domination of Chancellery, 93, 94; establishment of NSFOs, 100, 101, 102, 293n131
Brandt, Hans Jürgen, 78, 297n6
Brauchitsch, Walther von, 89, 93, 234
British Royal Air Force Chaplains Department, 216
Browning, Christopher R., 151
brutalization, 16, 133, 151, 206, 208
Buchenwald, 194, 313n124
The Bulletin (August 1939), 85–89, 91, 94, 96, 97
Bundeswehr, 223, 227, 240, 267n14, 283n10, 288n49
Bündische Youth, 26
Buttmann, Rudolph, 69, 70

329

camaraderie, 26, 102, 118, 122, 151, 181, 312n93
canon law, 83, 124, 157, 291n97
Catholic lay organizations, 36, 37, 42
Catholic Military Bishop's Office, 11, 240
Catholic newspapers, 24, 241
Catholic youth, 8, 25–28, 40–41, 47, 48–49, 76, 156. *See also* youth movement
Center Party, 19, 21, 34, 69, 73, 79, 275n86
Christ, 47, 309n47, 317n76
Christian culture, 97, 180, 187
collective guilt, 201, 211, 213, 214, 250
collective responsibility, 196, 222, 237
Communion (sacrament), 90, 138
communism, 8, 35, 161; Church condemnation of, 23–25, 42, 44–46, 185, 312n106
concentration camps, 46, 48, 113, 194, 212, 215, 237, 242, 299n50
concordat: with Nazi regime, 6, 15, 109, 229, 234, 251, 273n63; secret appendix, 10, 69–70, 107, 294n142, 296n1; history of, 31–35; effects on German bishops, 36–39, 45; effects on youth, 39–42; regime's breaches of, 47–50, 54, 60–62, 213; and pastoral care, 68–69, 76, 227; and conscription, 112, 135
Confession (sacrament), 90, 123–125, 127, 152, 299n42. *See also* Penance
confessional schools, 43, 47, 72
Congregation of the Council, 29
conscience, 11, 18, 23, 33, 159, 160, 209, 228, 249
conscientious objection, 114, 150, 296nn4–5
conscription, 4, 10, 17, 52, 69, 70, 103, 112, 114
Corpus Christi mysticum. *See* suffering
Council of Germany, 227
Council of Trent, 123, 156
crusade, 24, 25, 142, 179, 185, 187
Crusades, 152, 285n14

Dachau, 113, 119, 120, 201, 225, 242, 244
Das Schwarze Korps, 41, 44
Davidson, Eugene, 198

death camps. *See* extermination camps
de Jong, Jan, 244
Delp, Alfred, 7
demilitarization, 199
denazification, 199–201, 214, 219, 250, 315n20, 318n78, 322n35
denominational schools. *See* confessional schools
deportation: of Jews, 52, 58, 59, 146, 150, 318n78; of Jewish converts to Catholicism, 57; knowledge of, 113, 242; of priests to Dachau, 225
Deutsche Christen, 215, 292n114
divine service, 90, 96
Dohrmann, Franz, 76, 77, 80, 90, 215, 220, 221, 222, 317n69
Dönitz, Karl, 192

Eastern Front: atrocities on, 56, 145, 148, 150, 183, 242, 246, 307n16; losses on, 93, 103; front-line seminars, 98, 134; experience of, 102, 113, 125, 133, 135, 155, 163, 189, 212; POWs on, 309n52
ecumenism, 27, 91, 160, 291n97
Edelmann, Karl, 82, 86–89, 98, 107, 225, 234, 236, 318n78; and nondenominational services, 89–91
Edict of Milan, 227
education: religious, 14, 18, 30, 282n3; in concordat, 34, 37, 69; in seminary, 156–158, 203, 235, 306n6
Ehrenfried, Matthias, 43
Eisenhower, Dwight D., 194
encyclical, 23, 41, 44, 52, 54, 161, 277n119. *See also Mit brennender Sorge*
end-of-war period: definition, 192, 193, 267n10, 313n1, 200, 222, 231; and guilt, 208; priests in, 218, 224; physical devastation of, 225, 226
episcopate (Germany): as religious authority, 3, 5–6, 15; bishops as model for Catholics, 8, 15, 42, 61–63, 113; nationalism of, 9; internal discord, 15–16, 30–31, 58–60; commitment to education, 18; memories of Kulturkampf, 22; opposition to Bolshevism, 23–25, 43–44, 53, 151; views on Nazism, 28, 54, 68, 254; and concordat, 35–39, 60; silence of, 45–46, 51, 236; and

INDEX

pastoral letters, 46; and 1937 encyclical, 48–49; and war, 52, 54–55, 160–162, 173, 186; and "Catholic non-Aryans," 56–59; opposition to Rarkowski, 73–76; at end of war, 196–197, 201, 206, 234, 235, 237, 252–254, 257, 269n7; as postwar authority, 209–211, 219; and Church as victim of Nazism, 212–214; and collective guilt, 213–214; on wartime atrocities, 211–213, 242
Erfahrungsbericht (experience report), 130
ethics, 110, 133, 159, 160, 172
ethnic German, 110, 126, 194
euthanasia (T-4) program, 44, 55–56, 186, 209
Evangelical League, 21
exemption, 68–69, 73, 76, 83, 229, 283n8
extermination, 56, 109, 149, 242
extermination camps, 56, 58, 146, 148, 241
Extreme Unction. *See* Last Rites

Fatherland: Catholic loyalty to, 4, 61, 75, 85, 88, 110, 112, 151, 231, 254, 255; war as defense of, 52, 105, 114, 252; distinct from Nazism, 54, 177, 178–180, 183, 189–190; physical destruction of, 224
Fattorini, Emma, 47–48
Faulhaber, Michael von: and Bolshevism, 25; reactions to Nazism, 29, 31, 46; and the concordat, 35, 36, 39; meeting with Hitler, 44; influence on 1937 encyclical, 47–48; silence about Jewish persecution, 56–57; protesting anti-Jewish measures, 59–60; wartime correspondence, 178, 187, 188; at end of war, 202, 318nn77–78; during World War I, 267n12
Feder, Gottfried, 29
Feldseelsorge, 64, 223
field bishop, 9, 63, 65, 72–76, 105
Field Bishop's Office, 84, 136, 163, 166, 226, 229
field provost, 71, 72
field vicar-general, 9, 65
First World War: German bishops and, 8; military chaplaincy in, 9, 65, 70–71, 283n4; and youth groups, 26, 175; Georg Werthmann in, 79, 159; compared to Second, 105, 175, 203; chaplain veterans of, 141, 146
Fourth Lateran Council, 123
Freemason lodges, 82
Freikorps, 13
Fresnes, 140, 309n52
Frings, Josef, 195
Fritsch, Werner von, 66, 283n5
Fritz, Carl, 35
front-line training seminars, 98–99, 125
Führer. *See* Hitler, Adolf
Fulbrook, Mary, 16, 17
Fulda Conference of Bishops, 15, 18, 31, 43, 55, 59, 68, 229

General Army Office, 82, 289n72
generation, 17, 26, 105, 106, 144, 159, 186, 203, 269n11
genocide, 2, 65, 175, 196, 222, 235, 246; Church silence about, 59, 62, 236
German bishops. *See* episcopate
German Charity, 57
Gestapo: harassing clergy, 39, 44, 48, 49, 51, 276nn110–111, 278n134, 288n59, 301n94; harassing youth, 41; and *Gleichschaltung*, 50; informants in, 58; and chaplains, 137, 243
ghetto, 58, 150, 243
Gleichschaltung, 38, 40, 41, 79, 97, 110, 275n88
Goebbels, Joseph, 96, 103, 247
Goerdeler, Carl, 100
Göring, Hermann, 84, 93, 193, 247, 283n5
Great War. *See* First World War
Gröber, Conrad, 30, 35, 202, 209, 210, 212, 214, 235, 289n59
Groener, Wilhelm, 75
Guardini, Romano, 158–160
The Guidelines (1942), 94–97, 99, 134

Haeuser, Philipp, 7, 281n166
"Halsschmerz," 247, 322n27
Hamburg Institute for Social Research, 321n6
Häring, Bernhard, 143, 165, 181–182, 303n121
Hassel, Ulrich von, 100
Hauck, Jakobus von, 79, 275n88

Heimat: Catholic devotion to, 10, 55, 57, 110, 132, 252, 300n73; as distinct from Nazism, 54, 110, 177, 179, 189; definition of, 177; loss of, 214, 248
Heimtückegesetz, 278n134
Helbach, Ulrich, 237
Hess, Rudolf, 93
Heydrich, Reinhard, 96
Himmler, Heinrich: and SS, 50, 53, 125–126; as anti-Catholic, 81, 96; criticism from chaplains, 116, 193, 278n131, 297n15, 319n96
Hindenburg, Paul von, 73
Hitler, Adolf: and failed putsch, 27, 28; bishops' views of, 30, 36, 44, 46, 58, 285n20; Vatican recognition of, 32; and concordat, 33, 37, 38; enmity for communism/Bolshevism, 35, 45, 62; and 1937 encyclical, 49, 50; and war effort, 54, 61, 70; about religion in the military, 66, 72, 121, 234; and army leadership, 66, 93; and NSFOs, 100, 102; as lawful head of state, 113, 230; postwar chaplains' criticism of, 175, 179, 247, 251; suicide, 182, 193; Werthmann's interrogation about, 221–222
Hitler Youth, 16–17, 27–28, 90; antipopularity, 28; and double membership, 40, 41; Catholic activities of, 40–41; Law, 49, 52; and SS, 50; surveillance of priests, 51
Hoffmann, Hermann, 26
Holocaust, 12, 146, 320n110, 323n42
Holy See, 44, 82, 195; and German bishops, 16, 29, 37, 53; on socialism, 23, 48; and Nazism, 38, 48, 213; and field bishop, 68, 76, 96, 229
human rights, 58, 62, 174

ideological training. *See* indoctrination
immorality trials, 49, 50, 51, 276n101
indoctrination, 65, 84, 90, 92, 100, 102, 151
indulgence, 124
indult, 233
Innocent III, 123
institutional religion, 45, 66, 90, 97, 109, 185–186, 208
Interior Ministry, 69
Iron Cross, 79, 136, 247, 322n27

Jaeger, Lorenz, 202, 206, 211, 213, 214, 235
JCS 1067, 199–200
Jesuits, 7, 19, 55, 92–93, 96, 121, 124
Jewish converts (non-Aryans), 57–60
Joeppen, Peter Heinrich, 71, 72, 286n31
John Paul II, 321n15, 323n42
Judaism, 57, 273n62
Judeo-Bolshevism, 64, 133. *See also* Bolshevism
just war, 171–176, 251, 252

Kaas, Ludwig, 69, 70
Kameradschaft, 305n151. *See also* camaraderie
Katholische Jungmännerverband, 27, 50
Keitel, Wilhelm, 80, 86, 100–102, 107, 195, 230, 234
Ketteler, Wilhelm Emmanuel von, 272n59
Knight's Cross of the Iron Cross, 247, 322n27
Knights of Malta (Knights Hospitallers), 285n14
Kristallnacht, 45, 51
Küchler, Field Marshal Georg von, 99
Kühne, Thomas, 67, 240, 266n6, 305n151, 312n93
Kultur, 60, 190
Kulturkampf, 4, 18–22, 30, 41, 49, 61, 91, 252; waged by Nazism, 14, 36
Kursk, 128

Last Rites (sacrament), 115, 138, 222
Lateran Accord, 32
Lebensraum, 109, 159, 175, 180, 239
Lenin, V. I., 141, 185
Leo XIII, 20, 23
liberalism, 31, 45, 60
Lichtenberg, Bernhard, 7
living space, 64, 88, 176. See also *Lebensraum*
Luftwaffe, 84, 90, 117, 126
Luther, Martin, 123

Marist Fathers (Society of Mary), 73–74
mass, 120, 152, 232; of Thanksgiving, 37, 150; attendance, 71, 115, 118–119, 131–134, 142, 143, 145; kits, 82, 121; said by *Priestersoldaten*, 116, 117, 233; said by chaplains, 126; with

civilian populations, 131, 141, 144; inability to attend, 169, 227; postwar attendance, 201, 202, 234
Mauchenheim gen. Bechtolsheim, Gustav Freiherr von, 120
Mauthausen, 235
Mayer, Philipp Jakob, 29
Mayer, Rupert, 7, 276n111, 295n161
May Laws, 19, 20
medical orderlies, 103, 107, 117, 127, 134
memory, 20, 121, 252–253
Militärseelsorge, 64
military bishop, 11, 240, 283n10
military service, 135, 291n97
Missalla, Heinrich, 78, 297n5
Mit brennender Sorge, 47–50, 51, 62, 173
modernism, 8, 23
The Modifications (1940), 91–92, 94, 97
Molotov-Ribbentrop Pact, 53
moral manuals, 124, 159
Morgenthau Plan, 199
Mühlenbein, Joseph, 74
Münchmeyer, Friedrich, 80, 215
Munich Agreement, 279n143
Mussolini, Benito, 32–33
Myth of the Twentieth Century, 31

national identity, 3–4, 8, 11, 21, 54, 151
nationalism, 3, 6, 29, 45, 54, 198; and religion, 21, 154, 252; as impetus for service, 67, 178, 179, 241
National Socialist Civil Servants Union (NS-Beamtenbund), 79
National Socialist German Workers' Party (NSDAP): program, 29; Chancellery, 93, 94, 104, 224, 230, 233
National Socialist Leadership Officer (NSFO): purpose of, 100–103, 178, 248; rivalry with chaplains, 101, 113, 210–211; chaplains' reactions to, 128–131, 172, 231, 241
National Socialist Leadership Staff (NSF), 100
National Socialist People's Welfare (NSV), 76
National Socialist War Victims Provisions (NSKOV), 51
navy, 71, 116, 126, 142, 233
nazification, 101, 183, 239

Nazi propaganda, 102, 128, 130, 142, 182, 188, 194, 278n127
Nazi weltanschauung, 39, 49, 66, 109, 114, 164
Neudeutschland Bund, 27
Nietzsche, Friedrich, 231
Niewind, Heinrich, 149–150
"non-Aryans." *See* Jewish converts
nondenominational services, 89–92, 96–98
nonfraternization, 199–200, 215, 216
Normandy invasion, 100, 168, 193, 297n15
Nuremberg Laws, 45, 48, 51, 59
Nuremberg Military Tribunals, 293n126

Office for Replacement and Military Affairs, 82
OKH (*Oberkommando des Heeres*): and Karl Edelmann, 82, 86–88, 236; and chaplaincy regulations, 83–85, 98, 99, 103, 107, 115, 120–121, 134, 140, 171, 231, 232; and nondenominational services, 90–93; and chaplain shortage, 106
OKW (*Oberkommando der Wehrmacht*), 6; dismissal of Jesuits, 55, 92; anti-Catholicism of, 80, 103–104, 115, 232–234; and chaplaincy regulations, 95, 98, 99, 137, 230; and conscription of seminarians, 294n142
Order of Malta, 70. *See also* Knights of Malta
Order of the Brethren at the Hospital of the Virgin Mary, 79
ordination, 1, 72, 112, 135, 157, 284n12
Orsenigo, Cesare, 165, 202, 275n88
Orthodox church, 24, 25, 52, 61, 185
Ow-Felldorf, Sigismund Freiherr von, 15

Pacelli, Eugenio: and concordat, 10, 32–35, 38–39, 41, 70, 279n143; and German bishops, 14, 69; and *Mit brennender Sorge*, 48. *See also* Pius XII
Papen, Franz von, 35, 69, 70
pastors. *See under* Protestant
Paul, Saint, 43, 160, 218
Peifer, Rudolf, 117, 135–136, 143

Penance (sacrament), 123–125, 138, 157. *See also* Confession
Peschke, Karl-Heinz, 241
Peter, Saint, 123
Peterson, Edward, 199
Pius VII, 32
Pius IX, 32, 272n59, 312n106
Pius X, 23, 173
Pius XI, 23–24, 32, 44, 46, 47–48, 50, 69, 82, 157, 173
Pius XII: reaction to outbreak of war, 52, 54; critics of, 62; wartime encyclical, 161; on state authority, 173–174; correspondence with German bishops, 202, 211, 213, 214; and field bishops, 229, 314n8. *See also* Pacelli, Eugenio
"positive Christianity," 29, 273n61
postwar period, 2, 7, 9, 10, 151, 192–193, 204, 208, 250
POW, 56, 79, 81, 142, 148, 171, 190, 221; camps, 140
Preysing, Konrad von, 7, 31, 44, 47, 50, 54–55, 58–59, 62, 81
Priestersoldat(en), 115–117, 118, 137, 230, 246; and relations with other soldiers, 119, 121; and relations with chaplains, 130, 134; at end of war, 206, 208; Werthmann's judgment of, 232–233
protective custody, 119, 276n111
Protestant: Reformation, 21, 123, 156, 217; youth, 41; church, 61, 216; chaplains, 65, 163, 293n125; pastors, 97
Pulpit Law, 19

Quickborn, 27, 79

racism, 29, 39, 62, 109, 150, 151, 249, 254, 273n62
Rarkowski, Franz Josef, 63, 65, 130, 225, 247; and *Priestersoldaten*, 9, 233; and embracing military service, 68, 105; and interwar chaplaincy, 71; pre-1933 background, 72–76; education, 73, 75; and criticism as field bishop, 76–78, 81, 165; support for Nazism, 78, 166; appointment of Werthmann as field vicar-general, 79–80; and chaplaincy regulations, 83–84; and front-line seminars, 98; ill health, 195; and lack of independence, 227, 229
Reconciliation (sacrament). *See* Penance
reconstruction, 193, 199, 205, 216, 219, 226
Red Army, 100, 133, 193, 194, 225
Reich Air Defense Organization (Reichsluftschutzbund), 176
Reich Catholic field bishop. *See* field bishop
Reich Catholic field vicar-general. *See* field vicar-general
Reich Security Main Office (RSHA), 96
Reichsfeinde, 48
Reichskonkordat. *See* concordat
Reichswehr, 69, 71, 72, 75, 79, 165
Reinecke, Hermann, 81, 86, 100–102, 107, 128, 130, 165, 225
Reinisch, Franz, 252, 265n2, 296n5
Relief Committee for Catholic Non-Aryans, 57
Rempel, Gerhard, 16
Röhm putsch, 45
Roman Empire, 227
Rosenberg, Alfred, 31
Royal Air Force (Britain), 193, 216

sacraments, 10, 128, 161; access to, 22, 45; administration of, 92, 124, 126, 145, 157, 232, 234. *See also* Communion; Confession; Last Rites; Penance
Schachleiter, Albanus, 72
Schirach, Baldur von, 28, 40, 278n131
Schulte, Carl Joseph, 47
Schutzstaffel (SS): harassment of Catholic youth, 41, 278n131; anti-Catholicism of, 50–51, 116, 213; and atrocities during war, 53, 58, 142, 146, 148–149, 201, 212, 221, 242, 243, 245; and confessions to chaplains, 125–128; SS-*Totenkopfdivision*, 126, 163; *SS-Einsatzgruppe*, 148, 149
Schwamborn, Paul, 71, 74–75
seal of the confessional, 113, 124, 146
Security Service (SD), 51, 58, 82, 184
Seelsorge, 64, 101

Seelsorgebericht (pastoral care report), 130
seminary: in Freising, 2, 167; training and education in, 10, 173, 253, 282n3; director, 73, 141, 180; regulations, 124, 156–159, 232; propaganda in, 187. *See also* Westermayr, Johann
sexual: matters, 119, 131, 162; debauchery, 133
silence, 43, 109, 125, 155, 190–191, 253; of the bishops, 45–46, 56; of the Church, 62; as protest, 175, 178; interpretation of, 236
Simon, John, 284n13
Sittlichkeitsprozesse. See immorality trials
Social Democrats (SPD), 34, 158
socialism, 14, 23, 24, 60, 158, 185
Sommer, Margarete, 58–59
Spanish Civil War, 42–45
Sperrfrist, 287n44, 321n5
Spicer, Kevin, 165
Sproll, Joannes Baptista, 213
SS-Einsatzgruppe. *See Schutzstaffel*
SS-Totenkopfdivision. *See Schutzstaffel*
Staebe, Gustav, 43
Stalin, Joseph, 141
Stalingrad, 122, 167
Stein, Edith, 244
Stelzenberger, Johannes, 146–147
sterilization, 57, 274n84
Stock, Franz, 140, 309n52
Stohr, Albert, 202, 206, 235
Stunde Null, 197, 226
Sturmabteilung (SA), 43, 104
Sturmschar, 79
suffering, 253; wartime, 2, 121, 138, 174, 243; Catholic interpretations of, 23, 47, 178, 196–197, 203–205, 235; and *Corpus Christi mysticum*, 160–162; German, 213–214, 234, 237
suicide, 133, 162, 182, 193
Syllabus of Errors, 272n59

Tätigkeitsbericht (daily activity report), 130
Tewes, Ernst, 148–149
theology student, 10, 65, 69, 135, 178, 232
Tiso, Josef, 318n78
totalitarianism, 48
total war, 7, 69, 239

Treaty of Versailles, 15, 64, 71, 110, 176, 240
Treblinka, 235
troop morale, 64, 65; chaplaincy and, 67, 86, 88, 90, 92, 114, 131–134, 170–171, 254; officers and, 94; detriments to, 104, 171; NSFOs and, 128–129, 210
Truppenbetreuung, 64–65, 129
20 July bomb plot, 100, 104, 228

United States Army Air Force, 193
Untermenschen, 142
Urbani, Giovanni, 146

Vatican secret archives, 47
Velesmes, 149–150
veterans, 11, 117, 141, 146, 151–152, 172, 208, 241–256
Volk, 4, 103, 104, 105, 209, 234; racial conception of, 29, 150; Catholic loyalty to, 61, 108, 178–179, 183, 205–206; Nazi conceptions of, 64; service to, 110, 112, 189, 231, 248
Völkischer Beobachter, 43
völkisch movement, 28
Volksgemeinschaft, 90, 95
Volksgrenadierdivision, 116, 298n36
Volkssturm, 103

Waffen-SS, 126, 127, 221
Wandervogel, 26, 27
war crimes, 62, 65, 133, 184, 246, 254, 293n126, 299n50, 321n6
War Merit Cross, 80
wehrgeistige Führung, 64–65, 100
Weidemann, Alfred, 104
Weimar: constitution, 14, 18, 22, 23, 33, 34, 37; republic, 16, 18, 33, 71, 73
Werthmann, Georg, 10, 63, 65, 66, 78–82, 195, 240; notes for "Geschichte für Feldseelsorge," 11, 118, 136, 197, 203, 206, 222–225, 236–237, 253; on meaning of service in war, 68, 170, 177–178, 240, 255; on Rarkowski, 73, 76–78; chaplaincy duties, 82–83; on 1939 Bulletin, 85–86; on Karl Edelmann, 86–87; on expulsion of Jesuits from army, 92–93; on 1942 Guidelines, 94–98; on Nazi hostility towards churches and chaplains, 96–97, 99, 104, 210–211,

Werthmann, Georg *(continued)* 213, 230–232; and front-line training seminars, 98–99, 120–121; on NSFOS, 101–103, 129; on chaplain statistics, 106, 115, 134; reflections on Nazism, 107–109, 218, 225–226; on compromising with Nazism, 110, 152; on disappointing chaplains, 119, 161–166; on Ernst Tewes, 148; internment, 196, 220–222; on postwar period, 204, 205, 206–208, 219; on suffering, 204–205; on American occupiers, 215, 217; on military chaplaincy, 226–230; on *Priestersoldaten*, 232–234; on "Hitler's army," 248

Westermayr, Johann, 167, 168, 180, 181, 183, 187, 189. *See also* seminary: director

worldview, 3, 10, 155, 218; Catholic, 24, 156, 158–160; competition between Catholic and Nazi, 60, 210; during war, 119, 125, 179, 187; Nazi, 182, 235, 247

youth movement: Catholic, 4, 8, 37; in Germany, 17, 25–26; and backlash following 1937 encyclical, 49; Werthmann's involvement in, 79. *See also* Catholic youth

Zimmer, Gregor, 210, 215, 295n162

Printed in the USA
CPSIA information can be obtained
at www.ICGtesting.com
LVHW040927250724
786422LV00005B/62/J